Deadly Baggage

Deadly Baggage

*What Cortés Brought to
Mexico and How It Destroyed
the Aztec Civilization*

AL SANDINE

McFarland & Company, Inc., Publishers
Jefferson, North Carolina

LIBRARY OF CONGRESS CATALOGUING-IN-PUBLICATION DATA

Sandine, Al, 1938–
　　Deadly baggage : what Cortés brought to Mexico and how it destroyed the Aztec civilization / Al Sandine.
　　　p.　　cm.
　　Includes bibliographical references and index.

　　ISBN 978-0-7864-9700-3 (softcover : acid free paper) ∞
　　ISBN 978-1-4766-2222-4 (ebook)

　　1. Mexico—History—Conquest, 1519–1540.　2. Cortés, Hernán, 1485–1547.　3. Aztecs—History.　I. Title.

F1230.S19 2015
972'.02—dc23   2015025316

BRITISH LIBRARY CATALOGUING DATA ARE AVAILABLE

© 2015 Al Sandine. All rights reserved

No part of this book may be reproduced or transmitted in any form or by any means, electronic or mechanical, including photocopying or recording, or by any information storage and retrieval system, without permission in writing from the publisher.

Front cover: *The Conquest of Tenochtitlán*, unknown artist, representing the 1521 fall of Tenochtitlán in the Spanish conquest of the Aztec Empire, Mexico, painted in late 1600s, oil on canvas (courtesy Jay I. Kislak Collection, Rare Book and Special Collections Division, Library of Congress)

Printed in the United States of America

McFarland & Company, Inc., Publishers
　Box 611, Jefferson, North Carolina 28640
　　www.mcfarlandpub.com

For Ariel

Table of Contents

Preface   1

Introduction   3

1—Guests Without Baggage   11
2—Iberian Voyagers   26
3—Conquest as Romance   39
4—Crusaders in America   51
5—The Sword's New Cutting Edge   64
6—America's Gold and Silver Promote Slavery and Boost European Commerce   71
7—The Horse's New Footing   98
8—Transplanting a Work Ethic   108
9—A New Kind of Savagery   125
10—Hog Heaven   149
11—Micro-Invaders   154
12—Leftover Baggage: The Triumph of an Oxymoron   166

Conclusion   189
Chapter Notes   195
Bibliography   218
Index   229

"Wherever the European had trod, death seems to pursue the aboriginal."
—Charles Darwin, *The Voyage of the Beagle* (1839)

Preface

Deadly Baggage is an interpretation of the sixteenth-century conquest of Mexico that explains the success of the famous Cortés expedition not by description of the personalities and actions of the key players in a historical drama but in terms of the conquest's wrappings of biology, history, geology, technology, geography, and culture.

Like an earlier book of mine (*The Taming of the American Crowd* [New York: Monthly Review Press, 2009]), *Deadly Baggage* was born in a bookstore, an excellent bookstore that, like so many others of its kind, no longer exists. In its final days, Borders in downtown San Francisco held a book sale. I got there later than I might have and went directly to the shelves of World History. It was a shock to see the gaps in those shelves: clearly a lot of titles had already gone out the door. But I managed to grab a copy of J. H. Elliott's *Imperial Spain: 1469–1716* and, more or less to go with it, *Conquest, Tribute, and Trade* by Howard J. Erlichman. Soon these books began transporting me to an era that everyone learns something about early in life—the age of European discovery. Perhaps that lesson of childhood had convinced me that there was nothing else on the subject that I needed to know, for I'd never given it a second look. But what could be more compelling than the earliest documented encounters between representatives of the long separated people of the Eastern and Western Hemispheres? I fleshed out my reading with an old edition of Bernal Díaz's *History of the Conquest of New Spain* and Yale University Press's *Hernán Cortés: Letters from Mexico*, both of which I discovered on the shelves of Moe's Books in Berkeley.

As I read, questions arose, patterns emerged, and I began taking notes and making visits to the University of California libraries on the Berkeley campus. I was encouraged by the fact that major primary sources on the Cortés expedition are few: anyone can read them. With a book publication project in mind, a historian would need to supplement such reading with visits to Spain and Mexico to pore over archival records. Mastery of sixteenth-century Spanish would be a prerequisite, and a working knowledge of Nahuatl, the language of the Aztecs, would come in handy, too. Fortunately, as it is far too late for me to acquire such skills and find support for such archival research, I am not a historian. Thus, *Deadly Baggage* does not concentrate its focus on some overlooked particular of the conquest of Mexico. Nor does it pretend to be a comprehensive history of the conquest. Hugh Thomas's *Conquest: Montezuma, Cortés, and the Fall of Old Mexico* represents the definitive English-language version of that approach, in my opinion. Nor is this book another description of the conquest that weaves together all of the major elements of the familiar adventure story like William H. Prescott's *History of the Conquest of Mexico*, the classic version of this approach in English. *Deadly Baggage* is a reaction to such triumphalist romances. It draws on the insight of Jared Diamond, Alfred W. Crosby, and others that history puts on weight in the company of geography, geology, biology, archaeology, cultural understanding, and perhaps even meteorology.

For all that, *Deadly Baggage* would not be what it is without the work of historians like the aforementioned Thomas, J. H. Elliott, Matthew Restall, Anthony Pagden, R. C. Padden, and many others including the great Fernand Braudel. My reading of Inga Clendinnen, Davíd Carrasco, and Ross Hassig, among others, has given me some understanding of Aztec society. Archaeologist Geoffrey McCafferty provided important information for my Chapter 9. I should also acknowledge the contributions of friends and associates Ann Buchbinder, Erik Gleibermann, Pam Liu, Peter Moore, Noreen O'Brien, Bruce Page, and Carol Page, each of whom helped push this project forward in one way or another. Ethan Stan has been stalwart in devising the maps. Helpful, as well, have been Ed Beer of Sphinx Fine Art of London, Libros Latinos in San Francisco, and Crystal Miles of the Bancroft Library in Berkeley. Last but certainly not least, my wife and compañera Mary Bradford edited drafts of the manuscript, provided discerning comments, and gave this project her consistent and sustaining support. Such errors and gaffes as may remain are, of course, entirely my responsibility.

Introduction

Europeans didn't just "discover" the Western Hemisphere, beginning with Columbus's famous voyage of 1492. Discovery alone could have resulted in trade relations with the inhabitants of the "new world," cultural exchange, the diffusion of knowledge, or resumed separation. After all, the enormous fleets of Zheng He, the Ming Dynasty admiral, visited thirty countries of Southeast Asia, South Asia, and East Africa in the early fifteenth century, enriching them with Chinese treasure without making them parts of a Chinese empire. Castilian contact with the Americas that began a few decades later, however, resulted in the conquest of advanced civilizations, the enrichment of Europe, and a major shift in the course of world history. In Mexico, Europeans destroyed the Aztec Empire, setting the stage for the conquest of the entire hemisphere.

As has usually been told, the Aztecs were conquered by a few hundred Spaniards, the conquistadors, under the ingenious leadership of Hernán Cortés and aided by native disunity. For example, the *Conquista de México* by Francisco López de Gómara, Cortés's first biographer, is a celebration of the brilliance of the man who led a small band of Spaniards to topple an empire. Here is Richard Hakluyt, the sixteenth-century English geographer's capsule on the subject: "Let the doughty deeds of Ferdinand Cortés, the Castilian, the stout conqueror of New Spain … resound ever in your ears."[1] Writing his own history of the conquest in the seventeenth century to defend the glory of the conquistadors against foreign critics, Antonio de Solís depicted Cortés as the tool of God that dismantled the work of Satan. In *A Complete Collection of Voyages and Travels* (1744–1748), John Harris suggests that absent Cortés the Aztecs would have mastered European guns and driven the Spaniards from Mexico's interior, holding the region on a permanent basis. Alfredo Chavero's *Historia Antigua y de la conquista* (1886) contrasts the tremendous energy and shrewdness of Cortés to Moctezuma's "incredible torpor."[2] For William H. Prescott, whose *History of the Conquest of Mexico* has become an American classic, "[t]he history of the conquest is necessarily that of the great man who achieved it."[3] The unprovoked conquest of one people by another becomes a thrilling story when cast as the work of an illustrious hero.

The tendency to reduce the conquest of Mexico to a contest between two leaders or a near-miraculous victory of European ingenuity and Western values—as personified by Hernán Cortés—over Indian superstition and savagery has also colored more recent accounts. The title of Henry Dwight Sedgwick's 1926 book speaks for itself: *Cortés the Conqueror: The Exploits of the Earliest and Greatest of the Gentleman Adventurers*.[4] The same can be said of Salvador de Madariaga's *Hernan Cortés: Conqueror of Mexico*.[5] Fr. Ángel María Garibay Kintana, who pioneered the study of Nahuatl literary traditions, found Cortés to be "a man of marvelous genius, not only a conqueror but a builder."[6] John Manchip White writes that Spain would have conquered Mexico even without Cortés, but "[i]f Cortés had failed to reach his goal our world would be different."[7] For Tvestan Todorov, the key to Spanish conquest was Cortés's "superior understanding" of the Aztec world—superior to Moctezuma's of the Spaniards'—and his striking use of language as an instrument of manipulation.[8] Even Hugh Thomas's comprehensive *Conquest: Montezuma, Cortés, and the Fall of Old Mexico* pits Cortés against the Aztec emperor, as announced by the title, and "tells how a small party of well-led adventurers fought against a large static monarchy." With the fall of the Aztec capital, Thomas concludes, Cortés "had conquered an empire."[9]

Facilitating the amazing exploit of the conquistadors was a case of mistaken identity: the natives took the invaders for returning gods. Such an understanding exalts the boldness and ingenuity of the Europeans, enfeebles native intelligence, and diminishes all of the impersonal forces and cultural factors that made European conquest virtually inevitable. It reduces one of the most important conflicts in human history to a two-act drama in which, however cruelly, the forces of wisdom and light, as embodied in one man, prevail over error and ignorance, as represented by another. Henceforth, Cortés and Moctezuma, forever linked as conqueror and conquered. This literary gloss on history deserves the victims of what happened, as well as the truth. Nor were the Aztecs defeated because of cognitive limitations, lack of improvisational ability, or their commitment to a cyclical notion of time.

Geological and climatic changes of thousands of years ago established that the people of the earth's Eastern and Western Hemispheres—the Old and New Worlds—would undergo separate development. Not only would they develop in isolation, but the people of the Old World would accrue decisive advantages, such that by the end of the fifteenth century if not before, contact between them would prove destructive to the indigenous people of the Americas. The conquistadors were the beneficiaries of lethal advantages, and they arrived with them in the Caribbean.

Brought to the New World by the Spanish invaders were such Old World phenomena as (a) the steel sword; (b) the horse; (c) other large domestic animals, represented here by the pig; (d) deadly microbes, especially the smallpox virus; (e) the cross, representing an intolerant, proselytizing religion; (f) a determination to acquire precious metals, especially gold; (g) an aristocratic work ethic; (h) a willingness to engage in the indiscriminate slaughter of people deemed savages; and (i) a romanticized image of the heroic warrior with whom the conquistadors identified. All of these "fellow travelers" flourished in the New World as, presumably, had the earliest human invaders when they crossed the Beringian "land bridge" from Siberia thousands of years earlier and encountered herds of large, curious, approachable animals, the "megafauna" of the Western Hemisphere.

The fortunes of most of these Old World entities had gone into decline in Europe. For example, by the early sixteenth century the heroic warrior of the Middle Ages, the true knight, thrived mostly in the pages of chivalric novels. In fact, he was on the verge of becoming a literary joke. The armies of Roman Catholicism had shut down the last outposts of Islamic civilization in Iberia, but the Church would soon confront a Christian rival throughout much of Europe. The cannon and siege had largely superseded swordplay and the equestrian fighter in European warfare. Europe's demand for gold and silver could not be satisfied by drawing on available sources. The aristocratic prejudice against work would become an anachronism with the decline of feudal relations and the rise of Protestantism. State and Church, for better or worse, were gaining control of Spain's demons of indiscriminate violence by substituting the Inquisition for the pogrom and making vigilantism almost an arm of government. And the smallpox virus had about run out of victims.

In the New World, each of these items would become a lethal piece of the conquistadors' "baggage"—their mental and physical equipment. Each would experience a revitalized career. Armed with superior weapons as well as religious and moral certainty, the Spanish adventurers of the Cortés expedition could plausibly identify with the romantic heroes of familiar chivalric novels. With military backing, the Church would face no rivals, and it would gain the opportunity to convert millions of pacified pagans. Spanish America would also become the source of the enormous flows of precious metals, especially silver, that would lift Europeans—some Europeans—from the economic periphery to commercial dominance of the Early Modern world. Meeting only cotton armor, the sword would once again separate enemy warriors from their limbs and heads, and the Spaniards' propensity for unaccountable and unchecked violence would keep such weapons engaged. As the largest, strongest, and nearly the fastest animal that Indians had ever seen, the horse would become the decisive military asset it had been for Bronze Age warriors of the Eurasian steppes. In New Spain (or Mexico), any European might become a master, any Indian a slave. Following thousands of years of domestication, pigs and other barnyard animals would run wild in a lush new environment. And deadly Old World microbes would encounter a universe of vulnerable new hosts.

This list of contents of the conquistadors' deadly baggage is far from exhaustive. For example, an indigenous description of the invaders in a post-conquest source uses the Nahuatl word for iron or metal—*tepotzli*—more than any other, referring not only to the Spaniards' swords but to their knives, gear, and armor. The printing press made Europeans aware of the Cortés expedition as early as 1520, and books, going back to Marco Polo's account of Asian wonders, inspired them to come to the New World.[10] The brigantines that the Spaniards and their native allies built for the siege of Tenochtitlán could be rowed, paddled, or sailed. They could carry cannons and up to seventy-five men. They easily outmatched Indian canoes.[11] And without the larger ocean-going vessels that brought the conquistadors to the Western Hemisphere and the navigational equipment that guided them to the shores of Yucatan, there would have been no conquest, not in the early sixteenth century.

But what does it mean that key elements of the conquistadors' deadly baggage were losing lethality (or had never been lethal) in their Old World setting? One implication is that earlier contact might have had the same deadly outcome. But was there an earlier point at which contact between Europeans and indigenous Americans might have been benign? I take up this question in Chapter 1. As underlined in Chapter 2, once Iberian mariners began to sail down the west coast of Africa, it was only a matter of time before prevailing winds blew someone to the coast of Brazil or an island in the Caribbean. As things turned out, contact was made in the late Middle Ages by representatives of a country, Castile, that was on a permanent war footing with Islamic forces. The Castilian noble or adventurer still carried a sword and rode a horse, if he could afford one. He lived in a world that was preoccupied with obtaining the precious ores needed to gain access to the highly-valued goods of South and East Asia. If one's prospects were dull or uncertain, acquisition of gold or silver could transform them into a glittering future. As Columbus observed, with such precious metals one could do anything. For example, one might buy land to lease to peasants and enjoy the easy life of a rentier. Putting one's gold and silver away in a chest no longer made sense, and anyone who had such a treasure trove would have made an unlikely candidate for invasion of the Americas. Meanwhile, one stood ready to help keep a check on the enemies of the Faith that remained in Spain—by joining others in collective violence, if need be. As for the epidemics that had killed so many people in the past, they seemed a thing of the past.

Discovery and colonization of the Indies, so-called, put a few young Castilian males of the kind I have insinuated here on a collision course with members of a distant civilization of which they were completely ignorant. The latter might have continued to live as their ancestors had, to develop or not as they would, without the interference of powerful invaders with intolerant beliefs, overweening desires, and destructive biota. But historical developments and impersonal forces had piled change on top of change, bringing European invasion and multifaceted destruction to indigenous Americans. Superior numbers and "home field advantage" could not offset native disunity and the Europeans' accumulation of deadly baggage. Indians died of sword thrusts and gunshots, of fire and water, torture and overwork. Many were killed arbitrarily, and many died of Old World diseases without ever setting eyes on a European. In some cases, we don't even know what people called themselves before they were wiped out.

Beginning with sixteenth-century Franciscan scholars, researchers have pieced together a considerable body of information about the Aztecs. Our knowledge of the conquest, however, is mainly based on the narratives of the conquerors, especially Cortés's *Cartas de Relación de la Conquista de Méjico* (or *Letters to the Crown*, as these reports are usually called in English) and the *Historia verdadera de la conquista de la Nueva España* (*True History of the Conquest of New Spain*) of Bernal Díaz. But these sources leave us with a paradox: although the Aztecs had been capable of consolidating all of the social, economic, and technical means required to build and maintain a splendid pre-industrial metropolis—one far more populous than any in Spain—they were incapable of defending it against the boldness and ingenuity of a few hundred Europeans and an aggregation of Indian allies that the Aztecs had dominated for decades. Yes, they were suffering from a smallpox epidemic, but so must have been the conquistadors' native allies.

I think that these primary sources resolve this paradox by a distortion of the facts. As we will discover in Chapter 8, Díaz had reason to play up the heroism of the conquistadors and minimize the intelligence of the Indians. His popular narrative depicts the latter as savage and fearsome yet easily managed once subdued. Insofar as one identifies with the storyteller, the *True History* is a fascinating account. Not many readers will find their way to the indigenous take on the conquest, as primarily represented by Bernardino de Sahagún's *Florentine Codex*, and those that do will be struck by its strangeness, precluding easy identification with the people who were sickened, besieged, and slaughtered. Cortés's letters to the Crown are blatantly self-serving. On page after page, examples of his boldness are matched only by those of his cleverness and good judgment. The letters become a self-portrait of the indispensible conqueror. After all, he was writing to the only authority whose approval he needed to remain in command of the conquest and the colonization that followed.

For the reader who is unfamiliar with or forgetful of the story of that expedition that emerges from Cortés's letters and Díaz's narrative, the following is a bare-bones account.

After two earlier exploratory voyages to the Mexican mainland by others, Hernán Cortés led an expedition of around six hundred adventurers and sixteen horses that sailed from Cuba in February 1519, defying the wishes of the Cuban governor, Diego Velázquez, who tried to revoke his authorization for the voyage at the last minute. The Spaniards made land at various points along the Yucatan peninsula. Their use of horses, steel swords, and harquebuses proved decisive in early battles with Indians. Cortés further exceeded Velásquez's mandate by establishing Vera Cruz as a permanent settlement and putting the expedition under the immediate authority of Charles V, the Hapsburg emperor and (as Charles I) king of Spain. He did this by reporting directly to that monarch.

It soon became clear that the conquistadors had arrived on the periphery of a vast empire, that the center was a place called Culua or Mexico, and that many of the people of Culua's tributary states were unhappy with their imperial masters, the Mexica. At Cempoala, a city near the Gulf Coast, Cortés put on a bold display of cunning by persuading the Cempoalans to imprison a pair of imperial tax collectors, then secretly releasing them with a message to Moctezuma, the ruler of this Aztec Empire, that he sought his friendship. Accompanied by Cempoalans and shadowed by Aztec emissaries, the Spaniards proceeded toward Culua, the reported source of the gold that they sometimes observed as native jewelry, destroying idols and erecting crosses en route.

At Tlaxcala, an independent state surrounded by areas aligned with the Aztecs, the Spaniards fought ferocious battles to defend themselves, suffering heavy losses. Ultimately, the Tlaxcalans decided to ally themselves with the invaders, becoming the most numerous and faithful supporters of efforts to defeat the Aztecs, their traditional enemies. The conquistadors and their newfound allies soon committed a major massacre at the nearby holy city of Cholula.

Overcoming Aztec efforts to divert or destroy the expedition and ignoring the warnings of their native supporters, the Spaniards finally arrived at the island city of Tenochtitlán (identified with the ancient center of Culua), "capital" of the Aztec Empire. They were amazed by its size and magnificence. Moctezuma treated them as honored guests. According to his welcoming speech, he believed that they were representatives of an ancient ruler, come home to claim their birthright. In an act of unimaginable audacity, Cortés had the Aztec ruler put under the equivalent of house arrest. Then, instead of ordering their annihilation, the warrior-monarch attempted to conciliate his captors, even giving them the hoard of gold and precious gems they had discovered in their lodging.

In April 1520, while still in Tenochtitlán, Cortés learned that a large force of Spaniards under the command of Pánfilo de Narváez had arrived on the Gulf Coast. Leaving some of his followers under the command of one of his captains, Pedro de Alvarado, Cortés rushed east to confront this new expedition, rightly judging that Diego Velázquez had deployed it to bring the conquest under his control. Cortés planted dissension among Narváez's men and then staged a surprise attack in which Narváez was badly wounded. Narváez's men went over to Cortés, although some did so reluctantly.

Bad news arrived from Tenochtitlán. The conquistadors there had come under dire threat. In Cortés's absence, Alvarado had conducted a massacre of many members of the Aztec nobility during a ceremonial dance. Re-entering Tenochtitlán, Cortés and his new followers also became entrapped. The hostage emperor was killed under disputed circumstances. Under constant attack, the Spaniards and their allies attempted the desperate expedient of a nocturnal escape. Detected, hundreds of them and thousands of their native allies were killed trying to flee the city, an event that became known as the Noche Triste (sad night).

The survivors retreated to Tlaxcala where they nursed their wounds and began to rehabilitate their campaign, starting in about July 1520. Meanwhile, Tenochtitlán was hit by a smallpox epidemic, its inhabitants suffering huge losses. The Spaniards slowly approached the city again, this time with the launches with which they would gain control of the lake. They were joined by a growing number of native allies, including the warriors of a member of the Triple Alliance that had ruled the Empire. Cortés lay siege to the city, having cut off its supply of fresh water and food. Fierce fighting on the causeways followed over several weeks. The Spaniards and their allies gradually gained the upper hand, destroying the city and capturing the last Aztec ruler.

Native resistance to the colonizers outlasted the fall of the Empire by many years, but its demise in August 1521 roughly marks the end of the setting for most of what follows.

I think that the above outline faithfully summarizes and perhaps even expands the popular understanding of the conquest of Mexico. But of all the ways of explaining the fall of the Aztec Empire, this is probably the most Eurocentric and prejudicial. In this telling, conquest relied mostly on one man, Hernán Cortés, whose guile and audacity are counterposed to native gullibility and superstition. The Europeans prevail in what the primary sources describe as a close and exciting military contest. A better understanding must identify the complex of impersonal and less personal forces that came into play in Mexico in those crucial years of the early sixteenth century. My intent is to show that Mexico was conquered and the Aztec Empire destroyed by a gestalt of forces that flourished in the New World. Had Cortés never left Cuba, other Europeans would have come to Mexico bearing the same constellation of deadly creatures, motives, weapons, and immoderation in their desire to impose their aims. This suite of baggage, together with native disunity, was sufficient to destroy a civilization.

Am I saying that the Pandora's Box of obsessions, weapons, biota, and inhumanity was sufficient in itself to destroy a civilization? No, let's give Cortés and the conquistadors their due. Their swords didn't wield themselves. The earlier expeditions of Córdoba and Grijalva did not result in conquest. Until Old World pathogens could take effect, success of the venture needed the kind of boldness and luck that Cortés had in spades. It's just that Cortés's audacity, cleverness, and leadership are not the whole story or even its most important part. There is plenty more to it than that, as we will see.

A word on usage. The rulers of the Aztec Empire, the Tenocha and Tlatelolca people who lived in Tenochtitlán, called themselves the "Mexica." The problem with calling them what they called themselves is that, for me, the adjectival form of the word—"Mexican"—evokes the people of today's Mexico, the nation state that grew out of the Spanish colony. Thus, following popular usage, I refer to them as the "Aztecs." Many scholars now refer to what I call the "Aztec Empire" as the "Triple Alliance." For the sake of convenience, I often refer to the conquistadors as "the Spaniards," although the expedition included Genoese, Portuguese, Neopolitans, a Frenchman, a few African slaves, and some Cuban natives. (The number of the latter varies considerably from one source to another.) According to Frances Berdan, a few Spanish women also came along.[12] At least one of them participated in the fighting. Also, early colonization occurred under Castilian, not "Spanish" auspices. Spain was not yet a nation but a geographic and cultural entity. The name of the Aztec ruler has been variously rendered. "Moctezuma" is a compromise. I have not attempted to discuss the conquistadors' invasion from the indigenous side, except for the analysis of Chapter 12. The chapters that follow are of uneven length as befits their subject matter.

1

Guests Without Baggage

Consider the following:

- In 1916 an amateur geologist by the name of George Fraser photographed some petroglyphs that he found at the base of Navajo Mountain in the Utah-Arizona border region. Stephen G. Jett, a reputable geographer, discovered these photos nearly sixty years later and examined them in the light of David Diringer's *The Alphabet: A Key to the History of Mankind*. He then sent the photos to Barry Fell, a well-known if controversial interpreter of ancient inscriptions. Fell saw the script as ancient "Iberic" or "Semitic." In his interpretation of the markings, they appear to be a warning to the (westbound) traveler. Although Fell was, reportedly, unaware of the geography of the Navajo Mountain area, his translation made geographic sense. West of the petroglyph site lies a barren desert.[1] Did ancient Eurasians lose their bearings in the American Southwest?
- In 1976 a scuba diver, looking for lobsters in waters near Rio de Janeiro, found several large jars that Brazilian archaeologists identified as Roman amphorae. Although the diver was arrested for trafficking in ancient artifacts, his discovery was followed within a few years by the investigative efforts of Robert F. Marx, known as the "father of underwater archaeology." Marx brought up several similar storage jars and some bronze objects. He described an underlying shipwreck. On the basis of thermo-luminescence testing at the University of London, archaeologists determined that the jars were manufactured around 19 BCE. However, before any further investigation could be conducted, the Brazilian government buried the site under tons of sediment, thus salvaging the reputations of Christopher Columbus as the discoverer of America and Álvares Cabral as the discoverer of Brazil.[2] But did a Roman supply ship, carrying olive oil perhaps, visit the coast of South America?

- In 1992 German researchers announced that they had found traces of cocaine, nicotine, and hashish in mummies from ancient Egypt and South America. The question was not so much whether ancient rulers had drug habits but whether received history had it all wrong with regard to the discovery of America. Cocaine was unknown in Eurasia before Columbus's famous voyage; hashish was unknown in the Americas. Like cocaine and hashish, tobacco has been assigned a place in the so-called Columbian Exchange that took place between the hemispheres following Columbus.[3]
- In 1524, exploring the east coast of what would become the United States, Giovanni de Verrazzano entered Narragansett Bay in Rhode Island where he encountered people that he described as having brass-colored or white skin and long black hair that they carefully trimmed and coiffed. He found the women attractive, well mannered, and well educated, though how he could have determined their educational status is unclear. The older women dressed like those of Egypt or Syria, he thought. Men and women alike wore jewelry, like people in the East. The men had beards. The implication of these descriptive details is that these people were unlike other Native Americans. Examination of old skeletons of Narragansett people in more recent times has shown that, unlike all other natives of North America but like people from the Old World's crowded urban settings, some of the Narragansetts had resistance to tuberculosis.[4] Who were these anomalous people?
- Clearing his land in 1898, a Swedish immigrant in Minnesota discovered a two hundred–pound stone entangled in the roots of a tree. On a side of the object was a runic inscription, in what has been identified as Middle Swedish. Translated, the inscription identifies the author as a member of a party of eight Goths—that is, people from Gotland in the Baltic Sea—and twenty-two Norwegians, exploring the country west from Vinland. One day some of them went fishing. Returning to camp they found ten members of their expedition murdered—"red with blood." They have left ten men guarding their ships fourteen days away. The author calls on the Virgin Mary to save them from evil. He gives the year as 1362.

    The Kensington Stone, as it is called, has long been regarded as a hoax, yet there are some reasons for accepting its authenticity. For example, an English philologist argues that even with access to the kind of linguistic resources that were unavailable to anyone in the nineteenth century, much less a Minnesota farmer, a modern scholar would have considerable difficulty in producing the Stone's text. If it is a forgery, it is a work of genius, he concludes.[5] But could fourteenth-century Vikings have ventured into the American heartland?

To the likes of these, one could add dozens of other wonders, such as the sculpture of what appears to be a Roman head, found under a twelfth-century sealed floor in Mexico; the mysterious Newport tower in Rhode Island; and the Newberry Tablet, inscribed in what Barry Fell identified as an early form of Hittite. Such phenomena are not mysterious at all, for many people, but serve as evidence that Columbus's discovery was preceded by many others, some of which anticipated his voyages by thousands of years. The Kensington Stone proves, they say, that the Vikings did indeed visit the American heartland. They believe that ancient Sumerians, Egyptians, Minoans, Phoenicians, and Romans came to the western hemisphere to extract resources, engage in trade, and advise the natives. They see evidence of a pre–Columbian Israelite presence, African migrants, and Celtic settlers. These alleged forerunners had the means, after all. The Sumerians built seaworthy ships, capable of bringing them copper and tin from distant parts.[6] The Phoenicians drew on Minoan and Egyptian ship-building traditions to construct sailing vessels that were capable of taking them beyond the Pillars of Hercules and into the Atlantic. They learned to tack against the wind. They visited Britain.[7] Herodotus was skeptical of the Phoenician claim that they had circumnavigated Africa, but his description of their report has convinced some scholars that they did.[8] The oceans were not such a barrier as many people think. The earliest settlers of New Guinea and Australia forty thousand years ago had to cross at least two hundred miles of ocean.[9] In 1969 Africans crossed the Atlantic in a replica of the kind of reed sailing vessel that appears in ancient Egyptian illustrations.[10] Chinese sailing vessels of the early fifteenth century dwarfed those of Columbus and their technology was far superior. Why wouldn't some of these pre–Columbian seafarers have found their way to the Americas? Columbus wasn't the first to discover America. He was the last.

Academic researchers generally ignore or dismiss such claims. Their journals are closed to amateur investigators and reporters. But the latter have their own journal, *Ancient American,* a recent edition of which features an article on "King Arthur's Colony in Ancient America" and another on "Pre-Columbian Oil Mining" in Pennsylvania by ancient Minoans.[11] In short, amateur archaeologists offer explanations for fascinating mysteries that most academic researchers make no serious effort to comprehend. On the same side of the fence as the readers and contributors to *Ancient American,* albeit uncomfortably perhaps, are a scattering of academic researchers, such as

Betty Meggers and Paul Shao, that have found "striking parallels" between cultural elements of China's Shang Dynasty of the second millennium BCE and the Olmec civilization of ancient Mesoamerica.[12] Such scholars are known as "diffusionists." In the case of the Shang-Olmec connection, they believe that Pacific voyagers came to the Americas before Columbus bearing Far Eastern ideas, culture, artistry, and possessions that influenced Amerindians and created cultural blends. Their intellectual opponents, called "inventionists," insist that cultural evolution of the western hemisphere before Columbus was indigenous. They say that any cultural diffusion that occurred developed internally. Pre-Columbian cultural parallels between the Old and New World are merely coincidental, in their view. They flow from human commonalities, crudely expressed as "people are the same all over."

Inventionists will concede that on occasion pre–Columbian mariners of the Old World, driven by storms, may have landed on American shores. But they deny that there were any round-trips or repeated trading expeditions between hemispheres. The extensive copper-mining operations near Lake Superior that some say provided much of the material for the Old World's Bronze Age are non-existent in the inventionist universe. Perhaps Polynesians raided the Pacific coast of South America to obtain sweet potatoes: how else explain the Polynesian presence of a South American plant that doesn't reproduce from seeds and spoils in sea water? Other than this, than the Vikings (for whose North American presence there is archaeological evidence), and the possible shipwrecks mentioned above, the inventionists deny pre–Columbian contacts. For them the diffusionists are "cult archaeologists" or faith-based researchers.[13] Although there is no reason for us to take sides in this debate—that would be someone else's book—I should mention that genetic research appears to be making hard-line inventionism decreasingly tenable.[14]

Let's consider something of how this historiographic polarity has played out in the samples of mysterious findings described above:

- Specialists of the Southwestern region examined the photos of the Navajo Mountain inscription and thought that it could represent Indian scrawlings or even a list of cattle brands left by rustlers. Repeated efforts of Stephen Jett to locate the site of the petroglyph were unsuccessful.[15] But over two hundred other enigmatic inscriptions that appear to be of pre–Columbian Eurasian provenance have been found on American rocks.[16]
- As for the amphorae that were found in Brazilian waters, such items have also been discovered off the Atlantic coast of Honduras and

Maine, reportedly. These join reports of the discovery of Roman coins at various points on the Atlantic coast of the Americas and near waterways of the Midwest.[17] The traditional holding was that the ancients, including the Romans, were afraid to venture out of the sanctuary of the Mediterranean and that Caesar's crossing of the English Channel was extraordinarily bold.[18] Now a Roman trade post has been found on Lazarote Island in the Canary Islands off the northwestern African coast.[19] Columbus and the Iberian voyagers that soon followed him learned to sail to the New World via the Canaries, where they could pick up the trade winds that would blow them across the Atlantic. Were they preceded by ancient Romans?

- The German researchers, Svetlana Balabanova and Wolfgang Pirsig, who discovered traces of cocaine, nicotine, and hashish on various mummies, think that their findings can be explained without recourse to speculation regarding pre-Columbian contacts. For example, Erythroxylum species of South Africa, Madagascar, and Mauritius produce cocaine, although not in the quantities of South America's *Erythroxylum coca*. Cocaine-producing plants may have flourished in ancient Egypt and become extinct. Small amounts of nicotine exist in celery, belladonna, and jimson weed, and the Balabanova-Pirsig findings are within dietary limits for these sources. Besides, nineteenth-century museums used tobacco as an insecticide—to protect mummies![20]

- In his best-selling *1421: The Year China Discovered America*, Gavin Mendes claims that the light-skinned Narragansett people serve as evidence that Chinese mariners visited America. The people described by Verrazzano, he thinks, were descended from Chinese concubines and others who had to be jettisoned in New England when, because of shipwrecks in the Caribbean, there was no longer room for them aboard the remaining giant Chinese vessels that were sailing all over the world seven decades before Columbus.[21] A somewhat more cautious scholar suggests that the Narragansetts may have been descended from Leif Eiricksson and the Norse people who visited North America from Greenland.[22]

- As for the Kensington Stone, *Ancient American* contributor and author Frank Joseph traces the inscription to a Cistercian monk from Gotland who was a member of the Knights Templar.[23] A British archaeologist responds by asking, what were Scandinavians doing in the Midwest in the fourteenth century when the days of Norse exploration were in the past?[24] I describe one researcher's answer below.

Culture Bearers

When the diffusionist scrutinizes an advanced civilization in the pre-Columbian Americas, he or she tends to find Eurasian antecedents and influence. Archaeologist Terence Greider, for example, thinks that successive waves of migration out of Asia and into the Pacific Basin eventually reached American shores, bringing astrology, art, astronomy, and other forms of intellectual sophistication. Cultural traits that had long-since become outmoded in Asia put down roots in the western hemisphere. Betty Meggers has found Japanese (Jomon) cultural models in the Valdivian civilization of ancient Ecuador. Architect Paul Shao explains the sudden blossoming of Olmec culture in terms of Chinese influence.[25] Gavin Menzies describes exquisitely carved pieces of walrus ivory, typically representing animals, that have been found in the High Arctic, then asks rhetorically, "Could the Inuit have made them, or were they the art of a civilization almost as old as time itself?"[26] The reader is supposed to conclude, in support of Menzies' thesis, that only Chinese voyagers could have rendered such objects. However, archaeologists attribute these carvings to individual artists of the mysterious Dorset people who lived in the area for thousands of years before the Inuit.[27] Similarly, lacquer decoration flourished in pre-Columbian Mexico and southern California, but the process requires an intricate technique, long-practiced in China. How, Menzies asks, could the Indians have learned of it?[28] Well, maybe they invented it independently of the Chinese.

Diffusionist claims of amateur archaeologists may veer off into white supremacist fantasies. The founder of Andean civilization was a Sumerian, writes Frank Joseph, "a tall, red-bearded, fair-skinned culture bearer." Or was this "fair-haired culture bearer" Egyptian? In any case, the Incan irrigation system was a product of Roman expertise.[29] A monumental building unearthed in Tennessee was clearly not the work of local Indians, thinks Joseph. According to J. Rendel Harris, a scholar of ancient languages, "[t]he red Indian was superimposed on another race," long gone.[30] The language of the Micmac Indians of Canada's Maritime Provinces includes Egyptian words. Their oral traditions speak of "fair-skinned foreigners"—"master magicians"—that came across the Atlantic in ancient times. Indians told George Rogers Clark, American general and frontiersman of the Independence era, that "Fair-skinned Giant Sorcerers" had formerly lived in the Ohio Valley, built the mysterious mounds, brought them agriculture, and introduced metallurgy.[31]

Such pronouncements, here yanked out of a context of supportive claims, will not be made by someone who believes that people are more or less the same all over, however they may differ in terms of geographic, biological, historic, and other advantages. They *will* be made by someone who thinks that some people are qualified to bring cultural assets to others who would otherwise not acquire them. In this view, the high civilizations of the pre-Columbian Americas required seeding by representatives of the high civilizations of Eurasia. Given such assumptions, the conquistadors appear in a new light, as members of a long line of culture bearers that extends even into the present. But the diffusionist need not make racist assumptions. The problem with cultural diffusion, in the opinion of archaeologist David Kelley, is that when it occurs, it gets in the way of indigenous developments that might have flourished without such intervention.[32] Recipients of the external influence could have figured things out for themselves and done so in a way that was uniquely their own.

But this is beside the point that I want to make, which is that (aside from the Vikings, whom we will get to in a minute) if any of these pre-Columbians really did come to the Americas, their experience with Native Americans seems to have followed a very different course than that of the conquistadors. Some of them (the Sumerians and Phoenicians) allegedly came for mineral resources, some (the Chinese) for trade or tribute, and some (Israelites and Celts) to escape Old World others. It seems the only baggage that they left behind consisted of the advanced technology that they passed on to the Indians, strange petroglyphs, caches of coins, mysterious mounds, and a miscellany of marvels of the kind discussed above. Archaeologists ask where is the trash? People don't leave inscriptions and the like, and nothing else. If they spend much time in a place—enough to leave a monumental building, let us say—they leave discarded baggage in the form of litter, middens, garbage, and perhaps shell mounds.[33] On the other hand, past developments need not leave the kind of traces that archaeologists seek. Linguistic connections alone may expose the course of ancient migrations. Literary sources tell us that the ancient Romans imported Chinese silks that have long since turned to dust.[34] People traveling through an area in a hurry may not leave much trash.

Beyond the absence of preservable trash or other evidence of human habitation, why did the obvious hemispheric exchange of flora and fauna have to wait for Columbus if his voyages to the Americas were anticipated by many others? According to Frank Joseph, the ocean-going ships of the Sumerians could carry livestock.[35] Wouldn't they have brought their animals on a voyage that could have lasted for years? Some diffusionists assert that the African emperor Arubakari II organized a transatlantic expedition of two thousand boats loaded with people and livestock that landed on the coast of Brazil in 1312.[36] Sixteenth-century Europeans found "indigenous" blacks in what are now Brazil, Venezuela, and Panama, reportedly, but the expedition of

Arubakari II would gain credibility if they had also found the descendants of African domestic animals. The treasure fleets of early fifteenth-century China carried pigs, chickens, and thousands of cavalry horses. Three of these fleets supposedly made landings in the Americas. As noted above, they may have left voyagers behind in Rhode Island. What happened to the animals? Gavin Menzies says (without attribution) that the first Europeans to visit Peru found horses and camels.[37] What happened to those creatures? Certainly they did not turn into enormous feral herds, like the horses and oxen that were left to roam by the European colonists that followed Columbus, or the pigs that spoiled American wetlands (see Chapters 7 and 10). What Europeans did find, according to Menzies,[38] were four varieties of Asiatic chickens in South America. But this could be consistent with Polynesian contacts rather than proof of Chinese. Frank Joseph says that early Brazilian colonists encountered representatives of *Potamochoerus porcus,* also known as "Guinea hogs" which are native to Africa.[39] Because he says so without citation, we must take his word for it—or not.

According to Menzies, one of the objectives of the voyages ordered by the Ming emperor Zhu Di in 1421 was to find "healing plants" and medicinal remedies for the plagues and epidemics that were ravaging China.[40] What about the microbial agents of such plagues and epidemics that at least a few of the thousands of voyagers that the fleets supposedly carried must have embodied? Chapter 11 discusses the devastating impact on indigenous Americans of the microbial invaders carried by the conquistadors. It took just one infected person to cause the smallpox epidemic that probably did more than anything else that the invaders brought to Mexico to bring down the Aztecs. Yet skeletal findings show that, before Columbus, Amerindians were not afflicted by such "crowd-type diseases" as smallpox, measles, bubonic plague, and cholera, though they had their share of other illnesses.[41] In short, any pre–Columbian contacts with the "virgin populations" of the Americas seem not to have resulted in the transfer of pathogens of the kind that thrived in the crowded conditions of the advanced civilizations of Eurasia, such as China and Rome, nor did they leave free-ranging herds of Old World domestic animals. The implications for claims of pre–Columbian contacts are not so good.

In his *Why the West Rules—for Now,* historian Ian Morris plays with Gavin Menzies' thesis by imagining Admiral Zheng He as Cortés, presiding over the destruction of Tenochtitlán and the collapse of the Aztec Empire.[42] For the inventionist, the invasion of the Caribbean and Mesoamerica by the conquistadors is the only significant model for initial contact between representatives of Eurasia and the Americas that we have. Diffusionist claims offer many alternative models. Are such claims valid? Do they represent an unconscious attempt to mitigate what happened with the arrival of Iberians? What if such inveterate traders as the Venetians had gotten here first? Clearly the conquistadors were culture bearers of a different kind, as the following chapters will elaborate. Hernán Cortés, Pedro de Alvarado, and the rest who came to Mexico in 1519 were "fair-skinned" bearers of a culture that was lethal to the natives of America, and the material and organic portions of their baggage proved pernicious, as well.

Vikings in America

The Introduction poses the question of whether there was a pre–Columbian point in time when contact between Europeans and indigenous Americans might have been benign? With the Viking voyages to North America of around the year 1000, such undisputed contact did occur, and while it would not be described as entirely "benign," neither was it genocidal. Because far less is known of these contacts than we know of those that began with Columbus—in part because they did not result in permanent European settlement—the Italian navigator is usually credited with the Eurocentric feat of "discovering" America. But at least one of the earlier landfalls made from Iceland and more often from Greenland is supported by archaeological findings of Viking-style buildings at a site on the northern tip of Newfoundland, L'Anse aux Meadows. In addition, there are the transcriptions of oral traditions, the Icelandic Sagas, that were made two hundred and more years after the earliest Norse expeditions took place.

Where they discuss the visits to North American sites, the Sagas are, admittedly, an intriguing compound of the mundane and the marvelous. For example, "The Saga of the Greenlanders" states that the Vikings took "all sorts of livestock with them" to "Vinland."[43] We need not greet this statement with the kind of skepticism that we reserve for another Saga's story of a one-legged man who attacked the expedition with bow and arrows, then "ran off back north" before the Vikings could catch him.[44] Archaeological findings are a mixed bag, too. They include considerable information brought to light by excavations at L'Anse aux Meadows, but they have also given rise to various conjectures as to the location of Vinland and the settlements named in the Sagas, the purpose of the Norse visits to North America, the range of their explorations, and other perplexing matters. As much as possible, I hope to limit what follows to consideration of what the Vikings brought to America—their baggage—and the impact of this cultural and material mélange on the people they encountered there.

Following the accidental discovery of unknown lands west of Greenland, voyagers from Greenland and Iceland mounted a series of expeditions to the shores of these new lands, which they called Helluland, Markland, and Vinland. "Helluland" translates as Slab Land, presumably designating the rockbound wastes of Baffin Island and perhaps northern Labrador. "Markland" means Forest Land, the Norse name for southern Labrador and Newfoundland, in the opinion of most scholars. As for "Vinland," one might easily assume that this means Wine Land, named for the wild grapes that the Vikings collected. If these adventurers had been French, such an assumption would certainly be correct. But in Old Norse, "Vinland" translates as Fertile Land, says a linguist, Graeme Davis.[45] Where was Vinland exactly? An archaeologist thinks that L'Anse aux Meadows was no more than a base or transit point for visits to the St. Lawrence River Valley and perhaps areas farther south: these were the Vinland of the Sagas.[46]

If the Vikings were seeking fertile land (Vinland), their North American

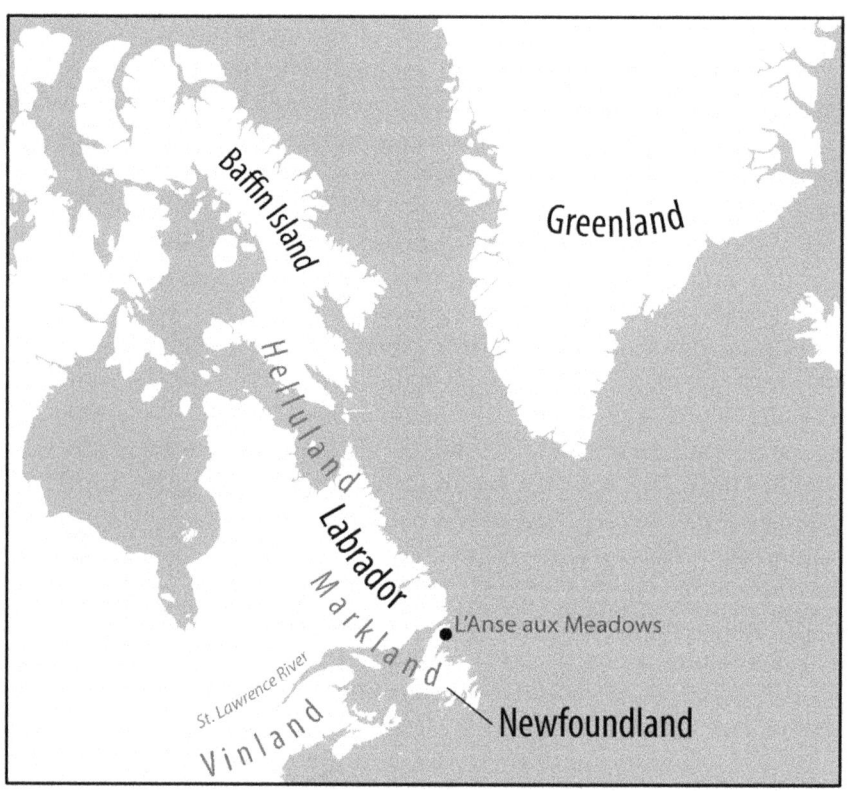

Viking America (author's collection).

venture may represent an effort to find new farm sites, at least at first. They were farmers and pastoralists, after all. Their settlement of a then-warmer Greenland consisted of a scattering of farms, with maybe twenty to thirty people at each site.[47] The "Saga of the Greenlanders" says "they intended to settle in the country [Vinland] if they could."[48] Finding an attractive spot, Thorvald Eiriksson announces that he would like to build his farm there.[49] Opposing the view that the Norse intended to settle in America is archaeologist Birgitta Wallace, who thinks that the expeditions described in the Sagas represent no more than exploratory probes, intended to bring back useful goods and gain prestige for the participants. According to the Sagas, the Greenlanders collected furs, obtained in trade with the Indians, as well as the aforementioned wild grapes. The latter would have been turned into wine, a highly prestigious item in the social world of the Norse.[50] In any event, there were not enough Greenlanders to sustain settlements in Greenland and in North America too. Colonization of North America would have meant abandoning the Greenland project; it would have put European luxuries nearly out of reach.

Native Encounters

The Sagas describe a fraught relationship with the indigenous North Americans that the Vikings encountered. Following a battle, the Vikings withdrew from an otherwise favorable site called Hop (meaning Tide Pool) because they realized that they "would be under constant attack from its prior inhabitants."[51] (Commentators place Hop at locations ranging from New Brunswick to Long Island.) The Vikings called the natives they encountered "skraelings," meaning "skin-wearers," according to one source. Another sees the term as a slur, meaning something like "scared weaklings." The Icelandic authors of the Sagas seem to have lost interest in the Greenlanders after describing a few expeditions of the earliest years, but there is every reason to assume that the latter continued their visits to America over the course of their four centuries-plus of Greenland settlement, perhaps making hundreds of voyages to obtain timber from Markland. Greenland had only stunted trees, and without timber there was no possibility of shipbuilding and repair. With the Roman Church and the king of Norway imposing trade and tax burdens on the Greenlanders after the early years, commerce with Europe became increasingly costly, forcing the Greenland settlers to depend more and more on whatever resources they could extract from North America.[52] In 1347 a Greenland ship bearing timber from Markland was driven off course and landed in Iceland.[53] In view of such venturing, the Norse would probably have encountered representatives of the shrinking population of the Dorset people; late-arriving Inuits who were moving east from Alaska and succeeding (if not displacing) the Dorsets in the High Arctic; and in the Vinland years, the Beothuks of Newfoundland, among others. (The Beothuks were the first Native Americans to be exterminated, not by the Vikings but by their European successors.)[54] All were *skraelings* to the Vikings, or so it seems. The Sagas depict the natives as alternately warlike and eager to trade, but they tell us little else about them.

Viking materials such as bits of smelted iron have turned up at Dorset sites from Labrador to the High Arctic. But there were few of the Dorset people and not many Vikings either: contact must have been sporadic. Norse material including a trove of valuables found at Inuit sites across the Canadian Arctic suggests more frequent contact with these migrants from the west. But the Arctic people traded widely among themselves. Did the Vikings enter their trade networks? Did these materials come from a wrecked Viking ship or an abandoned farm and become scattered through trade? Was it from the Dorsets or the Inuits that the Vikings got the walrus and narwhale ivory that they shipped to Europe as unicorn horns in exchange for timber and luxuries? At this point, the answers are speculative.[55] Graeme Davis seems to think that the widespread scattering of Norse materials represents the range of their explorations. The Inuit could not have left the stone foundations found at several sites, he says. This raises the intriguing possibility that the Vikings got as far as the western side of Hudson Bay, which could have provided an arduous riverine route to Minnesota and the Kensington Stone. Not that Davis believes they made such a trip.[56]

Religion

Efforts to convert Greenlanders to Christianity, ordered by King Olaf of Norway, had begun shortly before the voyages to North America. During this period of religious transition, people might consult with a prophetess during hard times, but only with great reluctance would a Greenland woman admit to knowing the magical chants required by the oracle's ritual.[57] Unlike Cortés and company five centuries later, the pagans and newly-minted Christians who traveled to Vinland and other American parts appear to have made no effort to convert the natives that they encountered to the new religion or to attack native religious practices. They were warriors but not holy warriors. This points up the fact that the Vikings were separated from the conquistadors by much more than the passage of time. Except for taxes that the Church levied on the Greenlanders to pay for crusades, such as the "Crusading Tithe" (1274–1282),[58] the Christian rivalry with Islam that put Spain on the frontline of sanctified war could hardly have been more remote. For the crusading Spaniard, on the other hand, non–Christians were akin to Muslims, the generic enemy, thus subject to conversion at the point of a sword.

Weapons

The Vikings had iron swords, spears, and axes. An archaeologist speculates that their swords would not have given them much of an advantage against "well-aimed" arrows.[59] (As we will see, the conquistadors' steel swords were highly advantageous against arrows that were only intended to wound.) According to the Sagas, the Indians coveted Norse weapons. Thorfinn Karlsefni, who led one of the early Vinland expeditions, had to dissuade others from trading them to the *skraelings* for furs. One of the natives supposedly tested a Viking ax by striking a companion with it. The blow killed him, and their chief threw the weapon into the sea. In another anecdote (or another version of the same incident), likewise probably intended to demonstrate the natives' relative lack of technological sophistication, the *skraelings* tested a Viking ax on trees. They liked the result, but when the ax struck a stone, it broke, and they tossed it away.[60] On the other hand, the *skraelings* had a weapon that was unknown to the Vikings and filled them with horror. Hoisting a large black object onto poles, the natives sent it flying toward them. It made a "threatening noise" on landing.[61]

Mineral Wealth

The Vikings were not seeking precious metals. In fact, their Greenland leader, Eirik the Red, hid a chest of gold and silver at his home when he decided to accompany his son, Leif the Lucky, to Vinland. In the absence of establishing a lasting settlement, the Vikings seem to have regarded the acquisition of timber, skins, and fruit-bearing vines as marking a successful Vinland venture, at least in the early expeditions covered by the Sagas. Securing food was their paramount concern: Vinland's wild grapes, herds of deer, and shoals of salmon were their gold and silver.

Uncovered at L'Anse aux Meadows was a smithy that the Vikings evidently used to make iron nails, presumably for ship repair. A twelfth-century source says that "[b]eyond Greenland, still farther to the north, hunters have come across people of small stature who are called Skraelings.... They do not know the use of iron, but employ walrus tusks as missiles and sharpened stones as knives."[62] These may have been Dorset people, for the Inuits that the Norse were also encountering prized iron including the spikes, nails, and rivets of Viking vessels. They converted these into spear tips, knife blades, and engraving tools.[63] Patricia Sutherland speculates that the Inuit may have been drawn east by the presence in northwestern Greenland of a large store of meteoritic iron.[64] Though their metallurgy was limited to the annealing process—pounding iron or copper into shape rather than smelting it— Graeme Davis wonders if their metal work was inspired by Viking contacts.[65] Imagine, if you will, the wary Inuit watching from a distance as the Vikings smelted nails and the like, becoming aware of the possibility of shaping ores but remaining ignorant of the best technique. Wouldn't the kind of people who invented the kayak, the igloo, and perhaps the Alaskan Husky—people that thrived under conditions that would kill almost anyone else[66]—have learned how to fashion things out of metal on their own?

Old World Domestic Animals

The Greenland settlers kept cows, horses, pigs, goats, and sheep[67]—the entire suite of European farm animals minus fowls. A literal reading of the Saga's statement that they brought "all sorts" of livestock to Vinland would have them filling their ships with representatives of all of these animals. The assertion that the male animals proved hard to handle, once the Norse reached land,[68] says that they brought males and females. The only such creature mentioned in the Sagas is a bull that came bellowing out of the forest to terrify the *skraelings*. In "Eirik the Red's Saga," the natives make a dash for their boats and row quickly away. In "The Saga of the Greenlanders," the appearance of the bull throws the Indians into such a panic that they try to hide in Karlsefni's house. Saga listeners must have gotten a chuckle out of that. To resolve the tension, Karlsefni has the Viking women bring out milk and other dairy products for which the natives are only too eager to trade furs. The Vikings later put the bull at the fore as they go into battle against the *skraelings*.[69]

The question is what became of the Viking animals? No corrals or pens have been discovered at L'Anse aux Meadows where archaeologists have found a bone of a domestic pig.[70] It appears that the Vikings' domestic animals either roamed freely like the bull in the woods or were soon slaughtered for food.[71] Unlike eighteenth-century settlers of Argentina, the English fishing families that settled Newfoundland centuries later did not encounter feral herds of the descendants of Old World domestic animals. Conditions there didn't favor their proliferation, it appears. Can the same be said of the Old World animals that disputed other pre–Columbian visitors might have left?

Old World Savagery

Besides what seem to have been primarily defensive battles, the Vikings demonstrated a capacity for arbitrary murder. The Saga says that members of the expedition of Thorvald Eiriksson killed eight natives that they found hiding under canoes and another five who were asleep in their skin sacks.[72] Like the conquistadors, the Vikings brought a willingness to slaughter others without good cause.

Labor as a Resource

There is no indication in the Sagas that the Vikings tried to capture Vinland natives for their labor power, although slavery was known to them. The conquistadors, on the other hand, were not interested in farming. They had aristocratic pretensions and despised farmers (peasants). An aristocrat did not work with his hands except to ride a horse and battle enemies. He made ignoble others work for him. But more on this in Chapter 8.

Micro-Invaders

Whether the Vikings, like the conquistadors, infected the Indians they encountered with disease-causing germs is unknown. At least one researcher thinks that disease agents carried by the Vikings might have caused or contributed to the puzzling decline of the Dorset people. Their last few survivors were killed by a European disease brought to them by whalers in 1902.[73] The Vikings themselves were beset by infectious disease, losing entire crews at various points in the narratives.[74] By the sixteenth century Europeans had acquired immunity to some of the Old World's most lethal microorganisms. This immunity and Indian susceptibility would convince many on both sides that Europeans enjoyed divine favor. Several other items in the conquistadors' suite of deadly baggage were already in place by the year 1000, if not borne by the Greenlanders. All in all, the centuries of Viking visits to the High Arctic and what are now Canada's Maritime Provinces left a negligible impact on the New World.

2

Iberian Voyagers

Joao Fernandez, a Portuguese pirate, explored the coast of Greenland around 1500, but for most Europeans the remote settlements and rumor of lands to the southwest of Greenland had by then become an all but forgotten dream. Some think that pirate depredations and tax raids caused or at least contributed to the demise of the Greenlanders. Payment of a crusade tax in 1327 alone would have required the tusks of some two hundred walruses.[1] The Breton, Basque, Bristol, and Portuguese fishermen that roved the waters off Newfoundland before John Cabot's better known voyage of 1497 may have put a squeeze on what remained of Greenland's export market, as well. But the cooling climate of the Little Ice Age that began around 1300 probably played a bigger role. Yet as late as 1623, pieces of a Greenland-type vessel washed ashore in Iceland.[2]

In any event, a modern map of the Atlantic and its shores suggests a more promising crossing route well to the south of these Arctic climes, where the bulge of northwestern Africa seems to strain toward the curve of northeastern Brazil. North East trade winds blow in this direction, too.[3] As noted in Chapter 1, some think that Africans took advantage of this geographic configuration, these trade winds, and the west-flowing ocean currents to visit the Western Hemisphere long before Columbus. Ivan Van Sertima, a controversial anthropologist and linguist, has presented many reasons for concluding that Africans were present in Mesoamerica at some point during the Olmec era (1200–400 BCE) and again during the fourteenth and fifteenth centuries. The most spectacular and perhaps the most compelling evidence that he adduces for this belief are the colossal stone heads found in Mexico in the nineteenth century that seem to bear facial features of sub–Saharan Africans.[4] Van Sertima also cites botanical evidence of a pre–Columbian exchange. Arriving in West Africa some decades before Columbus's discovery of America, Portuguese adventurers found cotton, indigenous to the Caribbean and South America, growing in abundance.[5] Besides the stone heads, Van Sertima describes linguistic, forensic, archaeological, cultural, and historical evidence of an African presence in the Caribbean, Mesoamerica, and South America. But it is his geographical considerations that should interest us here. Although he may exaggerate when he says that powerful Atlantic currents will "automatically, irresistibly" carry a craft lacking engine-resistance from the west coast of Africa to the Americas, the fact remains that in 1952 one Alain Bombard used a life raft to drift from the coast of Morocco to Barbados in the Caribbean.[6] We noted the Atlantic crossing of Thor Heyerdahl's Egyptian-replica reed boat, crewed by Africans, in Chapter 1. In 2011 a team of elderly Britons voyaged from the Canaries to the Caribbean on a raft of lashed-together plastic pipes with a sail on a phone pole.[7] More recently a South African couple crossed the Atlantic from the Moroccan coast in a row boat.[8] It looks easy, given these facts, but until European mariners sailed down the African coast to a point where they could pick up favorable winds and currents, they were prevented from crossing the Atlantic except at Viking latitudes. Columbus had to sail south before he could venture west.

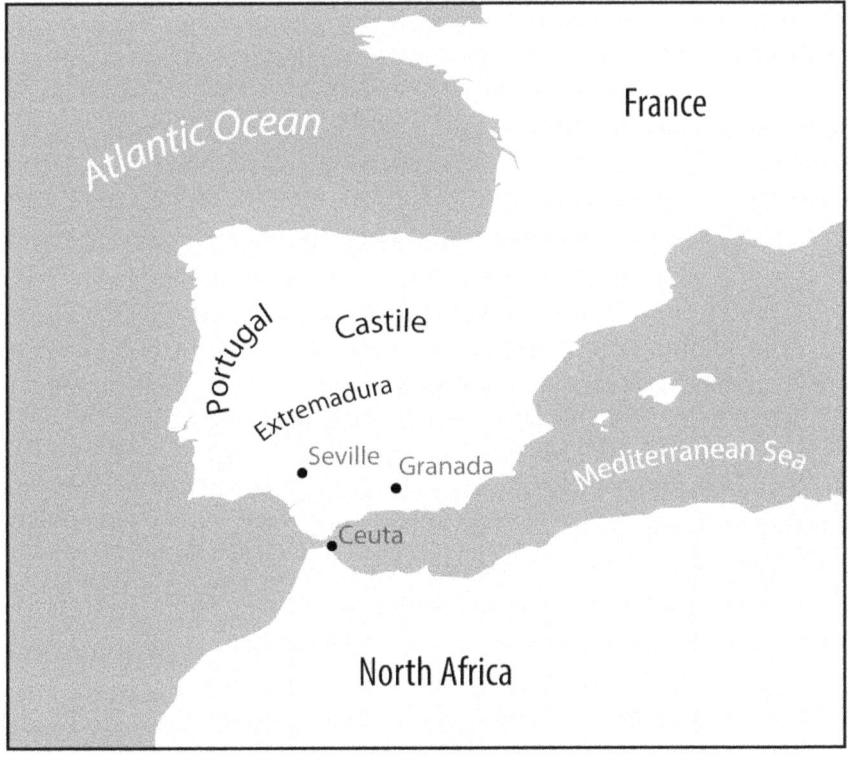

Iberia and surroundings, c. 1500 (author's collection).

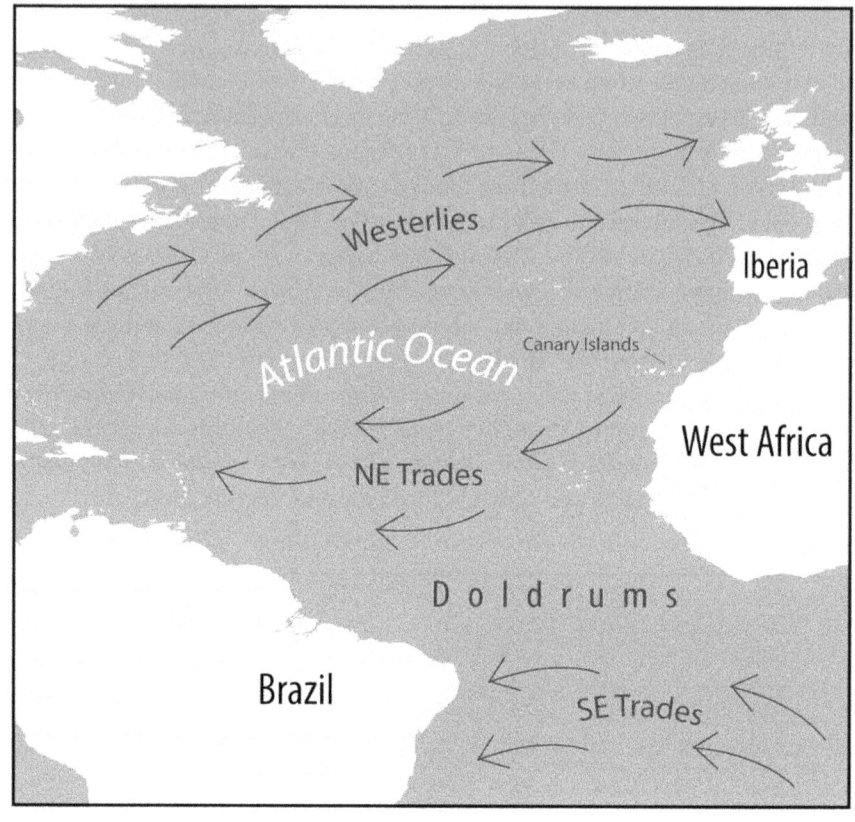

Atlantic wind patterns (author's collection).

Returning to the map, we may note the projection of Iberia out into the Atlantic. This geographic feature and perhaps Iberian idiosyncrasy, as well, inspired José Saramago, the great Portuguese writer, to imagine (in *The Stone Raft*) the region breaking off and drifting away from the rest of Europe. For medieval Genoese and other Mediterranean merchants bound for Flanders and other destinations in northwestern Europe, Portugal became a convenient place to put ashore and attend to any needed ship repairs. In the early fourteenth century, a Genoese admiral supervised the building of a Portuguese fleet to be used both for trading and crusading.[9] Christian mariners had long since mimicked their Arabic counterparts by adopting the lateen (or triangular) sail, greatly increasing the maneuverability of European ships. Mediterranean sailors of the fifteenth century then modified the square-rigged merchant ships (cogs) of the northern Atlantic to produce the barque, an ancestor of the square-riggers of the Age of Discovery. The caravel, a small ship of the kind that flanked the *Santa Maria* on Columbus's most famous voyage, was versatile but cramped. These were usually added to the fleet of larger European ships of early transoceanic voyages.[10] Reporting to Emperor Moctezuma, an Indian who had spotted some of these high-masted vessels off the Yucatan coast in 1518, described them as "a range of mountains ... floating on the sea."[11] (Or did he? Camilla Townsend argues that this oft-repeated story is based on a faulty translation.)[12]

Shipbuilding and design were important, but discovery of new lands also required the re-discovery of Ptolemy, the geographer and mathematician of the ancient world. For this, if nothing else, Iberian voyagers could thank the Turks, who sent Byzantine mapmakers fleeing to the west.[13] Also taking some of the guesswork out of sailing were advances in the compass, use of the deep-sea lead and line to gauge the depth of coastal waters, and adoption of the quadrant and astrolabe for stellar navigation.[14] All this might suggest that progress in marine technology guided American discovery and colonization. With such advances, the bigger ships of the Romans might have carried trans–Atlantic colonists. But technological progress was insufficient in itself. The giant ships of Ming China with their watertight compartments, reinforced bows, multiple keels, semi-submersible anchors, and four-sided sails—among other advanced features—had the capacity to sail around the world.[15] (Gavin Menzies argues that they did.) However, only western Europeans had the motivation to finance lengthy voyages into uncharted waters on a sustained basis. It fell to fifteenth-century rulers of Portugal and then Castile to encourage such ventures.

The Quest for Gold, Silk, Spices and a Christian Army

At the time of the famous Iberian voyages of discovery, Europe was suffering a "gold famine," pinching the import of luxuries. During this era of heavy meat-eating (at least in northern Europe) when, other than by ice or snow, refrigeration was not even a distant dream, Eastern spices were sought to cover up suspicious flavors. Affluent women longed for Asian silks, as they had since the salad days of Rome. But satisfaction of such demands had become increasingly difficult since the early fifteenth century when the sultans who ruled Egypt had prohibited Christians from traveling south of Cairo. This had the effect of banning them from the Red Sea and Indian Ocean. Add the fact that in 1421 the Ottomans had blocked the sea route through the Bosporus to the western end of the Silk Road, the ancient overland trade route that linked Europe to China.[16] The upshot was that Christian merchants could no longer bypass Islamic territory. They had instead to deal with Muslim middlemen and the canny Venetians who would deal with anyone. To make matters worse, European imports of spices, silks, ceramics, and other goods from the (East) Indies and distant East Asia required payment in precious metals. They almost always had, as Europe produced little else of interest to the producers of such goods or the merchants who now controlled the trade routes. But at this point Central European mines were almost played out.

Camel caravans carried African gold as well as slaves, spices, ivory, indigo, shellac, and other goods, plodding north from Mali across the Sahara via Marrakesh, Fez, and Meknes to Ceuta and other ports on the Mediterranean. Under the trappings of a Christian crusade, the Portuguese captured Ceuta in 1415, giving them some control over these gold shipments. From the viewpoint of European merchants and non–Portuguese monarchs, however, the gold caravans represented more of a bottleneck than an adequate supply of bullion.[17] Castile, in particular, was financially hard-pressed, as the expense of Reconquest was a drain on her treasury.

What Gavin Menzies calls Portugal's "stranglehold" on the trans–Sahara gold shipments[18] that came with the capture of Ceuta could not have lasted long, as soon Africa's gold began to call out to the royal sponsors of Portuguese maritime expeditions: Why wait for camel caravans? Why not go directly to the source? Imagining a truncated Africa, the Portuguese thought that by sailing south along the African coast they might find a backdoor to the Spice Islands (or East Indies), circumventing Egyptian and Venetian middlemen. Surely Portuguese sailors could get around such an abbreviated mass. Or could they? European efforts to reach the wealth of sub–Saharan Africa and India by sailing down the west coast of Africa had begun in 1291 when the Vivaldi brothers of Genoa led an expedition that passed through the Straits of Gibraltar and got as far south as the coast opposite the Canary Islands. But they were never heard from again. Fourteenth-century chroniclers like João de Barros saw Cape Bojador and the Canaries as the absolute limit of viable exploration. Beyond, they thought, was an uninhabitable "*torrid zone*" that was but a "*pasture for beasts.*"[19] But Portuguese rulers, seeking expansion, were spurred by rivalry with Castile, whose representatives argued that a realm known as Mauretania Tingitana, once ruled by Visigoths, extended all the way to the Canaries. Castilian penetration of this area, they maintained, would be a "natural extension" of the Reconquest.[20]

Thus prodded, Portuguese mariners sailed farther and farther down the African coast—Cape Branco, Cape Verde, Sierra Leone, the Grain Coast, the

Ivory Coast, the Gold Coast, the Slave Coast... The Portuguese then built a large fort at San Jorge da Mina (in today's Ghana). Sanctioned by papal bulls, this fort drew gold from the Sahara trade route, garnering profits that doubled the revenue of the Crown between 1480 and 1500.[21] At length, with a voyage that began in 1487, Bartolomeu Dias led two caravels around Cape Hope. The Portuguese were on track to capture some East Indian spice sources and establish a commercial empire. They appear to have had no interest in the potential of North East trade winds to blow them west to unknown parts from the coast of West Africa. That was left to Columbus, under the sponsorship of Castile.

Portugal's entry into the Indian Ocean suggested to many a grand strategy for the encirclement of the Muslim world and enrichment of Europe. Christians would establish a maritime link to India, thereby preempting the Muslim trade routes that made spices such expensive commodities as European imports. In addition, they would unite with the vast army of eastern Christians that, in their imaginings, marched under the command of the legendary Prester John. Some trace this belief to an actual event, the 1141 Battle of the Katvan Steppe, when Nestorian Christians were part of a Mongol force that defeated a Muslim army.[22] But the myth was so elastic that one of Portugal's incentives for sending voyagers down the west coast of Africa in the fifteenth century was the expectation that one of the rivers that empties into the Atlantic along that coast would prove to be a branch of the Nile that would take them to Ethiopia, where Prester John was also thought to reside.[23] When they finally got to India, Portuguese mariners announced that they were seeking spices and Christians.[24] Vasco da Gama began to venerate a statue of a Hindu goddess that he mistook for the Virgin Mary.[25] The Portuguese brought back spices, but the Christians they were seeking proved as much of a fantasy as the medieval travel guide of John Mandeville, which characterized Prester John as "the great emperor of India."[26]

While the Portuguese would not encircle the Ottoman Empire by linking up with an Asian (or African) army of Christians, Franciscan backers of Columbus imagined a different kind of encirclement. They thought that his initial voyage might enable Christians to enter Muslim-occupied Jerusalem through a "back door," thereby ushering in Revelation's "last age of humanity."[27] In addition to their quest for precious metals, their determination to escape the unhappy terms of Europe's luxury imports, and their desire to advance Christianity at the expense of the Islamic enemy, Iberians hoped to find new lands with the soil and climate for growing sugar. By 1500 or so, Portugal's plantations in the Azores and Madeira, and Castile's in the Canaries, were feeding a growing sweet tooth among Europeans. But sugar cultivation required lots of people to work under harsh conditions. Sugar fueled demand for slaves who could be made to work under such conditions.[28]

Ominous Doctrine

Suppose an Aztec sorcerer or priest had somehow learned of the kind of developments I've described above, the building of oceangoing vessels by distant Iberians and their entry of the even more distant Indian Ocean. Let us suppose, further, that this sorcerer had knowledge of Columbus's plan to visit China and its fabled riches by sailing south and then west from Europe. Were he geographically sophisticated as well as prescient, such a seer would realize that this course might bring Europeans into the Caribbean and its many islands. They might even get as far as the eastern coast of Mexico. If they could do that…

In fact, the Aztecs had no foreknowledge of the arrival of Europeans. And unlike the latter, they had no policy in place to deal with such perfect strangers, however imperfect they might prove to be. But these strangers they would soon encounter, these European Christians, had plans for dealing with them that went back over two hundred years. The Hostiensis doctrine, named after a thirteenth-century canonical lawyer, held that with the coming of Christ pagans had lost the right to rule themselves. Such natural rights as they may have formerly enjoyed—the right to liberty, property, and sovereignty—had devolved to Christians, and only the Church could confer legitimate political authority.[29] In a rather more ambitious version of this doctrine, Pope Innocent IV had declared that since God had created everything, the pope had dominion over "every human creature," both in body and soul. ("[E]very human creature" was later amended to "every Christian," but not in time to do great numbers of human creatures in America any good.)[30] Anticipating later discoveries or perhaps responding to Viking reports, Pope Clement declared in 1344 that the pope had the discretion to dispose of pagan islands as he chose. (Pagan continents were beyond imagining at the time.) Acknowledging Portugal's discoveries, a papal bull of 1454 known as *Romanus Pontifex* gave the king of Portugal the authority to "invade, conquer, dispossess, subjugate, and perpetually enslave" all non–Christians in Portugal's Atlantic possessions (the uninhabited Azores and Madeira), Muslim northwest Africa, and south through Guinea "toward the [as yet undiscovered] southern shore."[31] If, following a meeting at which Christians explained the interpretation of history to be found in both the New and Old Testament, non–Christians declined to accept these truths and also refused Christian colonization, Christians had a religious duty to kill them. In addition, under the doctrine of *terra nullius* (no-man's-land), Christians had the right to invade and conquer pagan lands, dispossess such non–Christians of all their goods, expel them from their lands, and enslave them.[32] Considering what followed in the Americas, such tenets do not represent antiquarian curiosities.

However, more benign elements of Church doctrine specified that while Christians could require any non-believers they encountered to accept missionaries and could punish them for natural law violations, they could not attack them for being infidels or force them to convert. Clerics and theologians would find ample grounds for recommending punishment of indigenous Americans for "natural law violations," as we shall see. In 1455 Pope Nicholas V issued a bull that promised "suitable favors and special graces" to Catholic monarchs who vanquished infidels "and their kingdoms and habitations, though situated in the remotest parts unknown to us."[33]

In sum, Christian rulers were thought to have "automatic dominion" over pagans and other non–Christians.[34] No wonder the log-book of Columbus's first voyage shows him appropriating one Caribbean island after another on behalf of Castile and Aragon.[35] Following the report of his discoveries, while Columbus was just beginning to organize his second voyage, Pope Alexander VI issued two bulls, dividing the oceanic world to the west between Castile and Portugal. Thus, the natives of the Indies and the American mainland subsequently encountered by Columbus and his successors were already vassals of the Castilian or Portuguese crown, or so they were regarded by Iberian voyagers and settlers. If they resisted the invaders, they were engaged in rebellion, not legitimate self-defense. The pontiff commanded Ferdinand and Isabel to continue the work of discovery begun by Columbus in order to subjugate and convert to the Catholic faith the inhabitants of the newly discovered lands and islands, as well as those yet to be discovered.[36] In effect, the Church had issued a license for Castilian conquest, and this at a time when the notion of universal human rights was not even a glimmer in the mind of Bartolomé de Las Casas.

Backward Discoverers

If the people of the Caribbean and Mesoamerica had had any choice in the matter, they would surely have preferred not to be "discovered" by anyone. In the event, they could not have done much worse than discovery by representatives of Castile, where the ideal of waging holy war, though largely forgotten in other parts of Europe, still flourished in the early sixteenth century. The Church had put the retaking of Spain from what were regarded as Muslim occupiers on the same footing as the liberation of Jerusalem. The Reconquest made Castile "a society organized for war" in which one's hopes and opportunities for advancement were bound up with military exploits.[37] Nobles were trained from childhood in the arts of warfare. As for commoners, every able-bodied man was obliged, at least in principle, to maintain readiness to go to war if so ordered, and military discipline was strictly enforced. For townspeople, the raiding of enemy territory for booty was "an industry."[38] Roman legal doctrine had held that the conqueror could claim conquered land, and as the Reconquest advanced, Christian emigrants quickly filled the lands that had been "cleansed" of Moors, just as the descendants of such settlers would colonize the Americas.[39] For hidalgos like Cortés who made up much of the leadership of the conquistadors—men who had inherited titles but not much else—warfare afforded the best and perhaps the only opportunity to obtain land, collect rents, and enjoy the higher status, income, and privileges that went with such ownership. The Reconquest had served as a seven-hundred-year rehearsal for the conquest and colonization of what would become Spanish America.

Much of this could be said of the Aztecs, as well. These fierce late-comers to the Valley of Mexico had only their military prowess to offer the rulers of Azcapotzalco, the city state that ruled the Valley in the fourteenth century. At length, the Aztecs led a rebellion against their patrons and, with powerful allies, became rulers of a vast empire that they held together by warfare and intimidation. As in Castile, accomplishment in battle afforded the Aztec male the greatest opportunity for social advancement. For the commoner, there was no other path to joining the ranks of the nobility.[40] Does the fact that both the conquistadors and the Aztecs were representatives of societies that were heavily invested in war mean that they faced one another from a position of rough parity? Not at all. The conquistadors' readiness to fight was hugely augmented by their lethal accoutrements. The deadly baggage that had piled up in the course of European history and the Reconquest would blow up in the Caribbean, Mesoamerica, and the Andes. Besides military and other advantages that we will examine in ensuing chapters, these Europeans would arrive with warring practices that were unknown to the indigenous Americans they would face, such as a willingness to starve people into submission.

In 1492 Castile and Aragon had been recently united under Ferdinand and Isabel, with Castile the dominant partner. Granada was the last bastion of Moorish Spain. When it fell that same portentous year, Spain had finally completed the Reconquest. But Christian Spaniards continued to live in fear. Their Mediterranean coastline appeared susceptible to seaborne reprisal by the Ottomans. Even after becoming Christian converts, former Muslims represented a potential fifth column. In addition, anti–Semitism was endemic. A century earlier there had been anti–Jewish riots in which crowds killed thousands and forced thousands of others to convert. When peasants and townspeople reacted against aristocratic privilege and oppression, they usually directed their collective energies against Jews and Muslims, or *Conversos* and *Moriscos*—Jews and Muslims that had converted to Christianity, at least nominally. Spanish place-names still bear witness to this intolerance. Whether a village in northern Spain named Castrillo Matajudos (Little Castle of Kill the Jews) was named that by anti–Semites or by Jews living there for self-protection, as some think, is unclear.[41] But the question speaks volumes. A world atlas shows three towns named Matamoros (Kill Moors), all in Mexico. Jews were said to be lazy, greedy, promiscuous, and malodorous people who practiced necromancy, sodomy, and ritualistic infanticide.[42] Spanish colonists would soon dust off such epithets and apply them to Indians.

Within two months of the fall of Granada, Isabel ordered the expulsion of Spanish Jews. Their confiscated property financed Columbus's voyages. Muslims who refused conversion were also expelled, as priests burned thousands of books by Moorish geographers, astronomers, mathematicians, poets, scientists, historians, and philosophers.[43] Irreplaceable Aztec records would receive the same treatment. "Burn them all," ordered a bishop in Mexico. "They are all works of the Devil."[44] Instead of the Renaissance, Spain got the Inquisition's search for secret Jews. In short, the Americas could hardly have been invaded by representatives of a more backward and intolerant society. The irony of this is that in Moorish Spain, Christians and Jews had peacefully co-existed with Muslims. The Ottomans granted religious minorities within their Constantinople-centered realm a kind of local autonomy and generally tolerated pagans, as well. However, although Muslim Morocco had an Atlantic coastline, a foray into ocean waters had no place on the Ottoman agenda. The Ottomans had their hands full in expanding their territory into southeastern Europe, the Fertile Crescent, the Persian Gulf, and Egypt.[45] In the Atlantic they would have run up against European superiority in weaponry and sea power. There was never any possibility of an Islamic Columbus.

Hernán Cortés and several of the other conquistador leaders hailed from Extremadura in southwestern Castile, a land of murders, robberies, brawls, illegal detentions, and unauthorized land occupations. There men who murdered prisoners and innocents became cult heroes. Organizations of commoners known as the *hermandades* (brotherhoods) maintained order by cutting off feet, hands, and heads.[46] Evidently such terror tactics were ineffective. Hugh Thomas calls Medellín, the region's principal city, "the most undisciplined of towns,"[47] and outside such towns, "everything was robbery and murder."[48] When a hidalgo like Martín Cortés, Hernán's father, wasn't fighting Moors he was serving his patron by battling his own kind for control of land, castles, and cattle. No one traveled without heavily-armed companions.[49] A crisis of 1502–1508 served as an "economic draft," impelling men like Hernán Cortés to seek their fortune in the Indies. If Spain had been a city, we could say that many of the invaders of the Caribbean and Mesoamerica came from its roughest neighborhood.

A Model for American Conquest

Ancient geographers like Strabo knew the Canaries as the "Fortunate Isles," in recognition of their mild climate when compared to the inferno-like conditions of the Saharan mainland. The Canaries were rediscovered in 1312 by Lancellotto Malocello, a Venetian.[50] The subsequent European conquest of these unfortunate islands provided basic training for the conquest of the Caribbean Islands, Mesoamerica, and much else of the New World.

The earliest historically-recognized landing in the Canaries by Europeans came in 1341 when three ships arrived from Lisbon with horses and heavily-armed men. Instead of the fortified towns that these expeditioners had expected to find and attack, they encountered people who swam out to their ships. Like Columbus in the Bahamas 150 years later, the Europeans were struck by their innocence, represented mainly by their unabashed nakedness. Guided by rumor of a River of Gold on the African coast, the voyagers questioned the natives, called Guanches, as to the whereabouts of the precious stuff, but the Canarians could only offer to trade them sealskins, goatskins, and fats. They made wickerwork and sculpted small figures of clay and stone but lacked metallurgy and had forgotten their Berber ancestors' use of boats. Thus, each of the Canaries' seven major islands was an isolated world unto itself. In an echo of the story that an Aztec scout mistook Spanish ships for floating mountains, the Iberians were alarmed by the appearance on one of the Canaries of a "strange mast," to which a sort of sail was attached.[51] What it was is unknown. The most recalcitrant of these Stone Age islanders would fight off European efforts to conquer them for a century, deploying weapons of hardened wood, sharpened bones, and splintered rocks.[52]

The Portuguese saw the Canaries in terms of their potential resources—

sealskins, orchil (a purple dye), and slaves. They thought they might also serve as an "offshore station" for the trade route that the Portuguese hoped to create to get around Muslim-controlled North Africa. Portugal soon lay claim to the Islands. The Kingdom of Majorca also claimed the Canaries, and a French explorer, Jean de Béthencourt, who had co-led an expedition to the Islands in 1402, cajoled Henry III of Castile to grant him title to the Canaries, too. The Church had plans of its own. Under the direction of Pope Clement IV, some native Guanches were abducted and brought to Europe for conversion to Christianity. Clement sent Franciscan and Carmelite friars to the island of Grand Canary (*Gran Canaria*) where they encountered people whose experience with slave hunters and pirates had left them embittered and highly suspicious of Europeans. Bubonic plague, probably brought there by slavers, had already wiped out a considerable portion of their population. When famine struck and the Grand Canarians could no longer feed themselves, their council ordered a massacre of the Europeans in their midst.[53]

Besides avaricious motives, writes David Abulafia, Europeans were genuinely convinced of the righteousness of their Christianizing project in the Canary Islands, just as the conquistadors would be in Mexico. In a letter to Pope Eugenius IV of 1436, King Duarte of Portugal described the Guanches as "nearly wild men" that needed to be conquered for their own good, to save their souls from hell. Meanwhile, slavers and pirates were killing and kidnapping even the Islands' Christian converts and pillaging native food supplies.[54]

In 1479 Portugal and Castile resolved rival claims to the Canaries, with the latter getting the Islands and Portugal all the uninhabited islands of the Atlantic to go with the Azores and Madeira that they had already turned into plantations for growing wheat and sugar. Never mind that, of the Canaries, Grand Canary and Tenerife remained unconquered. Castilians claimed that their occupation of Lanzarote stretched Castile's dominion over the entire archipelago. The Islands comprised a cultural union, in their estimation, and this included even those that were vacant. "Vacant," in this context, meant those without a Christian ruler.[55] (This self-serving doctrine reappears in Columbus's log-book where he asserts that "having annexed one [island] it might be said that we had annexed all.")[56] With the help of mercenaries from smaller Gomera, other native divisions, horses, European weaponry, and especially European diseases, the Spaniards put an end to the independence of the larger islands, but not without a protracted struggle. The building of a sugar mill on Grand Canary in 1498 coincided with its full pacification.

One of the perceived advantages of the Islands was that they had "a slave labour force on the spot."[57] But it seems that that labor force was insufficiently docile, for the Spanish deported many of the fierce native Guanches, exported many more as slaves to work on the sugar plantations of Madeira, then imported thousands of black and brown slaves to work in the Islands' transformed environment of sugar fields. The process of converting the Canaries into plantations had taken much longer than on unpeopled Madeira. There the Portuguese had cleared the land by burning down a primeval forest in a huge conflagration, then introducing cattle and pigs that, running wild, rooted and trampled out any possibility of forest renewal.[58] But the outcome in the Canaries was about the same: plantations of export crops, mainly sugar, worked by imported slaves. Although slavery had not yet been racialized, the Spanish preferred slaves from sub–Saharan Africa to the Berbers who were closer to hand. The latter were apt to be Muslims, representing a potential threat as their numbers multiplied. Portugal would in time turn its other possessions off the coast of West Africa, the uninhabited Cape Verde Islands and São Tomé, into stopping places for human cargos en route to Caribbean slave markets.[59]

As for the Guanches, disease, forced removal, and cultural dislocation pushed them over the edge. The last of their kind was gone by the middle of the sixteenth century.[60] The similar fate that awaited Tainos and other natives of the Caribbean can be read on early sixteenth-century maps: as yet unnamed islands of the region are designated "*Canarias*."[61]

Acquisition of the Canaries gave Castile the navigational key to discovery of America. Conquest and exploitation of the Canaries gave it the model for New World conquest and the plundering of its resources.

3

Conquest as Romance

Among the items of deadly baggage that the conquistadors brought to Mexico was a heroic self-image that shielded them from doubts regarding their enterprise and spurred them to acts of bravery. This was especially true of Cortés whose conduct at times, in the narrative of Bernal Díaz, resembles that of the "true knight," the hero of an earlier European era whose vocation it was "to combat the enemies of the faith and give aid to the weak and helpless."[1] At each encounter with emissaries of native tribes, Cortés delivers a mission statement: we come to right wrongs, such as idolatry, human sacrifice, cannibalism, sodomy, robbery, and tyranny.[2] The most famous of the chansons de geste, *The Song of Roland,* had accused Muslims ("the enemies of the faith") of praying to stone gods.[3] In Mexico the conquistadors encountered people who really did seem to worship stone gods. An avid reader of the ballads and romances of chilvalry, Cortés directed his followers to overturn these idols, free captives intended for sacrifice, and—when he deemed it necessary—limit the plundering activities of indigenous allies.[4] Not to exonerate Cortés and the conquistadors. In the course of helping to destroy a civilization they also tortured and mutilated prisoners, engaged in terrorism and collective punishment, branded and auctioned captives into slavery, and sometimes burned people to death. But the question here is not what we might think of the conquistadors but what they thought of themselves.

In none of his activities was Cortés following the orders of a superior. As discussed in some detail in Chapter 12, he had defied the authority of Diego Velázquez—his patron, former friend, and the governor of Cuba—by ignoring his request to return to that island. Instead he planted an outpost on the mainland and put himself directly under the authority of the Castilian Crown. But he was separated from the Crown by the Atlantic Ocean. A royal command or reply to one of his now-famous letters might take a year to reach him. Cortés was, in effect, his own sovereign.[5]

Who was this man who by turns sought the salvation and the destruction of natives of Mesoamerica? Born into a family with "little wealth but much honor," according to Francisco López de Gómara, his first biographer, Cortés had failed to find a career for himself in Spain and sailed to Hispaniola at the age of nineteen. He became a civil servant and acquired the labor of numerous Indians on an estate in Cuba, where arrogance, insubordination, and womanizing kept him embroiled in disputes. Yet he was charming and had many supporters. Another biographer describes him as chivalrous but cruel, pious yet sinful, generous but greedy, and belonging "to a world that had passed."[6] William H. Prescott thought that he was a true knight-errant.[7] Examples of his guile, his intuition of the hopes and fears of others, and his ability to exploit such insights crowd the pages of Bernal Díaz's *Historia* and Cortés's own letters to the Crown. Fluent in Latin, he was "an intellectual who dodged his destiny," in the words of Rebecca West.[8] Though hot-tempered, he could practice the rare gift of restraint, she writes. Or could he? According to Ramón Iglesia, Cortés failed in his desire to make peace with the Aztecs because of his *impatience*: given their obvious sophistication, he could not accept their unwillingness to embrace Christianity at first exposure to its light.[9]

Cortés could manage people, no doubt about that. His Letters even try to manage Holy Roman Emperor Charles V (r. 1519–1558), his sovereign. But his leadership is overrated, I think. For example, with regard to the seizure of Moctezuma (discussed more extensively in Chapter 12), Gómara writes, "Never did Greek or Roman, or man of any nation, since kings have existed, do what Cortés did."[10] But according to Bernal Díaz, Cortés agreed to seize Moctezuma only when urged to do so by his troubled captains and a delegation of trusted followers who argued that, having entered Tenochtitlán, the very heart of Aztec power, they were exposed to a deadly attack. In order to give themselves some protection, urged the frightened men, they must seize Moctezuma immediately, before his seeming affection for them turned to hostility. Cortés asked how they could possibly do such a thing without provoking an attack. His captains and confidants then told him how, offering to seize the emperor themselves if he would let them.[11]

But why did Cortés bring his expedition into Tenochtitlán in the first place? The reason he gave the Aztecs—that Charles V had ordered him to go there—was patently untrue. He had yet to hear anything from Charles V. So, what did he have in mind in defying the repeated warnings of his Indian allies that Tenochtitlán would become a trap? Was it only the city's reputed riches that drew him forth along its causeway into the danger-bound seat of Aztec rule? He could not have known in advance that Moctezuma would simply give the conquistadors much of the royal treasure, far more in fact than they could carry off in the desperate flight of the Noche Triste. (See Chapter 6.) Speaking of the debacle that nearly killed the entire expedition, what was Cortés thinking when he left his homey, the cruel and unstable Pedro de Alvarado, in charge of the conquistadors that were left behind in Tenochtitlán when he went off to confront Narváez and his army? Alvarado's actions—discussed more fully below—set in motion events that led to the Noche Triste. Prior to the arrival of Narváez, Cortés seems to have been waiting for something, even telling his carpenters to slow down the building of the ships that he might have used to carry off the Aztec treasure.[12] But what was he waiting for?

While he gained a title and great wealth through his deeds in Mexico, Cortés did not bask on this pinnacle of achievement but sought greater authority and honor. Like Columbus, he hoped to extend Castile's empire to China and the Spice Islands, and like Columbus he soured his declining years with complaints about lack of recognition and adequate rewards for his service to the Crown.[13] Unlike Columbus, Cortés did not think that he might encounter a land of one-eyed men or men with dogs' heads. Or if he did, he kept it to himself. Nor did he report the discovery of mermaids.[14] If he had one foot planted in the Middle Ages, Columbus had both. Although Cortés led the destruction of an advanced civilization, in a 1529 *recidencia* (investigation) of his activities in Mexico, he was charged with being "loved well" by the Indians.[15] Evidently this charge was not without a basis in fact. Except that Cortés was not a prince, Macchiavelli might have had him instead of King Ferdinand in mind when he wrote that "nothing brings a prince more prestige than great campaigns and striking demonstrations of personal abilities."[16] Cortés sought prestige, to say the least, but the heroic warrior who attacks evils and advances the good was also a component of the self-image of this complicated man.

Despite the Age of Discovery's medieval overhang, Europe was entering an era in which less would be credited to God's will and more to human effort. As Shakespeare has a character muse: "They say miracles are past; and we have our philosophical persons to make modern and familiar, things supernatural and causeless."[17] In *Amadis of Gaul*, God reverses the movement of the wheel of fortune that had allowed an arrogant knight to tyrannize "matrons and maids" and humiliate male rivals.[18] Cortés adopted as his emblem the image of a wheel of fortune and the figure of a man with a hammer and nail. His motto: "I shall hammer in the nail when I see that there is nothing more to possess."[19]

Medieval Revivals

Every age gives birth to its own kind of hero, but heroic types are not necessarily confined to the time and place of their birth. Let us indulge his biographer and suppose that Cortés, his up-to-date motto to the contrary, had a spiritual homeland in a "world that had passed." Had that world really passed? European nobles of the thirteenth century had experienced a loss of military importance without a corresponding decline in wealth and social status. Something was needed to justify their privileged existence, and that something was a new kind of hero, the "true knight" and the chivalric code that was thought to govern his actions.[20] Like the samurai who initially provided tax-collection and protection services for their betters, knights were originally dependents of feudal lords. Again like the samurai, many of them became landed lords themselves. All were obligated to seek the kind of opportunities to display individual valor that only one-on-one combat could provide. As members of the ruling class, they were able to "define its ostentatious and public manhood as the moral core of society."[21] This points to Johan Huizinga's insight that warlike aristocracies need a concept of masculine perfection, an ideology to disguise the aggression and self-interested action of violent men.[22] The Europeans who first sailed to the Canary Islands sought not only access to a rumored River of Gold and a way around Muslim-dominated trade routes. They also hoped to acquire fame through the performance of good deeds while serving Christ, which was the chivalric ideal.[23]

Huizinga defined chivalry as pride striving for beauty.[24] Its code of conduct was intended to coax violence into the circuits of morality and service to others, and to separate the "true knight" from the false.[25] But the code did not apply to merchants, peasants, or even women who were not members of the nobility. All such people were unprotected and vulnerable. Knights were supposed to defend the Faith, uphold justice, and protect the weak, but they themselves were a major source of violence and disorder. Away from the deadly tournaments that he might attend, the knight was expected to serve his lord by slaughtering peasants and destroying crops and other property in order to impoverish his lord's enemy,[26] as had Cortés's father. Huizinga wrote that the "illusion of society based on chivalry clashed with the reality of things."[27] Medieval Europe did have a tradition of protection of the weak. In time of war, a feudal lord might gather his serfs in his castle. But this had to do with custom and economic self-interest, not chivalry.[28] Chivalry provided a system of politesse for contending knights but otherwise functioned to obscure the crimes of Europe's warrior aristocracy and make them appear exceptional.

While knights had long since become ineffective in European warfare, they were not confined to the pages of books or the misty past in 1492 or 1519. On his return to Spain from his first transatlantic voyage, Columbus had accused a Portuguese official of the Azores of violating the laws of chivalry by detaining some of his men.[29] Columbus's second voyage specifically included twenty of the knights that had recently conquered Granada.[30] Knights also accompanied Cortés. One of the conquistadors was descended from Pedro Alvarez Osorio, a knight of some renown.[31] Twelve members of his expedition took vows of chivalry to emulate the Twelve Peers of France of the *chansons de geste*.[32] Some wore suits of shiny armor, terrifying Indians with their clamor and their "glistening iron from head to foot."[33] Charles V knew what was required by the chivalric code. He went to battle at the head of his troops and challenged royal rivals—such as Francis I, King of France—to single combat.

The conquistadors did not have to look far to find models for chivalric valor. Garci Rodríguez de Montalvo's reworking of the fourteenth century *Amadis* tales came out at the beginning of the sixteenth century, some thirty years after Gutenberg's press had found a home in Spain but within a decade or so of Columbus's initial voyage. The stories were a runaway success, enjoying international popularity for hundreds of years. The spell cast by books such as *Amadis of Gaul* and *Tirant lo Blanc*—books in which characters such as Urganda the Unknown do indeed cast spells—was not limited to the fictional Don Quixote. The chivalric novels described, at times, the deeds of actual people, and actual people (as well as Don Quixote) imitated what they read in them.[34] The conquistadors were first-generation readers, and they carried their copies of *Amadis* like prayerbooks[35]—or, to bring the simile up to date, like the hand-held devices that pre-occupy people in the world of today. And they were inspired by them.[36] In other words, American conquest was keyed to romance, as recorded in the rhetoric of Francisco de Jérez, a conquistador of the Andean expedition: "When in ancient or modern times ... have there been such great enterprises of so few against so many, through so many lofty climates and vast seas and endless lands, to conquer the unseen and unknown?"[37]

Some think that our most detailed source of information about the Cortés expedition, Bernal Díaz's *Historia*, drew on a reservoir of chivalric fantasies.[38] If true this would naturally have inclined him, along with other influences, to depict Cortés as a hero and the Indians as brutes. To give just one example, Díaz reports that their Cempoalan allies are sacrificing humans every few days, removing the limbs for eating. Ignorant of the nature of ritualistic cannibalism, he speculates that their allies may be selling such "cuts" in the marketplace.[39] In the morality play of the chivalric novel or the action movie, the villain is often marked out by repulsive behavior. But speaking of butchery, the conquistadors salved their wounds and caulked their brigantines with fat from the bodies of dead Indians.[40]

Absent consideration of the conquistadors' material and biological advantages and the cultural sources of their deadly attitudes, the conquest becomes a romance, with a native legend to add mystery and confirm Western prejudices (as discussed in Chapter 12). But it wasn't a romance. It was an early example of modern asymmetrical warfare.

Archetype and Conquistador

Although the conquistadors looked to the medieval past for heroic fashion cues, the archetype of the warrior-hero is rooted in prehistory. Both the *Rig Veda* and the works of Homer, for example, describe the hero as questing "fame everlasting."[41] Glory in battle confers a kind of immortality, perpetuating one's deeds, perhaps even one's name. Approaching the fearsome giant Humbaba, Gilgamesh seeks to calm his companion by telling him that if he, Gilgamesh, is slain, his name will endure.[42] In the *Iliad,* Hector resolves that his glory "will not be forgotten."[43] During the bloody Tlaxcalan campaign when some of his party want to return to safety, Cortés urges them to stay the course, saying that their exploits already exceed those of the Romans. Considering what to do about Narváez's campaign to take over the conquest of Mexico, Cortés decides to risk his life in the service of his king (as he writes Charles V), knowing that to die under such circumstances "would win for us all great glory."[44] Cortés explains in his Second Letter that he made Moctezuma a prisoner in his own palace because, considering the likelihood of provocative action by Cortés's companions, the emperor might otherwise "obliterate all memory of us,"[45] thus robbing them of the promise of glory.

The miraculous military victory, usually attributed to divine intervention, was a tradition in European culture going back to *The Iliad* and prehistory. Entrusting his destiny to an image of the Virgin, King Arthur is said to have slaughtered nine hundred pagans at the siege of Mount Badon.[46] He single-handedly slays 470 Saxons, wielding Excalibur, his mighty sword, and calling on God for support.[47] In another account of this battle, Arthur's knights suffer not a single casualty while the Saxons lose two thousand.[48] King Alfonso VIII of Castile made the preposterous claim that in the famous battle of Las Navas de Tolosa, the Christian army had killed 100,000 Muslims while sustaining losses of only twenty to thirty.[49] The Spaniards enjoyed similar outcomes in the Indies, at least in their narratives. When Hispaniola's natives rebel against the newly-arrived colonizers in 1495, Columbus leads two hundred "Christians" with twenty horses, twenty "hunting" dogs, and an unknown number of Indian allies against an Indian force allegedly amounting to a hundred thousand. Employing harquebuses and crossbows, cavalry charges and canine attacks—and "by God's will"—the Spaniards prevail, killing, capturing, and executing innumerable natives.[50] In Diego Mendez's account of Columbus's fourth voyage, twenty Spaniards defeat four hundred natives in a battle on the coast of Panama, thanks to divine intervention.[51] Cortés writes that as the badly outnumbered conquistadors battled the Tlaxcalans, "it truly seemed that God was fighting for us."[52] When the conquistadors inflict heavy losses on the natives of Mexico and suffer only light casualties themselves, they are living the legend of their romantic heroes.[53]

Don Quixote reprised this tradition in claiming that a single knight errant could destroy an army of two hundred thousand.[54] Such notions accord with the popular belief that Cortés and a few hundred followers brought down a mighty empire. The truth is that Cortés and a few hundred followers with advanced weaponry, destructive motives, self-serving ideology, horses, many thousands of native allies, and countless deadly microbes demolished a fragile empire. But the ethos of divine intervention and miraculous victory was very much in play. At a low point in their venture, Cortés assures his men that "God gives us the strength of many."[55] Bernal Díaz writes that Jesus Christ gave the Spaniards the fortitude to capture Tenochtitlán and win many other battles en route to that decisive victory, always against foes that vastly outnumbered them.[56] The conquistadors gave additional credit to St. James, the patron of Spanish Christians whose Spanish name—Santiago—was also their battle cry. Crusaders had credited the intervention of angels, saints, and slain colleagues for their victory at Antioch in 1098.[57] But ultimate credit for the victory or defeat of Christian armies was traditionally assigned to God, who determined winners and losers on the basis of the innocence or guilt of the warring parties.[58] By this logic, a victory could only be deserved and just.

As a single hero can supposedly slay thousands, with the aid of a female consort he can also spawn a host of future heroes. The archetypal warrior is so virile that the *Rig Veda* describes him as *sahasramuska*, which means "of a thousand testicles."[59] Thus the drill sergeant who, calling the roll, exhorts his male troops to "sound off like you got a pair" is asking each man to demonstrate, by the volume of his response, that he has at least one five-hundredth of the virility of the archetypal warrior. Cortés seems to have had at least fifteen children by various Spanish and Indian women.[60]

Finally, heroism requires a witness. Without Cortés's letters, Díaz's famous narrative, and some other, fragmentary first-hand accounts, the conquistadors' exploits might have been reduced to rumor and speculation.

The Berserker Versus the Infantryman

Cortés presented his followers with a vision of themselves as heroic warriors. The actual hero, however, may become a military liability. Aristotle questioned whether the military champion could also be a good citizen.[61] He saw in the example of Sparta the fact that to defend the existing order one must have the capacity to disrupt it. The quintessential warrior is free to do as he will, finding comfort only in absolute strength. At the extreme of this type, the berserker of ancient Scandinavian lore was thought to have a second being living within him—a bear, wolf, or other fierce creature—that his furor would release in battle.[62] The animal costumes favored by Aztec warriors[63] suggest a similar attempt to engage trans-human powers—or convince their enemies that they could. Yet the Aztecs levied harsh penalties on overly exuberant men who suffered a loss of self-control. They prized humility and modesty. Similarly, the samurai warrior whose ferocity found vent outside acceptable channels had no place in the Tokugawa order. He could only wander, masterless and hungry.[64]

The conquistadors did not include any berserkers in their ranks, but in Pedro de Alvarado they had what might be described as a very loose cannon. Called Tonatiuh—the Sun—by the Indians, Alvarado was blond, handsome, even radiant, or so we must assume. Already, in the 1518 expedition of Juan de Grijalva, he had provoked the ire of that commander by sailing off on his own.[65] Two years later, when Cortés rushed to the Gulf Coast to confront Panfilo de Narváez and left this man in charge of his forces in Tenochtitlán, Alvarez gave permission to Aztec nobles to hold the ceremonial dance of the Toxcatl festival, then ordered their slaughter. Here is an excerpt from the description of that massacre that was later given by Bernardino de Sahagún's informants:

> Then they surrounded those who were dancing, going among the cylindrical drums. They struck a drummer's arms; both of his arms were severed. Then they struck his neck; his head landed far away. Then they stabbed everyone with iron lances and struck them with iron swords. They struck some in the belly, and then their entrails came spilling out. And if someone tried to run it was useless; he just dragged his intestines along. There was a stench as if of sulphur.[66]

When Cortés returned Alvarado explained that he had known "for certain" that the Aztecs were planning to attack them. Cortés did not buy this, nor did any of the other Spaniards, it appears,[67] although the massacre of Cholula of a few months earlier had been similarly justified. (See Chapter 9.) As for preempting an Indian attack, the massacre of the dancers provoked the entire Aztec nation to assail them and led to the losses of the Noche Triste. Alvarado would order additional preemptive massacres in Guatemala.

Military commanders have usually tried to tamp down heroic or psychopathic impulses and shepherd them into the disciplined violence of the regiment. The invention of the smaller "recurved" bow (the Cupid's bow) and socketed arrowheads three thousand years ago transformed the mounted warrior of the Eurasian steppes into a member of a coordinated cavalry unit. The exploits of Achilles and Hector might have evoked a keen sense of longing in the infantryman of the armored phalanx, around the sixth century BCE.[68] The overlapping shields of the Roman testudo made soldiers indistinguishable. When the Romans compared the barbarian's quest for fame through honorable feats in battle that would "outlast death" to the legionnaire's self-restraint and dedication to the collective good, they found the barbarian sadly lacking.[69] Tacitus admired the Chatti, who alone among German tribes chose and obeyed their leaders, knew when to attack and when to hold back, planned their day's duties, and secured their nocturnal defenses. When they attacked, they did so deliberately, not in the kind of impetuous rush that is the brother of the pell-mell retreat.[70] In other words, they resembled Romans in their military comportment, leaving no room for outdated heroism.

In 1519 when Hernán Cortés and his followers landed on the Gulf Coast of what would become Mexico, the heroic warrior had all but vanished from the battlefields of Europe. Use of the long bow in the Hundred Years War and the artillery bombardments that demolished the last bastions of Moorish sovereignty in Iberia had made the hand-to-hand combat required for displays of individual prowess obsolete. The big infantry units of pikemen and harquebusiers that the *Gran Capitan*, Gonzalo de Córdoba, had assembled for Castile's Italian campaigns also lacked room in their ranks for the individual hero. If the medieval version of the heroic warrior, the "true knight," survived the Age of Chivalry in the mission statement, leadership, and occasional actions of Hernán Cortés, his followers survived the severest battlefield threats they faced by acting as a single unit, all for one and one for all. The member of such a unit had a greater affinity for the organization man than for Superman. When they were hard-pressed by waves of onrushing Tlaxcaltecan warriors, the conquistadors survived by fighting in closed ranks without individual sorties or retreats.[71] The romance of the hero's quest does not encompass battlefield conduct where collective action offers a better chance of survival. The Achaians defending the body of Patroklos also knew this.

The conquistadors adapted their tactics to the situation, attempting to kill their adversaries at a distance with their cannons and crossbows and shamelessly running away from danger at times. This meant violating native rules of combat that were intended to facilitate battlefield heroism.[72] In fact, the heroes were all on the Aztec side. In describing the final days of the siege of Tenochtitlán, Book Twelve of Bernardino de Sahagún's great compendium of Aztec life singles out those who distinguished themselves in the fighting: Tiplacatzin, "a great warrior" who assumed various disguises; the Tlappanecatl Ecatzin, an Otomi-rank warrior; Coyohuehuetzin, a formidable scraped-head warrior, et al.[73] The Indians fought like the heroes of the *Iliad*. The conquistadors identified with military heroes, but they fought in disciplined formations. As we will see in Chapter 5, this gave the Spaniards a decided advantage, militarily.

Cortés's Achievement in Perspective

We have seen that to a significant extent Hernán Cortés modeled the leadership of his famous expedition on a medieval ideal, the conduct of the true knight. He sought glory, as well as riches. He was imbued with Christian faith and a determination to contribute mightily to its advance among pagans. If we are to credit the account of Bernal Díaz, Cortés sometimes displayed genuine concern for protecting the weak against the strong, as when he freed native prisoners intended for sacrifice. Again, this is not to gainsay that Cortés was also capable of great cruelty against the weak and vulnerable. The question is did Castile require such a quasi-hero to defeat the Aztecs and gain a Mesoamerican empire?

According to Díaz, who may or may not have been a member of Juan de Grijalva's earlier expedition, Grijalva was a bold and courageous leader. Velazquez, the Governor of Cuba who became Cortés's archenemy, had given Grijalva a mandate to sail to the mainland, obtain precious metals, and settle there if he dared.[74] But unlike Cortés, Grijalva did not try to found a settlement there. His boldness did not approach Cortés's, and there is no reason to suppose that he could have matched Cortés in exploiting native divisions or that he had the supreme self-confidence to make a captive of an emperor in the seat of his own empire. Yet without the deadly Old World baggage that the Spaniards bore—their swords and their self-righteousness, their horses and their microbes and the other elements of their invasion that proved lethal to Mexico's indigenous civilization, Cortés's boldness and cleverness—his heroism, let us say—would have been for naught. In fact, some of the qualities that made him a hero nearly resulted in the annihilation of his entire company.

Given the forces that were then at work in Europe—the navigational advances of the Age of Discovery, revival of the crusading impulse (Chapter 4), the quest for precious metals (Chapter 6), and so forth—an unsuccessful Cortés venture would surely have been succeeded by other, probably larger expeditions. The men who might have led them would not have been the equal of Cortés perhaps, but they would have been capable, at the least, of bringing Europe's deadly baggage to the New World's continents and inflicting their contents on the people who lived there.

To a limited extent the achievements of the Cortés expedition made New Spain. But to a much greater extent, the Mexican expedition made Cortés the famous conqueror he has become in the pages of Eurocentric history. Military heroism requires the opportunity that only warfare confers, and war between nations offers the greatest legitimate and most honorific opportunity for the testing of masculine honor that heroism requires. For the would-be hero, the peaceful alternative is grim. Warfare is needed, wrote Geoffrey of Monmouth nine hundred years ago, because otherwise men will only "toy with women and play at dice and such like follies."[75] Without the opportunity to lead a bellicose force to Mexico, Cortés might have continued to prosper on his Cuban estate until he was run through by the sword of a jealous husband.

As for the adventurers who followed him to the center of the Aztec Empire, we might compare them to the squire and companion of Cervantes' comic version of the chivalric hero. We might, but without the brave but unheroic efforts of these followers, Don Quixote might have *lacked* a Sancho Panza. Sancho is credulous, but only in a world in which Europeans really are discovering uncharted lands and taking them over to exploit their human and natural resources would he believe that he could become the governor of an island by serving Don Quixote.

Warfare has continued to

Portrait of Hernán Cortés. **Oil on canvas by unknown artist, Emilian School, late 16th century (courtesy Sphinx Fine Art, London).**

produce military heroes—Napoleon, Washington, Andrew Jackson, Teddy Roosevelt, MacArthur, de Gaulle, Zhukov ... they come in a mixed bag. But except in science fiction, it appears unlikely that Cortés will ever be followed by another individual leading a small force of adventurers that will be credited, however accurately, with bringing down an empire. Without the publicity provided by a Bernal Díaz narrative or the eye of the TV camera, war can no longer produce the military hero. Leaked images seem only to result in scandal, not glorification. Who can name a member of the Joint Special Operations Command force that killed Bin Laden? Chris Kyle, the tragically murdered author of a best-selling memoir of his life as a Navy SEAL, was a hero to some, but his military prowess was based on his hundred and sixty confirmed kills as a sniper. The medieval hero had to defend his honor openly, against an equal. He could not have done that by shooting a suspicious somebody a mile away. The drone "pilot" has even smaller claim to the traditional ideal of military glory.

Today's heroes engage in fierce competition but not in warfare. They are known as superstars, and they tend to be athletes, the ones that make the crucial three-point shots, complete touchdown passes in the Super Bowl, and win homerun championships. And we watch them do it, too.

4

Crusaders in America

Lest we forget, the cross was originally an instrument of execution by torture—crucifixion. When a prophet, thought by many to be the Son of God, was crucified two thousand years ago, the cross became the leading symbol of a religion that, within a few centuries, gained dominance over almost all of Europe. Much of its European career was relatively peaceful, but at times the cross was placed at the head of armies. It was as such a militant cross that this potent symbol invaded the Americas and established a new career. Let us take a sprint through European history to consider something of what preceded that venture.

Constantine, the first Roman emperor to embrace Christianity, apprised a sword of its future partnership by declaring, "In this sign [of the cross] shalt thou conquer."[1] With the dissolution of the Roman Empire and the economic dislocations caused by the rise of Islam, Western Europe experienced a breakdown of central political authority. Inhabitants of the region were beset by a "habit of violence." Churchmen held from early on that it was the duty of the Christian ruler "to eradicate evil by the sword." Agobard of Lyon declared in the ninth century that the prince's sword was meant for the "subjugation of barbarous nations so that they may embrace the faith and widen the frontiers of the kingdom of the faithful."[2] The Church soon proclaimed holy war against Muslim invaders of Italy.

Gratian's *Decretum* (c. 1140) held that war could be authorized by God through the pope and that such a war was just.[3] That is, God could command violence, and the Church could use such authority to attack the enemies of the true faith and do so as an expression of Christian love. Such thinking embodied a concept of holy war, in which violence received religious sanction. Could there be a better excuse for making war? Clearly self-defense is a better excuse, and European nations might have combined to wage a war of self-defense against the leading threat to Christian Europe—namely, Islamic imperialism. But they were much too divided for that. Instead, they mounted a series of invasions, called crusades (from the cross—*crux*, in Latin— marked on soldiers' shields or breastplates). The cross was then worn or carried on banners into the margins, if not the heart, of successive Muslim empires. The Church put the "reconquest" of Islamic Iberia on a par with the retaking of Jerusalem, giving Spaniards a special crusading mission. The conquests by Castile and Portugal in the Age of Discovery represent, at least in part, an extension of these religious campaigns.

Like other crusaders, Iberian Christians had the assurance of the Church that if they died on the battlefield, they would go straight to heaven and eternal life.[4] Acceptance of such a guarantee can armor one against fear of death, making such a belief a formidable weapon,[5] as we observe in the age of the suicide bomber. In Mesoamerica, Iberians would battle warriors whose concept of an afterlife was quite modest in comparison.

Although crusading had lost its allure by the start of the fifteenth century—what with the Islamic recapture of Jerusalem in 1244, the disastrous invasion of Egypt by Louis IX, and other fiascos—the discoveries of Iberian seafarers injected it with new life. The century-long effort to conquer the Canary Islands (as discussed in Chapter 2) was regarded as a continuation of the war on Islam, as was even the occupation of uninhabited Madeira. Bethencourt and De la Salle, the French adventurers who visited the Canaries in 1402, gained recognition by the pope as crusaders.[6] Papal bulls of crusade gave Portuguese monarchs the authority to attack Islamic cities at will. Such encouragement, if any were needed, led to the assault on Ceuta (near the Strait of Gibraltar) in 1415. The sons of King João (1358–1433) saw such ventures as obligatory: infidels and pagans must be attacked. Portuguese forces approached Tangier with a banner showing Christ in a suit of armor, although this image failed to guard them against defeat. King Henry the Navigator (d. 1460) painted Portugal's great maritime project and slave trading expeditions down the coast of West Africa as a "Crusade of Discovery."[7] If a quest for slaves and gold could qualify as a crusade, what could not? African gold enabled the Portuguese to mint their own gold coin, the *cruzado* (crusade), in 1447. The sails of Portuguese caravels displayed the square red cross worn by crusading Templars three centuries earlier. The "Cross Patee" on the sails of Columbus's ships announced a crusading intent, and on the eve of his voyage of 1497, Vasco da Gama received the banner of the Crusading Order of Christ. He spent the night before embarking in a chapel, like crusading knights of an earlier era.[8]

With the fall of Constantinople to the Turks in 1453, many Castilian commoners had been ready to enlist in a crusade to reverse the Islamic tide that had swamped the remains of the Byzantine Empire, risen in the Balkans, and threatened to flood the Danube basin. They had to be restrained. Henry IV, King of Castile and Leon, was an Islamophile who dressed and dined in Moorish fashion. Christian nobles and commoners alike welcomed his successors, Isabel and Ferdinand. Spanish Christians embraced the new rulers' plan to complete the Reconquest through capture of the shrunken remains of Moorish territory in the south of Spain. Granada held out until 1492. When it fell—an outcome said to compensate for the loss of Constantinople—the Pope proclaimed Ferdinand and Isabel "the Catholic monarchs."[9]

A venerable argument held that the Reconquest of Iberia would result in the liberation of Jerusalem by providing overland access to the Holy Land via North Africa. Predictably then, with the fall of Granada, Castile extended the Reconquest to North Africa, consistent with Isabel's dying wish.[10] The Spaniards took Oran (1509), Tripoli (1510), and Tlemcen (1518), but the North African campaign did not generate much booty, the region did not attract Spanish settlers, Spanish troops were preoccupied in Italy, and continued North African expansion would have soon run up against a tsunami of Islamic "reconquest."[11] In any case, the discovery of America soon made Spain's North African venture beside the point.

Columbus Takes the Cross Across the Sea

As described in Chapter 2, Columbus's initial voyage to the Antilles took place in the midst of an ambitious dream of globalized crusade. Columbus won success for his long, frustrating campaign to secure royal financing for his plan to sail west and visit the Orient by telling the devout Isabel, during the assault on Granada, that his quest would bring Christianity to the infidels of the Far East described by Marco Polo two centuries earlier. He added that he would dedicate the profits of his venture to the funding of a new crusade to the Holy Land to recover former Christian sites. Having gained the backing of the Crown, he declared that he would help the Catholic monarchs cleanse the world of heresy and idolatry, becoming "the right arm of their crusade." Such formulations found no part in his pitch to would-be crew members, however. He based his appeal to them on the common desire for instant wealth.[12] Clerics had traditionally sent crusaders off to war by telling them that God was on their side and that their cause was just, often adding that crusading might provide the opportunity for them to get their hands on riches, too.[13]

Columbus was interested in finding gold, very interested in fact, but he was even more intent on advancing Christianity. In his mind, these objectives were linked as means and end. He declared (in his log for December 26, 1492) that he would seek gold to finance recovery of the Holy Sepulcher.[14] Following his initial voyage, he fantasized returning to the (doomed) little settlement he had left behind on Hispaniola to discover enough gold and spices to underwrite the conquest of Jerusalem.[15] Such priorities did not put him out of tune with clerical contemporaries like Bartolomé de Las Casas, who wrote that everyone was "awed by the concern God showed for [Columbus's] enterprise."[16] With Spain's invasion of America, writes Theresa Ann Sears, crusading found a new direction and a new era. The invasion was an "elaborate medievalist project."[17]

Eight years after Columbus first landed in the Caribbean, a Portuguese expedition led by Pedro Álvares Cabral spotted an island that turned out to be the coast of Brazil. Cabral named it "the land of the true cross."[18] Within a few years, Hernán Cortés would make "Vera Cruz" (True Cross) the name of a Gulf Coast settlement, as well.

Fighting Muslims in Mexico

For their participants, the expeditions to the mainland that were organized in Cuba were an extension of the Reconquest of Spain. Members of Hernandez de Córdoba's aborted expedition of 1517 had dubbed a city they had spotted on the coast of Yucatan "Great Cairo."[19] Perhaps as a result of a visual impairment, Fr. Juan Díaz thought that the Totonac Indians encountered by the Grijalva expedition to the mainland in the following year were circumcised. He concluded that there were probably "Jews and Moors nearby."[20] Cortés's more famous expedition also bore many of the markings of an Iberian crusade. The banners made for his voyage from Cuba bore the cross, and he proclaimed conquest under that sign in a speech to his followers.[21] The Indians of the Yucatan peninsula dressed in "Moorish fashion," he reports, and their habitations of small low rooms also mimicked the Moors."[22] The Europeans under his command referred to an Indian village where the natives had imprisoned a comrade before killing him as "Pueblo Morisco"—roughly, Moorsville.[23] Similarly, conquistador Vásquez de Tapia refers to a native temple at Cholula as their "principal mosque."[24]

Although most English translations of his letters to the Crown have Cortés counting "temples" in Cholula, what he wrote was *"Yo conté desde una mezquita cuatrocientas y tantas torres en la dicha cuidad, y todas son de mezquitas"*[25] ("I counted from a mosque four hundred some towers in said city, and all [the towers] were of mosques"). Members of the multinational force ("the Spaniards") that became the conquistadors did not regard themselves as Europeans but as Christians. Their religious identity made Moors the generic enemy, just as Robinson Crusoe's made him long for rescue by a *Christian* ship. Bartolomé de Las Casas referred to the conquistadors as "perfidious crusaders."[26]

Doctrine: The Cross and the Indian

As we saw in Chapter 2, Pope Alexander IV had divided the unknown hemisphere, on which Columbus's initial voyage had only touched, between Spain and Portugal, making inhabitants of those lands vassals of the monarchs of one or the other of those nations. His *Inter Caetera* bull of that same year (1493) had given highest priority to the exaltation and spread of Christianity, the care of the "health of souls," the overthrow of "barbarous nations," and the delivery of such nations to the faith.[27] By 1498 the Castilian Crown was requiring the "Indians" (as Columbus had called them from the beginning) to serve it peacefully "in benign subjection" in order to be converted to Catholicism.[28] But if the object were religious conversion, wondered Las Casas, "Why, instead of sending among them peaceful sheep, do you send hungry wolves?"[29]

Theological qualms about forced religious conversion in the Indies were resolved by a device suggested by the *Romanus Pontifex* discussed in Chapter 2 and employed in the conquest of the Canary Islands—the *requirimiento* (or requirement). Here is what was required. On first encountering New World inhabitants, the conquistador was to read them a summary of Christian doctrine beginning with the creation story of Genesis and continuing through the Crucifixion and papal inheritance of divine authority. The reading, often in un-translated Spanish, would conclude with a demand that the natives submit to the Church and Spanish rule or suffer attack. Assembled Indians would typically respond with a hail of arrows. Application of the *requirimiento* was soon reduced to a pro forma reading addressed to the forest or an empty village.[30] Cortés described reading it while under attack by javelins and arrows.[31] The opening question of the 1529 investigation (*Residencia*) of Cortés's conduct in Mexico reveals the concern for legal niceties of colonial administrators: Did Cortés have the *requirimiento* read to the Indians at Cholula before ordering the slaughter of thousands of them? According to Las Casas, Spaniards would read an abbreviated version of the *requirimiento* at a distance from a native village suspected of being near a site of gold. They would then attack the village before dawn, setting fire to its straw dwellings, torturing survivors as to the whereabouts of the gold, and enslaving the rest while searching through the charred ruins for booty.[32] Acknowledging the flaws of the *requerimiento,* historian and conquistador G. Fernández de Oviedo y Valdes thought that it might yet prove an effective educational tool if a captured Indian could study its theology "at his leisure" while caged, with the explanatory help of a bishop.[33]

European encounters with *"ignorantes"*—that is, people who had never heard of Christ and were unaware of Christian doctrine[34]—raised an important theological question: why would God allow people to live in a state of ignorance that condemned their souls to eternal damnation? For Oviedo y Valdes, Fr. Diego Durán, and others, the answer was clear: the Indians were actually lapsed Christians. Known to them as Quetzalcoatl, St. Thomas had blessed their ancestors with a visit, as had all other people who lived in parts of the world that were remote from Europe.[35] Jesuits in China would later look for evidence of his evangelizing presence there.[36] In short, the Indians were apostates, their paganism was a result of a memory lapse, and they could be punished for it.

Though no theologian, Cortés shared the dualistic world view of many others then and now. For him, the universe was divided between God's world, inhabited by Christians, and the realm of Satan with its non-believers. Satan maintained his grip on earth by deploying certain weapons. These included the ability to corrupt the understanding of many people with "idolatrous blindness," and God had chosen Spanish monarchs to cleanse the New World of this contamination.[37] Instances of drunkenness, cannibalism, sodomy, and child sacrifice proved that the Indians were victims of this blindness and slaves of Satan.[38] Cortés's Second Letter describes burning native villages under the sign of the cross and "fighting for our Faith" and monarch.[39] The native authors of the post-conquest "Annals of Tlatelolco" write that when one of Moctezuma's gift bearers met Cortés and paid him the signal honor of offering him a draft of blood "in an eagle vessel," Cortés cut him down with his sword.[40]

Practice: Evangelizing in Word and Deed

On sailing from Cuba, Cortés defied most of the parting instructions from his friend, patron, and governor of that island, Diego Velázquez, but not his injunction to "'serve our Lord God and increase the dimension of our holy Catholic faith.'"[41] He established a pattern of hard-ball evangelizing early on. Despite the Augustinian doctrine that the idol must be removed from the infidel's heart before being removed from his temple,[42] Cortés ordered the natives' idols at Cozumel, island-site of the adventurers' initial landing, broken and rolled down the temple steps like the bodies of sacrificial victims. His gear included a supply of Christian icons, crosses, and banners,[43] and he replaced the fallen idols with an image of the Virgin. His carpenters then constructed a wooden cross, which they installed in a chapel near the Virgin's altar. The intimidated natives agreed to revere it and to keep it clean and adorned with flowers, and Cortés told them that they would see what advantages accrued as a result.[44]

Following the conquistadors' first battle, Cortés gathered the defeated chiefs and asked them to give up their idols and their practice of human sacrifice. He then gave them an image of the Virgin and ordered them to build an altar. His carpenters built a tall cross.[45] At nearby Cintla (on the Gulf coast of the Yucatan peninsula), Cortés had several carpenters cut a cross on a massive Ceiba tree. Bernal Díaz promises his readers that with renewal of the bark, it would "show there forever." Next day the townspeople assembled to watch the conquistadors' Palm Sunday procession and mass. They observed them kissing the cross. Cortés left crosses and a Christian image in their care, promising that their solicitude would bring them good health and bountiful harvests.[46]

In erecting crosses Cortés was staking a claim like that of João Gonsalves Zarco, who took possession of Madeira on behalf of Portugal in 1419 by raising a cross.[47] Portuguese mariners had left crosses at various sites as they progressed down the west coast of Africa.[48] Columbus had done the same in the Caribbean. According to one chronicler, the conquistadors planted crosses everywhere they stopped.[49]

Envoys of Moctezuma called on the conquistadors as they camped in the dunes above San Juan de Ulúa (still on the Gulf coast), where they held Easter mass. When the adventurers fell to their knees before the cross, an envoy asked why they humbled themselves before such a tree. Cortés seized the opportunity to expound Christian doctrine and urged them to put the cross and an image of the Virgin in their temples. Then they would find out what the Christian God "would do for them."[50] Thus did the conquistadors proceed toward Tenochtitlán, battling Indians, destroying idols, erecting crosses, and offering defeated Indians the chance to take on the accoutrements of Christian practice.

Entering heavily-defended Tlaxcala, Cortés urged, "Let us follow our banner, which bears the sign of the holy cross, and through it we shall conquer!"[51] Though surrounded by client states of the Aztec Empire (or Triple Alliance), the Tlaxcalans were perennial enemies of the Aztecs—hard-pressed but fiercely independent. According to the interesting conjecture of Ross Hassig,[52] the Tlaxcalans saw these barbarians with their horses and advanced weaponry—these invaders whom they almost defeated—as presenting them with something more valuable than the chance to worship new gods. Alliance with these strangers might enable Tlaxcala, finally and definitively, to defeat the Aztecs. The cross installed at Tlaxcala was both "tall and sumptuous."[53]

The Tlaxcalan alliance was important, as the Tlaxcalans joined the Spaniards by the thousands in the later stages of their Mexican campaign. Aztec mastery had been harsh, and many others sought alliance with the invaders, so many others that in song and other native cultural productions the "Spanish conquest" has become "a native civil war."[54] Religious conversion could cement a vital partnership with the invaders. As for the invaders, they surely would have agreed with Tacitus that "fortune can bestow on us no better gift than discord among our foes."[55]

Texcoco, on the lake of that name, was a junior partner in the Triple Alliance, but its leading family was divided over subservience to Tenochtitlán, the island metropolis that ruled the Empire. Thus, when Cortés explained the mystery of the Baptism, Ixtlilxochitl, a dissident prince, "begged for the crucifix" and asked to be baptized. Although some of the Christians present thought that he needed more time and instruction, Cortés opted for his immediate baptism. Ixtlilxochitl took Hernando as his Christian name, after Cortés, his sponsor. His brother became Pedro after the murderous Pedro de Alvarado.[56]

Such an impetuous conversion was not a possibility in Tenochtitlán, but even as an unwanted guest of the Aztec emperor, Cortés did not for a moment put his light under a bushel. He had barely arrived when he began telling Moctezuma of the "one true God." Taken on a tour of the city's great temples by the emperor, Cortés tells him that he cannot understand how he has failed to realize that his gods are really devils, and he asks his permission to install a cross atop one of the temples.[57] Andrés de Tapia writes of climbing one of the great sacred towers as requested by Cortés and finding a room that was darkened by a thick veil. He and others used their swords to cut it down, revealing images of deities and walls caked with sacrificial blood. Roused by the ringing of the veil's bells, a crowd formed below and Aztec priests rushed to the scene. Through his interpreters, Cortés began to preach to them. He asked them to replace the idols with Christian icons and to wash away the blood. The crowd responded with a contemptuous laugh. "Well pleased am I to fight for my God against your gods which are nothing," announced Cortés, at which he leaped on an idol and began beating it about the eyes with an iron bar, breaking its gold mask, and shouting, "Something must we venture for the Lord."⁵⁸ (Tapia would later say of this frenzy that Cortés was just passing time.)⁵⁹

Moctezuma, by then a prisoner of the conquistadors, was brought forth. He reluctantly agreed to replacement of the Aztec icons with an image of the Virgin and a cross. The Spaniards deepened their "symbolic appropriation"⁶⁰ by holding mass there. As if this were insufficiently provocative of the large and devout population surrounding his band of adventurers, Cortés had the principal idols of the Great Temple thrown down the steps, as he had the ones at Cozumel, Cholula, and other cities on the path to Tenochtitlán. Or so Cortés says in his Second Letter to Charles V.⁶¹ But according to another chronicler, a condition of the agreement between Cortés and Moctezuma gave the Aztecs the opportunity to remove their idols to a place of their choosing, which they did a few days later using ropes, rollers, maguey mats, and the labor of several hundred priests to ease the idols down from the temple heights in a silent process that mightily impressed the European observers.⁶² In line with a Reconquest tradition of scrubbing away the "filth" of captured mosques,⁶³ Cortés then had the "chapels" cleansed of the sacrificial blood that fed the Aztec gods.⁶⁴ The Spaniards staged another religious coup at Tlatelolco (Tenochtitlán's sister city), putting themselves at great risk to capture the city's great tower and install Christian banners there.⁶⁵ Then they burned the tower's idols.

We might contrast such religious intolerance with the attitude of the Aztecs. Captured images of the gods of conquered cities were stored in Tenochtitlán's Coateocalli temple. R. C. Padden refers to this repository as a prison for captured deities, perhaps as needed to control their supernatural powers, as Davíd Carrasco suggests.⁶⁶ But according to Enrique Florescano, the eminent Mexican historian, the point of the collection was expansion of the Aztec pantheon.⁶⁷ A Christian version of such "religious syncretism," if such were possible, might have seen sainthood conferred on all the Hindu deities and Muhammad, too, with British colonization of India.

The Aztecs would complete a conquest by setting fire to the enemy's temple. They would then replace the captured idol with a stone image of their own deity, Huitzilopochtli, the god of war and sun god, leaving it in the conquered city's renovated temple for its inhabitants to venerate.⁶⁸ The Aztecs allowed the city that surrendered on demand to keep its own deity as an equal of Huitzilopochtli.⁶⁹ But religious conversion went no further than that. There was nothing like conversion at the point of a sword, nothing like an *encomendero* (colonial labor boss) to force defeated Indians to remain on their knees for hours of religious indoctrination. That would follow Spanish conquest.⁷⁰ On the other hand, the Spaniards did not drag the people of conquered cities off for sacrifice to their own deity, as did the Aztecs.

The clerical arm of Spanish empire-building would later take over the business of trying to mold native beliefs, but pending the fall of Tenochtitlán, European conquest had yet to develop such a division of labor. Although the expedition included two friars, Cortés was still the expedition's chief evangelist. But he was also an evangelist of wealth. As he told Narváez's men in his effort to persuade them to join him, in Mexico they could serve God and the king and get rich, too.[71] Within the context of a mania to find precious metals and other treasure, the Europeans' religious impulse has taken on the retrospective coloring of ideology. But the cross was not just a magnet to attract gold and silver. Cortés risked his life and that of others to destroy idols and install crosses. Later, as Spaniards were shipping silver to Europe and Asia, other Spaniards were dedicating their lives to the goal of Christianizing Indians.

For the Aztecs, the inconceivable destruction of their metropolis implied the defeat of their gods. Their goal became assimilation of the new god into their pantheon through submission, although surviving nobles and priests might resist the effort of Franciscans to impose Christian norms. For the Spanish, the conquest had been willed by God. The religious task took its cues from the Reconquest and Inquisition, becoming the total eradication of the native pantheon and the complete conversion of the pagan population to Christianity.[72]

Cortés explained the destruction of Cholula, Tenochtitlán, and other horrors, by writing that "we were fighting against a barbarian people to spread our Faith." He also wrote that "as Christians we were obliged to wage war against the enemies of our Faith."[73] Bearing the title Commissioner of the Crusade, a Franciscan was sent by Rome to sanctify the conquest of what was to become New Spain and to offer dispensation for any sins committed during battle by the conquistadors.[74] The Church had customarily conferred such indulgences on crusaders.

When one enjoys a monopoly on moral excellence, anything is permitted against others. Cortés had a native burned to death for eating human flesh, because—as he explained to the king—he "wished to see no one killed."[75] In short, the conquistadors were holy warriors, imbued with a sense of righteousness. For those in their path, this made them the most dangerous kind of men.

The Crusader Model

Earlier crusades had given the conquistadors a source-book for what to do with a defeated city and its people. With the conquest of Jerusalem in

1099, for example, knights slaughtered men, women, and children, cutting open their bellies to retrieve any gold coins they may have swallowed. Even the conquerors were covered in blood.[76] Constantinople was considerably larger and more magnificent than any other city in Christendom at the beginning of the thirteenth century. With its high walls, numerous towers, soaring church spires, and rich palaces, this Queen of Cities presented a fantastic image: "no one would have believed it to be true if he had not seen it with his own eyes," exclaimed a crusading chronicler[77] who evidently lacked the kind of literary reference available to Bernal Díaz when he came within sight of Tenochtitlán.[78] Once they had broken through its walls, participants in the Fourth Crusade engaged in a frenzy of murder, rape, and pillage, turning the Queen of Cities into a battered shell, thereby destroying the Christian world's greatest urban civilization. Cholula, already ancient, and Tenochtitlán, though not yet born, were on course to become the Mesoamerican version of Jerusalem and Constantinople.

The American career of the cross was just beginning with the fall of Tenochtitlán in 1521. Negotiating peace with the defeated Indians of Chiapas two years later, Luis Marin set up crosses and extolled the virtues of Christianity. The natives must give up their idols, their sacrifices, their sodomy and robbery, he told them, and must make an altar for an image of the Virgin.[79] By 1525, in the course of Cortés's ill-considered Honduran expedition, a Mayan leader, having already learned of European prowess, preemptively offered to burn tribal idols and replace them with a cross.[80] Other Indians would learn to do *La Conquesta*, the Dance of the Conquest.[81] In what had become New Spain, Franciscans used the same evangelizing methods that the Benedictines had employed in Britain and other parts of Western Europe nearly a thousand years earlier, except that "the Indian was usually under duress."[82] The experience of the Mexican native, demoralized and deracinated by conquest, cannot be described in milder terms than that.

In his Fourth Letter, Cortés asks Charles V to send religious zealots to attend the spiritual needs of the Indians, not bishops who would waste money on pomp, ceremony, "and other vices." He adds that the natives had been used to priests whose chastity and honesty were guaranteed by capital punishment for transgressions.[83] Certainly he got what he asked for. The Franciscan zealots who moved to New Spain saw Cortés as an agent of divine will. The conversion of the New World's millions would culminate in the Second Coming, or so they believed,[84] and "spiritual conquest" proceeded apace. Motolinía, the monk who became a chronicler of the Indians of New Spain, claimed that the Franciscans at Tlaxcala were baptizing as many as five hundred Indian children a week by around 1540.[85] "[G]reat and demented ascetics" implanted a doctrine of "metaphysical terror" at Cholula. Its tenacity remains in evidence today in ceremonial emphasis on penance and the cult of the Virgin. Today's Cholultecas reportedly think of their pre–Hispanic heritage as "a past possessed by the devil" from which they have been saved by Christian belief.[86]

In 1539 Franciscans at Tlaxcala directed a performance of "The Conquest of Jerusalem," with a cast of thousands of converted Indians. The plot featured miraculous victories by the Christian armies, the surrender and conversion of the Muslims, their baptism under papal auspices, etc.[87] By the late sixteenth century, Spain had established a Pacific trading center in Manila, to which Catholic missionaries flocked. For them the expeditions of Cortés and Pizarro represented a model for the conquest and conversion of China.[88]

In 1517, however, about the time that Bernal Díaz and others were sailing to Yucatan on Hernandez de Cordoba's ill-fated expedition, Martin Luther was posting his ninety-five theses on the door of the castle church. The Reformation would tear Europe apart. But the New World offered room for adherents of every kind of cross, and in the earliest centuries of European colonization, England still flirted with a return to Catholicism. Yet the cross bore heavily on the Indian. In John 10:16 the Evangelist writes, "And other sheep I have, which are not of this fold: them also I must bring, and they shall hear my voice; and there shall be one fold, and one shepherd." Juan Ginés de Sepúlveda, Castile's imperial chronicler, cited this passage to justify the conquest. The Puritans turned to Psalm 2:8 ("Ask of me, and I shall give thee the heathen for thine inheritance, and the uttermost parts of the earth for thy possession") and wrote it into law. Cortés distributed crosses; Walter Raleigh handed out shillings with an image of Elizabeth I.[89] For the native, the result was about the same: dispossession, despair, and death.

Catholicism now has more adherents in Latin America than anywhere else in the world. But because Latin America is "poverty-racked," many are drawn to evangelical and Pentecostal promises of material wealth,[90] just as some Indians may have been attracted to Christianity on the basis of Cortés's assurance that Christian faith would bring them "good health and bountiful harvests." As for America north of the Rio Grande ... suffice it to say that the cross in each of its major Western varieties has had a highly successful New World career.

In October 2011, Pope Benedict XVI joined other religious leaders in an international gathering to condemn the use of violence and terrorism in the name of God. "With great shame," the pope acknowledged that "in the course of history, force has also been used in the name of the Christian faith."[91] One man, at least, had recommended a different course with regard to the indigenous people of Spanish America. We might think of Bartolomé de Las Casas as a whistle blower, except that he did not need to leak news of Spanish atrocities to third parties. This great advocate of Indian rights and Bishop of Chiapas had the ear, if not the will, of the Holy Roman Emperor. Had his views prevailed, the Indians would have been allowed to decide for themselves whether to accept the Gospel that Christian missionaries preached to them. They would have retained control of their minerals and other resources unless they granted Castile the right to "develop" them. But the Crown might have had to go to war against Spanish colonists to enforce those rights and restore native sovereignty.[92]

The crusading ideal did not end in the sixteenth century. Following the attacks of September 11, 2001, President George W. Bush launched a war that he characterized as a "crusade" to defend civilization. On the basis of his choice of words (as well as targets), we can hardly blame the many who concluded that his War on Terror was really a war on Muslims.

5

The Sword's New Cutting Edge

On Watling Island (also known as San Salvador Island) in the Bahamas where Columbus first landed in the course of his most famous voyage, the great navigator concluded that the natives had no knowledge of weapons, citing the fact that "when I showed them swords, they took them by the edge and cut themselves."[1] A fifteenth-century European could hardly expect to meet with a greater display of innocence—or ignorance—than someone's grasping a sword by its blade. In the Eastern Hemisphere, the long metallic blade fixed to a hilt had served as a weapon for thousands of years. On the basis of cave engravings, it appears that the horse-borne warriors who invaded southeastern Europe and much of India and the Middle East from the Eurasian steppes some four millennia before the Age of Discovery may have worshipped the metal blade, though they did not yet have swords.[2] By the late Bronze Age, the extraction of ores for the production of tools and weapons, including what seem to have been ancestral swords, was proceeding on a "nearly industrial scale."[3] Shaft graves at Mycenae, dating back to about 1650 BCE, include swords, as well as images of men in chariots.[4] In the *Iliad*, swords "smoke" with the blood of slain enemies, though bronze-headed spears seem to do most of the damage. When aroused, the God of the Old Testament may wield a hungry sword that "shall devour from the one end of the land even to the other…: no flesh shall have peace."[5] The Roman soldier carried a sword, though his spear was a more important weapon. This priority continued into the Middle Ages, with the addition of the battle ax. But the sword was always a more celebrated, more prestigious weapon, and it was far more likely to be passed on from father to son for generations. Some, such as Arthur's Excalibur, even had names.[6]

Like the male infant of the Aztecs with his tiny bow and arrows,[7] the son of a European noble might be given a sword at birth or at his naming. He would play with it at first; later he would train to use it as a weapon. As a warrior, his sword would be his "constant companion," brandished for the swearing of an oath, for a duel, or for warfare. Unless he left it to a son or other relative, he might be buried with it.[8] When Childeric, the first major European king of post–Roman Europe, was lowered into the grave in 482, a ceremonial sword, "the symbol par excellence of elite male status,"[9] was placed at his side. Like the "gem-studded" sword that Hygelac presents to Beowulf and like swords found as far from Childeric's Belgian grave as Apahida in Romania and Blučina in the Czech Republic, the hilt and scabbard of King Childeric's sword were decorated with gold and garnets. Besides swords found in ancient burial sites, many were thrown into the Thames and other European rivers, presumably as votive offerings, though long after the inhabitants of some such areas had adopted Christian beliefs.[10]

A less exalted knight than Childeric might have had to make do with a plain iron (later steel) sword with a wooden or iron scabbard. Such a weapon would be the costliest he possessed, which is not surprising considering that the elaborate process of crafting a sword required a specialized smith. A knight who served in Iberia's Reconquest usually carried an iron sword, about three feet long and double-edged. Its primary purpose was to pierce an enemy's armor. While a sword was de rigueur for such a knight, an infantryman might carry one, as well, if he could afford to.[11]

In Europe and what would become European colonies, the career of the sword became closely linked to that of the cross, as we have seen in Chapter 4. An important date in this partnership was 758 when Pope Paul I sent a sword to Pippin, the Frankish king. When a successor, Lothar I of France, went to Rome to be crowned Emperor of the Romans, the pope handed him a sword as part of his coronation. The implication was clear to contemporaries: the secular ruler derived his strength from God through the pope and had the responsibility of protecting the pope and assisting him in the elimination of evil. But the power of the sword in medieval Europe transcended its use as a symbolic or actual weapon. The sword signified strength and justice. It was another form of the Christian cross. Some swords, such as that of St. Ferdinand (Ferdinand III) that was housed in the Seville Cathedral, were thought to work miracles, like the swords of legendary heroes. Cortés evoked something of this tradition when making three cuts in a giant ceiba tree that stood in the central plaza of a town on the Tabasco coast, thereby proclaiming possession of that town in the name of his sovereign and a willingness to defend his claim by force.[12] That sovereign, Charles V, was known as the "sword of Christianity."[13]

The sword regained some of its Old World magic in what would become New Spain and other parts of Spanish America. Without encountering the kind of metal armor that ordinarily might have deflected their blows, the conquistadors used their swords to slice off Indians' limbs and heads. Native drawings of the massacre at Cholula and of Pedro de Alvarado's surprise attack on the palace dancers show a scattering of neatly severed limbs, heads, and half-torsos.[14] When Cortés was captured during the assault on Tenochtitlán, a follower freed him by cutting off the hands and arms of the Indians who had seized him.[15] Swords versus clubs was perhaps not as much of a mismatch as guns versus knives, but as Jared Diamond points out, the metal weapons of the Spaniards—swords, spears, and daggers—could easily pierce the Indians' cotton armor, while steel helmets protected the adventurers from the blows of Indian clubs.[16]

In Bernal Díaz's account of the Córdoba expedition of 1517, Indians fled "when they felt the sharp edge of our swords," besides the impact of other European weapons. Two years later in an early battle of the Cortés expedition, Díaz writes that Indian warriors suffered "greatly from the strokes and thrusts of our swords," as well as from the Spaniards' crossbows, harquebuses, and cannon. Surviving natives were forced to retreat to a swamp.[17] At Tlaxcala, only "a miracle of swordplay" stopped a charging mass of Indian warriors from overwhelming the invaders.[18]

As acknowledged, the conquistadors did not have to rely on the mystique and cutting edge of swords alone in battling Indians. Collected from the canals of Tenochtitlán following the Noche Triste were cannons; harquebuses; spears; crossbows and arrows; steel helmets; coats of mail and breast plates; shields of metal, wood, and leather; and swords.[19] The Spaniards' horses made for a decisive advantage, at times, as discussed in Chapter 7, and their attack dogs were another fearsome weapon, early on. With their suite of superior weapons, the conquistadors didn't need travel visas or any other kind of permission to enter the territory of others. But cannons were cumbersome and, when used in Mexico, more likely to produce awe than casualties.[20] The harquebus was also unwieldy. Such weapons required dry powder that was not always available. Historian Matthew Restall goes so far as to say that the cannoneer or harquebusier was "lucky to get a single shot off."[21] An indigenous account of the post-conquest era says that in the battles of Tenochtitlán, attacking Aztecs learned to zigzag to avoid harquebus blasts and to hit the ground when the conquistadors fired a cannon.[22] In the following century in New England, Indian arrows often outperformed British guns in terms of accuracy and lethality.[23] Horses and dogs could be effective, but only under limited circumstances that, in the case of horses, did not cause them to founder or slip, or subject them to "cold-cramping."[24]

Members of the Grijalva expedition that preceded Cortés's encountered Indians with brightly polished metal ax heads. Taking the metal for low-quality gold, the Spaniards eagerly traded beads to acquire six hundred of them, giving the king's officers in Cuba a laugh at their expense when the metal revealed itself to be copper.[25] Indian metallurgy was limited to the crafting of jewelry, ornaments, and copper tools. The smelting of steel was out of the question, as Mesoamerica lacks deposits of iron ore.[26] But the metalwork of the Incas was quite advanced, enabling them to make stunning jewelry pieces, as well as bronze and copper tips and footrests for their plows, and to show Europeans how to smelt silver at low temperatures.[27] The Tarrascans of present-day Michoacan used advanced metallurgical techniques to fashion masks, bells, ornaments, and weapons out of copper and gold. The Mixtecs were also accomplished goldsmiths.[28] Perhaps in a more civilized world societies would be compared on the basis of their ability to turn metals into beautiful objects rather than weapons, but such a world did not exist in the sixteenth century, nor does it now, when noticeable advances in ornamental metalwork have not begun to keep pace with the manufacture of the metal tools, appliances, structures, and conveyances that provide much of the material basis for modern life. In an eerie parallel with the attitude of Bronze Age warriors toward the earliest metal blades, Aztec mythology linked the first flint knife to the origins of the Mexica people and the birth of numerous Aztec gods.[29]

In any case, Bartolomé de Las Casas surely exaggerates the arms imbalance between indigenous Americans and their conquerors when he describes the former's weaponry as consisting of bows and arrows and wooden lances that "could only wound and not kill."[30] The natives of Mesoamerica had spears with sharp obsidian points whose lethality was enhanced by the *atlatl* or spear-thrower. They had blowguns and wooden or fibrous shields, and they threw darts and stones. These stones were not the kind that lies strewn about by natural forces to be picked up off the ground or stumbled over. They were hand-fitted and round, they were stockpiled, and they came to the Aztecs as tribute from their client states. The Indians edged their wooden club, the *macama*, with bits of obsidian. Bernal Díaz claimed that these "two-handed swords" were better than the Spaniards' and that the "knives" set in their lances were so sharp that the natives could shave their heads with them.[31] Tlaxcalan warriors were able to decapitate a horse. The victor will often maximize the strength of the vanquished in order to polish the trophy of his own accomplishment, but native weaponry took a visible toll. According to a woman who came to New Spain after the conquest in the hope of finding a rich husband, the conquistadors' wounds made them "look like they have escaped from hell." She mentions amputated feet, hands, ears, the loss of an eye, the absence of "half a face." Even the handsomest were marred.[32]

Having fallen into the hands of Indians at Hispaniola and later in Mexico,

Spanish swords were not cast aside in favor of traditional native weaponry. According to Díaz, the Aztecs turned captured swords into sword-bearing lances, deploying them "like scythes" to attack the conquistadors' horses. At another point in his narrative, he writes simply that the Aztecs attacked them with captured swords. They also used captured crossbows against the attackers of Tenochtitlán, having forced European captives to show them how they worked.[33] Thus, the Aztecs acknowledged the superiority of such weapons by substituting them for their bows and arrows and their non-metallic spears and clubs when they had the chance. Canary Islanders had paid homage to European weapons by crafting swords and shields out of hardened wood.[34]

Ross Hassig argues that the invaders' suite of weapons did not give them a decisive advantage. Besides the fact that the Aztecs learned to avoid the line of fire of the Spaniards' cannons, the Spaniards had an insufficient supply of gunpowder for their guns to make a major difference.[35] But the technological advantage enjoyed by the Europeans was not limited to weaponry and armor. As Camilla Townsend points out, Spanish sailing vessels brought not only the disruption of the Narváez expedition: additional vessels bearing additional Europeans began arriving on the Yucatan coast as early as 1520. Cortés's father sent one. And as mentioned in the Introduction, without advances in navigational devices, Europeans could not have come to American shores except by accident. The multi-functional brigantine proved crucial in the struggle for Tenochtitlán. Books persuaded more Europeans to cross the Atlantic, and so on. The Indians recognized this technological superiority, saw that they couldn't match it, and realized that they were in no position to protect their noncombatants. Or so argues Townsend.[36]

Besides their technological deficits, the Aztecs were at a tactical disadvantage, even when greatly outnumbering the Spaniards. The goal of each warrior was to capture an enemy or enemies for sacrifice to their gods. The highest honors were bestowed on the valiant warrior who brought back multiple captives. The son of a noble who managed such a feat became a member of the military caste, thereby acquiring both a wife *and* a harem.[37] Thus, the Aztec warrior fought in competition with others of his kind, although a capture might require the help of a comrade or two. The premium put on capturing enemy fighters meant that the Aztecs did not try to kill their adversaries in battle but to inflict disabling wounds that would allow their capture. While they were hurling rocks and darts intended to deliver weakening blows, the Spaniards were firing crossbows and guns, often with lethal aim. Hassig's argument that it was the nature of Aztec weapons that made combat "an individual affair"[38] lacks plausibility in view of Aztec cultural priorities. Moreover, when they attacked the conquistadors in their barricaded

Tenochtitlán quarters following the massacre of the dance ceremony, the Aztecs fought in closed ranks. They may have lacked space for anything else. Conquistadors who had battled the French and the Turks in Europe said that this was the fiercest fighting they had ever experienced.[39]

The fact that the invaders could sometimes kill a warrior at a distance won them no more respect than that accorded the Achaian archer who would fire an arrow into the Trojan ranks and then retreat into his own, like a child who runs "to the arms of his mother."[40] The success of the Hispanic equivalent of the Achaian archer could devastate the morale of indigenous warriors by bringing down a great native hero from a distance, thus "trivializing" the death of a man who had not yet even entered combat.[41] Closer in, the Spaniard could use his sword to thrust and slash without restraint, while the Indian sought an opening to wound and capture this formidable barbarian. Even when the Aztecs were besieged at Tenochtitlán in the final weeks of fighting, they were still intent on the capture and sacrifice of invaders, as Díaz's narrative makes clear.

The conquistadors won battles by fighting by their own rules—or from the Indian point of view, no rules at all. For the Mesoamerican native, a battle was a "sacred duel," with its own preparation, warning ritual, regalia, and standards of conduct. They attached no virtue to winning an unfair fight. Fairness might even require that food and weapons be sent to an enemy. The Aztecs were outraged by the Toxcatl massacre but even more so by the fact that the Spaniards attacked without warning.[42] The tactical inventory of the Mexica did not include the pre-emptive assault.[43] When the Spaniards devised an ambush, it was to inflict casualties on the Indians with minimal risk to themselves. The intent of the Indian ambush was a dramatic confrontation with an adversary, preparatory to individual combat. The Spaniards campaigned out of season when the demand for agricultural labor was too high to permit the Aztecs to defend themselves at full force. Finally, in besieging Tenochtitlán, the Spaniards were applying the ultimate weapon of European warfare of that era. For the Aztecs, the siege was the opposite of warfare.[44]

Because the invaders refused to fight by the rules of native warfare, the Aztecs would not accord a warrior's death to a Spaniard who, for practical reasons, had to be killed rather captured. Instead they would bash in the back of his head. This was the mode of execution reserved for criminals of the Aztec world.[45]

For the Spaniards, an age that exalted heroic feats by individual warriors was fading into the misty past, as noted in Chapter 3. Concern for glory, honor, pledges to gods (or maidens), and desire for revenge had become battlefield liabilities,[46] despite Cortés's sporadic efforts to rally his followers with the promise of lasting fame. When the conquistadors advanced shoulder to shoulder behind the charges of their horsemen in a tight, disciplined formation, or when they defended themselves in such a body, they could effectively deploy their swords and spears to offset the numerical disadvantage that they usually faced. In Europe, advances in artillery had already pushed such weapons to the margins of military usefulness. New tactics, strategy, equipment, weaponry, fortifications, training, and military recruitment were beginning to give Europeans a "comparative advantage in violence" in Old World conflicts.[47] The celebrated sword weighed lightly in this growing military edge, but in Mexico, c. 1520, steel swords and spears remained important weapons.

Perhaps as important as Spanish weapons, tactics, and freedom from indigenous tradition was what happened during the conquistadors' initial visit to Tenochtitlán. Instead of deferring to Moctezuma, the great emperor before whom other Aztec nobles swept the ground on which he might alight from his litter and averted their gaze under penalty of death, the Spanish stared at him and prodded him. In what might today be called an act of "disruptive innovation," they took him by the hand, stroked his hair, and jostled one another for a better look.[48] They treated Moctezuma so familiarly that his authority began "to bleed away."[49] Cortés's decision to take him captive in the core of his empire was something "unimaginable," a possibility that could not have been anticipated,[50] not by the Aztecs, at least, though the seizure of an enemy ruler was an ancient war tactic of Europeans.[51] In Chapter 12 I will question the veracity of both the conquistador accounts and indigenous sources with regard to this central event. Perhaps for now it is enough to say that the Spaniards' greatest weapon may have been their shocking audacity. As a Catalan contemporary put it, Castilians "give the impression that they alone are descended from heaven, and the rest of mankind are mud."[52] The conquistadors' Old World baggage included an uncritical assumption of superiority.

As for the sword, its prestige has extended into the present-day Western world where students of traditional techniques face off against one another brandishing this "queen of weapons." Because their steel long-swords have unsharpened blades and blunted points, and because the competitors clothe themselves in body armor, no one suffers the fate of the cotton-clad Aztec warrior. These make-believe knights have a women's division, too.[53]

6

America's Gold and Silver Promote Slavery and Boost European Commerce

An important item in the Old World baggage that the conquistadors brought to Mexico was a lust for precious metals, especially gold. To understand this addiction we must go further back in time. People have valued certain metals from the earliest ages as material that could be turned into beautiful adornments of the human body and its clothing. Prior to Columbus, such ores enjoyed separate hemispheric careers; with Columbus these careers came together. When they did all the discoverable precious metals in the parts of the Western Hemisphere that Spain could control went east, across the Atlantic, to Seville, at least until the 1560s when the Spaniards established a Pacific Coast port at Acapulco and trading center at Manila. We will see what happened to the gold and silver when it reached its destination, but we must first note something of its European career.

To mention such a career implies a set of uniform practices that did not exist when Europe was, for its inhabitants, almost the entire world. While the Romans were paying their soldiers in gold coins and buying what they needed with gold, bronze, and silver currency, Germans near the Empire's frontier were using Rome's outdated silver coins for money. Those in remoter parts were putting silver to uses that Romans reserved for earthenware.[1] Britons, meanwhile, were ornamenting the remains of wealthy citizens with bronze and gold jewelry, also tucking in a few bronze and silver vessels for the long voyage ahead. The grave of an Anglo-Saxon king may yield numerous silver bowls, silver dishes, bronze cauldrons, as well as battle implements and even a large boat. Adorning the body of a woman buried at Cologne around 530 were a necklace of gold coins, gold beads, gold and garnet ornaments and earrings, a gold bracelet, etc.[2] In the life of a society, such adornments—whether shells, feathers, beads, copper, gold, or silver—may eventually gain use as money.[3] Or they may not. One can still see women in rural India wearing their wealth as jewelry.

Independently of any human burials, Europeans also deposited valued metalwork in grounds and riverbeds throughout the subcontinent, presumably as votive offerings. If humans valued such objects so highly, so might the gods—or God: some of these objects bear Christian symbols. Treasure troves dating from a later period and consisting of gold medallions, Roman coins, rings, and various other objects, appear to represent mere hoarding. Such was often the medieval endpoint of the precious metals taken as plunder and otherwise used for long-distance trade.[4] The Vikings sought gold and silver not only for their exchange value but—like weapons, ships, and feasts—for the prestige attached to them. Enhanced prestige could win a chieftain followers and allies.[5] Gold and silver were still sometimes hoarded in sixteenth-century Spain, where each kingdom (Castile, Aragon, Navarre, etc.) minted its own currency.[6] But always such glittery ore was seen as valuable. In the pre-modern world of *The Iliad,* the Bible (for example, Revelation 21: 18–21), *Morte D'Arthur, The Canterbury Tales, The Song of Roland,* even *Don Quixote,* the image of magnificence is always encrusted with gold and precious gems.

Looting the New World

What we have of Columbus's logs portray the Caribbean natives, initially, in terms of their physical appearance and behavior. Columbus found them "a very fine people" and altogether malleable: we can "make them do whatever we wish," he wrote.[7] Noting a bit of gold jewelry, Columbus wanted to know its source. The gold came from another island, he was told. This became a pattern. The source of the gold he spotted, whether on a person's nose or coiled around her arms and legs, was always on another island, somewhere else.

Members of Columbus's second voyage to the Antilles could not have read Amerigo Vespucci's description of natives who neither valued the New World's gold, gems, and pearls nor worked to obtain them, as it was yet to be written. But they seem to have anticipated landing in such a world. Besides finding themselves to be dependent on the natives for survival, at least at first, the Spaniards were frustrated by the absence of the "gold and riches everyone had longed for since the day of their departure."[8] After the invaders had used swords, crossbows, the ancestral muskets known as harquebuses, horses, and mastiffs to reduce Hispaniola to "peace and obedience," Columbus decided that there were goldfields in a region called Cibao. How were they to get that gold? Columbus imposed a gold quota. Every Indian over age fourteen was required to produce a quantity of gold dust (a "large bell-full") every three months or face punishment. But the area did not have nearly enough gold dust to go around, and Columbus had to punish those who came up short. Most sources fail to mention that the punishment consisted of having a hand chopped off. Whether anyone survived such "labor discipline" is unlikely.[9]

During his fourth voyage to the Indies, Columbus became reflective, musing that "[g]old is most excellent." With gold one could do "whatever he likes in the world," even bring souls to Paradise[10]—by discovering pagans and converting them to Christianity, presumably, if not by the sale or purchase of indulgences. Discovery of gold in Hispaniola drew gold-seeking adventurers across the Atlantic, 1,500 of them by 1502.[11] With exhaustion of gold deposits in the Greater Antilles, they would look to the mainland for better opportunities for personal enrichment. One such man was Juan de Grijalva, whose expedition to the mainland of Mexico preceded Cortés's by a year, as we have noted. When Indians in a canoe approached the ghostly vessels of his fleet to find out what the strangers wanted, Grijalva told them that they wanted gold, only gold.[12] That seems to have been all that any of them wanted. According to Bartolomé de las Casas, "nobody came to the Indies except for gold."[13] Thomas More would tweak this gold lust by having his Utopians use gold for chamber pots and similarly humble household items.[14]

The Cuban chief Hatuey thought that gold was the Christian god.[15] After all, it was what Christians seemed to worship. Bringing out a basket of gold jewelry, he had his followers perform a dance to it. Then, rather than risk an attack by Europeans who might come to rescue their god, he had them throw it into a river.[16] The conquistadors' gold lust was not, of course, a form of worship, and it was more than a case of human greed. Wealth had not become intangible as credit in this pre-modern world,[17] at least not for the likes of those who sought their fortune in the Indies. As Columbus recognized, gold was liquid wealth, good anywhere for any kind of transaction, its value heightened by the "gold famine" mentioned in Chapter 2. We need not wonder at the conquistadors' passion for gold. Yet one historian suggests that the conquistadors fevered for "the actual golden metal," not abstract wealth.[18] Moctezuma's emissaries and other New World natives would have had no argument with that. When the Aztec emperor's gift-bearers brought them gold necklaces and emblems, the Spaniards "were delighted, they were overjoyed. They snatched up the gold like monkeys … they hungered for that gold like wild pigs."[19] This from an Aztec survivor of the Empire's destruction.

According to Gómara, secretary to Cortés in his retirement, Cortés had wanted his men to feign ignorance of gold so as not to give the Indians the idea that that was what they sought.[20] "Gold? What is that?" or words to that effect should be their constant refrain. Evidently they were terrible actors. Cortés returned to this ploy after the fall of Tenochtitlán, instructing Diego Hurtado de Mendoza on the eve of his exploratory voyage up the Pacific coast, to observe people's ornaments, noting whether they wore gold, pearls, or gems, but without displaying any particular interest in what he saw.[21]

At any rate, Cortés was a wretched model for indifference to gold. He asked everyone encountered by his expedition where they could find the stuff. "México" or "Culua" would come the reply.[22] According to R. C. Padden, representatives of Moctezuma had given members of the Grijalva expedition some finely-wrought objects of solid gold. These seem to have gone unreported, but (speculates Padden) Cortés would have learned of them through his friend, Pedro de Alvarado, a rebellious member of the Grijalva venture.[23] Camping in the dunes above San Juan de Ulúa on the Gulf, Cortés asks Moctezuma's envoys to have the nearby villagers bring them gold to exchange for beads. The envoys are willing. Then one of them asks for a Spaniard's helmet to show their emperor. He thinks that it resembles one worn by Huitzilopochtli, the Aztec deity. Cortés agrees to let him have the helmet, but he wants him to return it filled with gold dust, saying that he will send it to *his* emperor to determine if their gold is like the Spaniards' gold.[24]

The conquistadors were clear as to their motivation. "We came here to serve God and the king, and also to get rich," declares Bernal Díaz, their chief chronicler.[25] Erasmus satirized the doubtful compatibility of these goals by having a character in a dialogue examine a map of the Indies marked with Christian symbols and observe, "I have learned that there one can bring back plunder. But I didn't hear that Christianity had been introduced."[26] Like earlier crusaders who had shucked off all restraint on their "consuming addiction" to acquiring other people's jewels and precious metals,[27] the conquistadors seemed unaware of any contradiction between their creed and their greed. Some even thought that God had planted treasure in the New World to attract Christians. Being apprised of these divine deposits, Christians would come and convert the natives to the true faith.[28]

If God planted precious metals in Mesoamerica, he did so by using the labor of Indians. Natives of Veragua, Columbus notes, were said to bury their dead with their gold.[29] This statement follows his observation that with gold, one can do anything. Does Columbus mean to imply that Christians make better use of their gold? I think he does. But as we have seen, Europeans had formerly engaged in similar burial practices. We have also noted the treasure troves found in Europe that seem to represent hoarding.

The conquistadors would discover such a trove of treasure behind a hidden door in the palace where they were ensconced as Moctezuma's guests. Somewhat contrary to the view (mentioned above) that the conquistadors valued precious metals per se rather than as a means to something else and to the comparison of gold-hungry conquistadors to monkeys, they did not pour beautifully crafted gold objects over their bodies or begin playing catch with pearl necklaces on discovering this treasure. Instead they "unanimously" opted "not to think of touching a particle of it," at least until a better time, and they quickly bricked the hidden door back up.[30] Such restraint matched a decision they had made early on, before leaving the Gulf Coast, to pool what gold they had so far collected to send it to Charles V "in the hope that he may bestow favours upon us." Under group pressure, all had agreed to this.[31]

Except for the sailors and pilots who were hired by Cortés, the most likely payment these adventurers could hope to receive consisted of the treasure they would seize.[32] Matthew Restall has argued that the conquistadors sought gold not because they worshipped the metal but because it could be turned into royal favor, which might be converted to a grant of the governorship of an imperial province,[33] perhaps an entire island like the one Sancho Panza expected to get by serving Don Quixote. Eventually, the treasure trove behind the hidden door did fall into conquistador hands. According to Bernal Díaz, Moctezuma simply gave it to them as a gift. Why would he do this? An Aztec Studies scholar writes that Moctezuma's gifts were tokens of dominance, glorified by extravagant humility.[34] If so, such cultural cues were lost on the conquistadors. But perhaps Moctezuma thought that with all this treasure the Spaniards would finally leave. In any case, he was no longer well placed to stop them from taking it, as by then he had reportedly become their captive. Besides handing over his father's treasure, Moctezuma complied with Cortés's demand that he collect all the gold in his gold-bearing tributary states and give it to the Spaniards. The conquistadors promptly melted it down into ingots, stamped with the royal arms.

From the perspective of Aztec survivors of the conquest, this treasure consisted of sacred objects—golden leg bands, gilded shields, arm bands, forehead devices, and so on. They write that the conquistadors set fire to "all the precious things," turning them into bricks.[35] But such ingots were transferable, and one could calculate their value in terms of other goods. They had exchange value, in other words. With ingots one could easily determine the *quinto real* (royal fifth) claimed by the Crown.[36] The conquistadors had plenty of precedents for such metallic transformation. Precious metal had poured into the Church in the Middle Ages in the form of reliquaries, candlesticks, censers, and the like—all given as offerings by the faithful in the hope of gaining saintly intervention in the affairs of everyday life. Clerics would melt such treasures down, turning them into the liquid capital that made the Church Europe's lender of last resort.[37] When crusaders sacked Constantinople in 1204, they stripped public buildings, imposing statues, and other monuments of their precious metals and smelted them into coins. Four teams of oxen were needed to drag the head of a giant bronze Hera to the fires.[38]

But it seems that the golden hoard behind the secret door was not the only treasure trove to fall into the adventurers' hands. According to conquistador Andrés de Tapia, Moctezuma also showed the Spaniards a huge collection of gold in various forms. This probably represented years of tribute payments. Cortés promptly took this treasure to his personal quarters.[39]

Having acquired a mass of gold, silver, and precious gems, the conquistadors had only to divide it up among themselves. During the Reconquest the division of plunder had become institutionalized, with (as always) a fifth going to the Crown, so much assigned to bereaved families for their losses, so much for participating officials, etc., but such firmly established practices had yet to take root in the entirely different soil of Mexico. According to Bernal Díaz, a third of what they had seen was already missing, stashed away by Cortés and his compadres in the conquistador leadership. And the available amount "went on diminishing,"[40] a fifth for the Crown, a fifth for Cortés (pursuant to a provision of the agreement of the San Juan de Ulúa sand dunes); allocations for the expeditions' two priests, for the seventy men left behind at Vera Cruz, and for Cortés's agents in Spain; additional amounts that Cortés claimed for various expenses that they had incurred and for special shares, until so little was left for men like Díaz that many of them refused the tiny allotments that were offered them. Much of the remainder was recycled in card games. Cortés placated the more disgruntled of his followers with secret shares and promises of future opportunities to strike it rich, but two of the conquistadors got into a sword fight over a set of gold plates.[41]

In his Second Letter to Charles V, Cortés describes his great reluctance to leave Tenochtitlán to deal with the arrival of Narváez, in consideration of the gold and jewelry that the conquistadors have amassed there for themselves and for the Crown. In his absence, the city's inhabitants are likely to rebel and the treasure be lost, he declares.[42] But he is writing several months after leaving the city and its treasure in the safekeeping of the homicidal Pedro de Alvarado. Tenochtitlán did rebel and much of its treasure was lost. Ironically, the supposed transportability of the gold ingots proved fatal to hundreds of conquistadors and many more of their Tlaxcalan allies on the Noche Triste, when Tenochtitlán became a trap from which the Spaniards and their allies sought to escape under cover of darkness. Cortés assigned the conveyance of much of the treasure to the Tlaxcalans, while the royal officers (given lame and wounded mounts) collected the royal fifth. Yet so many ingots remained that Cortés had his notaries witness the fact that he had done everything he could with them, then invited his followers to help themselves. Many responded by loading up on gold ingots. Under their weight, they could not avoid the volleys of arrows and rocks as they tried to flee the Aztec metropolis, and they fell into the watery gaps where the natives had removed sections of the causeway.[43]

Some of the gold they bore was recovered when Lake Texcoco was drained to make way for the metropolis that now spreads over the entire valley where all the different tribes had had their states. As for the windfall fortunes of the survivors, Cortés ordered everyone to declare his holdings. A third would be returned, he said, but any undeclared amounts would be seized. Many of the conquistadors followed the example of the captains and kept their gold without acknowledging it. Cortés could do nothing but force a few of them to make him "loans."[44]

With the fall of Tenochtitlán a year later, the conquistadors were understandably itching for their share of the loot. Bernardino de Sahagún's informants complained that as the starving survivors streamed out of the ruined city, Spaniards stopped them to look for gold, peering into people's mouths, under men's loincloths and women's skirts, and removing the most attractive women and ablest-looking men from the file of refugees. They branded the men for slavery.[45] According to another post-conquest indigenous source, surviving leaders among the defeated warriors presented Cortés with a collection of gold nose ornaments, pendants, lip plugs, and gold that had been stripped from shields and the like. The had hoped to buy Spanish protection against the fearsome Otomis, their traditional enemies. Cortés responded by demanding the gold that was lost on the Noche Triste and had them put in irons before Malintzin, his native interpreter, intervened on their behalf.[46]

The conquistadors' obsession with finding gold is understandable. Many of them badly needed it, having paid for their weapons and even treatment of their wounds with the future treasure that would surely be theirs. David Graeber argues that they were driven more by such debts than by greed.[47] The fact that they had to buy their own weapons—and horses, if they could afford them—reinforces the point that the conquistadors were not professional soldiers. They were more like fight-savvy entrepreneurs, investing their savings and their bodies in a risky enterprise with great potential returns.

Twentieth-century calendar illustration titled "*Toma Este Puñal y Matame Con El*" ("Take This Knife and Kill Me with It"), unknown artist, Landin Sol, *Ediciones de* Arte, Mexico (courtesy Bancroft Library, University of California, Berkeley).

When Cortés asked the captive Guatemoc, Moctezuma's successor and last ruler of the late Aztec empire, the whereabouts of Moctezuma's treasure, Guatemoc told him that the Spaniards in the brigantines had taken it.[48] Those in the boats had been able to invade the homes of affluent Aztecs. They had enjoyed access to hidden treasure in the reeds. They had also been able to intercept the boats of Indians who were fleeing with their valuables.[49] In addition, the Tlaxcalans and other Indian allies had enriched themselves. At length, the conquistadors gathered together all the gold, silver, and jewelry that was left. Bernal Díaz writes that it did not seem to amount to much. A rumor circulated that Guatemoc had thrown the rest of the treasure into the lake a few days before his capture, and the Royal Treasury officials declared that Guatemoc had hidden the bulk of the treasure. Cortés was delighted with this announcement, Díaz writes, as it meant that he would not have to give up what he had taken.[50] This is as close as Díaz ever comes to saying that Cortés had robbed the rest of them of their share of the spoils.

The officials proposed torturing Guatemoc and his cousin, the Lord of Tacuba, to make them reveal the treasure's location. Cortés, Díaz, and some of the others were opposed. They were not against torture per se: torture was standard practice, especially when there was thought to be hidden treasure.[51] But they were against torturing a *prince* "for greed of gold."[52] This suggests that they were inhibited by medieval notions of aristocratic privilege. But Cortés's opposition increased the suspicion of those who distrusted him, and apparently they were many. The torture proceeded, Díaz writes, so as "to avoid making any accusations against Cortés." Hot (probably boiling) oil was poured onto the prisoners' feet, and they confessed that they had thrown the gold into the lake.[53]

Díaz and others dove for the treasure, bringing up only some small gold pieces that Cortés and the Royal Treasurer confiscated as belonging to the king. Better swimmers were sent down. They brought up some necklaces and other small objects of insignificant value, at least in comparison to what was sought.[54] The Spaniards also went to Guatemoc's palace, pulling from a pond his private collection of jewelry and a large golden disc like one that Moctezuma had given them much earlier. Present-day curators, scholars, and interested others can only regret that they had had this magnificent object melted down. But all of these findings were thought to be of "small value."

Díaz concludes that the best of what Guatemoc had inherited of Moctezuma's treasure had already been sent to the king with one Alonso de Avila. What remained was quite disappointing. The conquistador captains suggested dividing it up among the wounded and disabled, and Cortés announced shares: eighty pesos for a horseman, sixty for a crossbowman or musketeer, etc. But again the amounts were so small that no one would accept them. There followed a graffiti war in which anonymous messages, some in cleverly written couplets, appeared on the whitewashed walls of the palatial lodging that Cortés had appropriated for himself. These accused him of taking far more than his share of Aztec gold. (Minor knights and foot soldiers had made similar accusations against the leaders of the sack of Constantinople some three hundred years earlier.)⁵⁵ Cortés responded with clever graffiti of his own, but the complaints persisted. At length, he lost patience with his accusers and sent them off to distant parts. Those who remained on good terms with him got their reward in the form of the allotments of Indian labor (*encomiendas*) discussed in Chapter 9.⁵⁶

But some of the conquistadors *were* able to send gold home, or try to anyway. According to Hugh Thomas, a good deal of it was captured by the French pirate, Jean Florin, between the Azores and Iberia.⁵⁷ Yet Aztec treasure continued to turn up. At some point in the years that followed, a work party strengthening the foundation of a church that was built on the site of the great temple (*Templo Major*) found a trove of gold, silver, and precious stones.⁵⁸

Graeber remarks that the more wealth that has been taken as plunder, the more must be given away in spectacular display.⁵⁹ What is described in the last chapter of Bernal Díaz's *Historia* seems to illustrate this point, for in 1538 Cortés, by then the Marques del Valle, and New Spain's Viceroy Don Antonio de Mendoza hosted an extravagant public celebration in Mexico City (née Tenochtitlán) to celebrate the Treaty of Nice between Charles V and Francis I of France. In Díaz's account of this "Roman Circus," the Zócolo (main plaza) was turned into a woods stocked with animals, which Indians hunted down before fighting among themselves. Other mock battles followed over succeeding days, including a fight between Turks and Christian knights, with Cortés posing as Grand Master of Rhodes. There were also bull fights, horse races, farces, and such exotica as African women nursing their babies. Díaz devotes pages to description of the elaborate dishes and wines of the feasts, the gold and silver service, and the efforts to control the revelry of this Europeanized potlatch.⁶⁰

Among the justifications for making war on the Indians cited by a leading ideologue of Spanish conquest, J. Ginés Sepúlveda, was lack of knowledge of the use of money.⁶¹ Aside from the many other problems with this idea, it would clearly not apply to the people of Mesoamerica. Juan de Grijalva's men discovered that on the mainland they could use cacao (chocolate) beans to pay for things, including Indian labor. Such beans were widely used in Mesoamerica at the time, and the near universal demand for them stimulated trade. Cortés thought that cacao beans served as a universal media of exchange.⁶² The cotton cloth worn by Aztec nobles, copper axes of the kind that fooled the Grijalva expeditioners, and quills filled with gold dust also served as media of exchange.⁶³ Díaz reports that people used these gold-filled quills to buy cloth, cacao, slaves, and other commodities, although any preoccupation that the natives might have had with the monetary value of things could not have approached his own.[64] For ceremonial purposes, the value of a banquet that an Aztec merchant might arrange was measurable in large capes, breechclouts, skirts, and other objects.[65] Decades after the conquest, Diego de Landa, Bishop of Yucatan, would compile a list of the benefits that Europeans had given the Indians. Included was the use of money.[66]

Aside from the small quantities of gold dust that the Aztecs used in everyday transactions, precious metals represented the adornments of their political power. Their founding myths projected a future in which others would pay tribute to them, and they would become "lords of gold and silver, of jewels and precious stones, of splendid feathers."[67]

Enslaving Miners

Gold became the New World's earliest export. An estimated twenty-three to twenty-seven metric tons of it had been shipped to Spain by 1525.[68] Forty-three tons of gold arrived in Seville between 1551 and 1560. This was huge compared to the seven hundred kilograms a year coming in from the west coast of Africa.[69] The bulk of these imports from the New World did not represent seizure of treasure troves by conquistadors but something more sinister.

David Graeber has identified an historic association of militarism and the capture of slaves to do the back-breaking and dangerous work of extracting precious metals from the earth.[70] Soldiers must be paid, after all, and they usually demanded gold. But for the centuries of Reconquest, Castilian monarchs had generally sidestepped this necessity by allowing their Christian warriors to turn conquered Muslim lands and people into plunder. About to besiege Valencia, the Cid sends out word that anyone "eager to exchange poverty for riches" should come join him.[71] Captured lands were parceled out along the kind of hierarchical lines that Cortés had improvised for what remained of Moctezuma's treasure: whatever a foot soldier was awarded, a knight was given twice as much, as determined by the area that a pair of oxen could plow in a day.[72] Not waiting for any such allocation, ordinary Castilians would sometimes move right into newly liberated areas with their flocks. Production of precious metals took on heightened importance with Charles V's wars against Protestantism and Islam. (More on this below.) By then, European armies consisted of the kind of hired combatants that had mastered the latest weaponry and infantry techniques.[73] And by then, Castilian use of slaves as miners was well established in America.

The people who acquired a Spanish American empire had no qualms about enslaving a conquered populace, especially if it consisted of non–Christians. Ownership of slaves had been common in ancient Greece and Rome. In the Middle Ages, Venetians bought female slaves on the Dalmatian coast and exported them to the harems of Egypt and Syria. Swedes had a similar trade in the Ukraine. Arab commentators of the tenth century thought that the Swedish Vikings known as the Rus lived entirely off slaving.[74] The Church authorized the enslavement of "infidels" and later even Christians of infidel origin. Captured Muslims were forced to provide domestic work in Iberia, enhancing the status of their owners.[75] When Christians conquered Muslim Minorca in 1287, they sold the entire population into slavery.[76] The Ottoman Empire ran on slave labor.

In 1441, Portugal's Prince Henry the Navigator presented the first known slaves to come from sub–Saharan Africa, ten of them, to Pope Eugenius IV.[77] Three years later, the first black slaves landed in Portugal.[78] Like the Indians that Columbus first brought to Spain, they were displayed as exotic creatures from another world.[79] There followed a flood of African slaves into Europe. In Spain they joined the thousands of enslaved Circassians, Bosnians, Poles, Russians, Guanches, and Berbers who were already working in the latifundia of Andalucia and elsewhere. Portugal became an African slave-trade middle man after 1444. Her ships had borne an estimated 150,000 sub–Saharans away from their homeland by the end of the fifteenth century.[80]

As blacks were shipped to Europe, slavery took on the racial dimension that had already become affixed to it in Muslim North Africa and the Middle East. The only sub–Saharan people that Europeans encountered in Europe were slaves and former slaves. In addition, the Biblical story of Ham (Genesis 9:21–27) inspired the idea that for some people, condemned by God, slavery could be perpetual. Slavery became identified with members of one race.[81] By the eighteenth century, when the African slave trade hit full stride, the sailors of a slave ship would be regarded as "white men," even though some of them may have been men of color. They were white because they were not intended for sale.[82] With the discovery of precious metals in the Antilles, Mesoamerica, and eventually the Andes, Castile greatly expanded the acquisition of slaves and oversight of slave labor. The New World's gold and silver financed the import of African slaves, who were used to extract additional mineral wealth.

Spanish Christians had gained plenty of experience in dealing with the inhabitants of conquered territory by the time Columbus planted a settlement on Hispaniola. Following their great victory over the Almohad army at Las Navas in the thirteenth century, they had gotten used to enslaving the population of conquered territories—the "non-productive" urban portion of it, at least. Labor shortages brought by the devastation of the Black Death made such acquisitions vital. Anyone captured in war or otherwise seized might be enslaved. Longstanding doctrine legitimized the enslavement of war captives. But in Africa as well as the New World, war would become "a euphemism for the organized theft of human beings."[83]

The natives of Hispaniola, the Tainos, reminded Columbus of the Guanches, at least in color. And he saw a potential slave in every Indian he encountered. He offered to bring all of the inhabitants of one small island to Castile or to hold them there as slaves, whatever the Crown preferred.[84] The problem for Columbus's business plan was that the natives did not travel well. Of 550 captives from his second voyage, two hundred intended slaves died en route to Spain; the rest were sick and dying by the time they arrived.[85] With the native population of Hispaniola already in rapid decline by 1499, Columbus still wrote of exporting four thousand slaves a year to Spain. He transported six hundred that May. But the Crown did not support his slave-trade scheme and even returned a few of those that survived.[86] His opportunism finds an echo in literature when Sancho Panza realizes that the kingdom he imagines he is about to acquire may be inhabited—and by blacks! He can get rid of them "in a flash," he sees, just by selling them into slavery.

The Spanish located their earliest settlements on Hispaniola in areas of greatest population density: the better to avail themselves of native labor—and women. By 1497, Columbus's brother Bartolomeo was doing out freeholds of land and the services of Indians to settlers from Castile. When Las Casas arrived in 1502, he was greeted with the news that he had come at a propitious time: the ongoing war on Hispaniola's natives would soon provide colonists with numerous slaves.[87] Two kinds of forced labor soon evolved. The settler with connections to a colonial official might be awarded an allotment of Indian labor, called an *encomienda*. Such a labor force, organized by the local tribal chief, could be made to work "wherever necessary," in the expansive phrase used by Queen Isabel in her instructions to the governor of Hispaniola. Although she advised the governor to see that the Indians were well-treated, they were not. Las Casas writes that if a Hispaniola settler was not inclined to walk to his destination, he would have an Indian carry him on his back or, perhaps for longer trips, he might lie in a hammock relayed along by Indians who would shade him with a large leaf and fan him with a goose's wing. There were reports of settlers using Indians to dig cassava mounds, which meant heaping the soil three or four feet high. Such workers would be released every third day or so to feed themselves by going into the hills to try to find some fruit.[88]

The encomienda system left plenty of room for an older and even more horrendous institution of forced labor. Slavery was worse for the worker because, typically, he had to risk his life in a mine where a Spanish overseer would set an intolerable work pace, driving his workers with "beatings, kicks, lashes and blows," in the words of Las Casas.[89] If an enslaved mine worker ran away, a special police force was on hand to hunt him down. A miner's life expectancy was twenty-five years. And unlike the person assigned to an encomendero, the slave could be bought and sold. Slavery was worse for the slave owner, too, in a way, for unlike the encomendero, he had to feed, clothe, and house the workers he acquired. At least in principle, he did. But he could minimize such costs. According to Motolinía, the Nahuatl-speaking Franciscan historian, the Indians had to bring their own food to the mines. When it ran out, they starved.[90] But the mine operator would at least have to bear the initial expense of buying (or capturing) slaves. Now admittedly such differences in forced-labor regimes might have been lost on the outside observer. And the overworked, underfed worker who was subject to transfer from one encomendero to another might have regarded the distinction between slavery and the semi-slavery of the encomienda as a white man's sophistry.

In 1500 the Crown banned the enslavement of Indians but made exceptions of those attacking colonists and those engaging in "atrocious habits," such as cannibalism, a practice that slave traders were quick to allege. We may judge the efficacy of this early prohibition on slavery on the basis of subsequent pronouncements. In 1526, for example, the Council of the Indies outlawed the enslavement of Indians and conditionally limited the authority to wage war on them to ecclesiastics. A Cuban settler, Rodrigo Durán, among others, warned that many settlers would soon leave. Our Indians like mining, settlers claimed. It was easier than working in the fields, and the enslaved miners were quite well-fed.[91] Or so settlers said. In 1530, Charles V ordered that "[n]o one must dare to enslave any Indian," either in war or in peace or by purchase or trade.[92] A papal bull of 1537 growled a similar command, as did the New Laws of 1542. However, the colonists of Spanish America needed workers and were unwilling or unable to become their own labor force, and by the mid-sixteenth century the Habsburg monarchs, Charles V followed by Philip II, needed precious metals to pay for their European wars.

Patricia Seed points out that under Spanish tradition and law, buried minerals could not be owned by individuals. The *minero*, then, was only a concessionaire of the Crown.[93] He could not hope to strike it rich by discovering what appeared to be an abundant deposit of gold or silver and staking a successful claim that he might sell to someone else. In short, she concludes, the profitability of New World mining operations *required* low-cost labor. But capitalist dynamics also compel private employers to minimize labor costs. Some argue that the negligible costs of Spain's production and import of enormous quantities of precious ores, especially silver from the mines of Potosí, had great consequences for world history. More on this below.

As more and more of New Spain was "pacified"—that is, its natives defeated in battle, overpowered without a fight, or felled by disease—a diminishing number of prisoners of war was available for enslavement. Would-be slave owners came to Indian villages to demand tribute. An impoverished chief might meet this demand by giving over some of his own slaves or, lacking slaves, by designating fellow villagers, even some of his own kin, as slaves.[94] But the would-be slave owner would as likely seek out a trader, for from the earliest days of colonization of the Indies, worker shortages (especially in the mines) spurred a hunt for slaves from other parts.

American slave hunters had initially plied their sordid trade in the "worthless" islands near Hispaniola—worthless because they lacked gold. In an effort to meet what seemed the limitless demand for slave labor in the mines of Hispaniola and then New Spain, later expeditions visited Panama and what is now Venezuela. Members of the notorious First Audiencia (the regime that ruled New Spain while Cortés was away in Honduras and presumed to be dead) induced their relatives and even their servants to accept slaves in lieu of wages. Besides appropriating eighty Indian women for himself, their leader, Nuño de Guzman, empowered colonists to take twenty to thirty slaves apiece to the Antilles for sale there. Later, relegated to governance of then-remote Pánuco, Guzman encouraged island merchants to come to that province to export Indians to the Indies. According to the reliable Fray Juan de Zumárraga, over twenty-one ships bearing thousands of captured Indians sailed from Pánuco's port.[95] In 1537, the year that Pope Paul condemned the enslavement of Indians, slaving expeditions to the Pearl Coast region of Venezuela still offered the greatest prospect of commercial profit.[96] Thanks to demands for labor for the extraction of precious metals, slave trading remained a major industry of New Spain until the middle of the sixteenth century.

Meanwhile, discovery of large deposits of silver in Guanajuato and Zacatecas in New Spain and especially at Potosí in what is now Bolivia encouraged Philip II (r. 1556–1598) to duplicate his father's commitment to unaffordable military ventures. Workers at Potosí toiled in poorly ventilated, poorly drained mines. The unwillingness of mine operators to invest in the safety features that could have prevented fatal cave-ins was matched by the crown's rejection of an amalgamation process that would have reduced fatal exposures to mercury. The Crown enjoyed a monopoly on the production of mercury at the time. The dangers of mine work were such that indigenous people would sometimes maim their own children to keep them out of the mines.[97] Eventually, mine operators found that they could externalize almost all of the costs of Indian mine workers by adoption of the Inca *mita* system, whereby feeding, transporting, and other expenses of the worker became the responsibility of his village.[98] Besides shortening the lives of workers and helping finance European wars, the silver mines of northern Mexico and Potosí supported the army of officials that was needed to weigh, stamp, and test the extracted bullion, and to collect the royal fifth.

With the Tainos of Hispaniola and other Indians succumbing rapidly to the Castilian regime of relocation, overwork under harsh conditions, and exposure to Old World microbes, even members of the first generation of colonists had begun to look to Africa and the Portuguese slave trade to supply them with hardier workers. A hundred African slaves were included in a copper-mining expedition to Hispaniola as early as 1505. By 1518, Hugh Thomas writes, "all responsible people" in Castile and the Indies saw African slaves as the only answer to chronic labor shortages in America,[99] and Charles V signed a major contract to obtain them. In 1523, Maria Toledo y Rojas, a leading financier of forced labor and Columbus's daughter-in-law, shifted her investments in Indian slaves to the African slave trade.[100]

The enslavement of indigenous others in the Age of Discovery is a legacy not just of Spain but of western civilization. Consider the mental apparatus of an archetypal (albeit fictional) European man of the seventeenth century. Robinson Crusoe is headed for Africa to obtain slaves for import to Brazil when he becomes stranded on a Caribbean island. There he regrets his venture. After all, he could have simply *bought* slaves in Brazil. He sets to work, turning a pelagic wilderness into a fortress even before discovering that his island is the occasional site of cannibal feasts. He is as terrified of being eaten by a cannibal as any of the conquistadors in Bernal Díaz's narrative. Yet in order to escape the island he needs "to get a savage into [his] possession," perhaps by rescuing a captive of the cannibals. But why just one? He decides that he can manage two or three, making them "entirely slaves" who will do whatever he requires them to without doing him any harm. At length, he manages to kill some of the "savages" and turn some of their captives into servants.

Under the principles of "natural law" of medieval Europe, God made all of the earth's goods for everyone, but it fell to representatives of the most advanced civilization to see that all such goods should be properly developed.[101] Naturally, these "advanced" people got to decide what proper development meant. The extraction of precious metals required slave labor. But subsequent prime exports from the Americas such as sugar, tobacco, and cotton would be seen as requiring slave labor for their production, too, as discussed below. In sum, with investors shifting from silver mines to plantation agriculture, capitalism would move to new frontiers of unpaid labor.

The European Magnet

With the fall of Tenochtitlán in 1521, Castile's New World project began to turn a profit. The success of the Cortés expedition inspired similar ventures, most of which came to nothing in the way of discovery of mineral riches, although such efforts extended the "plunder frontier" of recently conquered territories.[102] Meanwhile, Castilians were finding that having a monarch, Charles I, who was also, as Charles V, the Holy Roman Emperor, was hardly a blessing. Sharing their sovereign with much of Italy, Germany, Austria, and the Netherlands meant constant warfare and long royal absences from Spain. Charles' wars in Italy, the Low Countries, and Germany, and his campaigns against the Ottomans and France, were not fought on Spanish soil, but they were mainly paid for by increasing tax assessments on those who could least afford them, Castilian peasants and other commoners. It was not until the 1550s that American treasure began to provide some serious support for these military adventures, though the intake of precious metals coincided with a "price revolution." Economic historians disagree as to whether the flow of treasure caused this price surge,[103] though the fact that rising prices in Spain were followed by rising prices in neighboring countries with the expansion of this new money supply is more than suggestive.[104] The bonanza of Potosí, supplemented by production from northern Mexico (New Spain), soon made silver inflows more important than gold.

Some of the silver would be claimed by the viceroys of Peru and New Spain, as well as lesser officials, clerics, and colonists who sent remittances to their Old World relatives. Castilian and foreign merchants used around half of silver-based revenues to stock returning voyages with all the goods that Castile's American colonists required to enable them to live like their class contemporaries in Spain, eating the same foods, drinking the same wines, etc.[105] By mid-century the king's share (the royal fifth) of bullion arriving in Seville was going to the Genoese bankers who were his creditors. Eventually, Charles V resorted to financing his ongoing payment deficits by confiscating silver remittances bound for private individuals and replacing them with interest-bearing government bonds, called *juros*. He also mortgaged the cargos of future treasure fleets and tax revenues. Driving royal overspending was again a simple fact: soldiers, especially mercenaries like those who fought in the Spanish Netherlands, must be paid—and not in i.o.u.'s. In Austria in 1552, when Charles had to flee an advancing Protestant army, bankers refused him further credit. He could not pay his troops and, as a consequence, his son, Philip II, inherited a shrunken European empire.[106]

Philip was borrowing money at 54 percent interest in 1557,[107] when a royal bankruptcy obviated further war with France. However, he soon found it necessary to take on the Turks in the Mediterranean and to suppress rebellion in the Netherlands. But he could afford it, could he not? Potosí seemed to offer a limitless supply of silver, so much that the area's colonists shoed their horses with it. Although American silver comprised only about a quarter of royal revenues, that was enough to collateralize loans from the Genoese and the Fuggers of Augsburg.[108] Over the next eighty years or so, enslaved and semi-enslaved workers at Potosí, Zacatecas, and elsewhere in Spanish America tripled the amount of silver in the Old World. Imports from the Americas also increased the Old World's stocks of gold by about a fifth.[109] By one estimate, from Columbus's second voyage until the end of the eighteenth century, 85 percent of the world's silver and 70 percent of its gold were shipped from the Americas.[110]

Although Spanish America's treasure fleets had Seville as their destination, their cargos flowed out of Spain so quickly that contemporaries compared the bullion to rain falling on a slanted roof.[111] In fact, with Philip in England and the Netherlands from 1554 to 1559, shipments of silver bullion were redirected to Antwerp, sometimes arriving just in time to head off a riot by the Empire's German troops. Antwerp became a "distribution centre" for American silver bound for German, British, and other northern European sites. This dispersal of silver was "like an explosion," writes Braudel.[112]

By the 1560s, the silver was going to Italy, often via Barcelona.[113] *Asientos*, contracts issued by the Spanish government to Philip's Genoese financiers, gave the Italians control of the bullion as it arrived from America.[114] The Genoese would convert the silver into the gold that Philip needed to pay the troops of the Army of Flanders—aka the "Catholic army." They were able to do this not by alchemy but by selling the inferior metal to Venetians and Florentines, who paid for it with checks—bills of exchange, really—redeemable in Antwerp in gold. As for the silver, the Florentines and Venetians used it to pay for spices and silks from the East, as in the old days before the Portuguese took over some of that trade with their gunboat diplomacy in the Indian Ocean.

Between 1571 and 1575 the cost of maintaining the Army of Flanders came to more than twice the value of royal receipts from the mines of Spanish America. The deficit was paid for by "merciless" taxes on Castilians and by the kind of financial gymnastics described above.[115] Such an arrangement was bound to be short-lived. In 1574, with his credit in tatters, Philip tried to make peace in the Netherlands by offering the rebellious Dutch a pardon. Unpaid troops went on strike, turning his peace offering into a joke. Better that Philip should seek forgiveness from his creditors. Another bankruptcy sent his troops rampaging through Antwerp and grabbing its valuables. After 1580, Italy became the distribution center. Its financiers supported both sides in the Dutch Revolt. A contemporary observed that Naples, Sicily, and Milan were flourishing as never before.[116]

In 1586 the Cortes, Castile's parliament, asked the king to stop the import of "useless luxuries" like candles and glass trinkets in exchange for gold, "as if Spaniards were Indians."[117] But the same amalgamation process at Potosí that made mine work unnecessarily dangerous to workers had enabled a surge in silver production, beginning in the late 1570s.[118] Philip bet this mineral bonanza on "vast enterprises."[119] These included the fiasco of the Invincible Armada in 1588—an attack on England that was somehow intended to bring the Dutch into line.

For Spain the flows of silver had become a curse, creating "a false sense of wealth," promoting "imperial delusions," and diverting attention from the need for industrial, agricultural, and commercial development. In 1603, the Flemish humanist Justus Lipsius could write of Spain, "Conquered by you, the New World has conquered you in turn."[120] Subsequent to numerous additional mutinies by unpaid troops and other Castilian humiliations, a peace treaty of 1630 gave English ships the right to carry Spanish-American silver directly to the Netherlands, where it would finance the final, futile stages of Spain's war against "international Protestantism" and Dutch rebellion.[121] Eighteen years after that, the Dutch gained the right to transport American silver in the very ships that had preyed on Spain's for years—or the newer ones that they could then afford.[122]

By the end of the sixteenth century, the bankrupt Spanish monarchy had begun minting coins of copper. When copper, too, became unaffordable, the Crown devalued the copper currency.[123] But while Spaniards were complaining of shortages of gold and silver, currency in *New* Spain consisted of lead (coins, presumably), cacao beans (still!), and playing cards. Silver coins were an export item, "like dyestuffs or sugar."[124] They circulated in Europe as money that was "common to all nations"—except Spain.[125] But by then the largest payments made in Europe would consist of Amsterdam account entries that reflected transatlantic bullion production figures, not actual ingots or coins.[126] None such media of exchange bore a trace of the blood and sweat of the miners who were extracting this wealth at such great cost to themselves.

Miners have continued to tear ore out of *Cerro Rico*, the mountain of silver at Potosí, right up to the present. But the mountain has become so honey-combed with tunnels and shafts that today's miners, who include adolescents as young as fifteen, work under the threat of a colossal cave-in from the top down.[127]

Where It Ended Up

In 1621 a Portuguese merchant remarked that silver "wanders throughout all the world in its peregrinations before flocking to China, where it remains, as if at its natural center."[128] Let's follow some of these peregrinations and determine why the metal came to rest in China. Scraped from the insides of the *Cerro Rico* at Potosí, the silver might have to await the rains required to swell streams enough to power the mills that turned ore into silver bars. But with completion of that process, a llama train would carry it to Arica on the coast of what is now northern Chile. That would take fifteen days. Another eight days were needed for shipment to Lima's port of Callao, where the silver would be transferred to treasure ships for the twenty-day voyage to the west coast of Panama. Ideally, it would arrive there by March. A mule train would carry the silver across Panama to the galleons waiting at Nombre de Dios that would transport it to Havana. There it would meet up with silver from the mines of New Spain, arriving early enough, it was hoped, to avoid the hurricane season. By late summer or early fall, the silver would be shipped across the Atlantic to Seville, at least in the early stages of this sixteenth-century version of globalization, from where it went to England, France, and the Low Countries in exchange for manufactured goods. From these sites some was transshipped to Scandinavia and Russia along with the wine and cloth that Western Europeans used to pay for furs and timber, then sent on to Persia via the Volga and the Caspian Sea. The Safavid rulers of Persia, being Shia, favored trade with the West by this northerly route as it avoided conflict with their Sunni rivals in Syria.[129] (I resist the impulse to trot out the familiar French phrase.) Arriving in India, much of the silver would settle there where it paid for cotton exports and monetized India's economy. Aziza Hasan has found that the mintage of silver coins in Mughal India corresponded with its arrival in Europe, with a lag of ten or twenty years.[130] But much of the silver continued on to China to buy silks, spices, ceramics, and drugs.

As an alternative, a Spanish merchant might ship some silver to the Levant via the Mediterranean and familiar land routes in exchange for Asian goods. Silver might also go to India through the Red Sea or overland through

Turkey and Persia. Lesser amounts were shipped around the Cape of Good Hope to various Asian ports. And Spanish galleons carried silver from Acapulco across the Pacific to Manila, from where it proceeded to China and other trade centers in exchange for Chinese silk and porcelain and Southeast Asian spices.[131] The most common coins in the markets of Algiers circa 1580 were Spain's gold *escudos* and silver *reales*—in pieces of four, six, and eight. Chests of *reales* were sent to Turkey as exports.[132]

Why is China so often described as a "sink" for silver? China was the global leader in the production of such desirable commodities as silk, porcelain, quicksilver, and (a bit later) tea. China was also at the center of a "dense mercantile network" linking ports in Japan (another major source of silver), Southeast Asia, the Persian Gulf, the Red Sea, East Africa, and India.[133] Europeans had run a trade deficit with China going back to the days of the Roman Empire. Except for a period of the Middle Ages when they traded slaves for Far Eastern goods, Europeans paid for Chinese imports with exports of gold and silver, which they had begun sending east in exchange for silk and spices as early as 100 BCE.[134] Asian wealth enabled Venice and Genoa to grow rich in the role of intermediaries. The lure of spices from the (East) Indies and of Chinese goods spurred the Iberian voyages of discovery of the fifteenth century, including Columbus's, as we have seen. Long after that era had come to an end, efforts to find a better route to China prompted the search for a Northwest Passage.

Europe had been peripheral to this trading system of the Indian Ocean and the Far East, but in the sixteenth century, Western Europeans broke out of their isolation. Discovery and conquest enabled them to establish commercial linkages to the coast of West Africa, the Caribbean, Mexico, Peru, coastal Brazil, and the Atlantic seaboard of North America. American silver gave them entrée to the network of Asian and East African markets. But one should note that at the end of the long sixteenth century (c. 1450–1640) this globalized trade consisted of luxuries, not staples, and that the volume of trade was relatively small.[135]

China became a "sink" for American and Japanese silver with the collapse of her paper currency and bronze coins. Needing a new medium of exchange, the Mings made taxes payable in silver, though domestic production of this element was scant. Ultimately, American silver found a home in China because the Chinese paid twice as much for it in trade goods as anyone else. In the final years of the sixteenth century and the beginning of the seventeenth, when gold was trading for silver at a rate of 1:12.5 to 1:14 in Spain, it traded for 1:5.5 to 1:7 in Canton.[136] China's silver imports amounted to over a hundred tons a year at the time.

Fernand Braudel writes that China and India became "bottomless pits" for the New World's precious metals: "they were sucked in, never to re-emerge."[137] Does this mean that silver was "dug up in the Americas to be buried again in Asia,"[138] as some allege? No, it was put to better uses than that. Sixteenth-century China enjoyed a surge in population, largely attributed to the adoption of such New World food crops as sweet potatoes and maize. This made for an expanding economy with heightened demand for money. If around three-quarters of the New World's silver went to China in the Early Modern period,[139] it did so without boosting prices. Instead it made for greater liquidity.[140] As for its ending up there, Europe retained more of it than Asia, allowing for population differences, although ordinary Europeans got so few of the coins being minted from the flood of bullion that they often had to use the family silver to pay their taxes. After 1551, increasing amounts of silver stayed in colonial America.[141]

Gunder Frank maintains that only the precious metals produced in their colonies made Europe a player in an expanding world economy.[142] But was the export of precious metals really a symptom of European weakness? Braudel thinks not. Asia was dependent on American gold and silver; a gap in the treasure shipments could plunge Eastern economies into crisis. Besides, European purchases of Asian goods allowed European merchants to penetrate Asian markets.[143] At length, European financiers and manufacturers accumulated fabulous wealth from this globalized trade.

Europe's Leverage

The notion that Europe or "the West" has been the source of historical change and that less favored regions of the world need only emulate the West in order to catch up has by now been tossed into the trash can of chauvinistic illusions. Yet something must have happened to enable leading European nations to recapitulate the experience of sixteenth-century Spain by planting colonies in distant lands to extract their wealth for the presumed comfort and well-being of the "mother country." How was Europe, or at least northwestern Europe, able to move from the economic periphery of Eurasia to become, by the late nineteenth century, the vital center of the world economy, with political control over much of the Americas, Asia, Africa, and Australia? And what is the connection, if any, of this divergence and the silver-fueled commercial expansion of Europe in the "long sixteenth century"?

To ask this question is to risk entanglement in a thicket of controversy. In *The Communist Manifesto* (1848), Marx and Engels argue that European discoveries and colonization pushed feudalism into its grave, giving commerce, navigation, and industry "an impulse never before known," setting the stage for European industrialization and the making of a world market. On the other hand, the technologist will explain Western divergence in terms of European inventions and adoption of other people's inventions. Such an argument might even begin by reference to the appearance of the definite article in the language of ancient Greece, a development that facilitated abstract thought.[144] It might cite the unspectacular but cumulative technical breakthroughs of medieval Europe and the invention of scientific method. An argument from invention would surely underline that of the power loom, the mechanical spinner, the steam engine, and the presence of rich beds of coal in the English countryside. Although paper was invented in China, it took the English to use the absence of certain papers—written contracts—to force peasants off the land and, ultimately, into the "dark Satanic Mills" of early industrialization.[145] The invention of the proletariat also gave Europe an edge. But note that none of these or related developments has an apparent connection to the flow of precious metals that began in the sixteenth century.

Certain economic historians think that Europe started to separate itself from the rest about 1000 CE. Deploying an index of social development, Ian Morris finds that Western dominance got its start around 16,000 years ago![146] Others deny that Europe began its economic take-off before or during the long sixteenth century. They argue that European expansion was losing momentum by around 1620 and that European achievements to that date were matched by those of Ming China, the Ottoman Empire, Mughal India, and the Safavids based in Persia. The kind of conditions that would lead to continuing economic growth—that is, according to Adam Smith, the commodification of land, labor, and capital—did not yet exist. And the New World products of the "Columbian Exchange," such as maize, tomatoes, and potatoes, did not make Old World consumers dependent on European suppliers. Divergence of the West from the rest began later, around 1750 at the earliest, they say.[147]

Yet other economic historians think that the seeds of Europe's industrial transition *were* planted in an earlier period but were not embedded in the fruits of intercontinental conquest. Western Europeans already led Chinese workers in per capita production by 1500, according to a 2003 analysis,[148] although China was much bigger and more populous than any European state and had accumulated much more wealth. In this view, the engine of transformation was built on the peculiarities of Europe's own history in terms of culture, political and legal systems, property rights, commodity markets, and other factors. Freedom from arbitrary rule, argues Eric Jones in *The European Miracle*, meant that Europeans faced a lower threshold of risk. This stimulated industrial investment. People could devote less time to growing food and more time to working in the cottage industries that comprised a "proto-industrial" sector,[149] putting Europe on the road to industrialization.

Jones also credits accidents of geography and biology with giving *some* Europeans, at least, an economic edge. Western Europeans lived at such a distance from the Eurasian steppes that they escaped the periodic devastation visited on the Middle East, China, and Eastern Europe by the mounted nomads of Genghis Khan, his predecessors, and his successors. Besides, Europeans were less subject to the kind of disasters—for example, earthquakes and floods—that have as great an impact on capital as on labor. For example, the Black Death killed millions, but capital is not susceptible to germs, and the resultant labor shortages made for economic gains for many of those fortunate enough to survive, as well as for their descendents.[150] European diversity in terms of geology, climate, and topography, as well as the flow of major European rivers, encouraged trade in bulk goods, which rulers found more convenient to tax than to appropriate.[151]

In contrast, Europe's rivals for economic leadership—the Ottomans, the Mughals, and China's Ming and Qing dynasts—were "all alien, imposed military despotisms: revenue pumps [...] with little to offer when the spoils ran out."[152] To the question of whether the discovery and conquest of the West Indies, Mesoamerica, and other parts of the Western Hemisphere can explain the European edge, Jones replies that acquisition of this "resource bounty" resulted only in trade in luxuries and "colourful, but nugatory, rent-seeking"[153]—meaning piracy, one assumes. In other words, European discovery, plundering, conquest, infection, and colonization of the people of the Americas were beside the point of Europe's take-off.[154]

How does this compare, as an account of European divergence, with the fact that in the Americas, Europe acquired "a new transatlantic zone reserved exclusively for its exploitation," as John Darwin puts it?[155] Suddenly, with the import of vast quantities of silver, European nations were able to trade with Muslim merchants as equals, then superiors.[156] They could purchase Asian and other goods at negligible cost, thanks to the slave and semi-slave labor that was used in the extraction of that precious metal. European merchants could offer better prices in every market than was possible for anyone else, thus undercutting all competition. With this nearly free money from the Americas, European "proto-capitalists" could buy timber, grain, and iron from the Baltic, as well as Asia's silks, spices, and cotton textiles for European consumption and for re-export to Europe's American colonies. The endless

6—Gold and Silver Promote Slavery and Boost Commerce 95

supply of silver financed the further acquisition of slave labor, which Europeans could apply not only to mining but to the plantation agriculture that connected capitalism, colonialism, and sea power. Fusing the shackles of slave labor to the rich soil and sunshine of tropical America, they could produce and export sugar, tobacco, chocolate, cocoa, and cotton. The Americas were another source of the timber used for shipbuilding. (Some of the pine used to build slave ships in Liverpool was felled by African slaves in Virginia and the Carolinas.)[157] These imports freed Europeans to reduce the land and labor that they would otherwise have devoted to feeding and clothing themselves. They enabled proto-capitalists to invest in commercial agriculture, shipbuilding, sugar refining, the Atlantic fisheries, and urban development, as well as the import trade described above.[158]

Can Europe's penetration of Asian markets and the establishment of such favorable terms of trade, enabled by the mineral wealth produced by slave or semi-slave labor in the Americas, explain Europe's transition to industrial dominance, as Andre Gunder Frank and J. M. Blaut argue? If it could it would make for a tidy ending to this chapter's story of the new American careers of precious metals and slavery. But this attractive analysis cannot be made to carry that much explanatory weight. Their argument leaves Europe with a commercial revolution that concentrated wealth in big, interconnected port cities: London, Hamburg, Amsterdam. Such commercial success, as Charles Kindleberger has pointed out, need not have led to industrialization. In the case of seventeenth-century Holland, it did not.[159] Until at least 1750, seaboard Europe's commercial success was a prop for the *ancien régime* and its conspicuous consumption of exotic luxuries.[160] The prospect of acquiring such goods may have prompted some Europeans to work harder and spend more time producing goods for markets, as Kenneth Pomeranz suggests.[161] But such factors would not have led, necessarily, to new technologies or manufacturing of the kind that enabled Europe to separate itself from other regions. In addition, the argument that Europe's commercial revolution of the sixteenth century led to the industrial revolution of the nineteenth must contend with "the crisis of the seventeenth century" when European economic growth reversed gears.[162]

As late as 1750, per capita industrialization in India and China approached that of Britain. By 1913, industrial development in those countries had declined; British industry had surged ahead of them by a factor of forty or fifty.[163] This is the gap that needs to be explained. But an adequate explanation surely lies beyond the scope of this chapter. Instead we might compare two European regimes. The first is that of silver. Its rule lasted for a hundred years and more beginning about 1550. This was followed by what we might think of as the regime of cotton. The silver era required Europe's development of adequate sailing ships and knowledge of Atlantic wind patterns, and then it needed the Spanish conquest of the two most advanced civilizations in the Americas. It relied on slaves to work the silver mines of America, which meant that it had to have the means to assemble and compel such a work force. Europeans also needed to transport large quantities of silver to Europe: their sailing ships could accomplish this. During the reign of silver, Europeans were able to use their sea power to force their way into Eastern ports and eventually to dominate the sea lanes of the Indian Ocean, thus enabling them to dispense with Muslim (and Italian) intermediaries. But silver could only command small-scale trade in luxury goods. Except for its exports to colonial America, Europe was a subcontinent of elite consumers in terms of global commerce. The producers were in Asia. To mark the approaching end of silver's reign, some Europeans—for example, those of the Dutch trading company known as the VOC—found that they could dispense with silver altogether simply by using their military might to take over spice islands.

The Americas were also crucial to the cotton regime. Slave plantations in the West Indies and the South of what became the United States provided British manufacturers with raw cotton for the production of cotton fabrics. Some of these fabrics, perhaps a quarter of them by the 1780s,[164] helped pay for the African slaves who worked the cotton plantations of America. Forcible entry into the economies of the largest Asian producers, India and China, did not appear possible until the British East India Company conquered Bengal and gradually established a stranglehold on the rest of the subcontinent. The British then had an alternative to silver with which to break into Chinese markets—namely, Indian cottons and opium. Soon technical innovations and the use of steam power (from an abundance of coal) enabled British producers to swamp all markets with their manufactured cottons. These were followed by other industrial goods. Eventually, the non–European world was turned into the source of various raw materials to be used in European manufacturing. And the silver sent to China in the earlier era was flowing in the reverse direction. By 1832 China was exporting almost four hundred tons of it a year to pay for the opium habit that the British and other Western powers had forced on her.[165]

Silver brought Europeans to the doors of far-off producers of exotic goods. But like those of a suspicious shop owner demanding cash, the doors were only cracked open enough to permit the buyer to hand over a quantity of bullion in exchange for some luxury items. Europeans required guns, manufactured goods, and drugs to force their way in, take what they wanted of what was inside, and send home tea, silks, and some of the silver that was formerly required to buy tea and silks. Eventually, they might turn such Asian outlets into storage sheds for their own industrial goods. If the earliest lengths of the path from plunder to empire were paved in silver, cotton insulated the later argument for what was called Free Trade.

7

The Horse's New Footing

Columbus brought fifty horses to the Caribbean on his second voyage. Using transport techniques developed during the Mediterranean crossings of the crusades and voyages to the Canary Islands, the Spaniards loaded hundreds of superb mounts onto the ships of subsequent expeditions, tethering them to the deck for what was usually a two-month voyage. Not every horse would walk on land again. In the "horse latitudes" of the Atlantic, where calms would sometimes last for weeks, drinking water sometimes became so scarce that horses would have to be jettisoned.[1]

Nevertheless, from Hispaniola to Cajamarca, horses were a key factor in Castile's American conquests. For the natives of the Caribbean and the mainland who encountered them for the first time, they were fearsome beasts, larger and more powerful than any animals they had ever seen, and so foreign to their experience that they could only call them "deer." Their landing prompted the Tainos of Hispaniola to flee to the island's interior. By 1507 the governor of Hispaniola could write the king that they required no more mares. They had quite enough horses already to defeat any Indians in the island's vicinity.[2] Las Casas thought they were "the deadliest weapon imaginable" against the Indians. In his opinion, the sixty horsemen that participated in the massacre of Queen Anacaona and her people would have been sufficient to ravage all of Hispaniola.[3] Anyone who has been in a crowd that was divided and divided again, or perhaps entirely broken up, by mounted police will know what a difference a few horses can make.

The Indians of the Gulf coast of what would become Mexico, engaging Cortés's forces in their first battle, thought that horse and rider were one, like a centaur with two heads. These Indians suffered heavy losses, after which their chiefs came to talk peace. Cortés exploited their fear by letting a stallion scent a mare that had recently foaled, having him led off and then, while speaking with the chiefs, having him returned to the same spot. Scenting the mare again, the stallion became "wild with excitement." The scent came from the direction of the Indians. He looked toward them, filling them with terror. At this point, Cortés had the stallion led away, saying he had told him not to be angry with them. He also used horses to impress Moctezuma's envoys.[4]

Before long, however, the Cortés expedition began to encounter Indians who, though they may have feared the horses and their riders, clearly understood that they were a weapon that they could destroy. Battling the conquistadors, Tlaxcalans used what Bernal Díaz calls their "swords" (wooden clubs lined with sharp obsidian fragments) and "lances" (obsidian-pointed spears) to wound some of the horses and even to decapitate a mare. They appeared to consider this as much of a coup as killing a Spaniard, for (continues Díaz) they carried off the body of the mare to exhibit its parts and made an offering to their gods of the horseshoes.[5] The invaders were happy to receive another of their mares, wandering riderless and wounded by arrows, when she returned to their camp to die, as this deprived the Indians of a chance to celebrate.[6] In the temples of Texcoco, the conquistadors found an American version of the head-and-hoof funeral offerings made by people of the Eurasian steppes in prehistoric times: five tanned skins with hoofs of horses that the natives had evidently offered to their gods.[7] During the siege of Tenochtitlán, the Aztecs advertised a victory to their wavering allies by sending round a display of the flayed heads of two horses and those of some Spaniards. Besides occasionally killing a horse, the Aztecs learned to set up barriers to their advance.

For the most part, though, the Spaniards were able to use the speed, mobility, and size of their mounts to defeat the natives, at least in battles on open ground. Again and again, a few charging horsemen would penetrate the ranks of massed warriors, scattering them and then running down their spectacularly-clad chiefs. Harquebusiers, bowmen, sword-wielders, and native allies would quickly follow their lead. Cortés also deployed an old Muslim tactic by pretending to flee on horseback, then wheeling around to attack: "we always took a dozen or so of the boldest," he writes.[8] He constantly reminded his followers not to take any ground without securing it for the horsemen, "the mainstay of the fighting."[9] Cavalry charges were later used to defeat the Inca.

The Warhorse in Perspective

There are a couple of things to note about this equestrian invasion of America. The first is that in coming to the New World, the horse was returning to its birthplace. The second is that people on horses had been conquering people without horses for a long time.

The ancestral horse was indigenous to the Americas where it had evolved over sixty million years. Then, between ten and eleven thousand years ago, many animal species of the Americas became extinct. In North America, this great die-off included such "megafauna" as mammoths, mastodons, twenty-foot-long ground sloths, a giant armadillo, glyptodonts (unlike anything alive today) weighing up to a ton, camels, big capybaras, huge beavers, dire wolves, fifteen hundred-pound short-faced bears, saber-toothed cats, entire genera of other animals, as well as the horse. Some researchers, following the lead of Paul S. Martin, attribute the demise of these animals to overly-successful hunting by humans, Paleoindians so-called, who had begun to arrive in the Americas a millennium or two before. They reason that, having evolved without human contact, these Pleistocene animals would have had no fear of humans and been easy victims of organized hunting. They also point to extinctions, like that of the moa in New Zealand, which occurred in historic times when humans first settled a land mass. But this thesis is controversial; some think that the American megafauna fell victim to climate change.[10]

However that may be, horses did not become extinct with other large American animals. Many of them had migrated to Asia around twenty-three million years ago, crossing Beringia, the thousand-mile wide "bridge" that joined Siberia and North America in colder eras when much more of the oceans' waters were locked up in ice. Their herds spread far and wide in this new world, extending into Europe where Neolithic people hunted them for food. A "kill-site" in central France contained the remnants of tens of thousands of them. (Similar sites in North America include the remains of butchered mastodons, mammoths, camels, tapirs, horses, and other species, but the number of such sites is insufficient to convince kill-off skeptics.)[11] By seven or eight thousand years ago, thick forests had replaced the Ice Age steppe of Europe, presenting horses and other grazing animals with an even less favorable environment than that in which human hunters freely roamed. Horses disappeared from areas west of the Eurasian steppes.[12]

The horse not only survived but flourished on the steppes. Then, around six thousand years ago, people found that they could domesticate horses, using them like pigs as a "low-maintenance food source."[13] This brings us to the second point regarding the horse in America, its use as a weapon. To summarize developments that required thousands of years, the horse was eventually converted from a source of meat to a pack animal. It replaced the ox in pulling carts, requiring a redesign of such vehicles and encouraging the nomadism of people with horse-drawn wagons. Experimenting, people may have found that as a mount the horse could be used for herding cattle and sheep, enabling these early riders to acquire larger herds and facilitating the capture and management of entire herds of horses. The horse could eliminate natural barriers by swimming across rivers. But because of digestive limitations (compared to cattle), the horse needs fresh grass. A drought can prove fatal. To save their horses, these herders of the steppes would routinely seek better grazing lands. They often found them in the south, where the sedentary agriculturalists that they encountered were no match for horse-borne warriors. The grass was always greener on the other side of the Volga, the Indus, the Tigris, and the Amur. Development of the metal bit, advances in bridling, invention of the saddle, and use of the "mobile firing platform" of the chariot revolutionized warfare. The kinship of most languages of Europe and northern India suggests that these equestrian warriors held sway over a vast expanse, prehistorically.[14]

Just when and where all these developments occurred is controversial. Even more controversial is the question of whether and to what extent horse-borne warriors of the Eurasian steppe overran an agrarian civilization of southeastern Europe—aka Old Europe.[15] Following this disputed prehistory, in any case, were invasion and conquest by successive waves of horse-borne warriors—Scythians, Sarmatians, Persians, Parthians, Mongols, Huns, and others—invading and often conquering other, more sedentary civilizations. Genghis Khan wanted to turn all of northern China into horse pasturage.[16] The introduction of horses made the contending kingdoms of the West African savanna dependent on cavalry. Portuguese slave buyers of the fifteenth century found that the Wolof kingdom had a cavalry force of ten thousand to go with their hundred thousand infantrymen. The horse gave Islam its "striking force." Europeans could only hope to catch up.[17]

By the Age of Discovery, Castilians had caught up. In the centuries of Reconquest and its back and forth of cavalry raids, Spaniards had become horsemen. Their nobles had, anyway, and Spain had many more nobles than any other European country. The Spanish word for "gentleman"—*caballero*, from *caballo* (horse)—puts a person on a horse. If a foot soldier of the Reconquest could catch a horse, he could also become a mounted combatant,[18] although he would have to add a claim to aristocratic lineage to achieve nobility. Due to an absence of hay and oats, horses were scarce in Spain, so scarce that in the thirteenth century laws banned their export from Christian areas.[19] Enhancing the status of the horseman, conveyance by mule was a lot more common.[20] More commonly, one walked.

The place of equestrian martial skills in Spanish tradition is illustrated by the Cid's greeting of his wife and daughters after a three-year separation. Does he cover them with kisses and hugs? Not at first. Instead he jumps on his new horse and puts him through his paces for display. Only then does he embrace his wife and daughters.[21] Spaniards used two kinds of saddles, each of which required its own riding style. A man's ability to ride both kinds might be memorialized on his tombstone. The skills required for equestrian bullfighting are practiced and admired in Spain to this day.[22]

The horses of the conquest were short-backed with short, well-jointed legs. They are described as "tough, sturdy, [and] long-winded."[23] They had to be sturdy if they were to carry an armored rider with a sword, lance, and pistol on a heavy Moorish saddle that might include bronze stirrups.[24] But a Spaniard, even a foot soldier like Bernal Díaz, would have been more attuned to differences than likenesses among the sixteen horses that initially accompanied the conquistadors. Distinguishing between horses and mares, Díaz briefly describes each one in terms of its ownership, its color, and its martial capacities, using such phrases as "very fast and very easily handled," "not much good," "very handy," and "no good for anything."[25] Some of his meaning gets lost in translation from the equestrian slang of Spanish. "*Era muy revuelta*"—said of the mare called Bobtail (*La Rabona*)—does not mean that she was "very handy and a good charger," as the A. P. Maudslay translation has it. It means that she had a good mouth and could easily be turned when running at a gallop. This according to an inveterate horseman.[26] Not to split hairs: the point is that when it came to horses the conquistadors were connoisseurs. As these animals are always said to be intelligent, one wonders: how might they have graded their riders?

Horses in Cuba had been scarce and expensive. As in the classical world,[27] those who brought them were the few who could afford them. Ownership in some cases was limited to a half share. Cortés quickly cut through such proprietary relationships by distributing the horses to members of his expedition who were considered the best riders, including himself. With consolidation of forces from the Narváez expedition, the conquistadors would acquire additional horses, but their number never exceeded a hundred or so. Of course, this is a far cry from an army of tens of thousands of mounted Mongols, say, sweeping across the plains on course to conquer northern China. But the few horses that the conquistadors had made a big difference in their efforts to conquer an advanced civilization. Alive they served as chargers and as mounts for raiders who would thunder into villages and markets to snatch up food supplies. Felled by arrows, they themselves became food. Their fallen bodies bridged the shallow waters of Lake Texcoco for some of those who escaped from Tenochtitlán on the Noche Triste.

Riding a horse was bound up with Spanish notions of hierarchy, as suggested above. In Moorish Spain, the ruler had forbidden the Christian to ride a horse, lest he appear physically superior to his Islamic better. The Spaniards' memory of this lesson had, by the age of the American invasion, become culturally ingrained. A royal decree of 1528 prohibited the Indians of New Spain from having horses. Perhaps this ban was inspired by military concerns, but the privileges that the conquerors extended to Indian nobles—at Cholula, for instance—sometimes included riding horses.[28]

In Over Their Heads

In his unhappy expedition to Honduras across the Yucatan peninsula and into the Petén of present-day Guatemala (1524–1525), Cortés ignored a basic lesson of equestrian history: horses are stymied by rainforests, marshes, and swamps. Beginning with over a hundred mounts (sources vary as to the exact number), the Spaniards and their dozens of Indian laborers soon found themselves in what was literally a trackless wilderness. The Mayan inhabitants traveled only by canoe. In numerous crossings of rivers and marshes, the horses were often in water up to their ears. They sometimes sank in quicksand. They often had to swim or be led by the bridle around watery areas. Because of the horses, as well as the extent of their luggage and their numbers, the adventurers had no choice but to seek land-based routes. But the land was largely underwater. Besides water hazards, some horses died of heatstroke when made to chase deer for their riders to spear.

All this is described in Cortés's Fifth Letter to Charles V. Absent land routes, Cortés had to build over fifty bridges, or so he writes. What he means is that he directed his Indian workers to build over fifty bridges and, by amazing feats of arduous and, for some, fatal labor, the Indians complied. One of their bridges seems to have been over three hundred yards long. Without such efforts there was no getting the humans and horses across large bodies of water, and all would have starved.[29]

Spanish horses also foundered in the mud of the tropical forest of eastern Peru, during the ill-fated expedition of Gonzalo Pizarro. In the Andes, they could only be led up the steep grades and steps of Inca "roads," leaving the horse and its would-be rider vulnerable to Indian attacks from above via dislodged boulders.[30] Peasants of the Swiss cantons had used the same tactic in 1315 to rout a large horse-borne army of Rhineland nobles and Hapsburgs.[31] Europeans rediscovered the advantages as well as the limitations of warhorses when they invaded the Americas.

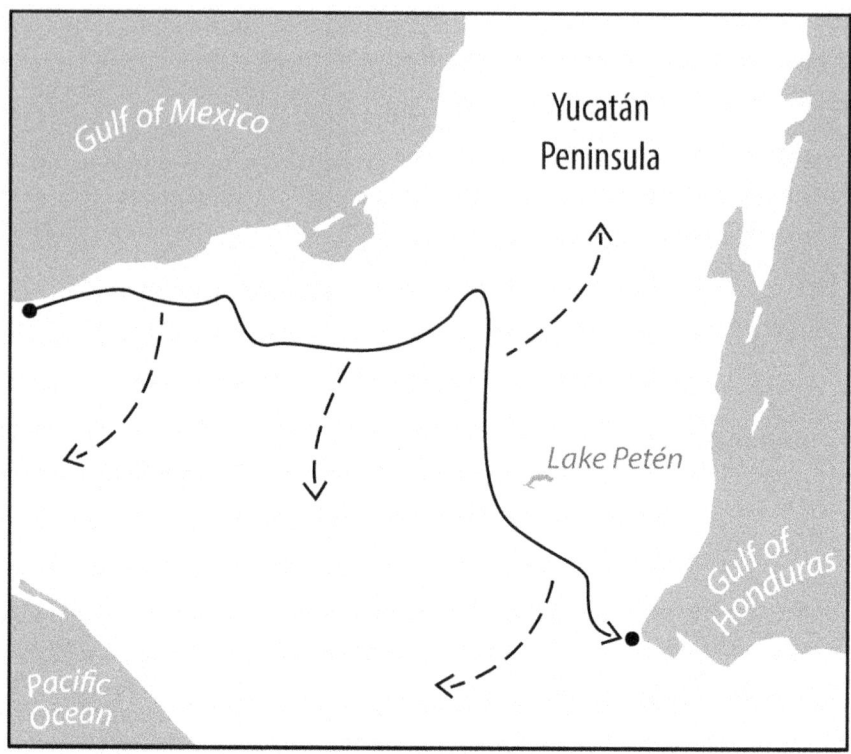

Cortés's route to Honduras, indicating dispersal of accompanying *biota* (horses, pigs, microbes, etc.) (author's collection).

The Deified Horse

In the course of the expedition to Honduras, Cortés's black horse became disabled by a stake in his foot. Cortés left him with a chief of the Itzas at Lake Petén.[32] Though he said that he would return for him, he returned to Spain instead, where in 1528 the Duke of Medina Sidonia presented him with some horses of a quality as to make him forget the horse he had left in the Petén.[33] Almost a century went by before some Spaniards came that way again. In 1618 a missionary expedition, following Cortés's route, entered a temple in the Mayan village at Lake Petén and encountered a large stone idol in the form of a horse, squatting on its haunches in a way that living horses never do. The Itzas called it Tziminchac, thunder and lightning, onomatopoetic for the flash and roar made by Spaniards on horseback firing harquebuses that their ancestors had observed almost a hundred years earlier.

According to the chronicler of this expedition, Juan de Villagutierre

Soto-Mayor, a meticulous researcher as well as lawyer and clerk of the Council of the Indies who never set foot in the New World, here is what had happened. The Itzas with whom Cortés left his horse, having had no experience with such creatures, treated it as they would an ailing noble, offering it choice cuts of meat and adorning it with flowers. The horse soon died, probably of hunger. Fearing the ire of a returning Cortés, the Itzas put a brave face on this disaster by worshipping the horse as a god. By the time of the arrival of the Spanish missionaries, Tziminchac had become their chief idol.[34]

One of the missionaries, Fr. Juan de Orbita, was so infuriated by the sight of this horse-god that he picked up a large stone and began smashing it to pieces, littering the temple floor with its fragments. Worshippers reacted by calling for the death of this iconoclast, as well as the other priests. One of the latter, Fr. Fuensalida, immediately flourished a cross, expostulating Christian doctrine in a loud voice and stating his readiness to die for his beliefs. Taken aback, the Indians listened mutely. The Christian chronicler interprets this as a sign of "Divine Favor," though death threats continued as the missionaries sailed away across the lake a few days later, having failed to convert Canek, the Itza chief, to their faith.[35]

Tziminchac was not the first sanctified horse, by the way. According to Tacitus, pre–Christian Germans kept white horses, "undefiled by any toil," in a sacred grove at public expense. On occasion they would yoke them to a sacred chariot and walk beside them, weighing their neighs and snorts for warnings and portents.[36]

Proliferation

Away from mountains and rain forests, certain parts of the Americas were ideal for horses, with year-round grass, infrequent drought, and many sources of water such as ponds and streams. The most obvious example would be the Pampas of Argentina, though parts of Texas, New Mexico, Arizona, and other regions offered similar conditions. In 1536 one Pedro de Mendoza abandoned seven horses, following an initial, unsuccessful founding of Buenos Aires.[37] Twenty years later there were so many horses in the area that a person could buy one for about two dollars. With the second founding of Buenos Aires in 1580, horses roamed the area in enormous herds. In 1744, a traveler in Argentina described being surrounded by horses for two weeks. A herd, speeding by at full gallop and threatening to trample him, would take two or three hours to pass. A slave in Buenos Aires might be sold for two hundred pesos, while a horse had almost no saleable value at all. Like the oxen that also roamed in wild herds, a horse belonged to anyone who could catch it.³⁸ Late-eighteenth-century travelers were in danger of losing their mounts to wild horses. With neighing and prancing, the latter would try to entice their domesticated cousins to join the herd. If they did, "they [were] lost forever."³⁹

Horses famously transformed the culture of the Plains Indians of North America. Native Americans began to capture escaped horses and to steal those of Spaniards in the Southwest in the late seventeenth century. They bred in large numbers, and Indian warriors became expert riders and bison hunters, preempting the communal hunting *à pied* of the Omahas and others that had formerly prevailed. Thus were they able to resettle the Plains that had been depopulated by drought in preceding centuries. Some, however, remained sedentary horticulturalists, their vulnerability to nomadic equestrians reproducing Old World patterns.⁴⁰

Horses undoubtedly changed the lives of those who became bison hunters and horse-borne warriors. For one thing, they had more meat than formerly, much more meat. Dakotas killed 1,500 bison in a "single surround" in 1830. Horse-borne Comanche, a scattering of tiny bands of nomads in the Great Basin when they were Shoshone, could range and raid from the Mississippi to the Rio Grande. Some Plains people became rich by accumulating numerous horses; others poor by failing to do so. Successful hunters could afford more wives. They needed them: curing a bison hide required three days of arduous work, a task assigned to women. Their workload greatly increased.⁴¹

Some Ironies

Jared Diamond writes, "Not until the First World War did the military dominance of cavalry finally end."⁴² Really? Reliance on cavalry had proven costly to both the French and English five centuries earlier in the Hundred Years War. Mounted knights were no match for English long bows, French catapults, or (later) Swiss pikemen.⁴³ By the middle of the sixteenth century, even the Ottomans had replaced their feudal cavalry with a "gunpowder army."⁴⁴ While the conquistadors were using horses (plus swords, attack dogs, guns, crossbows, native disunity, and—crucially but inadvertently—microbes) to destroy native resistance in the Indies and Mexico, Castile's *gran capitán* Gonzalo de Córdoba, campaigning in Italy twenty years earlier, had discovered that the only way to win battles against Swiss pikemen was to build up the Spanish *infantry*. He did this by giving his men better protective armor, increasing the number of those with long pikes, equipping some with sword and javelin, increasing the size of fighting units, etc. The *tercio*, first formed in 1534, consisted of three thousand pikemen and harquebusiers, organized such that they could face attack from any direction. This formation, which did *not* include horsemen, "dominated the battlefields of Europe for over a century."[45] Although the horse remained a major mode of transport and drayage into the twentieth century, its military usage had long since become marginal.

While the Spanish were breeding warhorses, the unromantic plow horse was effecting an "agricultural revolution" elsewhere in Europe, especially in the north. Use of the shoulder harness made the animal indispensable for plowing, harrowing, tilling, and transport, helping (along with triennial crop rotation, etc.) to almost double grain yields in medieval Europe. This contributed to population growth and the rise of the countries of northwestern Europe,[46] some of which would soon send their own invaders to the New World.

Today, whether rooting for a Derby winner or riding the cart behind the plodding nag that pulls the tourist family into Central Park, we use horses in multiple but inessential ways, as efforts proceed to cull the growing herds of feral horses in the West. In a crowning irony, the horse has come full circle in present-day Spain. During the real estate boom of the late 1990s newly affluent Spaniards bought large numbers of Spanish thoroughbreds, described as descendents of "horses that carried conquistadors into battle in the Americas." Hundreds of thousands were bred to answer this demand. Now that the bubble has burst, many horse owners can no longer afford their upkeep. Seventy thousand were sent to slaughter in 2012, and the end is nowhere in sight. Accompanying this news item is a photo of cured horse sausages hanging along the wall of a Spanish butcher shop.[47]

8

Transplanting a Work Ethic

Castile's earliest New World discoveries, known as the Indies, attracted men who were unwilling to dirty their hands with anything but the blood of Indians. They were gold seekers who hoped to enrich themselves at the expense of native labor. But before they could make the Indians produce any precious metals, they needed their help in addressing more basic needs. Following his second voyage to Hispaniola, Columbus required his followers to build a town. But that was going to be difficult. Bartolomé de Las Casas writes that the workers (servants probably) who accompanied the "gentlemen" were sick, hungry, and weak. In fact, they may have had malaria.[1] As for the nobles, birthright had exempted them from such work. Thus, "*A los unos y a los otros se les hacía a par de muerte ir a trabajar con sus manos*"[2] ("For both the ones [the workers] and the others [the nobles], to go to work with their hands would be like dying"). Without the help of Tainos, the Hispaniola natives, such would-be settlers would have starved. They depended on native labor to provide them with necessities from the very start.

The Spaniards knew nothing about the cultivation of New World crops, and—with a couple of exceptions noted below—none of them wanted to farm, in any case. All wanted aristocratic lives, however uneducated, coarse, and lowly in origin many of them were.[3] Cortés convinced each of his men that he could become a count or duke, "one of the titled," thus transforming them from "lambs to lions."[4] In the years that followed conquest, there was little need to risk one's life as the conquistadors had done. A man could live like a Castilian lord simply by commandeering Indians to work for him and otherwise serve his needs. Such labor served as a ladder up which one might climb to dizzying social heights.[5] Aristotle had even provided a philosophical rationale for such arrangements, and a prominent Spanish theologian, Francisco de Vitoria, had brought his thinking up to date: Indians are servants by nature and should submit to their natural masters, Spaniards.[6] In addition, the easy capitulation of Moctezuma (described in Chapter 12) was seized on by the likes of historian Juan Ginés de Sepulveda as evidence that the natives were cowardly by nature, thus meant to be enslaved.[7] In short, enslavement of Indians became "the principal goal of Spaniards … in the Indies."[8]

This was the real gold. Las Casas writes that when he gave up the Indians assigned to him, other settlers were shocked. For them the idea of not making extravagant use of Indian labor was like not using their domestic animals.[9] But "assigned" Indians? Who did the assigning? Initially, the victors in battles would parcel out surviving Indians—usually women and children—on the basis of settlers' relationship with the governor: thirty for this person, a hundred for that, etc. According to Las Casas, such distributions were rationalized as enabling Christian instruction.[10] With dwindling opportunities for seizing human plunder, colonial authorities distributed Indians as *encomiendas*, grants of labor and tribute to be performed and provided by all of the Indians living in a specified location, divided into work units of forty to 150.[11] Prohibited by royal decree from owning the natives' land, the *encomendero* (the holder of such a grant) became a lord of labor.

Roots of this system went back hundreds of years to the Muslim conquest of much of Iberia. The conquerors had allowed Christians to keep their farms and continue to produce goods in exchange for payment of tribute and displays of subservience, such as bowing to Muslims. Spanish Christians adopted this model as they reconquered Spain, allowing Muslims to remain on the land as oppressed, exploited laborers.[12] Then, coinciding with the overthrow of the last bastions of Moorish control, Columbus discovered a faraway world, rich in novel opportunities for coerced labor.

In 1503, reports reached Queen Isabel that Hispaniola's Indians were avoiding the settlers and Christian conversion. They were said to be enjoying "excessive liberty." She decreed that the native labor that the settlers were grabbing up for themselves would remain a royal trust. And she instructed Nicolás de Ovando, Hispaniola's governor, to "order each cacique [or chief] to take charge of a certain number of … Indians, so that you may make them work wherever necessary" to provide food for Christian settlers and mine gold, "and to have each one paid on the day he works the wages and maintenance which you think he should have."[13] The Indians were further required to live in towns, but close to the mines, each family in a house. They might have fiestas but only Christian fiestas, and no more naked or overly frequent baths. They were to serve Spaniards through labor assignments, the *repartimentos* of the encomienda system.[14] Thus did the encomienda system begin its New World career.

Allocation of Tainos reflected the Castilian social order. Around 1509, a noble (or caballero) with a European wife on hand was entitled to eighty.

A foot soldier of the same marital status got sixty; a married laborer thirty. But a high official or commander of a fortress might be assigned up to two hundred.[15] Thus, the inability of an ordinary settler to induce a wife or lover to join him in the far-off Indies could cost him the services of dozens of semi-slaves. Absent such a union, one had to look to plundering, slave-catching, or political connections to gain a livelihood. The premium that colonial officials put on transplanting the Spanish family reflected their desire to create a Greater Castile and perhaps, as well, a policy of trying to avoid unnecessary provocation of the Indians by appropriating too many native women. (The latter tendency may have led to the annihilation of the would-be settlers left behind on Hispaniola when Columbus returned to Spain after his first voyage.) Taking root instead of a Greater Castile were such New World hybrids as Cuba, Puerto Rico, Mexico, and the rest of Spanish America.

Besides reinforcing traditional marriage and the existing hierarchy, assignments of Indian labor were used for political leverage. Thus, we read that Francisco de Bobadilla, a judge who came to Hispaniola in 1499 to investigate complaints regarding the regime of the Colon brothers (Christopher and Diego), won support among the settlers by giving them Indians in exchange for a share of the profits that their labor might yield. Some twenty years and many similar arrangements later, Pedrarias Dávila (or Pedro Arias Ávila), the long-time strongman of Panama and later Nicaragua, responded to an overdue investigation of his conduct with a massive allocation of Indians to Spanish colonists—ten thousand to eighty-three settlers—thereby gaining a favorable outcome.[16]

In 1516 three Jeronymite monks were sent to the Indies in response to royal misgivings inspired by the tireless Las Casas's human rights campaign. They were to serve as "high commissioners for the protection of the Indians." Las Casas had complained that Hispaniola's commander was distributing Indians in allotments of fifty without regard to age or condition, sending the men off to work in distant mines and requiring the women to work the land with only a sharpened stick.[17] Under considerable pressure from the settlers, the Jeronymites acted on their mandate by polling some of Hispaniola's colonists to determine whether the natives were capable of self-government. (Never mind that they had governed themselves for many centuries without any help from Europeans.) The fifteen respondents told the clerics that the natives were habitually drunk and gluttonous, and that they preferred living in the forest eating spiders and roots to living with Spaniards. In sum, the Indians were altogether incapable of self-government and of finding Christianity on their own. The respondents also opposed any further changes governing Indian labor, such as putting the natives under the Crown's supervision. Optimal reform, they thought, would be elimination of the two-month rest period that enabled Indians to revert to idleness and their other customary vices. They recommended that the encomiendas be made perpetual so that encomenderos would see their workers as a long-term investment rather than a short-term lease.[18] In other words, the methodical foxes that the crown had sent to guard the chickens limited their effort to a survey of local foxes as to problems with egg production.

Export of the encomienda system to the Caribbean and, before long, the mainland gave rise to heated competition for Indian labor. One Cristóbal de Tapia complains as follows to the king regarding the allocation of Indians on Hispaniola that favored the governor's fellow Extremadurans: "the assistants to the assistants of the cooks have Indians in large numbers," he writes, but not he. Ovando intercepted his letter, jailed him, and confiscated his Indians.[19] According to Bernal Díaz, the Cuban soldiers and settlers who made up the Grijalva expedition to the coast of Yucatan were those "who possessed no Indians." The conquistador Juan de Escalante hated Diego Velázquez, the governor of Cuba, "because he had not given him good Indians."[20] Hernán Cortés accused Velázquez of impoverishing colonists who were out of his favor by denying them Indians.[21] He also wrote that many of the followers of Narváez, sent to Mexico to wrest command of the conquest from Cortés, were forced to accompany Narváez by Governor Velázquez's threatening to confiscate their Indians.[22] But denial of Indian labor is not what had prompted Cortés to venture forth. When they were still friends, Velásquez had given him control of land with many native inhabitants, as well as good mines.[23]

The request for permanent encomiendas became a perpetual refrain among encomenderos, both in the Indies and later in New Spain and Peru. As the impulse for reform mounted in Castile, representatives of the settlers would repeatedly assert that without encomiendas there would be no colonists in Spanish America. But in Hispaniola, Cuba, and other parts of the Indies, mine work and encomienda labor were proving incompatible with the survival of Indians. Las Casas mentions an official in Cuba whose regime of overwork left him with thirty Indians out of an allocation of three hundred, and this within three months![24] A demographer estimates the decline in Hispaniola's indigenous population under Spanish rule at between two and three hundred thousand. He does not find disease primarily responsible for this devastation, although illness due to unfamiliar microbes would have contributed. Instead, he relies on the reports of contemporaries to attribute this demographic collapse to such factors as overwork in the mines and elsewhere, the transfer of Indians from place to place and from master to master, and to the "concubinage" of native women, who were openly bought and sold by early settlers.

In short, the invaders rerouted indigenous labor from the ordinary activities of subsistence to the burden of supporting Spaniards at the expense of their own livelihood. As a consequence, Taino consumption levels decreased, living conditions deteriorated, and people could not meet their basic needs. They died, killed themselves, refused to reproduce, and engaged in suicidal rebellions. The result was the extinction of a people.[25]

Conquistadors' Reward

Nothing could be more telling than Article 45 of Castile's New Laws of 1542, which declared that any Indian *still alive* in Puerto Rico, Hispaniola, or Cuba owed no further tribute or services to Spaniards.[26] These islands, especially Hispaniola—"the Ground Zero of the New World"[27]—had served as a training ground for labor exploitation on the mainland. After the disastrous impact of the encomienda system on the Tainos, Cortés recommended against its use in New Spain. But as he was unwilling to give his followers more than minuscule amounts of plundered treasure (as discussed in Chapter 6), he could find no way of rewarding his men than by giving them Indians.

Toward the end of his letter of May 15, 1522, to Charles V (the Third Letter), Cortés declares that there are only two ways that Spaniards can maintain themselves in New Spain. The first is at royal expense. Cortés proffers this as a gambit, for he surely knows that the Emperor will not consider this option. He quickly withdraws it out of concern for his Majesty's "continuous and considerable" expenses. The second is by making the Indians work for them. He concedes that that the natives of Mexico are more advanced than those of the Caribbean. But wanting to reward the services of his followers, Cortés has been "almost forced," he writes, to distribute Indians to them.[28] He did not assign these "more advanced" Indians as slaves, though thousands of natives *were* being enslaved. Instead, he distributed them as encomiendas.

But Charles V had already decided to abolish the encomienda system, and by instructions to Cortés of June 26, 1523, he forbade such additional grants and revoked those already made.[29] In response, Cortés sent his monarch a copy of ordinances that he had already promulgated in an effort to ground an encomienda system in New Spain that would omit the most destructive features of that system's implementation in the Antilles.[30] In a separate letter of the same date, October 15, 1524, Cortés argues that the colonists are violent, vicious men. To allow the Indians free association with them would be disastrous for the Indians. Besides, without Indian labor, colonists would abandon the hemisphere and Castile would lose its new imperial possessions. As for the Indians, if they were not distributed to colonists, they would be enslaved again by other Indians who would sacrifice them to their pagan gods. He then goes on to describe how the use of Indian labor will be different in New Spain than it was in the Antilles.[31]

In actuality, the Spaniards would use Indian labor in New Spain for everything from mining to farming to manufacturing valuable commodities. Such use was limited only by the availability of Indians and, at least at first, by one's proximity to Cortés.[32] In Hugh Thomas's bland assessment of the relationship of settlers to natives, the former's survival required "some economic bond between the two races."[33] It is ironic that the Aztecs had maintained something of an encomienda system of their own. When they and their allies had distributed conquered lands (always giving priority to participating nobles), the labor of the people living on the land went with it, effectively reducing such residents to serfdom.[34]

Doling Out Indians

In 1522, about two and a half years after the conquistadors had massacred thousands of residents of Cholula, Cortés turned the ancient holy city into a work force as the first encomienda in New Spain. He awarded it to Gonzalo de Cerezo, who had served as his page and helped carry wood from Tlaxcala to Lake Texcoco, where it was converted into the brigantines that the Spaniards used to great advantage in their siege of Tenochtitlán. Cerezo became rich in the New World.[35]

Such grants often changed hands. Andrés de Tapia, one of the chroniclers of the Cholula massacre, also got Cholula as an encomienda. Cortés gave it to him in 1526, but the two later quarreled and Cortés took Cholula away from him, gave him some other (presumably less favorable) sites, and handed Cholula to one Rodrigo Rangel. A painting on Spanish paper[36] shows Cortés and Malintzin, his female companion and interpreter (better known as "Malinche"), holding the chain of a large dog that is attacking an Indian. In the *residencia* (investigation) of Cortés in 1529, Antonio de Carbajal testified that Cortés had had a Cholulan chief killed for refusing to give gold to Andrés de Tapia. The Spaniards sometimes killed Indians by dogging, though whether the painting depicts the incident described by Carbajal is unclear.[37] In 1532, one A. Proaño claimed half of the Cholula encomienda in a lawsuit.[38]

Another chronicler of the massacre, Francisco de Aguilar, also became an encomendero, though it seems that his ownership of an inn on a major route was what made him rich. At fifty he gave up his wealth to join the Dominican order. As for Bernal Díaz del Castillo, whose history of the conquest (*La verdadera historia de la conquista de Nueva España*) was destined to become a classic, he not only became an encomendero but a lobbyist for the rights of certain encomenderos. In fact, there is reason to think that his book was inspired, at least in part, by the frustrations he encountered as an advocate of such forced labor.[39] But more on this below.

Other conquistadors who got some of the first encomiendas in New Spain were the handsome and sadistic Pedro de Alvarado, who became the lord of Xochimilco. Azcapotzalco went to the charming Francisco de Montejo, the eventual conqueror of Yucatan. His confederate Alonso de Ávila, although imprisoned in France, garnered Cuautitlan, Zumpango, and Xaltocan. Cortés awarded himself Coyoacán, Chalco, Ecatepec, and Otumba. Before long he would gain control of a vast expanse of agricultural land in Oaxaca, as well as gold and silver mines. With the labor of 23,000 native "vassals" granted him by Charles V—a number that Cortés would inflate into 23,000 *households*—Cortés would convert his acreage into cotton and sugar plantations, orchards, mills, and pasturage.[40] But Cortés's forced-labor allotments to others drew greater attention from those taking notes at the time.[41] Flush with the triumph of the fall of Tenochtitlán, for example, he awarded various towns to surviving Aztec nobles, such as Pedro, Moctezuma's Christianized son. He gave "some pueblos of Indians" to a settler who had treated his broken arm.[42] He put the natives of the Tabasco region under the "protection" of colonists and gave other Spanish settlers the natives of another province. Cortés writes that the latter "were most willing to serve and to make themselves useful."[43] He also apportioned villages to settlers of Santistevan, near Tampico, and turned a conquered village in Oaxaca into an encomienda for a Spanish soldier.[44] Other conquest commanders also made labor allocations. Pedro de Alvarado, for example, awarded his brother Jorge the Indians of an entire region, Soconusco.[45]

Returning to Mexico City from his disastrous Honduran venture, Cortés found that his enemies, having happily concluded that he was dead, had redistributed his labor allocations to their supporters, along with other offenses. One can imagine the initial reaction of this clever, ruthless man. His subsequent response included the re-allocation of Tacuba from Pedro Almíndez Chirino to Isabel, Moctezuma's daughter and a former lover of Cortés. She got its inhabitants' services as a wedding present.[46] Was she thrilled? Appalled? One wonders. Rivalry between the Cortés faction and supporters of the Cuban governor Diego Valásquez was such that a preeminent historian of the encomienda system in New Spain declares that Spanish Mexico was "a victim of two competing gangs."[47] Competing gangs victimize Mexico today, as well, but their leaders have yet to occupy the president's chair.

Every grant of Indian labor seemed to elicit new antagonisms. Even Bernal Díaz, for the most part a great admirer of Cortés, eventually complains that he has given encomiendas to recent arrivals—many of them from Medellín, Cortés's hometown—instead of to veterans of the conquest like himself.[48] As for the conquerors' primary allies in the massacre and destruction of Cholula and the campaigns that followed, the Tlaxcalans also got their reward. The Spaniards exempted them from personal service, assigned them only token tribute obligations, and used them as New Spain's police.[49] Otherwise, as a contributor to the post-conquest *Annals of Tlatelolco* remarks, all of the *altepetl* (communities) were given out as vassals of the Spaniards.[50]

Large allotments of Indian labor coincided with a rapid decline in the native population of New Spain. Clearly there were not enough Indian villages to go around. And small farms being what one historian describes as "unsuitable," many a settler was left without a native force to work the land or otherwise provide him with a livelihood. Such a person could join the retinue of a successful labor lord, seek "fresh conquests" of his own, or begin the long and arduous voyage back to Spain.[51] He would not have disagreed with Juan de Zumarrága, the first bishop of New Spain, that Indians are "the good and wealth of this country,"[52] or with Cortés, who told the emperor in 1528 that they were the main resource of Spain's overseas domain.[53]

Thwarting Reform

During the early decades of Spanish America, settlers depended on Castile for imports, which included weapons, clothes, horses, textiles, foodstuffs, wine, books, oil, grain, and other things that their descendents would learn to produce for themselves. They also imported an archaic socioeconomic system, whose overthrow by reform the settlers resisted mightily. Criminals who chose exile over mine work in Spain, impoverished hidalgos like Cortés, failed planters, peasants, younger sons of aristocrats, mid-level professionals and craftsmen, and the diverse others who came to Spain's New World were bound to resist threats to their newfound lives as lords of dark-skinned vassals. Thus, when Charles V decreed in 1520 that, as God had created Indians as free people, they were under no obligation to work for Spaniards, implementation might have required a smackdown by the Castilian army.[54]

Resolutions of the Barcelona conference of 1529 would also have ended encomiendas. Their adoption would destroy New Spain, encomenderos argued, and the Indians would forfeit the salvation of their souls. Besides, most Indians were well-treated, they insisted, and were no worse off than feudal vassals.[55] The New Laws of 1542 expressed a determined effort on the part of Charles V to gain control of labor relations in Castile's distant possessions and to put a cap on what one historian has described as the "anachronistic feudalism" that had taken root in New Spain.[56] Surely the Emperor would have had no problem with such a growth if the settlers had acted like proper vassals and treated him as their liege lord, but beginning with Hernán Cortés they did not. Article 1 of the New Laws declared that the Indians were "free persons and vassals of the Crown." Article 26 forbade their enslavement, either by war, in response to rebellion, or by purchase. An Indian cannot be used "against his will." Article 32 ordered the redistribution of Indians from "excessively large encomiendas" to conquistadors who had none. Opposition to Article 32 was so furious that it was soon repealed. Another measure that was withdrawn after fierce resistance was Article 35, which would have precluded any new encomiendas. When an encomendero died, his Indians would have reverted to the Crown.[57] Death came to Article 35 instead.

With news of these New Laws, business came to a halt in New Spain. Prices shot up, and over six hundred colonists set out to return to Spain. Some proclaimed that, in view of their impending poverty, they had no choice but to kill their wives and daughters to keep them from becoming prostitutes.[58] One wonders about this threat: would the murder of wives and daughters have been required to preserve their reputations or to forestall the temptation of the paterfamilias to pimp them? Always a step or two ahead of his compatriots, Cortés arranged to import five hundred African slaves. Around 650,000 would follow them to Spanish America and Brazil over the next hundred years.[59]

Francisco Tello de Sandoval arrived in February 1544 with instructions to explain the New Laws and investigate the conduct of colonial officials. Besieged with complaints from the moment he disembarked, he passed off public proclamation of the New Laws to a notary. Leaders of the Franciscans, the Augustinians, and even the Dominicans who had most opposed the encomienda system announced their support for the encomiendas. Without them there would be no industry or stability, according to a statement of Mexico City's Dominicans. Not only encomiendas but perpetual encomienda grants would be best for continuation of agricultural projects then under way. Besides, added New Spain's Viceroy Antonio de Mendoza, the Aztecs had used others for personal services. And enforcement of the New Laws would depopulate New Spain. A fortiori, they were unenforceable.[60]

Don Juan de Zárate, Bishop of Antequera, complained to Prince Philip that the Indians were getting so much attention that "no Spaniard now dares to harm an Indian. On the contrary, the natives are so favored that they dare to mistreat the Spaniards, not giving them anything to eat except for money and at high prices, and only when they wish."[61] One is reminded of the mugger who grouses that his elderly victim tried to hit him with her purse. To avoid a civil war in New Spain, Tello de Sandoval was persuaded to suspend implementation of the New Laws pending an appeal to the Council of the Indies.[62] Meanwhile, an armed rebellion had broken out among settlers in Peru, where residents of Trujillo complained to Blasco Núñez Vela, the viceroy appointed to enforce the New Laws there, that unless they had slaves to attend them in old age, their wars had been for naught.[63] Núñez Vela's determination to compel obedience cost him his head.

A few of the New Law reforms, such as the ban on the use of Indians for personal services in lieu of their payment of (often unaffordable) tribute, survived colonial opposition. But prohibitions on the taking of slaves and the use of Indians as bearers of heavy loads were laden with exceptions.

Bernal Díaz began his *Historia* following a time when the exploits of the conquistadors were under attack by Las Casas and others. Here are the words with which he closes his long, adventure-filled account of conquest against great odds. Though he has served "as a very good soldier of his Majesty," he writes,

> I find myself poor and very old, with a marriageable daughter and my sons young men already grown up with beards, and others to be educated, and I am not able to go to Castile to His Majesty to put before him things which are necessary for his Royal Service, and also that he should grant me favours, for they owe me many debts.[64]

We need not look far to determine what Díaz hoped for in the way of favors. He had been to Spain in 1539 and 1550 to represent the interest of encomenderos like himself, making appearances at the court and filing petitions which argued for grants of encomiendas in perpetuity. Now it appears that his children and their children, on down the line, will not be able to inherit his wealth, which consists of Indian labor, and he laments it. Díaz's classic, which was not published in full and as written until the early twentieth century, represents a campaign in a "second war,"[65] a running battle for unpaid Indian labor.

As for Cortés, in his will he left his encomienda to Martín, a fifteen year old son (the *legitimate* Martín), with the proviso that should an investigation reveal that his "vassals" had given him greater tribute and services than they would have given their own native rulers, they should be "paid and indemnified" by that amount.[66] Martín surely lost no sleep over that.

An Allergy to Work?

Hugh Thomas notes that Diego de Ordaz had a "fortified farm" in New Spain on which he grew maize, beans, and cacao, besides raising ducks, and that Hernán de Barrientos ran a farm by himself in Zapoteca territory for over a year.[67] But these were exceptions to the general rule that in their dependence on the forced labor of Indians and resistance to reforms that might have required them to substitute their own efforts, the early settlers of Spanish America could hardly have displayed a greater distaste for arduous work. As one frankly stated, "I came here to get rich, not till the soil like a peasant."[68] To understand this aversion to manual work, we must consider the social world from which the Spaniards came—the tripartite order of the Middle Ages: knights, clerics, and laborers. These orders comprised a pyramid, and those who worked with their hands, the peasants and herders who made up eighty or ninety percent of the population, were at the base of it. In Spain, peasants were seen by their betters as vulgar, ignorant, even subhuman, just as Spanish settlers would come to regard New World natives. Besides, many of the Spanish colonizers were military men whose only occupation was making war and only income derived from the spoils of war. The importation of slaves to work the plantations of southern Iberia had reinforced their prejudice against manual work.[69] Such activity was for peasants, slaves, and … Indians. No less an authority than Aristotle had written that in an ideal state slaves would do the farming.[70] A mutinous member of Nuñez de Balboa's Panamanian venture suffered the humiliation of having to grind corn, like an Indian, in the streets of Darien.[71]

This prejudice against manual labor conformed to aristocratic modeling. Castilian nobles, especially those with large estates or courtly connections, traditionally enjoyed significant material advantages: tax exemptions, pensions, remission of debts, and the prospect of a lucrative career of tax-collecting for the Crown. A nobleman did not work with his hands or own a shop. For the impoverished hidalgo or disadvantaged other, Spanish America conjured a dream of living an aristocratic life. As one Spanish official put it, "No one comes to the Indies to plow and to sow, but only to eat and loaf."[72] With Indians to do his bidding, the former convict or other "quasi-military parasite"[73] could live out his fantasy of life as a prince. There *were* great rewards for a very few. Both Cortés and Francisco Pizarro acquired impressive titles, although the latter was illegitimate by birth, illiterate through neglect, and ill-mannered by disposition. We will resume contact with the American career of the aristocratic work ethic in the waning decades of Spain's—and then Mexico's—dream of a flourishing province up north on the Pacific coast.

Bernal Díaz describes how in New Spain, Cortés sent young Pizarro (which young Pizarro is unclear) on an expedition to explore a northern coastal area. He returned alone, having ordered his compatriots to start plantations and collect birds. Cortés reproached him for this. Spending one's time planting cocoa and collecting birds showed "weak character," he explained. He called for the would-be planters to return forthwith.[74] Cattle-raising, on the other hand, required equestrian daring and the kind of short bursts of energy that comported with the warrior mystique. New Spain's successful ranchers produced enough beef to feed multiple retainers and give marauding *chichimecas*—the nomadic Indians of northern Mexico—a taste for barbecue.[75]

For all this, there were circumstances under which these New World adventurers could become willing and even enthusiastic laborers, if we are to credit an incident described by Bernal Díaz. Early on in their expedition, Cortés wanted to establish a town on the Gulf of Mexico, to be called the Villa Rica de la Vera Cruz—now Veracruz. Without a word to his followers, he began digging trenches for foundations, carrying off the earth and stone on his back. Soon everyone was working—digging, building walls, hauling water, and making lime, bricks, tiles, boards, and nails. "In this way," writes Díaz, "we all labored without ceasing, from the highest to the lowest ... so that the church and some of the houses were soon built and the fort almost finished."[76] It seems that with the temporary suspension of hierarchy, manual labor ceased to be demeaning. But collective effort, in this case, was at least partly inspired by the threat or imagined threat of an attack by Aztec warriors, who were thought to number up to 150,000.[77] In any case, hierarchy was rarely suspended. The only other mention of such efforts comes in Díaz's description of the siege of Tenochtitlán. At one point, their Indian allies had abandoned the conquistadors, and "we ourselves began to fill in and stop up" the big opening in the causeway wrought by the Aztecs during the night. Even Cortés pitched in.[78]

How exceptional was the Spanish work ethic? Settlers in the colonies that became the United States and Canada did not attempt to enslave Indians, not as a major objective anyway. Tocqueville writes that people who came to the United States "realized that in order to clear this land, nothing less than the self-interested efforts of the owner [of the land] himself was essential." The land would not enrich both an owner and a farmer.[79] And the comparative ease of access to land made for ample opportunity for agrarian self-employment. Marx approvingly repeats the assertion that in the "new American settlements ... a passion for owning land prevents the existence of a class of labourers for hire."[80] (Even Defoe's Moll Flanders thinks that land in America can be snapped up with ease, though she hopes to return to England to live off the proceeds of her American holdings as a rentier.) In short, the earliest version of the American Dream involved owning one's own land and successfully working it, the point being that these northern immigrants wanted the Indians' *land*, not their labor. We can only guess what their attitude might have been if the native population they encountered had approached the density of Mexico's and if these colonists had been prohibited from ownership of Indian lands, as were the Spaniards.

In any event, some northern Indians *were* enslaved. Seventeenth-century New Englanders, for example, thought that like Spaniards they had the right to enslave "lawful Captives taken in just Wars."[81] But immigrants from northern Europe were generally not averse to working with their hands when they could neither hire nor compel other people's hands to do the work.

A Cultural Dead End

For people in other parts of the world, pre–Gold Rush California was one of the remotest places on earth. Even as a province of Mexico, California was a kind of Siberian penal colony with great beaches.[82] The few adventurous Yankees and Europeans who made the difficult passage around Cape Horn and up the Pacific coast to land on its shores found it lightly inhabited by various Indian tribes and by Spanish-speaking whites known as Californios. Whether some Californios were direct descendants of the conquistadors is doubtful, though they may have claimed that heritage. But the Californios seem to have inherited a *meme* of the conquistador, a meme being a unit of culture transmitted by imitation and functioning in the social sphere somewhat like a gene in the biological. Every note-taking visitor to Alta California describes the Californio male as indolent to an extreme. Here is what Fr. Ramón Olbes, Spanish Franciscan at Santa Barbara in 1812, says of him and his like. The Californios "are so lazy and fond of idleness that they do not know how to do anything except ride horseback; they hold that any kind of work is dishonorable and it appears to them that only Indians should do the work"—even cooking, washing, and gardening.[83] Auguste Duhaut-Cilly, captain of a French vessel that reached California in 1827, reports that the "Californios are lazy: the only work to which they give themselves with any inclination is that which consists in taking care of the herds, because, for this employment, one must be on horseback." Indians, reduced to "a kind of slaves," till the land.[84] We may safely assume that the sources of these descriptions would not have been Calvinists, for whom nonproductive idleness was among the greatest of sins.

8—Transplanting a Work Ethic

For Anglo-Saxons, the culture clash was pronounced. United States Navy Lieutenant Charles Wilkes, who headed a U.S. Exploring Expedition in 1841, writes that "[t]he whites are so indolent, and withal have so much pride, as to make them look upon all manual labour as degrading; in truth, they regard all those who work as beneath them."[85] Richard Henry Dana, whose *Two Years Before the Mast* remains the classic account of pre–Gold Rush California and the effort required to get there, describes the Californios as "an idle, thriftless people, [who] can make nothing for themselves." They export only hides, which Dana and his mates were collecting for shoe manufacturers in New England. The Californios import almost everything they use including wine, writes Dana, though grapes grow about them in abundance. Foreigners run the shops and other commercial endeavors. "The Indians ... do all the hard work," he writes; "even the poorest Californio keeps at least one as a semi-slave."[86] Dana also observes that with Indians doing all of the heavy work, the Californios have no working class: "every rich man looks like a grandee, and every poor scamp like a broken-down gentleman." The poorest man, though with nothing to eat, will appear well-dressed, have good manners, and ride a "noble" horse with fine trappings.[87] This is a portrait of the conquistador without an enemy to subdue.

The Californio was, first and foremost, a horseman. Duflot de Mofras, an attaché of the French Embassy in Mexico City who visited California in 1841–42, writes that the Californios "never walk when they can ride. Their first act upon arising is to saddle a horse." They will use it to travel less than fifty feet. Perhaps their only rival in this was the king of the Rus, described by the tenth-century Arab diplomat Ibn Fadlan as getting off his throne directly onto a horse and dismounting, when he did, back onto his throne.[88] Off their horses, the Californios would lie around smoking and drinking brandy. Their women did everything needed to maintain the household, including the hiring of Indians.[89]

Such a harsh portrayal deserves a second look. Had Henry Dana or Lt. Wilkes gotten away from the coast and availed himself of the generous hospitality of a ranchero and his extended family, he might have gained a more nuanced impression of the Californio culture. But he would probably not have liked what he observed. For one thing, the rancheros did cultivate grapes and make wine, at least for their own consumption. If they failed to exploit more of the abundant resources around them, it was because they saw no need, as "nobody starved in California" and some lived lives of luxury.[90] In the course of a day, their Anglo guest might have seen some of his hosts pick up guitars to play and sing, might have watched a cockfight or a horse race, might have observed a couple performing an elegant dance. At the end of such a day, he might have enjoyed (or endured) a great profusion of food and drink. Despite all this, he might have noted later, as did Lieutenant Wilkes, that the dancing was "coarse and lascivious."[91]

As for his hosts, they would never understand the Anglo fixation on work, profit, and saving for a future that might never come. The point of living was to enjoy life. Of course, the people that made such a life possible, the Indians and the Californio women, might not have agreed that this was such a good life. They might have said that it was a miserable and nasty life, replete with unfair burdens. No wonder Californio women were better disposed toward Yankees than were Californio men.[92] Or was that just a wishful thought on the part of certain gringos?

According to Richard Dawkins, the eminent ethologist and originator of the meme concept, a meme-complex is (like a parasite) self-perpetuating, though unconscious and "blind." Memes "compete" for the attention of the human brain "at the expense of 'rival' memes."[93] Before the Gold Rush brought people from all over the world to California, the area was so isolated that the Californio way of life had little exposure to compelling alternatives. Military conquest of California by representatives of the expanding United States in 1846 drove the ethos of languorous sociability into a cultural blind alley. As aggressive Anglos moved into the neighborhood, the anti-work ethic died a lingering death, to await a countercultural revival in the 1960s.

Elsewhere in the New World

Centuries before any Yankee sailor could encounter an indolent Californio, the native populations of Mexico and Peru had collapsed as a result of overwork, exposure to Old World diseases, and mercury poisoning in the mines. Whatever the pre–Hispanic population of Mexico had been—estimates have ranged up to twenty-four million—it had been reduced to less than a million by 1630. African slaves were imported to replace the mine workers, while members of a growing Spanish colony converted surviving Indians into low-wage laborers, debt peons, and people simply forced to work.[94]

I have said that unlike the Spanish colonists who relied on Indian labor, English colonists of America wanted only the natives' land, but the earliest settlers of Virginia had much in common with those of Hispaniola. The first generation of Jamestown colonists faced starvation amid an abundance of potential seafood. Ninety-two of the earliest 295 would-be colonists were "gentlemen," and many of the rest were their servants, all of whom abjured manual work.[95] Paradise "would not have been much better," wrote John Smith, yet Jamestown was "a misery, a ruine, a death, a hell."[96] Except for a man who killed and ate his wife, the colonists depended on nearby Indians to feed them. Then, becoming more self-sufficient, they sought to avoid the hard work of clearing land for planting by taking over land that the Indians had already cleared. Only by the adoption of native agricultural techniques were they able to stave off famine.[97]

English law made land ownership the first prize of colonists, and later English settlers seized on various rationales and expedients to force the Indians off the lands that they had hunted, cultivated, and occupied for millennia. Unlike any other European colonizers, the English believed that by working the land, with slaves if possible, they acquired ownership of it. Juan Ginés de Sepúlveda, Las Casas's opponent in the famous debate at Valladolid in 1550 regarding the legitimacy of Spain's American conquests, called this English doctrine "mere theft."[98]

Also in contrast to other Europeans, the English saw desirable native land as a commodity that they could obtain by giving the Indians something in exchange for it. As the Indians could not conceive of anything that could possibly bring about a permanent transfer of their lands, they innocently accepted such "gifts." Then, after the Revolutionary War, newly independent Americans asserted squatters' rights to land that congress was trying to auction to speculators. Tocqueville contributed to the myth that Americans had settled an empty land, "a desert land awaiting its inhabitants."[99] Small wonder that some natives characterized the invaders as "People Greedily Grasping for Land."[100]

Who did the work of clearing, cultivating, and maintaining all of this nearly free land that was acquired by Europeans or European descendants in the early decades of North American colonization? As already acknowledged, many settlers became their own labor force, although Daniel Boone, the archetypal frontiersman, left such efforts up to his wife and children while he went hunting and exploring.[101] But nascent manufacturers, merchants, and the English gentlemen who shared the conquistadors' allergy to manual work wanted a workforce. They might enslave an Indian when they could, but the native populations of the areas of settlement by northern Europeans were quite insufficient to meet their needs, due in part to the ravages of disease and massacres.

Was it only a coincidence that the wholesale maiming and execution of criminals ("blood sanctions") were replaced by sentences of indentured servitude and galley slavery (bondage punishments)[102] at a time when labor demands were overwhelming Europe's colonial administrators? The British emptied overcrowded prisons, exporting members of their "dangerous class" to America and later Australia and Tasmania. Between 1717 and 1775, an estimated forty thousand male and female convicts suffered the quasi-slavery of "transportation."[103] They arrived in America and elsewhere as indentured servants, no better off than slaves and in some cases worse, as the slave (like the worker of the perpetual encomienda sought by Spanish settlers) might be treated as a long-term investment. Moll Flanders' Lancashire husband, the gentleman thief, would rather have been hanged than transported into "Servitude and hard Labour." Unlike the African or Indian slave, however, the white servant could escape servitude by blending into the colonial population.

Not all of the indentured servants sent to British America had occupied prison cells. Many came voluntarily in pursuit of a better life. Many others came less voluntarily. The denizen of an English harbor might be plied with liquor to lure him onto an America-bound ship. Candy sufficed for children. The French used such trickery as misleading ads, as well as force, to fill their ships with emigrants. Similar practices would be deployed in the ports of southern China in the nineteenth century to meet the demand for cheap labor in the western United States and other parts of the world. But even though twenty-five thousand would-be Americans landed in Philadelphia alone in just four years,[104] there were not enough European immigrants to meet the labor needs of large-scale producers of sugar, cotton, and tobacco in the Caribbean and the American South—that is, plantation owners. That need, as well as that of Latin America latifundios, was met by the African slave trade. Between 1500 and 1840, more than three times as many Africans (11.7 million) as Europeans (3.4 million) came to the Americas.[105]

In sum, when forced labor by Indians proved inadequate, whites were used. When forced labor by whites became inadequate—or unaffordable, as in plantation agriculture—Africans were used. Racism served as rationale for their enslavement.[106] Those who provided their own manual labor were generally those who had no choice.

9

A New Kind of Savagery

Europeans so frequently referred to the indigenous people of the New World and other "new worlds" as *savages* that the word invites some scrutiny. "Savage" comes from "sylvan," meaning of the forest. (The Spanish *salvaje* comes closer to the original.) What lives in the forest is wild, untamed; hence "brutal," like a beast, "hence cruel."[1] In calling someone a savage, we are saying that he is like an animal, perhaps a dangerous animal. Juan de Matienzo, a sixteenth-century Spanish jurist, thought that the Indians were "animals ... ruled by their passions." He based this opinion on their appearance and what he knew of their behavior.[2] For him and for many of his contemporaries, the Indians were less than fully human. Had they been fully human they would have dressed, eaten, walked, and talked like Spaniards. They would have lived in houses, had a written language with an alphabet, had but one wife each, and enjoyed private property.[3] Pizarro urged the captured Incan emperor to "come out from the bestial and diabolical life" that he led, as God had invited him to do.[4]

Spaniards were not alone in making such judgments. In sixteenth-century English ideology, the Irish were a "savage nation" living "like beasts."[5] George Washington compared Indians to wolves, saying that they "are both beasts of prey, tho' they differ in shape."[6] English colonists of Australia saw the continent's native people as hardly more than "intelligent animals."[7] Europeans justified the slave trade by saying that Africans were "savage man-eaters."[8] Such examples of "political Augustinism"[9] could be multiplied indefinitely, but the point is that when you begin referring to others as "savages," you are implying that their behavior—their savagery—should be brought under control, domesticated, tamed—by exterminating them, if necessary. At the very least, they must, like children, be taught better manners.[10]

Are animals cruel? In perpetrating the massacre described in this chapter, the conquistadors were not acting like other animals but like human animals at their worst. Their conduct was a Spanish import. We will investigate this massacre, the massacre of Cholula, and the mystery of why it happened, reviewing the justifications given by eyewitnesseses and exploring the problematic character of their accounts. For there are bound to be problems when only the killers explain the reason for a killing. Under probing, we will see that their explanation takes on more and more of the coloring of a cover-up. Some commentators even suggest that the killers may have been serving an agenda of which they were unaware.

The ruthlessness of the massacre of Cholula had precedents, both in Europe and in Mesoamerica. Its seeming randomness was in line with atrocities committed by Spaniards in the Caribbean. But in the use of massacre as a medium of communication, the Cholula bloodbath looked to the future—in fact, to the kind of events that animate today's headlines. But I prejudge. Let us consider the reports of what happened and why it happened before drawing any conclusions. Before doing that, however, let's investigate the setting.

The Setting

Pre-Columbian Cholula was quite large for a preindustrial city. Some estimate that the city and its surrounding area had a population of a hundred thousand when the Spaniards arrived. No city in Spain approached this size. Its web of paths leading to the central marketplace and Quetzalcoatl Pyramid would have been crowded by day, with an estimated population density on the order of present-day Hong Kong's. Spaniards compared Cholula to congested Valladolid.[11] Cortés wrote that, on the basis of its proportions and hundreds of "towers" (that is, temple-topped pyramids), it was "more beautiful to look at than any in Spain."[12]

Cholula was also very old. There is archeological evidence that humans have inhabited the region for many thousands of years. The site itself was covered by a lake that slowly dried, enabling people to settle at its edge until, by the beginning of the current era, what would become Cholula was the largest settlement around. When the Spaniards arrived, people had continuously occupied the site for well over a millennium.[13] Today Cholula nestles up against Puebla, about seventy miles southeast of Mexico City.

Cholula had great regional importance, annually drawing hundreds of thousands of pilgrims from as far away as Guatemala to worship at its temples. Devotees of Quetzalcoatl, the feathered serpent, regarded Cholula with the same kind of reverence that Christians reserve for Jerusalem or Muslims for Mecca.[14] With each sunset the sound of trumpets would call worshippers to prayer. This call was repeated at midnight and at dawn when the devout ("all the common people") would join arriving pilgrims at the Quetzalcoatl temple with offerings of quail, rabbits, deer, incense, etc.[15] A newly appointed monarch would also visit Cholula, offering brilliant feathers, precious stones, blankets, or gold to Quetzalcoatl and swearing obedience to him. The city's high priests would then invest the monarch by piercing his ears, nose, or lower lip, following which five red-clad holy men would accompany him back to his own domain.[16] With this sketchy reconstruction, I should add that aside from archeological evidence, Europeans (or their descendants) are the only source of information on Cholula's pre–Hispanic past.

Entering Cholula, the Spaniards would not have seen its everyday face. The people who normally rubbed elbows in its narrow lanes—transients coming to market, slaves bearing the goods of accompanying merchants, pilgrims come to worship or to climb the Great Pyramid, bureaucrats and foreign officials—would have been displaced by the crowds that edged the passageways and filled the flat roofs of the houses to gape at the exotic strangers and their even stranger animals. Cortés noted poor people begging in the street, "as the poor do in Spain and in other civilized places."[17] The Spaniards could not have missed the Great Pyramid, called the "largest free-standing man-made edifice in the world."[18] With up to 430 meters on each side, its volume easily exceeded that of the Cheops pyramid, though certainly there are taller structures. By the eighth century, the Pyramid had been covered by large amounts of adobe, perhaps to make it look like a natural hill. When the conquistadors first sighted it, Cholultecas had largely abandoned the Great Pyramid as a place of worship, violently it appears. Toltec-Chichimeca rulers had built a new ceremonial center around their Pyramid of Quetzalcoatl, a few hundred meters away.[19] The Spaniards would also have noticed some of the additional pyramids (Cortés reported counting more than 400 of them), many of them small and privately owned, each topped with a thatched-roofed temple resembling a pointed mushroom on its stem.[20] These were scattered throughout the city and even in the fields outside of town.

The Massacre

Sojourning in Cholula en route to Tenochtitlán in October 1519, the conquistadors announced that they were about to leave, then posted guards at the exits of a courtyard near their quarters where thousands of Cholultecas had gathered, just as they would do several months later in a courtyard in Tenochtitlán where the Toxcatl dances were taking place.[21] The conquistadors then attacked and slaughtered those within. Participants who chronicled this event say that they killed two or three thousand. The Spaniards and over five thousand of their Tlaxcalan allies then formed killing squads and went throughout the city, killing, burning, and looting, although Cortés allegedly ordered them to spare women and children.[22] Following two days of this, Cortés directed an end to the destruction and divided the gold, cloth, salt, and slaves obtained as booty with the Tlaxcalans, the Spaniards taking the gold and unspecified "precious objects," leaving their native allies with clothing, salt, and cacao.[23] (Because of a blockade imposed by the Aztecs, the Tlaxcalans generally lacked access to salt.) In Bernal Díaz's telling, Cortés ordered the Tlaxcalans to free their captives. Although such an order "went against [their] grain," they did free some.[24] Cortés also commanded peace between Cholula and Tlaxcala, began turning pagan temples into churches, and within fifteen or twenty days, the city was back to normal and "it seemed as if no one was missing."[25]

A year after the massacre and destruction of much of Cholula, Cortés wrote to Charles V that he had seen "no city so fit for Spaniards to live in."[26] The conquerors leveled the top of the Great Pyramid to install a cross, which lightning twice knocked down. In 1847, during the Mexican War, a U.S. Army band mounted the Pyramid to play "Yankee Doodle Dandy" and "The Star Spangled Banner." Today the Great Pyramid draws tourists and students on field trips. Archaeologists have discovered a network of tunnels inside it covering a cumulative distance of seven kilometers.[27] They have also turned up numerous ritual burials, including evidence of decapitation and dismemberment. These include children.[28] On its flattened top today sits *Nuestra Señora de los Remedios*, a pastel yellow chapel with splendid frescos, stained glass, and a painting of an upside-down crucifixion. As for the Quetzalcoatl Pyramid, it was replaced in the years following the massacre by San Gabriel, a huge convent, though no longer used as such, that includes three churches.

The Conspiracy

Well-known eyewitness descriptions of events leading up to the Cholula massacre are included in Hernán Cortés's long letter to Charles V of October 1520—the so-called Second Letter—and in Bernal Díaz del Castillo's *History of the Conquest of New Spain*. Not so well-known are the chronicles of Andrés de Tapia, published in the 1550s, and of Francisco de Aguilar, completed around 1580. Francisco López de Gómara was not a witness (he was only eight years old in 1519), but he served as Cortés's private secretary and chaplain from 1541 until 1547 when Cortés died. Gómara's biography of him, published in 1552, discusses the massacre. Although inconsistent in detail, the meta-narrative of these accounts has guided popular histories of the conquest of Mexico for centuries. Neither the victims, for obvious reasons, nor those surviving in another part of the city contributed to this narrative. Yet, as we will see, the victims left something more eloquent than the silence of the grave.

Twentieth-century calendar illustration titled "Xicotencatl," unknown artist (courtesy Bancroft Library, University of California, Berkeley).

The Warning

Among the elements commonly reported by the Spanish participants is the assertion that their Tlaxcalan allies advised them not to go to Cholula. Cortés's Second Letter describes such a warning in some detail: Moctezuma, say their allies, has sent fifty thousand warriors to the Cholula area and created an alternate route that the Spaniards will need to take. That route is studded with horse traps. The Cholultecas have barricaded many of their streets and piled stones on their roofs. Cortés writes, a bit later, that he observed this alternate route with its disguised horse traps and that he saw stones piled upon Cholultecan roofs and noted barricaded streets.[29]

In Gómara's telling, Tlaxcalan leaders gave the Spaniards several women to seal the Tlaxcala-Conquistador alliance that developed following several days of bloody but inconclusive warfare between the conquistadors and the Tlaxcalans. One of these gift-women reported overhearing a disloyal Tlaxcalan "captain"—her own brother, supposedly—discussing a plot to kill the Spaniards in Cholula. Cortés had him quietly strangled. Gómara adds that then, coming into Cholula, Cortés saw evidence of "what the Tlaxcalans had told him."[30]

Andrés de Tapia was twenty-four at the outset of the expedition and became a trusted captain of Cortés. Regarding the Tlaxcalan warning, Tapia writes only that as they parted with their Indian allies outside Cholula (leaving the Tlaxcalans to set up camp in the countryside), the latter warned them to be on guard against the tricky merchants within the city.[31] Did they mistake the Spaniards for tourists?

Francisco de Aguilar was known for his integrity. At the age of fifty, he gave up the wealth he had acquired in New Spain to join the Dominican order. Writing his account of the expedition when he was eighty years old, the only thing that he recalled (or described) on the subject of Tlaxcalan warnings was that their reception outside Cholula by priests burning incense without ceremony was, according to the Tlaxcalans, a sign of war and an intention to sacrifice or kill the Spaniards.[32]

Here we come to the *History* of Bernal Díaz. Díaz was a common soldier who composed his still popular account in his declining years, decades after his participation in the expedition. Regarding the Tlaxcalan warning, he wrote only that the Tlaxcalans advised them not to go to Cholula.[33]

The Food Supply

The next common element in these primary accounts of the Cholula massacre has to do with the food supply. Cortés complains that the food provided by their Cholultecan hosts got worse with each passing day. Gómara writes that although the Cholultecas gave them each a turkey on the night of their arrival, the Spaniards got nothing more to eat for the next three days. Andrés de Tapia is silent on this issue. Aguilar says that they got nothing but jugs of water and wood, presumably firewood for cooking their own food. The Tlaxcalans (meaning, apparently, the few that the Cholultecas had let enter the city with the Spaniards) had to attend their needs. In Díaz's narrative, the Cholultecas cut off the Spaniards' food supply after two days, saying that they had no more corn. After that they gave them only firewood and water.[34]

Besides the food embargo, Cholultecan officials drastically reduced the frequency of their visits to the Spaniards (according to Cortés, Díaz, and Gómara), and Díaz noticed that the natives seemed to be laughing at them. Gómara has the Cholultecas thinking, "Why do these men want to eat, when they themselves will soon be eaten?"[35] For the most part then, Spanish chroniclers interpreted a Cholultecan unwillingness to feed them more than once or twice to be a hostile act, anticipating the sinister events that followed.

An Empty City

Aguilar is alone in noting that the city was "empty of people," although Gómara mentions the evacuation of women and children "to the mountains," and Díaz writes that some of the Tlaxcalans who were camped outside Cholula came to them to warn them of this development.

Sacrifices

The Tlaxcalans also informed them that the Cholultecas had sacrificed five children and two adults to their war god, an inauspicious sign if ever there was one. They sacrificed ten three-year-olds, in Gómara's account.[36] Díaz adds that the Spaniards' Cempoalan allies (Indians who had accompanied them all the way from the Gulf Coast) reported seeing horse traps—covered pits with sharpened stakes embedded in them—as well as stones and breastworks on the roofs and barricaded streets.[37]

Malintzin's Informants

Here Malintzin, aka La Malinche or Doña Marina, the famous native translator and, for many Mexicans, symbol of national betrayal, enters the picture. In Cortés's telling, a native woman informed Malintzin (not mentioned by name in his letter to the Emperor) that numerous Aztec warriors were gathered nearby, ready to attack and kill the Spaniards, that the women and children of Cholula had already been evacuated, and that she, Malintzin, should take shelter with her. Malintzin relayed this information to Gerónimo de Aguilar, their Spanish-speaking interpreter, who informed Cortés of the danger. Cortés then grabbed a passerby, who confirmed the existence of the plot.[38]

In Gómara's version, a nobleman's wife not only revealed the plot to Malintzin but the identity of the plotters, who included her own husband. Malintzin and Aguilar informed Cortés, who had two Cholultecas seized "and examined." They confirmed what the Cholultecan woman had said.[39] Andrés de Tapia also mentions Malintzin's revelation.

Always more detailed, Díaz's narrative first has Malintzin using charm and gifts to induce two Cholultecan priests to visit Cortés for a frank discussion. They tell him that the Aztec gods, Huitzilopochtli and Texcatlipoca, have advised Moctezuma to have the Spaniards either killed or brought to Tenochtitlán, presumably for sacrifice. They say, further, that there are twenty thousand Aztec warriors, half of them already sequestered in Cholula, ready to pounce on them. The Aztecs have even agreed to give the Cholultecas twenty of the Spaniards for local sacrifice. Díaz then tells the story of the "old Indian woman" who revealed the plot to Malintzin and invited her to save herself by sheltering with her. She could even marry one of the woman's sons. Malintzin slyly pumped her for additional information on the conspiracy and informed Cortés, who had the woman brought to him for confirmation of what she had told Malintzin.[40]

Contradicting Díaz's mention of the thousands of Aztec warriors who had hidden themselves in Cholula, Gómara writes that the Cholultecas would not allow the Aztecs to enter their city. For good reason: the Aztecs had a habit of commandeering any town that allowed their warriors to enter. (As noted, the Cholultecas had also refused to allow the thousands of Tlaxcalan warriors accompanying the conquistadors into Cholula.) The Cholultecas (says Gómara) intended either to capture the Spaniards while they slept or to lead them out of town and into a trap.[41]

The Leaders Confess

Cortés writes that at this juncture he sent for some of Cholula's leaders and imprisoned them when they arrived. Meanwhile, he told his men to attack the Indians who were gathering in the courtyard outside the Spaniards' quarters at the firing of a harquebus. As the "punishment" of Cholula was about to begin, according to Díaz and Gómara, Cortés confronted the Cholultecan leaders with the conspiracy and they confessed in detail—"without torture of any kind," adds Tapia.⁴²

In the Courtyard

But wait a minute. Who were these Indians gathered in the courtyard outside the Spaniards' quarters? Gómara says that when the Cholultecan chiefs learned of the intended departure of Cortés and his men on the following morning, they offered to supply them with servants and an armed escort. Cortés responded that he would settle for a few baggage slaves (*tamemes*) and some provisions. Next morning many men appeared bearing hammocks, to be used as capture nets, thinks Gómara.⁴³ They assembled in the courtyard, where Spaniards guarded the exits, and at the prearranged signal, the Spaniards attacked.⁴⁴ Tapia claims that the hammock-bearers had weapons; Aguilar calls them simply "the Indians who brought wood and water," and he says nothing about a plot.⁴⁵

Post Facto Justifications

Díaz recalls the prisons that they found in Cholula after the massacre and of freeing boys being fattened for sacrifice. A Franciscan investigation corroborated his account of the massacre, he writes.⁴⁶ He reiterates the great danger that the expedition was in. Its destruction, he writes, would have set back the conquest of New Spain. As a clinching argument, Díaz cites the opinion of Motolinía (Fray [Brother] Toribio de Benavente), the Franciscan historian of New Spain, who like Fray Bernardino de Sahagún learned Nahuatl and employed native informants. Motolinía regretted the massacre, writes Díaz, but thought that it accomplished something positive in demonstrating to the Indians that their idols were powerless, "evil and lying."⁴⁷

Popular English-language histories of the "conquest of Mexico" continue to explain the massacre of Cholula by reliance on this meta-narrative of a thwarted plot to kill and sacrifice the conquistadors. We need not revert to the nineteenth century and the literary embellishments of William H. Prescott for examples. Buddy Levy writes that Cortés's "uncharacteristic and perplexing" slaughter of thousands of Cholultecas was "[a]mazingly" driven by Malintzin's "chance encounter" with the nobleman's wife. Borrowing the language of the United States' attack on Iraq in 2003, he describes the massacre as "a punitive preemptive strike."⁴⁸ Peter O. Koch has an "army of porters," well over two thousand, showing up on the morning of the Spaniards' announced departure, although members of this army had "little in the way of weapons or shields to defend themselves." As for the thousands of Aztec warriors who had waited outside of Cholula to ambush the Spaniards, he follows Díaz in declaring that they "returned to Tenochtitlán with nothing to show for their effort."[49] According to Richard Lee Marks, Cortés wanted to avoid killing women and children, but some Cholultecas and their Aztec allies, who came out of hiding, fought back. The result: six to ten thousand Indian deaths. He adds that "[w]ith this lesson Cortés tried to pierce the veil of Moctezuma's indifference toward human life." With regard to Cortés's assertion that Cholula bounced back to life within a few days and that the (surviving) Cholultecas seemed unscarred, Marks explains that their ceremonies "exalted terror."[50]

Some Doubts

Information from diverse sources regarding various aspects of the massacre of Cholula throws this meta-narrative into confusion, if not doubt.

The Warning

Diego Muñoz Camargo was a mestizo, born ten years after the massacre, who married into the Tlaxcalan nobility. After making peace with the Spanish invaders (in his account), the Tlaxcalans sent envoys to Cholula, urging the Cholultecas to receive the Spaniards without belligerence and warning them against provoking the Spaniards into using their superior weapons or unleashing their "wild animals." The Cholultecas not only rejected this advice, but to illustrate their intransigence, they flayed the face of the Tlaxcalan ambassador, Patlahuatzin, and sent him home with his all but severed hands dangling from his wrists. He (somehow) reached Tlaxcala "in great agony," dying there and becoming a martyr. Thus, the Tlaxcalan army that joined Cortés in his march to Cholula was bent on obtaining revenge. When the Tlaxcalans arrived, the Cholultecas provoked them even further by calling them sodomites who had gotten "foreign savages" to defend themselves.[51] It would not be easy to reconcile this story with the Spanish accounts discussed above, which make no mention of a disfigured ambassador and state that the Tlaxcalans warned them *against* a visit to Cholula.

Bernardino de Sahagún's Aztec informants tell a different story. The Tlaxcalans were afraid of their enemies, the Cholultecas, they say, and they planted damaging rumors with Cortés about them, "so that he would destroy them."[52] The Tlaxcalans did fill conquistador ears with warnings and alarming reports, at least in the Spaniards' chronicles. But again, if they were trying to use the Spaniards to destroy the Cholultecas, why would they have warned them against going to Cholula?

Evidently Tlaxcala and Cholula were not the "ancient" enemies that William H. Prescott imagined them to be.[53] Cortés acknowledges that they had enjoyed a friendly relationship until shortly before the conquistadors' intervention.[54] Their enmity dated from something that had happened in the recent past. While they and the Cholultecas were still allies, the Tlaxcalans had been battling the Aztecs in one of their so-called Flower Wars. These formal battles fought by nobles, with an equal number on each side, were intended to obtain prestigious captives for sacrifice and to provide opportunities for individual valor. The Aztecs may have intended the Flower Wars to bleed Tlaxcala slowly of its strength, as well.[55] Anyway, in the midst of this recent battle, the Cholultecas had attacked the Tlaxcalan warriors from behind, catching them in a deadly vice between Cholultecas and Aztecs. As a result, the Tlaxcalans suffered a crushing defeat.[56] Tlaxcala's alliance with Cortés and the Spaniards may have represented an opportunity for revenge for this bitter blow and enormous breach of military decorum. But again, such a possibility cannot peacefully coexist with Spanish reports of Tlaxcalan warnings against their going to Cholula.

Cholula itself may have been divided in its political sympathies. Many foreigners had taken up residence there, worshipping at their own altars and shrines. Included was a small Tlaxcalan community. According to Torquemada, a seventeenth-century historian, three of Cholula's barrios were linked to the Aztecs; the other three may have been aligned with Tlaxcala.[57] Would the punishment inflicted by the Spaniards and their allies have respected any such boundaries? According to Bernal Díaz, "certain Caciques [leaders] and priests who belonged to other districts of the town" appeared after the massacre, asking forgiveness for the insult suffered by the Spaniards. They denied any involvement in the plot, a denial that Díaz found credible, for (he adds parenthetically) "it is a large city and they have parties and factions among themselves."[58]

Ross Hassig has advanced a Tlaxcala-centric interpretation of what happened in Cholula, arguing that in the fighting that preceded the Tlaxcala-Conquistador alliance the Tlaxcalans were not forced to make peace with the Spaniards. They could have defeated them but at great cost and at the risk of driving the (surviving) Spaniards into an alliance with the Aztecs against themselves. Instead, the Tlaxcalans formed a tentative affiliation with Cortés and his adventurers. Cholula was intended as a "litmus test" of the Spaniards' loyalty. This accords with the fact that the Tlaxcalans were willing to accompany the venture with thousands of their own warriors and that, following the massacre, thousands of Tlaxcalan warriors continued to accompany Cortés, sticking with the Spaniards through the horrible losses of the Noche Triste right up to the fall of Tenochtitlán.

The Tlaxcalans might also have seen a successful attack on Cholula as a chance to win back a traditional ally against the Aztecs.[59] But whether the massacre represents a test of Spanish loyalty to the Tlaxcalans or a strategic maneuver in the ongoing war between Tlaxcala and Tenochtitlán or both, the alleged Tlaxcalan warnings to avoid Cholula make sense only as reverse psychology or as part of a conquistador cover story. In any event, aside from Tlaxcalan interests, Cortés had a good reason of his own for going to Cholula, in that he needed to secure the route to (and from) Tenochtitlán. Cholula was not out of his way.[60]

The Food Supply

As noted above, some of the chroniclers of the massacre say that after some initial hospitality, the Cholultecas failed to provide them with food. They interpret this as an ominous message. Might there be another explanation? Imagine: hundreds of armed men have responded to Cholula's reluctant invitation to visit the city by taking up indefinite residence there and expecting to be fed. The harvest is under way, but it must produce enough of a surplus to feed a large and unproductive urban population. Food must be stored to meet the lean times that may follow, and much of the harvest is owed as tribute to Tenochtitlán. Alliance with the Aztecs bore a price.

In Aguilar's account, this food shortage drove the nobles and captains of the expedition to demand that Cortés either somehow obtain food for them or make war on Cholula. They importuned him with such urgency that he ordered the death of the men who brought them wood and water, although (says Aguilar) some thought that this was a bad decision. The slaughter ensued, and the expedition then headed for "Mexico," meaning Tenochtitlán. There is no mention in this account of the destruction that followed the initial massacre.[61] But if this is what inspired it, the Spaniards would understandably want to fabricate a better reason for what took place.

Horse Traps

Hassig questions the Spanish allegations about horse traps: how could people who had never before seen horses devise a European-style defense against the cavalry charge? Yet in the summer of 1521, the Aztecs were able to make some effective adaptations in their defensive war against the Spaniards and their allies—for example, by embedding sharpened stakes in the bottom of Lake Texcoco in the hope of sinking Spanish boats.[62] Were the Aztecs more innovative than the Cholultecas? Hassig also dismisses reports of stones piled on roofs and barricaded streets as being too obvious and probably having nothing to do with the Spaniards.[63]

The Invisible Aztec Warriors

Hassig denies that the Aztecs could have raised an army and gotten it to Cholula between the time Cortés announced his decision to go there and his arrival. Cholula was much closer to Tlaxcala than it was to Tenochtitlán. Hassig thinks that the peasants who made up the bulk of the Aztec forces would have been preoccupied with harvest activities. Warfare had a 120-day season for the Aztecs, and October was not part of that season.[64] On the other hand, the Tlaxcalans were quick to field an army of several thousand at this same time of year—a hundred thousand, if we are to believe Cortés.[65]

In any case, we have no eyewitness accounts of these thousands of enemy warriors. That was the presumed point of their being hidden. Reports of their nearby presence rely on information provided by the conquistadors' Indian allies. Certainly these hidden warriors did nothing to mitigate the attack on Cholula. They disappear like flies in a wind storm without any of the chroniclers having seen them.

The Porters

According to Tapia, on the day of the Spaniards' announced departure, many bearers (*tamemes*) came, as Cortés had requested, but they had weapons, and they were really warriors.[66] Others noticed only their hammocks, which Gómara assumed were for capturing Spaniards. He follows Cortés in asserting that besides the ill-fated porters (or warriors) in the courtyard, the Cholultecas "had occupied all the streets and placed all their people at the ready."[67] In what many may have mistaken for an eyewitness account, Bartolomé de las Casas, the great defender of indigenous Americans and Bishop of Chiapas, wrote that the Spaniards

> demanded of them [the Cholultecas] six thousand Indians, to carry the Luggage which they had with them.... It was a sad spectacle to behold this poor people preparing themselves to carry those burdent [sic]. They came naked, covering only their secret parts, and at their shoulders hung a little Net wherin they kept their food; and thus while they stooped under their

burdens, they lay open to all the cuts and blows of the Spanish weapons. Now being in this manner gathered together in a great and wide place, part of the Spaniards all in arms, stood at the doors to keep the rest out, while others with Swords and Lances killed the innocent Lambs, so that no one escaped.[68]

Las Casas goes on to describe how the Spaniards butchered those who were wounded and lay hidden among the slain when they revealed themselves by begging for mercy; how they burned at the stake all the Cholultecan nobles; and how they set fire to a temple, burning to death all those trapped inside. But Las Casas was not a witness to these events.

Later Testimony

In 1529, Cortés's conduct was the subject of an investigation, called a *Recidencia*. One of his former captains, Bernardino Vásquez de Tapia (not to be confused with Andrés de Tapia) testified that he did not know why Cortés had asked the Cholultecan chiefs to provide bearers or why he had assembled four or five thousand of them in the courtyard. It was also testified, probably by Vásquez de Tapia, that Cortés ordered them killed "without any reason." Following the massacre in the courtyard, Cortés and his men went into the city, breaking into the homes of nobles, setting fire to temples, and killing everyone they met, although the Spaniards had been well-treated and given adequate food (according to this testimony). Vásquez de Tapia thought that twenty thousand may have been killed or captured. In his testimony, there was no mention of Malintzin and her would-be benefactress.[69]

Why the testimony of Vasquez de Tapia would stand so at odds with the accounts of other eyewitnesses is unclear. A biographer describes him as "an old enemy" of Cortés, though without further elaboration.[70] Cortés himself was away in Spain at the time of this inquiry. His agents testified that at Cholula he had learned of a conspiracy to kill the Spaniards with the help of the Aztecs. Accordingly, he "executed justice" on "some" Indians to inspire fear and give them "the law."[71]

The massacre did inspire fear. Muñoz Camargo wrote that after Cholula "our armies" marched forth "causing terror wherever they went," as news of the Cholula massacre spread.[72] Sahagún's informants wrote that when news of the massacre reached Tenochtitlan, "[i]t was as if the earth quaked.... There was terror."[73] The Sahagún text appears to be alone in asserting that those slaughtered in the courtyard were Cholula's noblemen, rulers, captains, chiefs, and other prominent men of the city, as well as commoners "and everyone," gathered there on orders of the Spaniards.[74]

Foregrounding Malintzin

Malintzin (Malinche) may have played a much greater part in events that unfolded at Cholula than that of translator and elderly woman's confidant. Understanding such a possibility requires a bit of background. Early in the expedition, the conquistadors won battles in Tabasco, and the Tabascan chiefs made peace by giving them many presents. Among other valuables were twenty women. These included "one very excellent woman called Doña Marina."[75] Actually, the Spaniards gave her that name; her real name was Malintzin, and she was thought to be of noble birth. Cortés assigned her to one of his men, but she soon became so important to the success of the expedition—not just as an interpreter but for her diplomatic skills, equanimity, and good judgment—that Cortés appropriated her for himself. In fact, since she was always at his side, Cortés became known to the Indians as Malinche, meaning Malintzin's captain. The same name has stuck to her in her transformation from historical figure to feminine archetype.

Archaeologist Geoffrey McCafferty points out that she not only gave an early warning of a Cholultecan conspiracy against the Spaniards, as discussed above, but as interpreter of the questioning, she controlled the communications. Secondly, she was a noble of the Olmeca-Xicallanca people. As such, she had probably acquired negotiating skills and learned multiple languages. Because her mother remarried after her father died and then bore a son, Malintzin was eased out of the line of succession and into exile, where she was probably assigned to a temple in Potonchan as a priestess. Because she was not a member of a local household, she became expendable as a gift to the Spaniards.[76] Now, a few centuries earlier Cholula had been the highland capital of the Olmeca-Xicallancas. The elderly woman may have recognized Malintzin's nobility in offering her (in Díaz's account) sanctuary and marriage to her son. In putting the onus for the plot on Cholula's ruling faction, Malintzin may have been attempting to advance the fortunes of an Olmeca-Xicallancan faction, as represented by the chiefs and priests who surfaced after the massacre, against the dominant Toltec-Chichimeca descendants.

All this is quite speculative, but such speculation gains substance from a native drawing of the massacre (from *El Lienzo de Tlaxcala*) that shows Malintzin, without Cortés, seeming to direct the attack. The drawing was made a few decades after the massacre, but there is also this. To distinguish themselves from the Cholultecas, the Tlaxcalan warriors wore plaited-grass headdresses.[77] Was there another reason for this twisted-grass (*malinalli*) motif? "Malintzin" translates as "Lady Grass."[78] In this conjecture, the conquistadors become the tool of an Olmecan-Xicallancan restoration rather than a weapon of Tlaxcalan revanchism.

The Franciscan Investigation

Recall Bernal Díaz's claim that a Franciscan investigation corroborated his account of the Cholula massacre. The Franciscan Sahagún wrote that no such investigation took place.[79]

Out of the Ground

Not everything known about the Cholula massacre is based on textual or graphic material. Because of the city's pre–Hispanic cultural importance, Cholula has drawn archaeological interest for over a century. In the early 1970s, 671 skeletons were excavated from a small area on the property of the Cathedral of San Gabriel that occupies the site of the Pyramid of Quetzalcoatl. Many of these remains show decapitation and dismemberment. There are cut marks on many of the bones and some of the skulls seem to have bullet damage. The remains were "stacked like cordwood" in a mass burial, with bodies piled on top of one another on their backs, their heads to the east. Such burials were contrary to Indian practices. Researchers found few burial goods.

These remains could easily have been buried outside of the city but instead were buried within the central temple precinct. This together with the mode of burial, the cut marks on bones, and the other factors cited strongly suggest that the people interred in this small area were some of the victims of the Cholula massacre of 1519. Researchers suspect that there are thousands of additional bodies buried there. Thirty-eight percent (256/645) of the remains were of children under age seven. The remains also include pregnant women.[80] Still, in 1980 the mayor of Cholula characterized the Cholula massacre as a myth.

Archaeologists David A. Peterson and Z. D. Green have pondered the fact that so many of the victims were small children and so relatively few were juveniles. They speculate that young children would have been attracted to the location by the announced departure of the colorful strangers and their large animals, whereas juveniles would have been employed elsewhere in the city.[81] In any case, these findings appear to demolish both the notion that the Cholultecas had evacuated their women and children as well as the Prescott fantasy that all the participants in the massacre respected Cortés's ban on violence against women and children.[82] Why did the Spaniards need to slaughter women and small children if the aim of the massacre was to preempt an attack on themselves? The Toxcatl massacre of the following year was similarly indiscriminate. According to the *Annals of Tlatelolco*, after the Spaniards slaughtered the nobles who had gathered in a courtyard, they attacked palace workers—water carriers, corn grinders, sweepers, and even the people who fed the Spaniards' horses.[83]

A Nasty Habit

"It was always the determination in every country the Spaniards entered," declared Las Casas, "to perpetrate a cruel and outstanding *matanza* [massacre], so that these poor sheep should tremble."[84] What might he have had in mind? Spain's armies in Europe, though quite active in the Early Modern era and notorious for their arrogance, were not in the habit of cutting down large numbers of noncombatants except following a successful assault on a besieged city that had refused to surrender. Then all inside the walls would be killed or enslaved.[85] But we must distinguish between professional soldiers and the adventurers (including former soldiers) who flocked to the Americas. Still, in the New World, things were quite different. Averting our gaze, for now, from the horrors that Spaniards inflicted on the natives of Hispaniola, we might accompany some conquistadors to Cuba where, around 1509, they were expected at a large settlement called Caonao. The natives had prepared cassava bread and fish, then gathered by the thousands to behold these strange creatures from another world, especially their horses. At some point, a Spaniard ran amok, killing some of his hosts. Other Spaniards followed suit in a killing spree that continued until blood flowed in the street.[86] According to Las Casas, who *did* witness this massacre, the Spaniards were just testing their recently sharpened swords.[87] During the Vasco Nuñez de Balboa expedition across Panama in 1514, the Spaniards cleared their path of a resistant native force by cutting off arms, legs, and heads at a single sword stroke, "like butchers cutting up beef and mutton for market," slaughtering six hundred.[88] They had forty Indians who were "said to be transvestites," killed by their attack dogs.[89]

Las Casas saw indigenous men, women, children, and infants burned alive, hacked to death, drowned, and tortured to death in "novel ways," all done with impunity, without accountability, and sometimes acted out as sport.[90] His *Short Account* of such cruelties was addressed to the future Philip II. A lie, writes Anthony Pagden, would have been "unthinkable."[91]

In Chapter 3 we discussed what happened in Tenochtitlán when Pedro de Alvarado was left in charge. If there were no such gratuitous massacres as the Toxcatl slaughter under the command of Cortés, it was because every one of them had a purpose. He describes a dawn attack on a large town of Tlaxcala before the alliance that brought Spaniards and Tlaxcalan warriors to Cholula. The inhabitants "rushed out unarmed, and the women and children ran naked through the streets, and I began to do them some harm."[92] As their leaders preferred to become vassals of Charles V to seeing "their houses destroyed and their women and children killed," this tactic gained compliance.[93]

Following the Noche Triste, the Spaniards acted out their rage on the inhabitants of Calacoyan, butchering people without warning or provocation.[94] With the conquistadors' defeat, the city of Tepeaca had realigned itself with the Aztecs. Cortés decided that reform of Tepeaca required "a great and cruel punishment" that would also "strike some fear into the people of Culua [i.e. Tenochtitlán]."[95] Accordingly, Tepeaca—renamed Villa Segura de la Frontera—became a "slave town," serving as a base for hunting slaves and branding those captured in nearby towns.[96] Cortés also describes falling upon "an infinite number of people" in the devastated streets of Tenochtitlán, most of whom turn out (as one reads the text) to be starving and unarmed women and children.[97] The massacre at Cholula begins to look unexceptional.

An indigenous informant of the seventeenth century, Fernando de Alva Ixtlilxochitl, argues that Cortés had become annoyed at efforts of the Aztec ambassadors to discourage him from proceeding to Tenochtitlán and had the Cholultecas slaughtered to send a message to Moctezuma.[98] Or the message may have been intended for wider distribution. But killing noncombatants in order to intimidate others is usually considered an act of terrorism, is it not?

How New?

There is no way that we can know for certain that Aztec warriors and their Cholultecan allies were not plotting to kill the Spaniards at Cholula in 1519. Would Cortés have angrily confronted Moctezuma with authorizing such a plot if he had not believed that he had?[99] He might have. The conquistadors' leader was clearly capable of such a performance. All that we can do is consider the various accounts, as described above, together with the forensic evidence, also described above, and decide whether the story of a self-defensive attack represents a plausible explanation of the Cholula massacre. If this story is implausible, the attack may represent something else, perhaps something without pre-Columbian precedent in the New World.

In his seminal revision of the historiography of Indian-European relations, Francis Jennings points out that warring Indians generally spared noncombatants. As a rule, they tried to integrate the women and children of a defeated village into their own tribe.[100] There were exceptions. Archaeologists have discovered evidence of a fourteenth-century massacre of nearly five hundred Central Plains people at a South Dakota site known as Cow Creek.[101] In the deadly rivalry between Pawnees and the Sioux and Cheyenne that extended well into the nineteenth century, warriors sometimes took the scalps of women and children. Such scalps signified a warrior's daring entry into the heart of enemy territory. Massacre Canyon in Nebraska is named for a Sioux attack of 1873 that left twice as many dead women and children (49) as men (20).[102] But such exceptions to the rule are thought to have sprung from competition over dwindling resources, not an intent to instill fear in absent others.

Surely the greatest exception to the general rule that warring Indians spared noncombatants occurred in the pre–Hispanic history of the Aztecs themselves, along with other natives of Mesoamerica. For example, Aztec warriors punished Yancuitlán for killing Aztec merchants by slaughtering men, women, and children of all ages and burning the town.[103] According to the *Crónica Mexicana*, the Aztecs killed the elderly, women, children, and infants of Cuetlachtlán until that city's nobles ended resistance and agreed to pay tribute to Tenochtitlán.[104] Hassig describes degrees of conquest in which death and destruction could be precluded or stopped at any point by a town's surrendering to Aztec forces. Such surrender could be costly, however, in terms of obligations to provide tribute and sacrificial victims.

"Terrorism" has by now become a highly inflated term, carrying much more than a descriptive function. At minimum, though, it refers to an act that is intended to terrify others.[105] Aztec cruelty was notorious, and the Aztec empire was held together by intimidation, but the Aztecs do not appear to have slaughtered noncombatants merely to send a message to enemy others. Did American Indians *ever* engage in such acts? Even Jennings allows that the Iroquois practice of torture was "a terrorist device" addressed to neighboring tribes. But such Iroquois practices were, again, exceptional. The authors of "indiscriminate cruelty" intended to foment a reign of terror were far more often Europeans, such as English settlers in seventeenth-century Virginia.[106]

What about economic warfare? Jennings states that before the European invasion, American natives did not destroy their enemies' food supply or property.[107] This may be true, although the Aztecs rerouted substantial food supplies of their client states to Tenochtitlán as tribute. The Sioux and

Cheyenne attacked Pawnee women on their way to their corn fields, Pawnee buffalo hunters, and Pawnee storage pits.[108] But probably not in pre-Columbian times. As for Europeans, Caesar had no compunction about destroying all the crops of the "rebellious" Morini when they hid from the Romans in the woods. He set fire to their buildings, too.[109] The legendary Spanish hero and warlord, Ruy Díaz de Vivar—better known as the Cid—cut down the Valencians' crops, not once but year after year, so that the men of that city had to watch their wives and children die of hunger.[110] Behind the bluster of the epic poem is the fact that during the Reconquest, raiders would put off their raids until the summer or fall so as to destroy the enemy's crops before the harvest.[111] In the final stages of that centuries-long war, Castilian soldiers would so devastate the Moorish countryside that they had to transport their own food from distant sites.[112]

The siege warfare of the Middle Ages encouraged the selection of economic targets. Cortés began his siege of Tenochtitlán by cutting off the city's drinking water. The Christian army had done the same in besieging Ronda in 1485. All in all, writes Harold Driver, "the greed, cupidity, deceit, and utter disregard of Indian life on the part of most of the European conquerors surpassed anything of the kind that the Indian cultures had been able to produce on their own in their thousands of years of virtual independence from the Old World."[113]

Europeans made heavy propaganda use of Indian violations and alleged violations of European taboos. Such offenses as nakedness, sexual promiscuity, easy divorce, tolerance of homosexuality, and daily and communal bathing seemed to confirm the supposed superiority of whites and justify their oppression of Indians. Cortés claimed that the Indians were all "sodomites."[114] In the minds of Spaniards and other Europeans, violation of the one taboo was associated with others, especially with regard to sex.[115] Sixteen years after Queen Isabel authorized the enslavement of Indian cannibals, Cortés defended his enslavement of Indians at Tepeaca on the grounds that "they are all cannibals."[116] Some natives of the area did engage in the consumption of human flesh as an "aspect of sacrifice"—he who was offered as food for the god became the god, in Aztec theology[117]—but no one thought to condemn Europeans of that era for their occasional resort to "famine cannibalism."[118] Encountering something akin to long forgotten practices of their ancient ancestors—ancestral practices that every member of the Cortés expedition would have fervently denied—the conquistadors could summon only revulsion and opportunism.

As I have argued in Chapter 4, the Indians were, in some respects, a stand-in for Muslims, the generic enemies of Christian Spain. Fourteenth-century Castilian cultural productions had charged Muslims with cannibalism.[119] English colonizers had accused the Irish of cannibalism.[120] Mesoamerican Indians might have faced the same accusation regardless of their actual practices.

Aberrant practices ascribed to New World natives served as a *causa belli*. One of the justifications for war on Indians advanced by the philosopher Ginés de Sepúlveda in his famous debate with Las Casas at Valladolid in 1550 was that military action was needed to stop them from eating human flesh. Similarly, the sixteenth-century humanist and theologian Francisco de Vitoria thought that Spanish intervention was warranted when native laws or rulers sanctioned human sacrifice or consumption of the flesh of the victims of human sacrifice.[121] We might commend such concern for human rights, but no one urged foreign intervention to stop the *autos-de-fe* taking place in Spain.

Unlike Europeans, the Indians had not inherited Agamemnon's advice to Menelaus to spare none of the Trojans, not even the fetus in the womb.[122] None of their gods had urged an Indian version of Samuel to "smite Amalek" and "slay both man and woman, infant and suckling, ox and sheep, camel and ass."[123] More to the point, no one had even falsely accused America's natives of large-scale massacres and the wanton destruction of a major city such as Jerusalem, Constantinople, Cholula, or Tenochtitlán. "Civilization" became a club with which Europeans could annihilate "savages."[124]

Unchecked Aggression

Violence was endemic and ongoing in medieval Europe, and nearly everyone was affected by it. Besides random attacks on peasants and their property in connection with feuds between magnates, and besides the dangers of traveling outside one's own domain, there was the official violence of wars and the dramaturgy of public executions. This was matched by the micro-violence that occurred within the patriarchal family. Subordination of women and children was extended to servants, slaves, and eventually Indians, all of whom were "feminized" and infantilized. Absent strong central authority, people responded to hard times by trying to extract goods or other forms of satisfaction from those below them in the social order.[125]

Although Isabel sought to import the Renaissance, in multicultural Spain there was a counter-tendency to such openness: growing intolerance of difference—especially religious difference, as remarked in Chapter 2. As Cortés and company were entering Cholula, social tensions were coming to a head in the guilds of faraway Valencia. As was often the case, this build-up was heated by resentment of the privileges and actions of nobles and compounded by fear of a landing by Turks. Many Valencians viewed the Moriscos among them as an internal enemy with aristocratic patrons. In 1520 the guilds (*Germanías*) rebelled against the existing order, but they attacked mostly Moriscos, invading Muslim districts to offer the inhabitants a choice: baptism or death. The Revolt of the *Germanías*, so-called, continued into 1521.[126] If the Crown could not control events in a major Spanish city, its subjects in distant Mesoamerica were clearly on their own and could do as they pleased.

Civilized Warfare

By the time that Cortés and his followers had slaughtered thousands of men, women, and children at Cholula, Old World armies had found more sophisticated, less direct means of attacking noncombatants. The siege warfare that characterized military tactics in the Middle Ages lent itself to artillery assaults, and the artillery attacker need never even see the bodies of his victims. The impact of cannonballs weighing up to fifty kilograms had superseded the sword thrusts of conquistadors. By 1500 or so, the biggest guns could hurl their projectiles two thousand meters through the air and over (or into) fortified walls.[127] Artillery had become an elite unit in the final phases of the Reconquest, with an engineer in command and recruits drawn from France, Germany, Italy, and elsewhere. The Moorish town of Ronda was uniquely defended by its spectacular placement on a high ridge, but once Ferdinand's bombards and catapults got within firing range, it was only a matter of time before Ronda's commanders succumbed to the pounding of cannonballs and the cries of its terrified noncombatants. This took ten days.

Having seen the effects of Christian artillery on other towns, captains of Moclin, another Moorish site, evacuated women, children, and the elderly. Firing eight to ten cannonballs at a time, however, the Christian forces scored a direct hit on the Moors' store of gunpowder, ending that battle in one day. At Velez-Málaga, the only question was whether the Christians could drag their "doomsday machines" through the mud left by heavy rains. They could. Braudel writes that "[n]o fortified city, where the action had hitherto consisted of defending or surrendering the gates, resisted such point-blank bombardments."[128]

Residents of Málaga itself had to endure a three-month siege because King Ferdinand hoped to take that city intact. He confined his artillery to bombing its Gibralfaro fortress. After three months (in 1487), Málagans were reduced to eating cats, dogs, horses, and even palm fronds. With their surrender, the Christians entered the city to an unbearable stench—from human corpses, presumably. Ferdinand had the mosque converted to a church and four thousand survivors sold into slavery. Christians then moved in.[129]

Given the development of military technology that could deliver distant death, the Cholula massacre might appear to be an anachronism, except that at Cholula there was no need for a siege. The Spaniards were invited into the city. If instead of hacking thousands of people to death, they had peacefully exited the city, leaving behind a large cache of gunpowder with a short fuse and a volunteer to light it, we might see that far from being an anachronism, Cholula was a portent of things to come. The mediated killing of noncombatants by cannonballs was also a portent, a foretaste of such contemporary horrors as strategic bombing, the nuclear option, and "signature strikes" by drones. Cortés got a chance to wage siege warfare at Tenochtitlán, which his forces ultimately destroyed without benefit of a "doomsday machine," although their cannon played a minor role.

For the sake of fairness, we should consider the Cholula massacre in the best possible light, short of swallowing whole the story of a preemptive strike. Consider that the Spaniards had lost over forty-five of their comrades to arrows and illness at Tlaxcala.[130] The rest had barely survived the waves of Tlaxcalan attacks. By the time they got to Cholula, might they have been suffering post traumatic stress, some of them? Hearing the rumor of an Indian plot to capture them and stuff them into cooking pots, might they not have been inclined to strike the first blow? Once that blow was struck, a kind of frenzy may have taken hold, an intoxication that clouds the judgment and numbs the conscience. As to the force of that blow, better to kill too many than too few—or so the Spaniards' thinking might have run.

Others become dehumanized in a social order that considers their kind—read race, religion, ethnicity, sexual preference—"to be excluded from the moral order of being a human person."[131] While some Spaniards were battling New World natives, others—based in the court and academy of Castile—were asking whether Indians were even human, as noted above. A fair and final assessment of the culpability of Cortés and his followers for the death and destruction wrought on Cholula and its residents in the course of those bloody days of October 1519 would take the deliberations of the Hague Tribunal or the like. But it is far too late for that.

Cholula Today

Today's Cholula is a quiet workaday town with a Volkswagen plant but little to remind the visitor of the city's lost importance and former splendor.

In population and industry, it is grossly overshadowed by nearby Puebla, which was founded by officials in the early career of New Spain to give the many transients who were roaming the land and abusing Indians, a place to settle down.[132] What was known as the Great Pyramid appears to be an undistinguished natural feature in the form of a steep, brushy hill. Locals call it "*El Cerrito*" or, in full, "*El Cerrito de la Virgin de los Remedios*"—the Little Hill of the Virgin of Remedies, after the church on its summit. For the purchase of a ticket, you can make your way through the inner tunnel that is open to the public. Once you are inside, unless there are no other visitors pressing from behind, there is no turning back: the (approximately) 2.5' × 7' chamber confines the visitor to a one-way course. In a half-kilometer or so, you will emerge at a point about halfway up the hill where there are the remains of ancient foundations. It is difficult to see how these might correspond to the whole.

If you visit Cholula's Office of Culture and ask just where the massacre occurred, an official will point to a spot in the *zócolo*, the main plaza, bordering the San Gabriel convent, where self-absorbed young couples loll on the grass and children play.

10

Hog Heaven

Along with hundreds of would-be settlers and the fifty horses that accompanied Columbus on his second voyage to the Western Hemisphere were eight sows that he had obtained in the Canaries. Within a few years, there were so many pigs running wild in the hills of Hispaniola that Peter Martyr described their number as *"infinitos."*[1] Were they all descendants of Columbus's original octet? Bartolomé de las Casas thought so. But conquistadors brought pigs to the mushrooming Spanish settlements as a matter of official policy. Soon they flourished on other islands of the Caribbean. There were pigs on Cuba before there were cattle or sheep.[2]

In 1519 when the conquistadors landed on Cozumel, off the coast of Yucatan, some of them went hunting, as there were wild pigs. These were probably representatives of the pig-like peccary (genus *Tayassu*), not the easily-domesticated Old World pig (*Sus scofa*). I say "probably" because Spaniards of the Grijalva expedition had spent some time on Cozumel the previous year, though whether they had pigs with them, as well as salt pork, is unclear. In fact, they may have left some domestic pigs on Cozumel, as conquistadors did on other islands to provide future settlers with a source of food.[3] Members of the Cortés expedition may have been hunting domestic pigs gone wild. Bernal Díaz mentions buying pigs for the earlier, disastrous expedition that was captained by Francisco Hernández de Córdoba. He paid the equivalent of three dollars each for them.[4] Cortés bought Cuban pigs for his expedition, as well.[5]

Though seldom mentioned elsewhere in the chronicles, pigs figured in the conquests that became the basis for Castile's American empire. After the fall of Tenochtitlán, Cortés arranged a celebration and supplied it with recently-arrived wine from Spain and pigs from Cuba, whose governor bragged to Charles V that a hundred pigs there had become thirty thousand in just three years.[6] The ill-considered Honduran expedition included a herd of swine, at the outset. A herd of swine also accompanied the expedition to the Incan empire led by Francisco Pizarro, himself a former swineherd, some say.[7] In Panama, where demand for meat outpaced supplies, settlers were required to raise pigs in numbers proportionate to the number of Indians in their encomiendas, not to feed the Indians, surely, but to feed themselves and to stock ships bound for Peru.[8]

An Aztec drawing from the *Florentine Codex*, c. 1550 or later, depicts a landing of European settlers with horses, a dog, a ram, a cow, and pigs.[9] Except for the dog, which they used as a food source, the Mesoamerican natives had no domestic equivalent of any of these animals. We might skip ahead to 1619 to note the report of one of Virginia's English colonists that "an infinite number of Swine [had] broken out into the woods," where they were getting fat on tuckahoe, a root on which local Indians depended, as well as maize, nuts, and fruit.[10] One can imagine the desperation of people suddenly forced to compete with feral pigs for food.

The relationship of pigs and humans has a long history, but until Columbus's second voyage, this association did not extend to the Americas—or Australia, to which Europeans brought pigs even later. Domestic pigs are descendents of the wild boar, native to Europe, Asia, and North Africa. Going back perhaps nine thousand years, the earliest agriculturalists of the Middle East may have had pigs along with the first domesticated sheep and goats.

The wild boar is fierce: according to Tacitus, a Germanic tribe known as the Suiones wore an image of a boar instead of armor. Richard III, who briefly ruled England in the fifteenth century, used the same image, but he wore it on his shield.[11] Domestication could not have begun with such a dangerous animal except in infancy: piglets are easily tamed. Researchers think that the isolation of domestic from wild pigs may have followed a long period of semi-domestication when pigs were allowed to forage freely in nearby forests as a "harvestable meat source" for humans.[12] With inattentive human owners, they will continue to "run where they list and find their own Support in the Woods without any Care," as a Virginia planter complained in 1705.[13] People may need pigs, but pigs don't need people.

The pig is the ideal barnyard animal, in many respects. It will eat anything left over from humans and their dogs, and it will eat for hours, then sleep for hours, precluding the need for a nocturnal feeding. Oriented to food and not territory, pigs are easily led for short distances. They convert a fifth of what they eat into edible food for humans, about five times the rate of beef steers. Unlike other hoofed animals, the sow gives birth to a large litter and can do so twice a year. The poor family with a pig has its own food bank. The Romans saw pigs as pending feasts, and that view has not changed much.[14] What a pig might say of this relationship would depend on whether or not she knew why humans were giving her so much free food.

Pigs flourished in Mexico, some more than others. March 1950 Cerveza Monterrey calendar illustration, unknown artist (courtesy Bancroft Library, University of California, Berkeley).

Domesticated pigs require sedentary management. They are "notoriously unaccommodating" to efforts to drive them from place to place.[15] One wonders how far Cortés got with the pigs he tried to drive across the Yucatan peninsula. They disappeared as they were eaten, of course, but how many others melted into the morass of forest, rivers, and swamps that made his Honduran expedition such a debacle? How many pigs were left when Francisco Pizarro got to Cajamarca? We can assume that those that escaped human control multiplied rapidly and transformed the environment. Pigs destroy the undergrowth of forests by uprooting saplings and eating seeds and by digging out hollows for their beds and covering them with branches. They devastate lagoons, ponds, and floodplains with their wallowing. They eat amphibians, reptiles, mollusks, worms, small mammals, nesting birds, various kinds of plant life: there is probably nothing organic that they will not eat. Feral pigs cannot live in deserts or plains, or in areas with frigid winters, but they may otherwise be found wherever there are sufficient food resources. Considering all this, as well as the destructive habits of other domesticated animals that Europeans brought to the Americas and Australia, Alfred Crosby writes that if the colonists had arrived with modern technology but without their animals, they could not have had a greater impact on the environment.[16]

In Chapter 7 we observed the proliferation of horses on the pampas of South America. Spaniards encouraged the spread of other domestic animals—goats, sheep, cattle, and pigs—leaving pairs of them in remote places in a reversal of Noah's famous conservation program. Colonists were amazed by their resultant numbers. The unchecked exponential increase of hoofed animals over several generations when allowed to roam and forage freely in a new environment is now termed "ungulate eruption."[17] The fact that there's a word for it makes it no less destructive, of course.

Not only conquistadors but explorers, pirates, whalers, and other maritime itinerants assisted the proliferation of pigs by leaving a few on remote islands for the pleasure of future visitors. But it was ranchers, not pirates, who brought pigs to Santa Cruz Island off the coast of southern California in the 1850s. According to the National Park Service (NPS), which administers part of the island, feral descendants of these pigs had become a threat to rare native species in recent times. They had uprooted native plants, clearing the ground for the proliferation of fennel, which the NPS classes as an "invasive weed." They had also destroyed some sacred sites of the Chumash Indians who had formerly lived on the island. In addition, their piglets had attracted golden eagles, which were carrying off not only baby pigs but members of a dwarf fox species that lives nowhere else. In a controversial campaign, the NPS killed over five thousand of the porcine invaders in the mid-2000s. But as someone wondered, what could be more invasive and less indigenous than the hordes of human tourists that the NPS was trying to attract to Santa Cruz Island.[18] In the United States today, the descendants of escaped domesticates, together with those of the wild boars that were introduced in the nineteenth century for hunting, comprise a population of perhaps four million so-called "razorbacks."[19]

What about the pigs that stayed behind in Europe? Meat, around half of it pork, was available to the great peasant majority of northern Castile only sporadically and in minuscule portions. Meals consisted mostly of coarse bread. The villager who could "bring home the bacon" was a man or woman of some renown. A single pig might contribute a bit of bacon to a dozen or more peasant families.[20] The owners of such an animal would have valued it far too highly to allow it to get loose and return to a state of nature. For the family that was lucky enough to have one, a pig might be their most valuable possession, especially in Castile or the sun-baked scrubland of Extremadura, from which Cortés, Vasco Nuñez de Balboa, Pedro de Alvarado, the Pizarros, Hernando de Soto, and several other prominent conquistadors emigrated.

To the assertion that Extremadura produced only hogs and sheep might be added, "and adventurers."[21]

Considering how cheaply a family could maintain a pig, the fact that the meat of a peasant diet consisted of no more than the occasional bit of bacon (or mutton, with fish or salt fish on meatless days), it appears that there were not enough pigs to go around. Not after the overconsumption of pork and other kinds of meat that was typical of lords, merchants, and monks.[22] In America, on the other hand, there were soon too many pigs for European settlers to eat, although the New World's "lords and masters" stuffed themselves with meat without restraint, as Fernand Braudel writes.[23] Pork was "particularly abundant," so much so that settlers put a crimp in Castile's export of olive oil by substituting lard when cooking.[24] That bit of bacon on the Spanish peasant's dish was a symbol of social inequality with a geographic dimension.

Today the descendants of some Spanish pigs enjoy a short but pampered life. As piglets, those destined to become the substance of Spain's famous ham, *jamón ibérico*, are fattened on barley and maize for several weeks. They are then allowed to roam at will in pastures and oak groves, eating grass, herbs, acorns, and roots. As they near the end of this idyll, their diet may be restricted to olives or acorns. The drying and curing process that follows the slaughter can take up to forty-eight months.[25] The visitor to Madrid cannot fail to notice the crowds of hams that hang from the ceilings of numerous bars and restaurants.

Elsewhere, especially in the United States, the life of the domesticated pig has followed a different course. The typical American pig will spend its short life with perhaps five thousand other such animals, each of them confined to a box that may lack room for it to turn around or even stand up. Each will be fed an unvarying diet of taxpayer-subsidized corn (or soy). This is life in the kind of Concentrated Animal Feeding Operation (CAFO) that, at least for pigs, has all but replaced the family farm. Such an operation turns live animals into food the way a high volume assembly line produces manufactured goods. Or that is the intent. Anyone who has stumbled or driven into the vicinity of one of these corporate food factories will have known it by the stench. The horrors of these operations for the animals that represent their raw materials have been widely documented.[26]

11

Micro-Invaders

The unwelcome immigrants who turned the Antilles and much of Mesoamerica into colonial enterprises of Castile in the late fifteenth and early sixteenth centuries had considerable, even decisive, help from invisible organisms. Here we consider the first and most deadly of the "eruptive fevers" that more than decimated Caribbean and Mexican populations—namely, smallpox. Other invisible killers preceded it. Pathogens of Old World diseases, such as typhus and cholera, accompanied every passage from Castile to Hispaniola that followed Columbus's initial voyage of discovery. The seventeen ships of the second voyage, for example, brought a debilitating illness that devastated Spaniards as well as natives. In its disregard for hemispheric distinctions, this illness was almost unique, but the Spaniards were weakened by lack of food, and the natives, the Tainos, were only too vulnerable. But what was this illness? Was it typhus, as some suspect? Swine flu? The voyage had included eight sows, as noted in Chapter 10. Whatever it was, the Tainos constituted a virgin population in terms of pre-existing resistance to Old World diseases: they had none.

The settlers, animals, and plants that arrived with every subsequent fleet introduced new disease entities. Ships embarked for the Indies even as plague raged in Seville, their point of departure. Bartolomé de las Casas thought that because of illness, starvation, and massacres less than a third of the Tainos alive in 1494 remained so in 1496.[1] Weakened by overwork and lack of food, crowded into settlements to facilitate their exploitation by Spanish overseers, Hispaniola's remaining Tainos fell victim to a smallpox epidemic in 1518.

When introduced to a close-packed population without prior exposure to the disease, the virus will infect almost everyone and kill, on average, about 30 percent of those infected, though deaths may range up to 100 percent with the most virulent strain. The disease is communicated in air-borne droplets or dust that the victim inhales. During a two-week latency period, the virus multiplies in the lymph glands, then enters the blood stream to attack major organs. The victim experiences a sore throat, fever, and excruciating pain. He or she is infectious even before the appearance of the disfiguring pocks that give the disease its name. The pocks then become "virus factories" in which the virus reproduces. It stays alive in the scabs that form over them and in mucus from throat and mouth ulcerations. The victim remains contagious until the last scab drops off. The corpse of a victim is highly contagious, too.

Under ideal conditions, the smallpox virus can live for many months without a human host—for example, in blankets. Yet it required twenty-five years after Columbus set foot on Hispaniola to make an entry of its own. Explanation for the delay lies in the fact that the Atlantic crossing did not provide ideal conditions for the virus. Outside a human host, it cannot tolerate moisture, and sunlight kills it. Because the crossing took several weeks, an infected voyager would be dead or no longer infectious by the time his ship made landfall in the Antilles.[2] But what if such a voyager infected another in the course of the voyage? It appears that that did not happen before 1518.

Although few Spaniards were affected by the smallpox epidemic of 1518, the Tainos didn't stand a chance. From an original population of perhaps half a million, no more than a few thousand remained by 1530. Soon thereafter the Tainos became virtually extinct.[3]

In 1520 smallpox breached the Mesoamerican mainland. According to tradition, it arrived on the east coast of Yucatan in the infected body of a slave, Francisco Eguia, who participated in the expedition of Pánfilo de Narváez that was sent by the governor of Cuba to seize control of the conquest of Mexico from Cortés. The post-conquest informants of Fray Bernardino de Sahagún remarked that

> Large bumps spread on people; some were entirely covered. They spread everywhere, on the face, the head, the chest, etc. [The disease] brought a great desolation; a great many died of it. They could no longer walk about, but lay in their dwellings and sleeping places, no longer able to move or stir. They were unable to change position, to stretch out on their sides or face down, or raise their heads. And when they made a motion, they called out loudly.... Starvation reigned, and no one took care of others any longer.[4]

The informants called the disease "the great rash."[5]

Motolinía (aka Toribio de Benavente), a Franciscan monk who arrived in the country in 1524, thought that the virus had killed over half the people in most provinces. He attributed this alarming mortality rate to the fact that the Indians continued to bathe, even when infected. (Contemporary Spaniards considered bathing to be an unhealthy Moorish practice.) In any case, he wrote, "they died in heaps, like bedbugs." Many others died of starvation, as so many were afflicted that there was no one to feed them.[6] Writers who say that in its initial visit to the Valley of Mexico smallpox killed half the population rely mainly on Motolinía.[7]

Thus, as the conquistadors were beginning to lay siege to Tenochtitlán in 1521, smallpox had already carried off as much as a third of an urban population estimated at 150,000 to 200,000.[8] As one member of the Cortés expedition put it, "when the Christians were exhausted from the war [of the Noche Triste and the following months], God saw fit to send the Indians smallpox." Thus, the city had been struck by "a great pestilence," leaving the people, "especially women," without food, and—what with so many starving and diseased Indians—making it hard for the Spaniards to get about.[9] When they had destroyed the city and finally defeated the Aztecs, the conquistadors found that the desperate residents had dug up the roots of herbs and even eaten the bark of trees in their effort to stay alive. Lizards, swallows, corn straw, grass, leather, plaster, and even ground-up adobe bricks had also been consumed.[10] "[T]he land and the lake and the palisades were all full of dead bodies ... and even Cortés was ill from the stench."[11]

While estimates of the population of the Valley of Mexico in 1518 range up to twenty-five million, the native population had dropped to one million or so by 1605.[12] Indian vulnerability to smallpox and other Old World diseases was such that a German missionary could declare in 1699 that "the Indians die so easily that the bare look and smell of a Spaniard causes them to give up the ghost."[13] Subsequent smallpox outbreaks killed tens of thousands in Mexico City over the next 430 years.

A Skeptic

Despite a general understanding that the conquistadors and their native allies had considerable, many say crucial, pathogenic help in their destruction of the Aztec Empire, historian Francis J. Brooks has questioned the role of smallpox in what transpired. "Nothing in the historical record allows us to feel confident that one-third to one-half of the Aztec population died of smallpox in 1520," he writes in a 1993 journal article. "No such catastrophe actually occurred."[14] While subsequent researchers have found his article easy to ignore, we may find it instructive.

First of all, Brooks questions the more than 90 percent loss of population cited above on the grounds, established by physical anthropologists, that the agricultural capacity of the area could not have supported any twenty-five million people. In fact, recent researchers have drastically reduced their estimate of the population of the Valley of Mexico in 1518.[15] More troublesome is Brooks' assertion that there is no empirical basis for assuming that Indians of central Mexico were more vulnerable to smallpox than any other group whose members had not been exposed to it in their lifetime, though he concedes that they may have been. What about the observations of Cortés, Bernal Díaz, and Sahagún's informants? What about the conclusion of Motolinía? Brooks finds all of these sources suspect, selecting a single statement from the Sahagún text that serves his argument. But there *are* some grounds for thinking that the Indians of central Mexico, especially the Aztecs, could have been uncommonly vulnerable to the disease, could have transmitted it more easily than others, and could have suffered fatalities at an exceptional rate.

The disease is usually spread by face-to-face contact—for example, by a smallpox victim to a person who lingers at her bedside. Sleeping in the same small room as the victim or, worse, in the same bed also invites infection. Most natives of central Mexico ate and slept together in one-room structures. The idea of quarantining a sick person was a "completely alien notion."[16] Indians were culturally averse to it. Their impulse was to try to help the sick, and they suffered new infections as a result. In the eighteenth century, a native crowd "rescued" infected Indian children from isolation in a hospital.[17]

Brooks argues that smallpox is relatively slow to spread. It can infect everyone in a household, but then everyone is laid low by illness and cannot get around to cause additional infections. But smallpox can be transmitted by people who are infected but not yet ill. At any rate, support for the idea that the Indians of central Mexico suffered a severe epidemic of smallpox does not rely on the assumption that the disease spread quickly. According to Nahuatl sources, smallpox erupted in Tenochtitlán in late September or early October of 1520, a few months after the Noche Triste. It had arrived on the coast of Yucatan in April or early May.[18] In other words, it took about five months for a human chain of transmission to bring the virus to the capital.[19] The Cortés expedition needed a little more time than that to make the trip, but they intermittently stopped to fight, and they sojourned at various places along the way.

An epidemic will strike a community, not just individuals in a community, assaulting a web of relationships and disrupting the existing hierarchy. When members of multiple generations are sickened at the same time, nursing care may become impossible. The horrors of smallpox may cause some to panic and flee, spreading the disease to new parts.[20] Dehydration may lead to death for victims of a fever-causing viral infection like smallpox.[21] As we have seen, Cortés cut off Tenochtitlán's link to fresh water as a prelude to attacking the island-metropolis. When resistance finally collapsed, the Spaniards discovered that "there was no fresh water to be found, only saltwater."[22] In any event, because so many had succumbed to the disease, "there was no one who could give even a jar of water."[23] We have noted the infectiousness of the bodies of smallpox victims and the fact that corpses littered the land, lake, and palisades of the fallen city. James C. Riley, for one, concludes that, contrary to Brooks' assertion that smallpox "was incidental" to the outcome, the reports of Indian fatalities that were greater there than anywhere else that the disease has struck "would seem plausible."[24]

We will never know how many of the tens of thousands of natives who died at Tenochtitlán were victims of smallpox, as distinguished from starvation, neglect, sword thrusts, harquebus blasts, or some combination of such deadly blows. Examination of skeletons from numerous American sites suggests that, because their maize-based diets lacked nutritional diversity, the health of urbanized Indians in pre–Columbian Mesoamerica was less than optimal.[25] Survivors of smallpox would have had lifetime immunity, but enough residents of the Valley of Mexico avoided infection to permit a second smallpox epidemic in 1531–32.[26] This was followed by epidemics of measles, German measles, typhus, whooping cough, dysentery, mumps, meningitis, and, causing the highest death rate yet in the remaining population, an outbreak of what may have been pneumonic plague.[27] These epidemics came one after another, as "high points along a disastrous continuum,"[28] and they were not confined to the Valley of Mexico. For example, an outbreak of plague or typhus killed around 150,000 people of Tlaxcala in 1545.[29] The combined impact of Old World diseases was such that some think that the indigenous population of the Americas may have suffered a 90 percent loss.

Lacking a germ theory, many sixteenth-century Europeans saw America's epidemics and their own immunity to them as a matter of divine judgment. Gerónimoi de Mendieta, a Franciscan friar and associate of Motolinía, wrote that "God is telling us: 'You are hastening to exterminate this race. I shall help you to wipe them out more quickly.'"[30] Or as John Winthrop, governor of the Massachusetts colony, would write a century later, "For the natives, they are neere all dead of small Poxe, so as the Lord hathe cleared out title to what we possess."[31] Recall that unlike the English who only wanted the Indians out of the way, the Spaniards regarded them as no-cost workers and potential Christian converts. As the natives, too, saw divine intervention in diseases that sickened them and left Europeans untouched, the "situation was ripe for … mass conversions."[32]

Thus, deadly germs, invisible to the naked eye, bulk larger than guns and steel in many readings of the European invasion. In a book subtitled "A Medical History of the Conquest of America," P. M. Ashburn anthropomorphizes the epidemics as an army with smallpox as the captain of death, typhus his first lieutenant, and measles as his second, acting together to make "the conquest a walkover as compared to what it would have been without their aid."[33] J. M. Blaut goes so far as to say that absent Old World diseases, the Indians would have eventually prevailed in defense of their homelands, given their greater numbers and the diffusion of European military technology.[34] Brooks' contrary reading of the conquest of the Aztec Empire collides with what many of us regard as historical fact. It may also run afoul of one's unacknowledged investment in the implications of that fact. However cruel and rapacious the Europeans may have been, the genocide that they unleashed on the Americas was mostly inadvertent. It was their germs, we like to think, not superior weapons or their cruelty that enabled them to take over entire continents.[35]

Immunity's Growing Pains

In terms of immunity to the deadliest effects of smallpox, Europeans and Asians were only ahead of America's Indians by a few hundred years. But the Indians had missed any brush with the disease, prior to Columbus and company, by several millennia. Smallpox-like skin lesions have been found on Egyptian mummies dating from 1570 to 1085 BCE. These are among the earliest indicators of the disease.[36] Smallpox may have caused the plague of Athens of 430 BCE and several epidemics in republican Rome. The Antonine plague of 166 CE was probably a smallpox epidemic, brought to Rome by troops returning from Mesopotamia. Smallpox spread throughout the Empire over the next fifteen years, making for a significant drop in population and setting off a century of disorder and decline. Or was measles responsible, and another epidemic, that of 251–266 when five thousand Romans died daily, the work of smallpox? Until the sixteenth century, European and Arabic commentaries fail to distinguish the one disease from the other and sometimes confuse both with scarlet fever.[37]

Smallpox and measles arrived in China from the northwest in 37 CE, causing epidemics, political chaos, and in the fourth century, massive population loss. Buddhist missionaries brought smallpox to Japan in 552 CE. All of Honshu suffered an epidemic in 737 that killed a third of Japan's population.[38] Europeans and East Asians were as vulnerable to smallpox in these centuries as American Indians were at the time of Columbus's first voyage.

However, with the possible exception of China, these smallpox epidemics did not support foreign invaders. The viruses *were* the invaders. And in the case of China, human invaders from the northwest were eventually absorbed; they did not become members of the Han majority, but they became Chinese. In America only a scattering of individual Europeans was happy to join the Indians.

It takes a large and vulnerable population to sustain an epidemic. Otherwise, the virus will soon run out of victims. By about the beginning of the tenth century, contact between the most "civilized" parts of Eurasia had permitted an "epidemiological adjustment," meaning that (pending the outbreak of such new diseases as AIDS and Ebola) there were no longer any populous areas of the Old World that had had no experience with the kind of epidemic diseases that were spread by person-to-person contact. Like measles, chicken pox, whooping cough, and mumps, smallpox was on its way to becoming a disease of childhood. The immune system of anyone who survived an early bout of it would "remember" it, retaining antibodies or what a biologist defines as "microbe-specific lymphocyte clones" against a second infection. Contracting even a mild variety of smallpox would generally provide lifetime immunity. A more limited immunity is passed from a pregnant woman to her fetus. Smallpox was described as a disease of childhood in Japan as early as 1243. By the sixteenth century (until 1544 when a new, more lethal form of smallpox broke out in Italy), a mild strain of smallpox had become the European norm. Children survived it at a rate of 90–95 percent. In contrast, the Indians were like a European population made up entirely of newborns without any inherited defenses.[39]

Although humans have been its only host, smallpox is related to cowpox. As with other "diseases of civilization," the virus is thought to have been initially acquired through contact with domesticated animals. Actually, the nearest relatives of the deadliest strain of smallpox, *Variola major*, are camelpox and gerbilpox. Perhaps the virus that causes the three of these poxes had a common ancestor. In any case, the virus seems to have "jumped" to human members of an agrarian civilization, maybe in India.[40] Although this transfer of hosts took place thousands of years ago, the people who became the first settlers of the Americas, the Indians, had long since left the Old World for the New. Living in salutary isolation for thousands of years, they were not exposed to smallpox until much more recently, as described above. Except for the people of the Andes with their llamas, they had no large domestic animals.

All this is not to say that Eurasia had a monopoly on deadly microbes before Columbus's discovery. Europeans were quite susceptible to yellow fever, Chagas' disease, sleeping sickness, and other afflictions of the tropics of America and Africa against which tropic-dwellers are, to some extent, epidemiologically armored. Tropical ailments killed Spain's would-be colonizers by the hundreds in what would become Panama, Venezuela, and Colombia.[41]

A Viral Exchange?

Returning from his initial voyage to the Caribbean islands that he mistook for the outskirts of Japan in 1493, Columbus ran into high winds and stormy seas, and barely managed to find anchorage on the coast of Portugal. He was compelled to appear before King João II, who inspected his Indian captives with a suspicious eye. Had they been Africans, Columbus's voyage might have touched off an international incident, as Portugal was trying to maintain a monopoly on the resources of West Africa. But the Indians' straight hair and lighter skin persuaded João that they were not.[42]

Meanwhile, Martín Alonso Pinzón, the captain of the *Pinta* and Columbus's rival for the honors of great discovery, had arrived quite ill at a Castilian port where he soon died. In a biography of his famous father, Ferdinand Colon declared that Pinzón died of heartbreak over the refusal of Ferdinand and Isabel to grant him an audience,[43] but this was surely a misdiagnosis. Pinzón's physician, Ruy Diaz de Isla, wrote that Columbus "had relations and congress with the inhabitants of this island [Hispaniola] during his stay, … and since the disease is naturally contagious, it spread with ease, and soon appeared in the fleet itself."[44] Las Casas, who came to Hispaniola in 1502, reported that the Indians had long suffered from the same disease, whatever it was, but not as severely as Europeans.

In 1495 what seemed to be a new disease broke out among the mercenaries of Charles VIII of France who were battling Spanish troops for control of Naples. The disease caused sharp pain in joints, swelling, a rash, an excruciating headache, and tissue-destroying pustules. It was virulent in the extreme, causing loss of the eyes, the nose, reportedly even the hands and feet, and it often resulted in death. As it raced through Europe, it was called the French disease, the German disease, the Spanish disease, and the disease of Naples. Entering China in 1505, it was known as the ulcer of Canton. The English called it the great pox, to distinguish it from smallpox. In 1585 half the patients entering a London hospital had this pox. The appearance of this new disease was attributed to planetary conjunctions, to something one had eaten or drunk, and to contact with an infected person, probably through sex.[45]

Eventually, this disease came to be known as syphilis, and much later still it was discovered to be the work of a microorganism, a spirochete (spiral-shaped bacterium) named *Treponema pallidum*. This organism continues to find victims, but in the sixteenth century, syphilis was far more destructive than what it has become today,[46] and not just because of penicillin. The question is where did this new infection come from before it appeared in southern Europe and all those other places that gave it its geographic names? A tradition holds that it was an American export, brought to Europe by Castilians returning from Hispaniola with Columbus. Some of these adventurers had promptly joined the Italian campaign where, presumably, they passed syphilis on to Charles VIII's mercenaries through women with whom members of both armies had sex, whether voluntary or forced. The earliest link in this causal chain, according to this analysis, would have been a native of Hispaniola. As Gonzalo Fernández de Oviedo insisted in a letter to the Holy Roman Emperor Charles V (Charles I as King of Spain, not to be confused with Charles VIII of France), "Your majesty may rest assured that this disease came from the Indies." Oviedo claimed that the Tainos cured it with guaic wood ("Holy Wood"), and he arranged to share monopoly rights to this cure with German financiers, thus becoming the first European to offer for-profit medical treatment.[47] But if Fernández Oviedo was right about the origin of the disease, then the mixing of long-separate ecosystems known as the Columbian Exchange[48] was not quite as one-sided as it would otherwise appear.

Despite the outbreak of a syphilis epidemic in Europe at the time of first contacts by Europeans with natives of America, and despite the assertions of Alonso Pinzon's physician, Oviedo, and Las Casas' informants, some researchers deny that syphilis was an American export. For them the coincidence of epidemic and initial contact is just that, a coincidence. Or at least the relationship between epidemic and inter-hemispheric contact is a lot more complicated than appearances suggest. But here I must enter a caveat: opposing opinions and schools of thought on the "enigma of syphilis," as some have labeled it, present such a tangle that, without a lengthy and inappropriate discourse, I can do no more than sketch an overview.

Proponents of what is known as the unitarian theory point out that treponema spirochetes cause various diseases—venereal syphilis, endemic syphilis, yaws, pinta (a skin condition of the American tropics), and bejel (another kind of non-venereal syphilis). These spirochetes all look the same under the microscope. They can be distinguished only by the symptoms they produce. Moreover, the setting, whether tropical or temperate, seems to determine the kind of disease they cause. Even DNA testing cannot distinguish yaws from syphilis microbes.

The first of these treponemal diseases broke out in Africa in the remote past as yaws, which is transmitted by skin to skin contact with a bacteria-filled lesion, typically on the arm of a child at play with another child. Slave-trading is thought to have spread the disease into Egypt by perhaps 3000 BCE, and on into the Arabian Peninsula and Mesopotamia. Although it is usually confined to hot climates, some think that yaws entered Europe in the Middle Ages via returning crusaders. In a variant of this hypothesis, slaves transported yaws to Iberia.[49] Some exponents of the unitarian hypothesis think that the treponema spirochete that found expression in Europe as yaws may have adapted to improved living conditions in Europe that followed the Black Death by becoming venereal.[50] How could this happen? For one thing, returning crusaders brought not only germs from the east but soap, which Syrians and others of that region had been using for many centuries. As Europeans practiced better hygiene, the treponema bacteria were forced to adapt by moving to the moist body parts that favor endemic (or non-venereal) syphilis.[51] Other researchers point out that yaws is spread through skin contact of the kind that provided a source of warmth for people, especially children, on Europe's cold winter nights. In short, cuddling is thought to have transmitted yaws. But by the end of the fifteenth century, most Europeans had access to woolens, reducing the need for people to cling together for warmth. Here again the yaws spirochete faced a crisis. It had to discover another way of finding hosts or it would die out. It did find another way, infecting the mucus membranes of the sex organs, which enabled it to launch a disreputable new career.[52]

In a related argument, some maintain that venereal syphilis existed in Europe before Columbus, but it was confused with Hansen's disease—aka leprosy. The symptoms are similarly described, and "lepers" were treated with mercury. Mercury has no effect on leprosy, but it was used to mitigate syphilis symptoms until the early twentieth century. Cases of syphilis mounted as reports of leprosy waned. In other words, many syphilitics were misdiagnosed as lepers, and the perception of syphilis as a new disease represents an "error of reclassification."[53] Some have followed this line of argument further, pointing out that in 1490 the pope abolished Europe's leprosaria. Did the former inmates of those institutions touch off the syphilis epidemic?[54]

The treponema that cause syphilis and yaws may attack the bones in the later stages of such diseases, though this rarely happens with yaws. There are many findings of such pre-Columbian skeletal damage from the Western Hemisphere, but evidence of relevant bone lesions from the cemeteries of Eurasia is almost non-existent before Columbus. Nor do findings from leper cemeteries support the reclassification argument.[55] However, the findings from an archaeological dig at the site of a medieval Augustinian friary at Hull, England, in the 1990s seemed, initially, to resolve the "syphilis enigma" in favor of the unitarians. Pathological deformities in the leg and other bones of 60 percent of the 240 skeletons exhumed there were "consistent" with syphilis, and three had lesions that were held to be indicative of the disease. One of these three skeletons had supported a man who lived a century before Columbus's voyage, according to carbon dating. But 60 percent? Even with congenital syphilis, such a high rate of infections is otherwise unknown. And how would so many of the mendicants who served the poor of this port city have contracted syphilis? Perhaps the friars had some form of endemic syphilis, which can be spread "socially" in close-knit, impoverished communities through poor hygiene and the sharing of drinking utensils. The same diagnosis has been proposed with regard to a scattering of other suggestive findings in Europe.[56]

Proponents of the "Columbian" position that the bacterium originated in the Americas are careful to deny that treponematosis existed in the New World as a venereal form of syphilis. Skeletal evidence convinces them that yaws was present there before Columbus. Transmitted to Europe, the underlying spirochete responded to the new conditions it encountered by mutating to become "syphillitic,"[57] just as the mild strain of smallpox prevalent in Europe c. 1500 mutated in the American tropics to become *Variola major*. Researchers also cite the abrupt onset of the syphilis epidemic and its decreasing lethality as evidence that it was a new disease. The deadliest strain of a pathogen will soon run out of potential victims.[58]

Is the connection between Columbus's first voyage and the syphilis epidemic that began in 1495 a matter of cause or coincidence? Offering something for both sides, anthropologists T. D. Stewart and Alexander Spoehr have speculated that Europeans and Indians may have *traded* treponemal strains on early contact, with representatives of each of these long-separated populations acquiring an infection against which they lacked immunity.[59] This matter remains far from settled, but one is struck by the effort of partisans of all sides of this dispute to avoid reinforcement of the ugly stereotype that the Indians *had* syphilis and *gave* it to Europeans, making for a bit of revenge for what the Europeans did to them. The standard seems to be, no mitigation of the holocaust. Morally, this is appropriate. Syphilis has caused considerable suffering and death, but unlike the microbes that Westerners unleashed on the New World, *Trepomena pallidum* did not shape world history.

As for the smallpox virus, it survived well into recent times, killing an estimated 300 million people worldwide in the twentieth century. Its eradication arguably represents modern medicine's greatest triumph. Smallpox had taken perhaps a billion human lives over all by 1975 when it claimed its last victim, a toddler in Bangladesh whose immune system fought it off. Smallpox is now confined to a few viral samples in special labs.

12

Leftover Baggage: The Triumph of an Oxymoron

If you had read none of the foregoing and knew nothing else about Castile's sixteenth-century conquest of Mexico, you would probably have heard, at least, that a small band of Europeans led by one Hernán Cortés was able to conquer the Aztec Empire because the Aztecs mistook Cortés for Quetzalcoatl, the feathered serpent of native tradition (and oxymoron of the chapter's title), and thought that the Spaniards were returning gods. As a result, the Aztec ruler Moctezuma despaired of opposing these foreign invaders, welcomed them into his capital, and treated them as honored guests. As R. C. Padden has him saying (or thinking), "What good is resistance when the gods have declared against us."[1]

This mistaken-identity explanation of the conquest is reminiscent of the Russian mayor who, accused of flogging the corporal's widow, stammers, "I didn't flog her. She flogged herself!"[2] Of course, she didn't flog herself. But did the Aztecs flog themselves by mistaking the conquistadors for returning gods rather than human invaders? If they did not, then the widely accepted Quetzalcoatl story amounts to a piece of retrospective baggage in which native superstition mitigates European aggression. The Quetzalcoatl story is also supportive of the assumption, whether consciously held or not, that the natives of the Americas and, by implication, the people of other parts of the world that fell under the sway of Europe, were mentally inferior to whites. This makes it all the more important that we try to get the story right. In this chapter, I want to go over the various elements of the Quetzalcoatl story, then hold them to the light of recent scholarly analysis.

Omens

According to Bernardino de Sahagún's Book Twelve of the *General History of the Things of New Spain*, perhaps better known as the *Florentine Codex,* a series of omens and portents preceded the arrival of the Spaniards. Ten years prior to that event, a fiery light throwing off sparks and rising in the east invaded the nocturnal sky, reappearing every night for a year. A second omen took the form of a spontaneous fire that broke out in the temple of Huitzilopochtli, the Aztecs' tribal god. Then, under no more than a light rainfall, a drizzle really, another temple was struck by lightning. No one heard any thunder. Similarly uncanny events followed until there were eight. In the seventh, "water folk" brought a freakish ash-colored bird to Moctezuma. There was something like a mirror on its head in which he could make out a stellar constellation known as the Fire Drill. When the emperor looked again he saw a crowd of people coming, equipped for war and riding deer-like animals. The eighth omen consisted of the appearance of "thistle-people," each with two heads. They vanished once Moctezuma had seen them.[3]

Book Twelve also says that in approaching the first shipload of Spaniards to come to Aztec notice—surely Grijalva's expedition of 1518—Moctezuma's envoys believed that Topiltzin Quetzalcoatl had arrived. They exchanged gifts with the voyagers, elaborately-woven cloaks for the Spaniards' green and yellow beads.[4] But the strangers sailed off without touching land. The following year, 1-Reed in the Aztec calendar, was associated with the birth of Topiltzin Quetzalcoatl and feathered serpents, among other phenomena.[5] This was the year of Cortés's arrival.

Taken for Gods

Bernal Díaz says at several points in his *Historia* that the Indians they encountered called them "teules," which he took to mean gods or demons. For example, while the conquistadors were encamped in the sand dunes above the port they had named San Juan de Ulua, they were approached by gift-bearing representatives of Moctezuma who asked them to divide the gifts among the "teules."[6] Describing the resistance of Gulf Coast Indians to Spanish depredation that Cortés used as a pretext for the capture of Moctezuma, Díaz writes that formerly the Indians had taken them for "Teules" but now the natives were "like wild animals."[7] After the fall of Tenochtitlán, when the conquistadors had captured the emperor Cuauhtémoc ("Guatemoc" or "Guatimucín" in conquistador narratives), Sahagún's Book Twelve has people saying that he had surrendered to "the gods, the Spaniards."[8] Another post-conquest source has a representative of the defeated Aztecs address Cortés as "our lord the god."[9] Columbus had made a similar claim: the natives of the Indies thought that he and his crew came from heaven.[10]

The Mystified Ruler

With the second sighting of Spanish ships on the Yucatan coast, Moctezuma (whose name means "angry lord")[11] again decided that this must be Topiltzin Quetzalcoatl. He again sent envoys to the Gulf coast, instructing them to tell the legendary leader of the voyagers that he had arrived in Mexico, his home. Having hurried to the coast, the envoys paddled out to the strangers' ship, boarded it, and dressed the Spaniards' captain—that is, Cortés—in the mask, jewelry, and garments of a god. (It is hard to imagine Cortés holding still for such treatment, but perhaps he thought it was his due.) Book Twelve goes on to say that Cortés responded by putting the envoys in irons, terrifying them by firing a cannon, and challenging them to a fight to test their manliness. Meanwhile, awaiting the return of these messengers, Moctezuma neither slept nor ate. He felt tired and weak, and he was given to frequent sighs. When his messengers did return, Moctezuma had some captives killed for their blood, which was sprinkled on the messengers, as they had come from a dangerous place and looked on the faces of gods. They then described the Spaniards' cannon fire, their horses, their attack dogs, and their metal armor, bows, shields, and lances. Moctezuma became faint with fright.[12] He was so rattled that he imprisoned a messenger who had earlier reported the arrival of the Spaniards on the coast. When Moctezuma heard that he had disappeared from his cell, he said only that it was "a natural thing, for almost everyone is a magician."[13] (This from a late sixteenth-century source.)

Apparently trying to cover all bases, Moctezuma sent witches, elders, and warriors to meet the Spaniards and attend their needs, including their need, if any, to drink human blood like the Aztecs gods. Although the blood that his envoys sprinkled on their food nauseated the conquistadors, Moctezuma continued to take them for gods, according to Book Twelve. (The Aztecs regarded the Africans among them as "soiled gods.")[14] Still, Moctezuma thought to challenge them, sending wizards "to see what they ... were like," perhaps to enchant the Spaniards, cause them to break out in sores, make them sick or die, raise a violent wind against them, and somehow cause them to go away. But his wizards found that they had no power over them.[15]

As the Spaniards advanced, Moctezuma tried to dissuade them from coming to Tenochtitlán, sending envoys to try to buy them off or talk them out of it. But Cortés insisted that they must go there, that his sovereign required him to meet with the Aztec emperor. The Spaniards asked questions about Moctezuma: How old is he? What does he look like? According to Book Twelve, Moctezuma was anguished that the approaching gods wanted to see his face. He wanted to hide or run away, and everyone else in the capital was at a loss, shocked, frightened, and in tears. People sought to console their children in view of the coming catastrophe.[16] One set of wizards and priests that was sent to meet the strangers instead met a man who pretended to be drunk. He scolded them for pursuing a meaningless objective. Turn around, he said, and behold Tenochtitlán. They did and they saw temples, houses, and other buildings on fire. They recognized the man as young Tezcatlipoca, the most powerful Aztec deity. When the priests reported what they have seen to Moctezuma, he sat deathlike in despair. "What can be done...? Where can we go?" he asked.[17]

As the conquistadors neared the great center, one town after another submitted to them, either out of fear of experiencing the fate of Cholula or because Moctezuma had ordered non-resistance. This stands in striking contrast to the fierce reaction of other Indians, such as the Tlaxcalans and the Maya of Yucatan. Having been invaded, they knew how to respond to invaders.[18] Book Twelve has the Spaniards asking an Aztec envoy, where will Moctezuma hide? Will he fly away like a bird?[19] In Tenochtitlán people took to their houses to await the worst, and the roads were deserted.

The Spaniards entered Tenochtitlán in the Aztec year 1-Wind, a sign of Quetzalcoatl as a whirlwind but also a time of robbers who may put people to sleep and enter their homes to take their things.[20] Although Moctezuma, along with other nobles and his retinue, had peacefully met them on the edge of the city, Book Twelve has the Spaniards making a barbarian entrance to the ruler's palace, firing off their harquebuses and darkening the air with smoke.[21] Moctezuma then made the welcoming speech that has not only pumped life into the Quetzalcoatl story but has seemed to transform the conquest into an enormous concession. Here is the bulk of Cortés's account of what he said:

> For a long time we have known from the writings of our ancestors that neither I, nor any of those who dwell in this land, are natives of it, but foreigners who came from very distant parts; and likewise we know that a chieftain, of whom they were all vassals, brought our people to this region. And he returned to his native land and after many years came again, by which time all those who had remained were married to native women and had built villages and raised children. And when he wished to lead them away again they would not go nor even admit him as their chief; and so he departed. And we have always held that those who descended from him would come and conquer this land and take us as their vassals. So because of the place from which you claim to come, namely, from where the sun rises, and the things you tell us of the great lord or king who sent you here, we believe and are certain that he is our natural lord, especially as you say

that he has known of us for some time. So be assured that we shall obey you and hold you as our lord in place of that great sovereign of whom you speak; and in this there shall be no offense or betrayal whatsoever. And in all the land that lies in my domain, you may command as you will, for you shall be obeyed; and all that we own is for you to dispose of as you choose. Thus, as you are in your own country and your own house, rest now from the hardships of your journey and the battles which you have fought.[22]

Moctezuma then raised his shirt to show his guests that, like them, he was made of flesh and blood, and like them he was mortal. However, as Glen Carman points out, the Spaniards were under no illusions about Moctezuma's human status. In "dis-closing" himself before the fully clothed and armored Europeans, the Aztec ruler added to the abasement established by his speech.[23] Bernal Díaz's summary of Moctezuma's speech is consistent with Cortés's quote. The only other comprehensive version of his speech is that of Sahagún's Book Twelve. In view of the influence that this has had, it seems worth quoting in full:

> O our lord, be doubly welcomed on your arrival in this land; you have come to satisfy your curiosity about your altepetl [roughly, "community"] of Mexico, you have come to sit on your seat of authority, which I have kept a while for you, where I have been in charge for you, for your agents the rulers—[names of former Aztec rulers]—have gone, who for a very short time came to be in charge for you, to govern the altepetl of Mexico. It is after them that your poor vassal [myself] came. Will they come back to the place of their absence? If only one of them could see and behold what has now happened in my time, what I now see after our lords are gone! For I am not just dreaming, not just sleepwalking, not just seeing it in my sleep. I am not just dreaming that I have seen you, have looked upon your face. For a time I have been concerned, looking toward the mysterious place from which you have come, among clouds and mist. It is so that the rulers on departing said that you would come in order to acquaint yourself with your altepetl and sit upon your seat of authority. And now it has come true, you have come. Be doubly welcomed, enter the land, go to enjoy your palace; rest your body. May our lords be arrived in the land.[24]

A few weeks later, Moctezuma will repeat key elements of his welcoming speech in an address to his leading lords, telling them that Charles V is the ruler for whom they have been waiting and that Cortés is his captain in Mexico. He will ask them to give Cortés the obedience and tribute that they have been giving him. They will shed tears, but all will agree, together and separately, to comply. And Cortés will have their agreements notarized.[25] Meanwhile, between these speeches Moctezuma reluctantly agreed to become a prisoner of the Spaniards. Hugh Thomas has called his kidnapping "the critical [action] in the history of the expedition."[26]

Cortés had no sooner made the ruler of the Aztec Empire his captive than he attempted to force-feed him a diet of Christian doctrine. He scolded him for allowing the continuing ritual of human sacrifice. When he threatened to compel the replacement of Aztec idols with an image of the Virgin and a cross, Moctezuma conferred with his priests and sadly agreed to set aside some temple space for Christian icons.[27] But Cortés was not content with this. As mentioned in Chapter 4, he threw the Aztec idols down the steep temple steps and had the blood of countless sacrifices scrubbed from their "chapels." His Second Letter to Charles V has Moctezuma saying that as the Spaniards had more recently arrived from the Aztec homeland, they would better know what the Aztecs should believe.[28]

With Christian icons installed in their temples, Huitzilopochtli and Tezcatlipoca, the premier Aztec deities, told the Aztec priests that unless they killed the invaders their gods would abandon them. (This according to Bernal Díaz.) Moctezuma responded by ordering protection for the image of the Virgin.[29] He also asked Cortés to show mercy toward some of the conquistadors that Cortés had put in chains. In fact, to credit conquistador sources, the "angry lord" fell completely under the control of his captors. He became a "passive instrument," preferring to remain with them even when Cortés removed the irons he had briefly put on him and told him he was free to go. Beyond passivity, he seemed to fall in love with the Spaniards, especially Cortés, who administered alternate doses of charm and brutality.[30] One is reminded of the "learned helplessness" of the victim of Stockholm syndrome: Moctezuma as Patty Hearst.

Quetzalcoatl

Modern scholarship has cast considerable doubt on the idea that Moctezuma mistook Cortés and the Spaniards for representatives of Quetzalcoatl. Before getting to that, however, I want to consider an exception to this near-consensus of doubt. Davíd Carrasco, a leading authority on the Aztec world, has sought an understanding of the collapse of that world that honors the story of the return of Quetzacoatl. I lean heavily on his analysis in what follows.

The Aztecs were late-comers to the Valley of Mexico, arriving from the north as one of the many nomadic *chichimeca* tribes that cosmopolitans of the Valley regarded as barbaric. Such arrivistes might today be described as "hicks from the sticks," though one would not have whispered the Nahuatl equivalent of such an epithet in the presence of an Aztec warrior. To mitigate their sense of inferiority and "cultural illegitimacy," Aztec rulers arranged marriages with the offspring of aristocratic others who claimed descent from the people of Tollan, the Toltecs, who had dominated central Mexico until the end of the thirteenth century. The Aztecs saw the rule of Topiltzin Quetzalcoatl, the "man-god of Tollan," as a kind of golden age, a period of "enduring arrangements." In short, Aztec rulers looked to Toltec tradition for legitimation.[31] Their empire was less than a century old when the Spaniards arrived.

Here the story becomes confusing. Although Topiltzin (or Lord) Quetzalcoatl is regarded as a historical or quasi-historical figure, Quetzalcoatl was also a Mesoamerican god of ancient provenance. He was the wind god, associated with Venus as the morning and evening star. He was the god of merchants and of twins.[32] Some Europeans claimed him as St. Brendan, the Irish cleric (c. 484–577) who supposedly founded a New World paradise inhabited by monks.[33] In other post-conquest sources, he would become St. Thomas or, as racism gave the Mesoamerican deity a distinctive skin color, "the white hero of the break of day"[34] or a "white god." Ross Hassig thinks that the Quetzalcoatl story's explanation of Moctezuma's cave-in derives from a conflation of the god with the historical Toltec ruler,[35] and he may be right.

But if the quasi-historical Quetzalcoatl—Topiltzin Quetzalcoatl—was the founder, creator, and archetype of rulership, he also represented the abdication of authority. In one tradition, the Toltec ruler suffers what we might call an identity crisis, becoming appalled at his own reflection and losing his sense of authority, and Tollan falls. In a more dramatic reading, Tezcatlipoca, the supreme power of the Aztec pantheon, organizes a coup against Quetzalcoatl to defeat his efforts to abolish human sacrifice. He gets the Tollan ruler drunk, whereupon he has sex with his own sister. Waking in disgrace, Quetzalcoatl abandons Tollan, the city falls, and the demi-god retreats to the Gulf coast where in one account he immolates himself; in another he sails east on a raft, vowing to return.[36] There are other accounts, but every one of them has Quetzalcoatl struggling to gain power, then suffering a fall, usually at the hands of the brother or double that Tezcatlipoca represents. He must then leave Tollan and its people.[37] As a sacred model for Aztec rule, Topiltzin Quetzalcoatl was both legitimating and subversive. The Aztecs had a pre-invasion fear of devastation, says Carrasco, much of which can be charged to their identification with Tollan and Quetzalcoatl.[38]

But during the Aztec era, the cult of Quetzalcoatl was centered not at Tenochtitlán but Cholula, whose residents had failed to display recognition of any godlike qualities in Cortés and his companions either before or after they slaughtered thousands of them, as discussed in Chapter 9.[39] Quetzalcoatl was traditionally regarded as a lover of peace and compassion, virtues that the Aztecs didn't prize, and Quetzalcoatl did not occupy a prominent place in their pantheon. Carrasco argues, nonetheless, that the influence of Quetzalcoatl pervaded Aztec culture, as seen in rituals, coronation speeches, carvings, and the sacred history that was taught in Tenochtitlán's priesthood schools. In this he has the support of Enrique Florescano, the prolific Mexican historian, who writes that the Aztecs transformed Quetzalcoatl from a "pious, peaceful character" into a conquering warrior and legitimizer of Aztec rule. This linkage formed the content of a constant flow of propaganda.[40]

Carrasco maintains that one can see the influence of Quetzalcoatl "especially" in the dilemma of Moctezuma and his reaction to the appearance of the Spaniards.[41] Never mind that Moctezuma's reaction cannot be used to explain itself, Carrasco has a more intriguing argument to make regarding Quetzalcoatl. If I understand him correctly, this proceeds along both political-historical and cosmological tracks, corresponding to the quasi-historical Quetzalcoatl and the ancient Mesoamerican deity. To take the first of these, the Aztecs exalted the past. For example, half of the Templo Mayor is devoted to Tlaloc, a pre–Aztec god of the land and of rain. A shrine included a prominent sculpture of Chac Mool—a reclining figure with a bowl on his lap to receive human hearts. The image of this god is typically found at Toltec and Mayan sites.[42] In sum, the past was embedded in Tenochtitlán. And as with other pre-moderns and the novels of William Faulkner, the Aztecs saw the past as not really past: at least at the level of rulership, the authenticity of a practice or an act required its prior existence or performance, ideally by a supra-human being. The current event was prefigured in the past.[43]

In addition, the Aztecs were heirs of the tradition of the great capital city that had dominated life in the Valley of Mexico for over 1,500 years: Teotihuacán, Tollan, Cholollan, and now Tenochtitlán. Their challenge was to measure up to this great heritage. However, they hoped not only to measure up but to become the last of this line, the ultimate Tollan. The irony, writes Carrasco, is that if ancient traditions were needed to legitimize Aztec hegemony, the most exalted of these traditions included a king who had failed. Topiltzin Quetzalcoatl was a part of the "enduring arrangements" that affected current events.[44]

The analysis that runs along the second track is grounded in cosmology, according to which the Aztecs were living in the age of the "fifth sun." Quetzalcoatl was instrumental in starting the era of the "fifth sun" by spotting its appearance in the east. As Ecatl, the wind god, he blew on it and set it moving on its course across the sky. Four previous "suns" had ended in cosmic destruction. This kind of thinking did not originate with the Aztecs. The idea that the universe is everlasting but periodically destroyed goes back to ancient times. The flood of Genesis divides time into a before and after this universally destructive event, for example. The Chaldean doctrine of the "Great Year" spread throughout the ancient Greek and Roman world beginning in the third century BCE.[45] A pattern of cosmic destruction followed by new beginnings implies a cyclical view of time in which catastrophe becomes normal, meaningful, and never final. A single event recurs with each turning of the wheel of time. Such a view requires reference to the past in order to interpret the present: history is prophetic. For survivors of the conquest, Aztec history had to be transformed to accommodate that great event and the colonization that followed it.[46]

Although the Aztecs lived with a sense of impending doom, they were also so bold as to think that they might disrupt the cycle of cosmic destruction and rebirth, thus locking their imperium into an enduring order. But their gods, Huitzilopochtli and Tezcatlipoca, were insufficiently powerful to maintain the fifth sun by themselves. To ward off total destruction would require human help, Aztec help in the form of ongoing warfare. As the first Emperor Moctezuma put it, "if war is not going on the Mexica consider themselves idle."[47] How else but by making or threatening war could the Aztecs obtain the steady flow of captives whose lifeblood was vital to the dietary needs of the gods? Always depicted as famished, Cihuacoatl (Snake Woman) alone required a fresh captive every eight days.[48] If the age of the fifth sun were to persist (writes Carrasco), the over-compassionate, boundary-marking Quetzalcoatl would have to be marginalized in favor of Huitzilopochtli and Tezcatlipoca. Although the link to Quetzalcoatl conferred legitimacy, Quetzalcoatl also signified destruction, the end of an era. His return would animate the wheel of catastrophe and rebirth. The cycle that the Aztecs thought they had transcended would be re-engaged, and Aztec civilization would come to an end. For the Aztecs, the return of Quetzalcoatl was "inconceivable."[49]

But if, as Carrasco argues,[50] the arrival of the conquistadors turned Tenochtitlán into a stage on which a myth of royal destiny was performed, who took the role of Topiltzin Quetzalcoatl? Was he played by Cortés? What did Cortés have in common with this quasi-human Hamlet of a ruler except that he came from the east in a year, 1-Reed, associated with feathered serpents? Prior to the appearance of Cortés, Moctezuma had been a strong ruler, as harsh as any Aztec *tlatoani* (or Great Speaker, his actual title) was expected to be, if not more. In order to fulfill the destiny reserved for the greatest of Mesoamerican man-gods, it was *he* who had to become Quetzalcoatl, "the king who failed."[51] Although the primary sources identify Cortés as the leading actor in this drama, it was Moctezuma who played the most important part. From this standpoint, Cortés was merely the necessary barbarian and lever of destiny.

Considering the Sources

The Aztecs used pictographic symbols on bark or animal-hide "paper" for record-keeping, but none of their writings survived the conquest. Historic traditions were preserved by memorization and in song, hymn, and prayer. Native accounts of the conquest in Spanish, Nahuatl, or another indigenous language using Latin lettering were not written until a quarter century and more after the events described. Understandably, all such writings show signs of distortion and "legend formation."[52] One of these sources—namely, Book Twelve of the *Florentine Codex*—has served as primary inspiration for the Quetzalcoatl story, and I will have more to say about that below. This leaves conquistador accounts and the post-conquest writings of Spanish clerics like Diego Durán and Toribio de Benavente (aka Motolinía), Cortés's secretary and initial biographer Francisco López de Gómara, and the many that followed these secondary commentators. Of the conquistadors who mention Quetzalcoatl or the return of a godlike leader, Bernal Díaz's *Historia* provides an abbreviated version of what Cortés wrote in his Letters, adding nothing of importance to the subject. Other conquistador narratives have less relevance. This leaves the eyewitness account of Hernán Cortés.

I have reproduced, above, a translation of Moctezuma's welcoming speech and described the second version of this speech that he made to other Aztec nobles. Note that the Spanish original that Cortés included in his Second Letter to Charles V was itself the result of at least one translation. Malintzin, his native interpreter, may have been proficient in Spanish at the time of Moctezuma's speech. But if she was not, she would have had to translate the *tecpillahtolli* that Moctezuma would have used into Chontal Maya for Géronimo Aguilar, the former captive of Yucatan Indians, to translate into Spanish. *Tecpillahtolli* was the elevated rhetoric of diplomacy, full of indirect statements and even reversals of meaning; its use was de rigueur for the high-ranking noble who would make a courteous welcome to guests.[53] Besides the fact that the speech that Cortés put in Moctezuma's mouth may represent an interpretation at two removes, Cortés's Letter was written almost a year after the conquistadors entered Tenochtitlán, when Moctezuma was supposed to have made his speech. At most, the speech can be no more than a rough translation, drawn from memory. How far can we trust Cortés to have given his monarch even that? As I will point out below in discussing Moctezuma's apparent concession of sovereignty to the Spanish crown, Cortés had reason to distort the content of what was said.

Cortés's Letters to his king are replete with descriptions of his own duplicity, glaring inconsistencies, and what appear to be outright lies. These begin in his First Letter, which purports to express the general will of members of the unauthorized settlement that the expedition had planted at Vera Cruz. The settlers urge the king to grant them the right to depart from the exploratory probe into Mexico that was authorized by Governor Velázquez of Cuba in favor of the colonial project that they have already begun. Though surely written or dictated by Cortés, the Letter refers to him in the third person, describing how the settler community has prevailed on him to set aside his interest in trying to recoup his investment through trading and the like, and instead serve the interests of his sovereign, the king.[54] More egregious, Cortés has the settlers beg Charles V not to grant Velázquez the authority to explore and conquer areas of the Mexican mainland or, if he already has—and Cortés knew full well that he had—to revoke such a grant.[55] For Cortés to let the king know that he was aware of the grant would have meant acknowledging that he was acting in defiance of royal authority.

Would Cortés really lie to the king and Holy Roman Emperor? In narrating his departure from Tenochtitlán to confront the arrival of Pánfilo de Narváez on the coast, he says that he left five hundred men behind. Three witnesses later testified that there were no more than 120, many of them disabled or untrustworthy (though sufficiently able-bodied and reliable to help slaughter the Toxcatl dancers under the direction of Pedro de Alvarado). Presumably, Cortés did not want the king to think that he would fail to secure the gold and jewels that the conquistadors had amassed (see Chapter 6), 20 percent of which had become the property of Charles V.[56] Though writing only five months after the losses of the Noche Triste, with the fall of Tenochtitlán too far off to be reliably foreseen, Cortés claims in his Second Letter that Mexico has been "conquered and subdued." Speaking of that recent disaster, he puts Spanish losses at 150, with over two thousand Indian allies killed. Anthony Pagden calls the first of these numbers "obviously false." He thinks Spanish casualties amounted to something on the order of six to seven hundred.[57]

If Cortés could lie to the king, he could certainly lie to others, and he did, as when early in the expedition he grounded his ships, telling his men the whopper that they were no longer seaworthy, his object being to puncture the hope that any of them might have harbored of turning back to Cuba.[58] In his Second Letter, he writes that as they were battling the Tlaxcalans he rallied his followers by reminding them of all the Indians that had died at the hands of the conquistadors, "and none of us" at theirs.[59] The Tlaxcalans made peace with them shortly thereafter. But Díaz notes that over forty-five Spaniards had died of disease or were killed at Tlaxcala.[60] Even if this figure represents a doubling of the actual number, Cortés could not have told his men that they had suffered no casualties, as they could not have failed to know better. Again he is lying to his sovereign.

It follows that Cortés would have had no compunction about lying to the Indians. For example, when Aztec nobles meet the conquistadors to try to dissuade them from coming to Tenochtitlán, Cortés tells them that it is not in his power to call off their advance: Charles V has ordered him to "give an account" of their city, of which the king has long known. The Spaniards will do them no harm, he assures them. The Aztecs can ask them to leave at any time and they will comply. Besides, the Aztecs will greatly profit by their visit.[61] I count six lies in this anecdote. Once they have become guests of the Aztec ruler, Cortés supports Moctezuma's alleged belief that Charles V is the legendary Aztec leader whose return they have long expected. He exploits that illusion by telling Moctezuma that Charles V needs gold—Aztec gold— for certain unnamed projects.[62]

Cortés writes that shortly after arriving in Tenochtitlán he decided to take Moctezuma prisoner. He wanted to prevent him from changing his mind about serving Charles V, keep him from overreacting to the actions of the "obstinate" Spaniards, and gain better control over Aztec tributaries. The challenge was to take him captive "without causing a disturbance." Cortés says that he remembered a report he had received while in Cholula regarding some events in Nautla, a town on the Gulf north of Vera Cruz that the Spaniards had renamed Almería. It seems that Cuauhpopoca, Nautla's chief, had lured some Spaniards there by announcing that he wanted to become a vassal of Charles V. He then had two of them killed, following which a larger force of conquistadors and indigenous allies had marched on the town, burned it down, and killed many of its inhabitants. Six or seven Spaniards were killed in the fighting. A captive said that Moctezuma had ordered Cuauhpopoca to kill Spaniards. Cortés confronted Moctezuma with this allegation, demanded that he bring Cuauhpopoca to the capital for questioning, and told the emperor that he wanted him to stay in his (Cortés's) quarters until the matter was resolved.[63]

Moctezuma reluctantly complied, thus beginning his captivity. Cuauhpopoca was brought to Tenochtitlán and, in the course of being burned to death, confessed that Moctezuma had ordered the killing of the Spaniards. Cortés writes that he then had the emperor briefly put in irons. Moctezuma was "very pleased" when the Spaniards' captain had them taken off.[64] According to later testimony, the real reason that the Spaniards went to Nautla was to look for gold and to prevent Francisco de Garay, the governor of Jamaica, from settling on the coast. A fight broke out and some Spaniards were killed.[65] Cortés could not have failed to know all this. Thus, he seems to have lied to the king and Moctezuma both about what had happened in Nautla/Almería, and tortured a lie out of Cuauhpopoca about Moctezuma's culpability. But perhaps his account of taking Moctezuma prisoner at this time was also a lie, as we shall see.

I could go on, recounting various instances of Cortés's self-described duplicity[66] or discussing the possibility that Cortés fabricated the claim that he wrote an initial letter to his monarch—a letter that has never been found.[67] But I think I have sufficiently established the point that Cortés, though one of the two most influential primary sources of the Quetzalcoatl story, is an unreliable witness. His object was never to provide a historically accurate narrative of the conquest but to legitimize his claim that he represented the Spanish crown in the conquest of Mexico. Cortés controlled the discourse, and his version of key events in the conquest was reinforced by Sahagún's Book Twelve of the *Florentine Codex*, in which the returning "natural lord" of the Aztecs becomes identified as Quetzalcoatl.[68] Every succeeding commentator who has accepted the idea that Moctezuma mistook the Spanish invaders for representatives of Topiltzin Quetzalcoatl has, directly or not, relied on these two sources. Cortés's control of the message may not have done as much to facilitate the destruction of the Aztec Empire as the conquistadors' swords, horses, Old World viruses, and other elements of their deadly baggage, but it legitimized the conquest in the eyes of generations of intrigued Westerners.

Sahagún and his young indigenous contributors began Book Twelve in 1547, completed a first draft of the Book around 1555, and arrived at a text that was close to the present version only in 1569. The contributors were Christian converts, bilingual and quick to learn. No doubt they would have identified with the Franciscan friars who were their mentors and represented the winning side in events of 1519–1521. The Aztec informants that they interviewed would have been young warriors in 1521. As such they would not have had access to Moctezuma or his inner circle. The questions these informants were asked followed a format devised by Sahagún, whose rewriting shows up in the occasional reference to native temples as "houses of demons" and the like.[69] For Susan Gillespie, Book Twelve and the other Codices that were compiled by Spanish clerics and indigenous scholars during the post-conquest decades represent a dialogue that became "frozen in time," fusing two traditions.[70] James Lockhart regards the Cortés and Moctezuma of Book Twelve as symbolic figures, freighted with meanings and associations that they acquired only after the events described.[71]

Note that the young contributors on whom Sahagún relied were not randomly selected. All or nearly all were natives of Tlatelolco where Sahagún had his academy. To explain the significance of this I have to point out that Tenochtitlán was not a single political entity, though its inhabitants were all Mexica. The island traditionally consisted of sister cities—Tenochtitlán, home of the dominant Tenocha, and Tlatelolco, site of the island-city's biggest market and home of the Tlatelolca. The latter had maintained independence until 1473 when the Tenocha crushed their challenge to Tenochan dominance and made Tlatelolco part of Tenochtitlán. The point is that a residue of Tlatelochan resentment and preoccupation colors the content of Book Twelve. Indications of this take the form of a focus on events that occurred on the island, the depiction of Tlatelolca as heroes and Tenocha as cowards, and—consistent with this—the characterization of Moctezuma as the weak and vacillating leader described above. He weeps and mourns when he learns of the Spaniards' prowess; the Tenocha flee in terror of the conquistadors' boats; and it is Tlatelolcan warriors that capture the Spaniards' banner.[72] All of these descriptions may be accurate, but Tlatelolcan bias makes them suspect.

Tlatelolcan animus toward the Tenocha becomes more prominent in the "Annals of Tlatelolco," that date from about 1545. There the Tenocha fight among themselves as the conquistadors approach Tenochtitlán. They disappear during the fighting, leaving the Tlatelolca to battle the Spaniards alone and to maintain the canals that serve the city as barriers. Tenocha warriors even disguise themselves to avoid recognition, inviting the scorn of Tenocha women. As the siege goes on, allies advise the Tlatelolca to let the Tenocha die alone. The Tlatelolca respond that they should have done that weeks earlier.[73] The Tlatelolca had a heavy ax to grind.

Book Twelve's description of the conquistadors' reception in Tlaxcala may serve as a marker of just how distorted that source's account of Moctezuma's relationship with Cortés and company may be. Recall that the eyewitness accounts depict fierce, bloody, and extended resistance to the Spaniards' intrusion. In Book Twelve, the Tlaxcalans—whom the Tlatelolca had reason to hate even more than they did the Tenocha—learn of the conquistadors' defeat of the Otomis and become "limp with fear." They quickly decide to submit to the invaders without resistance, bringing them food, honoring them, attending them, and giving them their daughters.[74] In sum, we can no more rely on Book Twelve than we can on Cortés's Letters, yet these are the principal sources of the Quetzalcoatl story.

Reconsidering the Omens and Portents

Only Book Twelve of the *Florentine Codex* describe these phenomena. They do not appear in other post-conquest sources. They do, however, show up in some of the Greek and Latin texts that were available to Sahagún's students.[75] James Lockhart finds significance in the fact that the omens number eight. This corresponds to the canonical number of assemblages in the Nahuatl world: things come in units of eight.[76] Some scholars attribute the omens and portents to the Franciscans' sense of approaching apocalypse.[77] But perhaps they are better understood as representing the attempt of a conquered people to explain their downfall, the equivalent of saying, "We should have seen it coming."[78]

Taken for Gods?

Did the Indians that they encountered really think that the Spaniards were gods? Recall that Bernal Díaz thought that they were addressing them as "teules," which he took to mean gods or demons. It seems that what he was really hearing was the Nahuatl word "*teotl*," but Díaz's definition may have been near if not on the right track. Clendinnen writes that *teotl* refers to something that is surpassingly good or evil, or as we might say (using her example) "weird."[79] So maybe the natives were calling them "weirdos." But *teotl* seems to have several meanings, including "lord" in the sense of a feudal lord.[80] The *teotl* could also be an ancestor or ruler, writes Lockhart. In any case, in Book Twelve the Spaniards are not depicted as vastly different from other enemies of the Aztecs. They are seen as another *alteptl* group like the Otomi or the Tlaxcalans, outsiders defined by the place from which they come, except that the Aztecs lacked a name for that place, at least at first. The Tlaxcalans had such a name and soon learned to add "Castile!" to their war cries.[81] Whatever the invaders' origins, the Aztecs assumed that they had the same objectives as themselves—conquest and the extraction of tribute. In this they weren't badly mistaken. In short, suggests Lockhart, the Aztecs saw the invaders as part of the world of outsiders that included traditional enemies and not as sui generis visitors from a radically different cosmos.[82]

If Moctezuma's emissaries dressed Cortés as a god, Cortés never mentioned it. Nor did the sacred accessories in which they supposedly draped him—the quetzal-feather head-fan, the plaited green-stone neckband, etc., that Book Twelve so lovingly lists[83]—ever appear on an inventory of items sent to Spain, as was required. Grijalva did receive gifts, including mosaic masks, but there is no basis for thinking that these represented the vestments of Quetzalcoatl.[84]

Speaking of Grijalva, we might note that Moctezuma was not guided by a prophetic year when he mistook that voyager from the east for Quetzalcoatl.[85]

Book Twelve has Moctezuma treating the Spaniards as gods yet sending wizards to try to sicken them and make them go away. Does this signify the bizarre pairing of an Aztec version of Pascal's wager and national defense? Carrasco sees it as evidence of Moctezuma's resilience: unconvinced that Cortés is Quetzalcoatl, he seeks more information.[86] This reading makes the spells of wizards the work of an experiment. But perhaps Book Twelve consists of two parts, as Lockhart believes, with the first of these, which takes the reader up to the Toxcatl massacre, reflecting "a late reconstruction" based on fragments of old oral accounts combined with "legend formation" and "embroidery"?[87] If it does, the idea that the arrival of the conquistadors was announced by omens and portents and that the Spaniards were taken for gods and Cortés for an ambassador of Quetzalcoatl sheds plausibility.

Contrariwise, the usually down-to-earth Ross Hassig thinks that the Aztecs might indeed have seen Cortés as Quetzalcoatl and the Spaniards as gods, not as a fact but as a "disturbing possibility." How else explain these powerful strangers with their formidable technology and ferocious animals?[88] Bronislaw Malinowski, the eminent anthropologist, believed that people deploy magical beliefs to explain an "unbridgeable gap" in their knowledge or ability to exercise control of something. Such beliefs can serve as an acceptable alternative to the anxiety and frustration of feeling powerless.[89] Is that what happened? Did Moctezuma mistake Cortés for a returning god as a cognitive stopgap? The question welcomes only conjecture.

I have described above how conquistador accounts have Moctezuma following his controversial and consequential welcoming speech by raising his shirt to show his outlandish guests that, like them, he is made of flesh and blood. J. H. Elliott has pointed to the biblical parallel of which Cortés would probably have known but Moctezuma could not have known—Jesus telling his disciples, "a spirit hath not flesh and blood as ye see me have."[90] Of greater relevance to the question of whether Moctezuma took the conquistadors for gods is Bernal Díaz's description of what the emperor said before he raised his shirt, which was that, contrary to the exaggerated reports that had come to him from others, he knew that the conquistadors were not "angry *Teules*" but made of flesh and blood.[91] Perhaps even more relevant is that, again according to Díaz, Cortés had sweetened his effort to make peace with the Tlaxcalans some weeks earlier by assuring them that the conquistadors were not "*Teules*" but Christians and "men of flesh and blood like themselves."[92] To think that Moctezuma would use the same words to offer the same assurance tortures credulity, and once more we are left in the dark as to what he really thought.

Moctezuma Reconsidered

We have seen the post-conquest portrayal of Moctezuma as a ruler whose reading of certain omens and portents leave him panic-stricken and unmanned, and how he can hardly wait to turn over his empire to people that he takes for representatives of a legendary ancestor. This characterization grafts smoothly onto the figure of the compliant and easily controlled ruler of Cortés's Second Letter. The sum of these portrayals is the widely accepted explanation of the improbable outcome of the Cortés expedition—overthrow of a Mesoamerican empire by a small band of Europeans. As argued above, however, the sources of this image and its corollary are questionable. The real Moctezuma remains an enigma. Cortés assumed that he was an absolute ruler, but we don't really even know the extent of the authority of the official—here Moctezuma—whose title was the Great Speaker.[93]

Moctezuma may (or may not) have become rattled by the approach of the Spaniards, but there were military and political reasons for him to allow them to enter Tenochtitlán. According to Bernal Díaz, word came to the conquistadors as they neared the great capital that Moctezuma's advisers had pointed out that if he refused them entry, the Spaniards and their indigenous allies would battle the Aztecs in their tributary towns, presumably meaning the towns around Lake Texcoco.[94] Defeat there or even a prolonged battle could have drawn allies if not members of the fragile Triple Alliance to the side of the Spaniards. Moctezuma's nonresistance may represent a realistic appraisal that the Aztecs were outmatched.[95] Perhaps the question of why Moctezuma let the Spaniards into Tenochtitlán should be turned around to ask why the conquistadors entered the trap of which their allies had fervently warned them, a trap in which they came close to being annihilated. Hassig suggests that, on the basis of his string of military successes up to that point and his prior knowledge of the cities and the towns of Europe and Mesoamerica, Cortés underestimated the size and density of the population of Tenochtitlán.[96] Militarily, he didn't know what he was getting into.

According to a conjecture of Francis Brooks, the conquistadors may not have taken Moctezuma prisoner until several months after their arrival in Tenochtitlán. Certainly this challenges conquistador accounts and ignores the fact that immediate seizure of the ruler was a standard practice of the conquistadors in the Caribbean and Panama, not to mention its future application in Peru. But, argues Brooks, the peremptory seizure of Moctezuma in his seat of power makes sense only if he did, in fact, succumb to a sense of fate—just as the Quetzalcoatl story specifies. Such an explanation would support the Spaniards' assumption of natural superiority, but for Moctezuma to submit so passively would have made him as useless to the conquistadors as the puppet ruler that he did in fact become following the Toxcatl massacre. Assuming that the Spaniards placed Moctezuma under house arrest when Cortés said they did, it caused nary a wrinkle in the city's social fabric. The round of ceremonies continued and life went on as usual, by Cortés's own admission. According to Andrés de Tapia, the people didn't even know that Moctezuma had been arrested. Assuming the veracity of conquistador accounts, why would they? Moctezuma was free to come and go and to confer with his lords and priests: his restraint was "almost invisible."[97]

Book Twelve tells a very different story, in which the arrest of Moctezuma prompted the rulers of allied cities and Tenocha lords to go into hiding, abandoning Moctezuma in anger. A general panic ensued, as if "everyone had been taking mushrooms." The Spaniards' needs were met, but outside their quarters, fear was the order of the day, "as though a wild beast were loose."[98] In this telling, Moctezuma *does* become a useless puppet of the conquistadors, beginning just after their arrival in Tenochtitlán.

Brooks thinks that the Spaniards eventually made Moctezuma their captive but not until some five months after Cortés said they did. In this he relies on Diego Duran's estimate that Moctezuma was confined by the conquistadors for eighty days before he died. His death came at the end of June or early July 1520. The later arrest would have coincided with the arrival of Narváez on the Gulf coast and his reported effort to stir up a native rebellion against Cortés, while promising freedom for Moctezuma. For this scenario to work, Narváez would need to have arrived in April, and he probably did.[99] To understand why Cortés might have faked an earlier date of Moctezuma's arrest, we must consider the political implications of the welcoming speech that Cortés said he made, which we will do below. Ultimately, the focus of the post-conquest sources on Moctezuma and his collapse in the face of Cortés's blandishments and bluster may simply represent scapegoating by survivors of the collapse of the Aztec world, the all-too-human tendency to blame the leader for a disaster.[100]

Moctezuma Speaks—Or Does He?

In welcoming the conquistadors to his great city, did Moctezuma really say what Cortés says he did? Here is an overview of the speech that I have presented almost in full above:

- We Aztecs know from our ancestors that we come from distant parts. A great chief led us here, then went back to his own land.

- After many years that chief returned to lead us away.
- But we were settled here by then, having acquired families and political dominance. We refused to follow him.
- He left, but we have long expected his descendants to come here from the east and conquer us.
- You and your great chief (Charles V) are they. This, then, is your land. What is ours is yours.

Worth noting is the implication that the Aztecs' ties to the land are based on marriage. Thus, their in-laws would seem to be the "natural" heirs of what Moctezuma seems to be giving away. But this is an aside. More important is how Moctezuma's speech served Cortés's purposes. Remember that his Second Letter was written after the disastrous Noche Triste but before the conquest of the Aztec Empire. Cortés can minimize the defeat of a few months earlier if he can assure Charles V that, legally speaking, he has already won an empire. Prevailing legal norms limited the acquisition of new, inhabited territory to that won in a just war *or that voluntarily given*. According to Cortés's Second Letter, Moctezuma has donated an entire empire to the Spanish crown. Moreover, since Moctezuma's speech has made the Aztecs vassals of Charles V, they are now in rebellion and subject to legitimate conquest. This follows from a legal doctrine known as *dominium jurisdictionis* and the assumption that Moctezuma is the equivalent of a defeated Moorish ruler.[101] Whether Moctezuma said what Cortés said he did or his speech was an act of "historiographical ventriloquism,"[102] the words ascribed to him could not have better served Cortés's aim of winning Charles V's support for his otherwise unauthorized enterprise. The conquistadors repeated this tactic in the 1570s to delegitimize self-rule by the Inca.[103] Dialog and communication were deployed to sanitize Castile's conquests in America.

At this distance we cannot know what Moctezuma really said or, following from that, judge the accuracy of the translation of what he said. Historians of the Renaissance commonly invented the speeches that they put on others' lips, writing what they thought would have been appropriate to the situation.[104] The conquistadors may have mistaken the ruler's "obsequious politeness" for a statement of submission.[105] Linguistic analysis of Moctezuma's speeches reveals the syntax of the *Siete Partidas*, Castile's legal charter and much of Cortés's focus as a young law student in Salamanca. The speeches also resonate with biblical motifs.[106] The return of the hero is a universal theme, from Jason to Rip van Winkle.[107] Besides, in the chivalric novels such as *Amadis of Gaul* that many of the conquistadors read with the enthusiasm of a Don Quixote, the encounter of strangers is seldom fortuitous. As in

"Oedipus Rex," strangers who meet are often related without knowing it. Cortés not only read these romances, he may have taken them for "'true histories.'"[108] Elliott concludes that the "donation" speeches ascribed to Moctezuma were "founded more on fantasy than facts."[109]

Hugh Thomas, on the other hand, argues that Cortés had no need to lie when he could bully Moctezuma into doing his bidding. But the "donation speech" of Cortés's second letter was unprompted: the bullying had yet to begin. One conquistador who was there, Juan Cano, once expressed doubt that Moctezuma had understood the import of the translated version of his speech. Cano later recanted, however, declaring that Moctezuma had voluntarily surrendered his empire. As for the tearful native leaders who seemed to agree to become the vassals of Charles V, they were already in chains.

None of the conquistadors took issue with the content of what was said when the Second Letter was published in 1522 and widely circulated. Gerónimo Aguilar gave evidence against Cortés at his *residencia* of 1529, but as an Augustinian monk in the 1560s, he wrote that Moctezuma had declared before a notary that ancestors had foretold the arrival of bearded men from the east who should not be resisted, as they were the "future lords of the earth," and that he would serve as Charles V's vassal. Six other conquistadors, testifying under oath, affirmed Cortés's version of what was said.[110] But as Francis Brooks points out, to have taken issue with what soon became the official narrative would have questioned Castile's right to rule New Spain, thereby committing a potentially dangerous act of lese majesty. Besides, if Moctezuma really agreed to hand over the Aztec Empire to Charles V on the conquistadors' arrival in the Aztec capital, why didn't Cortés write immediately to his sovereign to announce this amazing windfall, instead of waiting almost a year?[111]

If, as Hugh Thomas thinks, Cortés took only minor liberties with what Moctezuma said, later commentators went beyond that. A conquistador who witnessed the proceedings with the Aztec lords maintained that they agreed to become not merely vassals of Charles V but his slaves. Citing Aguilar, Diego Duran declared that Moctezuma also said that he would become a Christian.[112] According to Alva Ixtlilxochitl, a native historian writing in the seventeenth century, the nobles also pledged their brothers and children to the Spaniards as hostages to this compact.[113] We have examined Sahagún's account.

Construction of a Myth

Susan Gillespie has convincingly shown that the identification of Cortés with Quetzalcoatl, the man-god ruler of ancient Tollan who was prophesied to return and rule the Aztecs, was a post-conquest construction that served the purposes of both surviving Nahuatl speakers and Spanish clerics. The germ of this myth is embodied in the welcoming (or "donation") speech that Cortés attributed to Moctezuma, although there is no mention of Quetzalcoatl in that speech. Nor is there mention of such a prophesy in pre-Hispanic Nahuatl traditions or in the earliest post-conquest documents. Mayan traditions do include such a prophesy, and Cortés may have learned of it through his interpreters.[114] Topiltzin Quetzalcoatl was not a central figure in the Aztec pantheon, as we have seen, though the Aztecs appear to have tried to counter his popular appeal and even to undo the belief in his traditional opposition to human sacrifice.[115]

The earliest identification of Cortés with Quetzalcoatl in the mind of Moctezuma appears in the *Annals of Tlatelolco* of 1528, according to Hugh Thomas.[116] An account of 1532, *Relación de la Genealogía,* has Topiltzin Quetzalcoatl dressed like a Spaniard. Other early sources refer to Topiltzin but not Quetzalcoatl. Some de-emphasize Tollan in favor of Culhua, a city that (like Tenochtitlán) claimed to be the successor of Tollan, with descent from Quetzalcoatl. In Fr. Andrés de Olmos's version of the myth, the *Historia de los Mexicanos por sus Pinturas* (c. 1535), Quetzalcoatl is a deity and Ce Acatl (1-Reed) a great human warrior who leads people out of Tollan and leaves them in Cholula. Motolinía's Quetzalcoatl is the god of the air associated with Cholula whose prophetic return is keyed to the appearance of the Spaniards. Conquistador Andrés de Tapia's account of the conquest (1542 or 1543) describes Quetzalcoatl as a monk-like figure in a white tunic with red crosses. Such descriptions probably influenced the identification of Quetzalcoatl with St. Thomas, the Christian apostle who, in an apocryphal text that was widely accepted in Europe at the time, evangelized beyond the Ganges.[117]

Writing in the late 1550s, Las Casas makes no mention of Quetzalcoatl's link to Tollan but does identify him with the Spaniards in fulfillment of his prophesied return. In the *Codex Ríos* (1566–1589) Quetzalcoatl, like Jesus, is the issue of a miraculous conception. When mature he leads people out of Tollan and ultimately enters a "Red Sea." The final form (1575–1580) of Sahagún's Book Twelve brings some of these and various other strands of the Quetzalcoatl story together. A contemporary text, *Anales de Cuauhtitlan,* written by indigenous scribes, also synthesizes this disparate material and some additional elements into the familiar story. Bernal Díaz, writing some decades after the events he witnessed, repeats the prophesy of conquerors arriving from the east, but he says that the story was told by *Tlaxcalan* leaders, who added that if the Spaniards were these prophesied conquerors, they could only applaud their bravery.[118] The massaging of this narrative continued into the next century, with Ixtlilxochtl, the indigenous historian, writing that Moctezuma mistook Cortés not for Quetzalcoatl but for Huitzilopochtli.[119] Gillespie characterizes this long process as a "negotiation" of Aztec history.[120]

The Moctezuma that identifies the leader of a band of European invaders with the semi-divine ruler of a golden age, the Moctezuma that emerges from the most influential text in this extended project—Sahagún's Book Twelve—surely represents, at least in part, the effort of Sahagún's informants to levy blame for the loss of Aztec eminence.[121] But the Quetzalcoatl story also brings the conquest within the purview of the old gods: if the fall of the Aztec world was preordained, the traditional gods still rule. Moctezuma's dithering becomes a vehicle in which fate rides out its course. Description of such behavior also reinforced Cortés's narrative of Moctezuma's early submission and capture.[122] Those that survived the carnage of 1521, as well as their descendants, surely found comfort in the thought that successful resistance would have been impossible. As Clendinnen has it, the story of Quetzalcoatl's return was an Aztec "emollient myth"—salve for a people's wound. And for the Spanish clerics who participated in its construction, the story of the prophesy that served the conquest helped demonstrate that the Spanish triumph was sanctioned by God and that the Indians were inferior by nature to Christian Europeans.[123]

The Quetzalcoatl story also represents an Aztec projection of recent events onto the distant past: the fall of Tenochtitlán was anticipated by the fall of Tollan. To be conquered was the Aztecs' destiny. Moreover, if Aztec sacrifices had been insufficient to arrest the all-destructive, all-regenerative cycle of history, time's wheel still turned. And because Cortés had proven to be a false Quetzalcoatl, Aztec descendants might look to the dawning of a new "sun," a new age, and with it a new Quetzalcoatl figure—perhaps in the guise of a Moctezuma III—whose return would mean the defeat of their Spanish overlords.[124]

The recent scholarship that I have summarized above has largely discredited the Quetzalcoatl story, yet it remains the leading explanation of the conquest of Mexico in the popular imagination. Is the notion that this momentous event turned on Indian gullibility and European cleverness too tempting for Westerners to discard, as Clendinnen suggests?[125] Or is it merely the case that popular assimilation of a scholarly consensus requires a lengthy period of incubation? It seems to me that as long as a mythical belief serves the values and prejudices of a vast majority, its perpetuation is pretty much assured. Take the notion that the United States had to drop atomic bombs on Hiroshima and Nagasaki in order to save the thousands of American lives that would have been lost in a ground invasion of Japan. Revisionist historians have persuasively debunked this idea without putting a scratch on the surface of the popular belief.[126] No one wants to think that her country unnecessarily and summarily killed over a hundred thousand civilians to send a message to a third party. And with regard to the conquest of Mexico, Westerners can take some comfort in thinking that, to some extent, the Aztecs brought disaster down on themselves. As usual, the truth is more complicated.

Conclusion

To say that the Cortés expedition brought deadly baggage to the Aztecs and other Indian nations is another way of saying that various factors—historic, geologic, geographic, technologic, economic, and political—determined that contact between these particular Europeans and Mesoamerican natives at this historic moment would inevitably take the form of a devastating invasion and conquest. The earliest such determinant happened around 15,000 years ago when the remote ancestors of the Aztecs and other indigenous Americans crossed the Beringian land mass from Siberia and began a southward trek into the Americas. Had the mammoths, mastodons, and many other large animals that they encountered not become extinct within a few thousand years, they might have domesticated at least the horse. Whether there were others that fell within the narrow range of species that humans can domesticate is something we can't know. The upshot was that unlike all the people who remained behind in the Old World, the Indians had no large domesticated animals except for the llama. This had the consequence of making them vulnerable to horse-borne invaders and susceptible to the kind of infectious diseases that originated in contact between humans and certain of their Old World domesticates.

Concurrently, with the waning of the most recent Ice Age, sea levels rose to cover Beringia, isolating these earliest Americans from further contact with people of the Eastern Hemisphere. Until Columbus, the Viking expeditions described in Chapter 1 were a rare and perhaps singular exception, underlining the point that any contact with the Indians would have to be made by seafarers. Indigenous Americans found no reason to develop the kind of navigational skills and maritime technology that might have led them to transoceanic ventures of their own.

As discussed in Chapter 2, Iberia's projection into the Atlantic made the peninsula a breeding ground for mariners. And Iberian shipbuilders were ideally placed to combine Mediterranean designs with northern European features to produce ships that, while not intended for transoceanic voyages initially, proved capable of them. Demand for spices and other goods from the (East) Indies and East Asia determined that Portuguese mariners would venture south along the west coast of Africa in hopes of rounding that continent and entering the Indian Ocean. In the course of these ventures, they discovered that at the latitude of the Canary Islands and beyond, prevailing winds might blow a ship far to the west.

Enter Columbus, who thought to take advantage of these winds and the smaller earth that his geographic understanding assumed: he would sail to China and its riches by heading south and then west instead of east. Sponsorship of his project came not from Portugal but from Castile, a state that was organized for war against Muslims. Castile's centuries-long struggle had periodically spilled over into popular violence against real and suspected non–Christians, and this continued even after the ouster of the Moors. Reconquest had also expanded the ranks of Spanish nobles, men with the leisure and wherewithal to devote themselves to military campaigns. Downgraded were all those who labored to produce food and other material conditions of human existence.

Meanwhile, people of Eurasia had gradually acquired immunity to some of the infectious diseases that had formerly devastated entire regions. In addition, they had long since developed metal weapons that could cut and pierce even armored bodies. The Indians had comparable weapons, but being nonmetallic theirs were less effective. What Europeans lacked, c. 1500, were adequate supplies of gold. Without it they could not afford to buy such cov-

Kneeling Female Figure, fifteenth-early sixteenth century, Mexico, Mesoamerica, Aztec, stone, pigment, overall 21½ × 10½ inches. Museum purchase, 1900 (image copyright © The Metropolitan Museum of Art. Image Source: Art Resource, New York).

eted Asian goods as spices, silks, and porcelain. When European invaders reached Mexico, they arrived with not only horses and Eurasia's superior weaponry but a determination to find gold, acquire vassals or slaves, and live like lords. They also brought a predisposition to identify non-Christians as the enemy. For reading material, they carried some of the earliest "best sellers," novels that exalted combat, adventure, and the righting of other people's wrongs. When a conquistador opened such a book, he found a mirror inside. As an incidental aim, they sought to stock the land with useful animals.

In the Introduction, I pointed out that various elements of the conquistadors' suite of deadly baggage were losing their lethality in the Old World at the time of the invasion. And in the first chapter, I compared such European items and impulses to their role, hundreds of years earlier, in the Viking contacts with indigenous Americans. Except for siege warfare, the latest developments in European history, culture, and military tactics were irrelevant in Castile's invasion of the New World. The predispositions, biota, and technology that the conquistadors brought with them were sufficiently lethal to assure successful domination of indigenous defenders. Separate development had not been equal.

What if Europeans had not invaded Mesoamerica when they did? Would the Aztecs and their rivals have achieved some higher level of social organization, eventually catching up with Europe? Who can say? The question is loaded with assumptions with regard to stages of development and what "eventually" might mean. Just as the Aztecs looked to ancient Tula and the Toltecs, Europeans looked to the classical world for examples of an advanced civilization, prior to 1500. For good reason: until the eighteenth century at the earliest, the Romans had consumed more meat, built more cities, used more and larger merchant vessels, and (in a more dubious indicator of economic success) created more industrial pollution than any Europeans that followed them.[1] Greatness was in the past. Or if it coexisted with late medieval Europe, it did so in some distant place—in China perhaps, or in India. Better to ask would Europeans and their diaspora have achieved global dominance by the second half of the nineteenth century absent the seizure of Mexico, Peru, and the rest of the Americas in the sixteenth and seventeenth centuries? With Iberia's discoveries and exploitation of its discoveries, followed by the colonizing projects of other European states, "the dialectic of development and underdevelopment intensified, and the world economy fixed itself in place,"[2] leaving Europe on a divergent course from the rest of the world.

If it makes no sense to lament the higher stages of development that the Aztecs might have achieved, what was lost with the fall of Tenochtitlán? Some would say that the Aztec nation survived in the shouts of "Moctezuma!

Cuauhtémoc!" by José María Morelos, the radical priest who sought to revive the Aztec nation three centuries after its fall. Some might say that it continued to live until 1919 when Emiliano Zapata was assassinated. Yet for others, the Aztecs live on in the magnificent murals of Diego Rivera on the walls of Mexico's National Palace, in the idealized images of twentieth-century Mexican calendars, and in the dreams of every barrio dweller in the southwestern United States who regards that region as "occupied" Mexico.[3] But certain practices that died in the ruins of Tenochtitlán have not had many mourners. Human sacrifice and ritual cannibalism were central to the Aztec culture. Although such practices figured in the lives of distant ancestors of practically everyone alive today, the great temporal distance between their lives and ours has made all the difference. By the sixteenth century, Europeans had a foot in the modern world where human sacrifice and ritual cannibalism survived only remotely among people that Europeans would find comfort in regarding as savages.

Yet something distinctive and probably irreplaceable was lost with the conquest of Mexico. Life in the Aztec world was generally unfair, insecure, and uncomfortable, but the daily life of the Aztec people was saturated with meaning. Such meaning was reinforced at frequent intervals by the ceremonies of the Aztec calendar, events whose repetition recreated what the Aztecs saw as the natural order. These events ranged from the spectacularly grotesque to domestic rituals involving food preparation. Begin with the doctrine that food comes from the earth gods and that what is given must be returned. Then, from the weaned child to the warrior, maiden, or merchant, human flesh becomes no more than the conscious episode of the vegetative cycle that runs from the gods to the earth to the harvest and human consumption, returning to the gods with the sacrifices of the next festival. People were potential "drinking cups of the gods."[4] Sahagún doubted that there had "been in the world idolators [who were] to such a degree venerators of their gods."[5] Through their rituals, the people of Tenochtitlán and elsewhere in the region transcended everyday reality and achieved a conscious merger with the divine. Falling victim to the Spaniards and their deadly baggage was a culture of life as epiphany, frequently renewed.

But it's not my intention to counter the romance of European invasion that has served as the leading narrative of the conquest of Mexico with a romance of Aztec culture. Some maintain that commoners seldom participated in events of the Aztec calendar or even got to watch.[6] Some would say that the epiphenomena of Aztec religious ceremony and sacrifice were a cover for priestly dominance or would argue that the Aztecs required constant warfare and a large and super-exploited class of undernourished peasants to sustain a bloated military aristocracy. All of this may be true. But as we are no longer children, let us cast aside the fairytale version of history that suffuses the leader of a small band of Europeans that landed on the edge of an Indian empire with reason and boldness and drenches the ruler who presided over that empire in ignorance and superstition, holding this out as an explanation of how the Europeans prevailed. Failure to highlight the comparative deadliness of European weaponry, biota, and culture is no explanation at all.

The early sixteenth century saw a collision between two societies heretofore separated by the space of an ocean and several thousand years of time. The results are with us yet. We might loosely call each side in this encounter a warrior society, for each was geared for warfare. One ran on ceremony and terror, the other on greed and fanaticism. Power and privilege in each comprised a pyramid, with agricultural workers at the base and a supreme ruler at the apex. Each had nobles and commoners. Beyond this the similarities seep into the differences that made contact by Europeans a mismatch for Native Americans. For whether we consider weapons, tactics, disease, the use of animal species, or any of the other factors discussed in the foregoing chapters, one side was holding all the trumps. The Aztecs may have exceeded most Europeans in religious fervor, but this only made their losses more devastating and inexplicable. Their gods provided no protection against the lethality of Old World baggage.

Chapter Notes

Introduction

1. Qtd. in Benjamin Keen, *The Aztec Image in Western Thought* (New Brunswick: Rutgers University Press, 1971) 172.
2. Keen 82, 176, 258, 431.
3. William H. Prescott, *History of the Conquest of Mexico* (New York: Modern Library, 1843) 666.
4. (Indianapolis: Bobbs-Merrill, 1926).
5. (New York: Macmillan, 1941).
6. Qtd. in Keen 535.
7. John Manchip White, *Cortés and the Downfall of the Aztec Empire: A Study in a Conflict of Cultures* (New York: St. Martin's Press, 1971) 19.
8. Tvestan Todorov, *The Conquest of America: The Question of the Other*, trans. Richard Howard (New York: Harper & Row, 1984) 121–23, 127, and passim.
9. Hugh Thomas, *Conquest: Montezuma, Cortés, and the Fall of Old Mexico* (New York: Simon & Schuster, 1993) xi, xiv, 533.
10. Camilla Townsend, "Burying the White Gods: New Perspectives on the Conquest of Mexico," *The American Historical Review* 108.3 (June 2003) 680, 686.
11. Thomas, *Conquest* 315.
12. Frances F. Berdan, *The Aztecs of Central Mexico: An Imperial Society*, 2d ed. (Belmont, CA: Thomson Wadsworth, 2005) 173.

Chapter 1

1. Eugene R. Fingerhut, *Explorers of Pre-Columbian American? The Diffusionist-Inventionist Controversy* (Claremont, CA: Regina Books, 1994) 27.
2. Frank Joseph, *The Lost Colonies of Ancient America: A Comprehensive Guide to the Visitors Who Really Discovered America* (Pompton Plains, NJ: New Page Books, 2014) 104–08.
3. Duncan Edlin, "The Stoned Age? A Look at the Evidence for Cocaine in Mummies," undated but posted after March 2002, http://www.hallofmaat.com/modules.php?name=Articles&file=article. Retrieved April 17, 2014.
4. Gavin Menzies, *1421: The Year China Discovered America* (New York: Harper Perennial, 2003) 327; Graeme Davis, *Vikings in America* (Edinburgh: Birlinn, 2009) 160–65.
5. Davis 120.
6. www.fsmitha.com/h1/ch01.htm.
7. http://www.flowofhistory.com/category/export/html/193.
8. Herodotus, *The History* 4.42, trans. David Grene (Chicago: University of Chicago Press, 1987) 296.
9. David H. Kelley, "An Essay on Pre-Columbian Contacts between the Americas and Other Areas, with Special Reference to the Work of Ivan Van Sertima," *Race, Discourse, and the Origins of the Americas: A New World View*, Vera Lawrence Hyatt and Rex Nettleford, eds. (Washington, D.C.: Smithsonian Institute Press, 1995) 106.
10. Joseph 42; Ivan Van Sertima, "African Presence in Early America," *Race, Discourse* 89.
11. *Ancient American: Archaeology of the Americas* 16.97 (December 2012).
12. Fingerhut 113, 117.
13. Fingerhut x, xii, xiv, 5, 17, 40; Arthur C. Gibson, "Batatas, Not Potatoes," undated, http://www.botgard.ucla.edu/html/botanytextbooks/economicbotany/Ipomoea/index.html. Retrieved April 17, 2014.
14. See, for example, Lutz Roewer et al., "Continent-Wide Decoupling of Y-Chromosonal Genetic Variation from Language and Geography in Native South Americans," April 11, 2013, http://www.plosgenetics.org/article/info: doi/10.1371/journal.pgen.1003460; Simon Romero, "Discoveries Challenge Beliefs on Humans' Arrival in the Americas," *New York Times International* 28 March 2014: A5.
15. Fingerhut 27–28.
16. Kelley 111–12.
17. Joseph 113–120.
18. See, for example, N. K. Sandars, Intro-

duction, *The Epic of Gilgamesh*, rev. ed. (New York: Penguin, 1972) 39.
19. Romeo H. Hristov and Santiago Genovés T., "The Roman Head from Tecaxic-Calixtlahuaca, Mexico: A Review of the Evidence," revised and extended version of paper presented on April 22, 2001, http://www.unm.edu/~rhistov/calixtlahuaca.html.
20. Edlin.
21. Menzies 327.
22. Davis 65.
23. Joseph 247–48.
24. Keith Fitzpatrick-Matthews, "Old World People in the New World Before Columbus?" Sept. 22, 2012, http://badarchaeology.wordpress.com/tag/ogham/.
25. Fingerhut 86, 92–3, 109, 113.
26. Menzies 354–55.
27. Daniel Odess et al., "*Skraeling*: First Peoples of Helluland, Markland, and Vinland," *Vikings: The North Atlantic Saga*, William W. Fitzhugh and Elisabeth I. Ward, eds. (Washington, D.C.: Smithsonian Institute Press, 2000) 194.
28. Menzies 257.
29. Joseph 25, 42, 111.
30. Joseph 56, citing Jane Hopping, "A Temple in Tennessee," *Ancient American* 10.75 (May/June 2010).
31. Joseph 63, 126–7.
32. Kelley 105.
33. Fitzpatrick-Matthews; Fingerhut 40.
34. Kelley 108–9.
35. Joseph 24.
36. Joan Baxter, "Africa's 'greatest explorer,'" December 13, 2000, BBC News at http://news.bbc.co.uk/2/hi/Africa/1068950.st.
37. Menzies 460.
38. Menzies 156–57.
39. Joseph 153.
40. Menzies 67.
41. Suzanne Austin Alchon, "The Great Killers in Precolumbian America: A Hemispheric Perspective," *Latin American Population History Bulletin* 27 (Fall 1997), www.hist.umn.edu/~mccaa/laphb/27fall97/laphb271.htm.
42. Ian Morris, *Why the West Rules—For Now* (New York: Picador, 2010) 410–11.
43. "The Saga of the Greenlanders," trans. Keneva Kunz, *The Sagas of Icelanders: A Selection* (New York: Viking, 1997) 646.
44. "Eirik the Red's Saga," trans. Keneva Kunz, *The Sagas* 672.
45. Davis 74–75.
46. Birgitta Linderoth Wallace, "The Viking Settlement at L'Anse aux Meadows," *Vikings: The North Atlantic* 213.
47. Davis 43.
48. "Greenlanders" 646.
49. "Greenlanders" 642.

50. Wallace, "An Archaeologist's Interpretation of the *Vinland Sagas*," *Vikings: The North Atlantic* 226.
51. "Eirik the Red's," 671.
52. Davis 49, 52; Kirsten A. Seaver, "Unanswered Questions," *Vikings: The North Atlantic* 272.
53. Robert Ferguson, *The Vikings: A History* (New York: Penguin, 2009) 297.
54. Peter Schledermann, "A.D. 1000: East Meets West," *Vikings: The North Atlantic* 192; Odess et al., *Vikings: The North Atlantic* 203; Davis 48.
55. Patricia D. Sutherland, "The Norse and Native North Americans," *Vikings: The North Atlantic* 241–246; Odess et al., *Vikings: The North Atlantic* 193, 199–200.
56. Davis 114, 128–29.
57. "Eirik the Red's" 658–59, 661.
58. Davis 52.
59. Schledermann, "A.D. 1000" 192.
60. "Eirik the Red's" 671.
61. "Eirik the Red's" 670.
62. *Historia Norvegiae*, qtd. in Brian Fagan, *The Great Warming: Climate Change and the Rise and Fall of Civilizations* (New York: Bloomsbury Press, 2008) 103.
63. Schledermann, "Ellesmere: Vikings in the Far North," *Vikings: The North Atlantic* 254.
64. Sutherland 242.
65. Davis 137.
66. Cf. the account of the Franklin Expedition in Davis 106–7.
67. Ferguson 284.
68. "Greenlanders" 646.
69. "Greenlanders" 646–48.
70. Davis 77.
71. Wallace, "Viking Settlement" 211.
72. "Greenlanders" 242.
73. Odess et al. 197; Davis 134–35.
74. "Greenlanders" 641, 644; "Eirik the Red's" 657, 663.

Chapter 2

1. Brian Fagan, *The Great Warming: Climate Change and the Rise and Fall of Civilizations* (New York: Bloomsbury Press, 2008) 104.
2. Graeme Davis, *Vikings in America* (Edinburgh: Birlinn, 2009) 62, 103, 142; Robert Ferguson, *The Vikings: A History* (New York: Penguin, 2009) 291; Eugene R. Fingerhut, *Explorers of Pre-Columbian America? The Diffusionist-Inventionist Controversy* (Claremont, CA: Regina Books, 1994) 56 ff.; Kirsten A. Seaver, "Unanswered Questions," *Vikings: The North Atlantic Saga*, William W. Fitzhugh and Elisabeth I. Ward, eds. (Washington, D.C.: Smithsonian Institute Press, 2000) 279.
3. See Figures 5 and 6 in Alfred W. Crosby,

Ecological Imperialism: The Biological Expansion of Europe, 900–1900 (New York: Cambridge University Press, 1986) 109–110.

4. Ivan Van Sertima, "African Presence in Early America," *Race, Discourse, and the Origins of the Americas: A New World View,* Vera Lawrence Hyatt and Rex Nettleford, eds. (Washington, D.C.: Smithsonian Institute Press, 1995) 73, 76.

5. Van Sertima 70.

6. Van Sertima 71; Frank Joseph, *The Lost Colonies of Ancient America: A Comprehensive Guide to the Visitors Who Really Discovered America* (Pompton Plains, NJ: New Page Books, 2014) 162.

7. Margalit Fox, "Anthony Smith, Explorer With Zest for Land, Sea and Air, is Dead at 88," *New York Times* 25 July 2014: A19.

8. Corey Kilgannon, "Couple Arrives in New York From Africa, Merrily, Merrily," *New York Times* 21 June 2014: A19.

9. David Abulafia, *The Discovery of Mankind: Atlantic Encounters in the Age of Columbus* (New Haven: Yale University Press, 2008) 83.

10. J. H. Parry, *The Age of Reconnaissance: Discovery, Exploration and Settlement 1450 to 1650* (Berkeley: University of California Press, 1981) 58–63.

11. Hugh Thomas, *Conquest: Montezuma, Cortés, and the Fall of Old Mexico* (New York: Simon & Schuster, 1993) 48.

12. Camilla Townsend, "Burying the White Gods: New Perspectives on the Conquest of Mexico," *The American Historical Review* 108.3 (June 2003) 681 note.

13. Gavin Menzies, *1421: The Year China Discovered America* (New York: Harper Perennial, 2003) 396.

14. Parry 80–81, 91.

15. Menzies 93–94.

16. Menzies 115, 139.

17. Pierre Chaunu, *European Expansion in the Later Middle Ages,* trans. Katharine Bertram (New York: North-Holland, 1979) 103.

18. Menzies 387.

19. Qtd. with emphasis in Nicolás Wey Gómez, *The Tropics of Empire: Why Columbus Sailed South to the Indies* (Cambridge: MIT Press, 2008) 300, 304.

20. Wey Gómez 295, 319.

21. John Darwin, *After Tamerlane: The Rise and Fall of Global Empires, 1400–2000* (New York: Bloomsbury Press, 2008) 52.

22. Bernard Lewis, *Cultures in Conflict: Christians, Muslims, and Jews in the Age of Discovery* (New York: Oxford University Press, 1995) 60.

23. A. J. R. Russell-Wood, "Before Columbus: Portugal's African Prelude to the Middle Passage and Contribution to Discourse on Race and Slavery," *Race, Discourse, and the Origins of the Americas: A New World View,* Vera Lawrence Hyatt and Rex Nettleford, eds. (Washington, D.C.: Smithsonian Institute Press, 1995) 137.

24. Barnaby Rogerson, *The Last Crusaders: The Hunded-Year Battle for the Centre of the World* (New York: Overlook Press, 2009) 38; Nigel Cliff, *Holy War: How Vasco da Gama's Epic Voyages Turned the Tide in a Centuries-Old Clash of Civilizations* (New York: HarperCollins, 2011) 2, 84, 115.

25. Darwin 53.

26. *The Book of John Mandeville with Related Texts,* Iain Macleod Higgins, ed. and trans. (Indianapolis: Hackett, 2011) 161.

27. Rogerson 138.

28. Lewis 62; Fernand Braudel, *Capitalism and Material Life: 1400–1800* (New York: Harper & Row, 1973) 156–57.

29. Abulafia 72–73; R. C. Padden, *The Hummingbird and the Hawk: Conquest and Sovereignty in the Valley of Mexico, 1503–1541* (San Francisco: Harper Torchbooks, 1967) 138.

30. Walter Ullmann, *A History of Political Thought: the Middle Ages* (Baltimore: Penguin, 1965) 19–21, 104, 115 note.

31. Qtd. in Wey Gómez 307–8.

32. Valentin Y. Mudimbe, "Romanus Pontifex (1454) and the Expansion of Europe," *Race, Discourse* 60–61.

33. Francis Jennings, *The Invasion of America: Indians, Colonialism, and the Cant of Conquest* (Chapel Hill: University of North Carolina Press, 1975) 44.

34. Wey Gómez 318.

35. See, for example, Bartolomé de Las Casas, "Digest of Columbus's Log-Book on His First Voyage," *The Four Voyages of Christopher Columbus,* J. M. Cohen, ed. and trans. (New York: Penguin, 1969) 60.

36. James Reston, Jr., *Dogs of God: Columbus, the Inquisition, and the Defeat of the Moors* (New York: Doubleday, 2005) 325; Wey Gómez 324; cf. Jonathan Riley-Smith, *The Crusades: A Short History* (New Haven: Yale University Press, 1987) 152.

37. James F. Powers, *A Society Organized for War: The Iberian Municipal Militias in the Central Middle Ages* (Berkeley: University of California Press, 1988) 242–43.

38. Joseph F. O'Callaghan, *Reconquest and Crusade in Medieval Spain* (Philadelphia: University of Pennsylvania Press, 2003) 128; cf. 127, 129.

39. Padden 135; Thomas, *Conquest* 58.

40. Frederic Hicks, "Mexica Political History," *The Aztec World,* Elizabeth M. Brumfiel and Gary M. Feinman, eds. (New York: Abrams and the Field Museum, 2008) 5–21; Ross Hassig, *Aztec Warfare: Imperial Expansion and Po-*

litical Control (Norman: University of Oklahoma Press, 1988); Inga Clendinnen, Aztecs: An Interpretation (New York: Cambridge University Press, 1991) 119–21.
41. Rafael Minder, "A Hard Sell to Tame a Name in Spain," New York Times 11May 2014: 6.
42. Teofilo F. Ruiz, Spanish Society, 1400–1600 (Essex: Pearson Ed., 2001) 97.
43. Jan Carew, "The End of Moorish Enlightenment and the Beginning of the Columbian Era," Race, Discourse 199–201.
44. Bishop de Landa of Yucatan, qtd. in Van Sertima 68.
45. Darwin 73–76.
46. Sheldon Watts, Epidemics and History: Disease, Power and Imperialism (New York: Yale University Press, 1997) 95; J. H. Elliott, Imperial Spain: 1469–1716 (New York: Penguin, 2002) 87.
47. Thomas, Conquest 117.
48. Qtd. without attribution in Thomas, Conquest 118.
49. Thomas, Conquest 117–18.
50. Wey Gómez 297.
51. Abulafia 38.
52. Abulafia 36–43, 58.
53. Abulafia 65–67, 74–78.
54. Abulafia 79, 86–87.
55. Wey Gómez 319.
56. Las Casas,"Digest" 60.
57. Chaunu 98.
58. Crosby, Ecological 76–78.
59. Abulafia 84, 95, 98, 100–101.
60. Crosby, Ecological 82–103; Ronald Findlay and Kevin H. O'Rourke, Power and Plenty: Trade, War, and the World Economy in the Second Millennium (Princeton: Princeton University Press, 2007) 146.
61. Abulafia 296.

Chapter 3

1. Joseph R. Strayer and Dana C. Munro, The Middle Ages: 395–1500 (New York: Appleton-Century-Crofts, 1959) 387.
2. Bernal Díaz [del Castillo], The Conquest of New Spain, trans. J. M. Cohen (London: The Folio Society, 1963) see, e.g., 85, 98, 107, 124, 154.
3. The Song of Roland, trans. Frederick Bliss Luquiens (New York: Macmillan, 1952) 1, 31.
4. Díaz del Castillo, The History of the Conquest of New Spain, trans. A. P. Maudslay (Albuquerque: University of New Mexico Press, 2008) e. g., 159, 173.
5. William Weber Johnson, Cortés (Boston: Little, Brown, 1975) 4.
6. W. Johnson xii.
7. William H. Prescott, History of the Conquest of Mexico (New York: Modern Library, 1843) 907.
8. Rebecca West, Survivors in Mexico (New Haven: Yale University Press, 2003) 113.
9. Ramón Iglesia, Columbus, Cortés, and Other Essays, Lesley Byrd Simpson, ed. and trans. (Berkeley: University of California Press, 1969) 155; cf. R. West 112.
10. Qtd. in Francis J. Brooks, "Motecuzoma, Xocoyotl, Hernán Cortés, and Bernal Díaz del Castillo: The Construction of an Arrest," Hispanic American Historical Review 75:2 (May 1995) 168.
11. Díaz, History 185–86.
12. Hugh Thomas, Conquest: Montezuma, Cortés, and the Fall of Old Mexico (New York: Simon & Schuster, 1993) 333, cites the testimony of conquistadors collected in the Conway papers housed in Cambridge, England, and Francisco López de Gómara, La Conquista de México, José Luis Rojas, ed. (Madrid: Historia 16, 1987) 213. But cf. Díaz, History 206–7, who says that the work had begun "in haste," as the conquistadors in Tenochtitlán quaked in fear of an impending attack; cf. Inga Clendinnen, "Cortés, Signs, and the Conquest of Mexico," The Transmission of Culture in Early Modern Europe, Anthony Grafton and Ann Blair, eds. (Philadelphia: University of Pennsylvania Press, 1990) 100–1.
13. Iglesia, citing the nineteenth historian Lucas Alamán, 168; cf. Cortés, Letters from Mexico, Anthony Pagden, ed. and trans. (New Haven: Yale University Press, 1986) 327.
14. Tzvetan Todorov, The Conquest of America: The Question of the Other, trans. Richard Howard (New York: Harper & Row, 1984) 15.
15. Iglesia 206.
16. Qtd. in Hugh Thomas, Rivers of Gold: The Rise of the Spanish Empire from Columbus to Magellan (New York: Random House, 2003) 10.
17. Lafeu in "All's Well That Ends Well," II, iii.
18. Amadis of Gaul, rev. by Garci Rodríguez de Montalvo, trans. Edwin B. Place and Herbert C. Behm (Lexington: University Press of Kentucky, 1974) 75.
19. J. H. Elliott, "The Mental World of Hernán Cortés," Transactions of the Royal Historical Society, Series 5, vol. 17: 49 (1967).
20. Strayer and Munro 385ff.
21. Leo Braudy, From Chivalry to Terrorism: War and the Changing Nature of Masculinity (New York: Alfred A. Knopf, 2003) 66; Eiko Ikegami, The Taming of the Samurai: Honorific Individualism and the Making of Modern Japan (Cambridge: Harvard University Press, 1995) 48, 69.
22. Johan Huizinga, The Waning of the Middle Ages (Harmondsworth: Penguin, 1955) 77.
23. David Abulafia, The Discovery of Man-

kind: *Atlantic Encounters in the Age of Columbus* (New Haven: Yale University Press, 2008) 76.
24. Huizinga 69.
25. Braudy 74.
26. Barbara W. Tuchman, *A Distant Mirror: The Calamitous 14th Century* (New York: Ballantine, 1978) xix, 8–9; Henri Pirenne, *Economic and Social History of Medieval Europe* (New York: Harcourt, Brace & World, 1937) 196.
27. Huizinga 67.
28. Pirenne 63.
29. Hernando Colon, *The Life of the Admiral by His Son, Hernando Colon*, excerpted in *The Four Voyages of Christopher Columbus*, J. M. Cohen, ed. and trans. (New York: Penguin, 1969) 106.
30. Thomas, *Rivers* 121.
31. Thomas, *Conquest* 314.
32. E. C. Riley, *Don Quixote* (Boston: Allen & Unwin, 1986) 63.
33. Sahagún, *General History of the Things of New Spain*, excerpted in *The Broken Spears: The Aztec Account of the Conquest of Mexico*, trans. (from Spanish) Lysander Kemp, Miguel Leon-Portilla, ed. (Boston: Beacon Press, 1992) 41.
34. Teofilo F. Ruiz, *Spanish Society, 1400–1600* (Essex: Pearson Education, 2001) 220.
35. Thomas, *Conquest* 61.
36. Richard Lee Marks, *Cortés: The Great Adventurer and the Fate of Aztec Mexico* (New York: Alfred A. Knopf, 1993) 15.
37. Qtd. in Henry Kamen, *Spain, 1469–1714: A Society of Conflict*, 3d ed. (Harlow: Pearson Education, 2005) 97.
38. Stephen Greenblatt, *Marvelous Possessions: The Wonder of the New World* (Chicago: University of Chicago Press, 1991), cited in Theresa Ann Sears, "Spain's Medievalist Project in the New World," *Medievalism in Europe: Studies in Medievalism*, Vol. V, Leslie J. Workman, ed. (Cambridge: D. S. Brewer, 1994) 205.
39. Díaz, *Conquest* 107.
40. Díaz, *Conquest* 126; Gary Kamiya, "Cabrillo made his name with bold, bloody exploits," *San Francisco Chronicle* 18 October 2014: C-2.
41. David W. Anthony, *The Horse, the Wheel, and Language: How Bronze-Age Riders from the Eurasian Steppes Shaped the Modern World* (Princeton: Princeton University Press, 2007) 56.
42. *The Epic of Gilgamesh*, trans. N. K. Sandars, rev. ed. (New York: Penguin, 1972) 71; cf. 77.
43. *The Iliad of Homer*, trans. Richmond Lattimore (Chicago: Phoenix Books, 1951) 7–90: 170.
44. Cortés, *Letters* 125.
45. Cortés, *Letters* 88.
46. William of Malmesbury, *Gesta Regum Anglorum*, trans. E. K. Chambers, excerpted in *Arthur, King of Britain*, Richard L. Brengle, ed. (New York: Appleton-Century-Crofts, 1964) 8.
47. Geoffrey of Monmouth, *Historia Regum Britanniae*, trans. Sebastian Evans, excerpted in *Arthur* 64.
48. Layamon, *Brut*, excerpted in *Arthur* 130.
49. Joseph F. O'Callaghan, *Reconquest and Crusade in Medieval Spain* (Philadelphia: University of Pennsylvania Press, 2003) 147.
50. Hernando Colon, *The Life* in *Four Voyages* 189–91.
51. Diego Mendez, "Account by Diego Mendez of Certain Incidents on Christopher Columbus's Last Voyage," *Four Voyages* 309.
52. Cortés 59.
53. Thomas, *Conquest* 168.
54. Miguel de Cervantes, *Don Quijote*, trans. Burton Raffel, Diana de Armas Wilson, ed. (New York: W. W. Norton, 1999) 1.13: 69; 2.1: 364.
55. Díaz, *Conquest* 140.
56. Díaz, *Conquest*, e. g., 325.
57. Jonathan Riley-Smith, *The Crusades: A Short History* (New Haven: Yale University Press, 1987) 31.
58. O'Callaghan 201.
59. Georges Dumézil, *The Destiny of the Warrior*, trans. Alf Hiltebeitel (Chicago: University of Chicago Press, 1969) 65.
60. W. Johnson 219–20.
61. Aristotle, *The Politics of Aristotle* VII. xiv §19, trans. Ernest Barker (New York: Oxford University Press, 1962) 319.
62. Dumézil 61, 106–7, 141.
63. See Fig. 14, *The Aztec World*, Elizabeth M. Brumfiel and Gary M. Feinman, eds. (New York: Abrams and the Field Museum, 2008) 150.
64. Inga Clendinnen, "The Cost of Courage in Aztec Society," *The Cost of Courage in Aztec Society: Essays on Mesoamerican Society and Culture* (New York: Cambridge University Press, 2010) 26; Ikegami 206.
65. Díaz, *Conquest* 32.
66. "Book Twelve of the Florentine Codex," *We People Here: Nahuatl Accounts of the Conquest of Mexico*, James Lockhart, ed. and trans. (Berkeley: University of California Press, 1993) 134.
67. Díaz, *History* 213.
68. Anthony 223–4; Braudy 45.
69. Braudy 35–6.
70. Tacitus, *The Agricola and the Germania*, trans. H. Mattingly and S. A. Handford (Baltimore: Penguin, 1970) 127.
71. Díaz, *History* 94.
72. Clendinnen, *Aztecs: An Interpretation* (New York: Cambridge University Press, 1991) 269–71.
73. "Book Twelve" 198–236.

74. Díaz, *Conquest* 26, 36.
75. Geoffrey of Monmouth, in *Arthur* 76.

Chapter 4

1. Eusebius, *Life of Constantine*, qtd. in Rolena Adorno, "The Polemics of Possession: Spain on America, Circa 1550," *Empires of God: Religious Encounters in the Early Modern Atlantic*, Linda Gregerson and Susan Juster, eds. (Philadelphia: University of Pennsylvania Press, 2011) 19.
2. Qtd. in Walter Ullmann, *A History of Political Thought: the Middle Ages* (Baltimore: Penguin, 1965) 40, 76.
3. Jonathan Riley-Smith, *The Crusades: A Short History* (New Haven: Yale University Press, 1987) 93
4. Leo Braudy, *From Chivalry to Terrorism: War and the Changing Nature of Masculinity* (New York: Alfred A. Knopf, 2003) 75.
5. Richard Dawkins, *The Selfish Gene* (New York: Oxford University Press, 1989) 331.
6. David Abulafia, *The Discovery of Mankind: Atlantic Encounters in the Age of Columbus* (New Haven: Yale University Press, 2008) 79, 82.
7. Barnaby Rogerson, *The Last Crusaders: The Hundred-Year Battle for the Centre of the World* (New York: Overlook Press, 2009) 19–20; James Reston, Jr., *Dogs of God: Columbus, the Inquisition, and the Defeat of the Moors* (New York: Doubleday, 2005) 13.
8. Rogerson 34, 62; Reston 115–16, 278.
9. J. H. Elliott, *Imperial Spain: 1469–1716* (New York: Penguin, 2002) 46.
10. Riley-Smith 209, 237; Elliott, *Imperial* 53–4.
11. Fernand Braudel, *The Mediterranean and the Mediterranean World in the Age of Philip II*, Vol. 1, trans. Siân Reynolds (New York: Harper & Row, 1972) 474.
12. Reston 166, 220–1, 253–4, 275–6.
13. Joseph F. O'Callaghan, *Reconquest and Crusade in Medieval Spain* (Philadelphia: University of Pennsylvania Press, 2003) 177–78.
14. *The Book of John Mandeville with Related Texts*, Iain Macleod Higgins, ed. and trans. (Indianapolis: Hackett, 2011) xx.
15. Theresa Ann Sears, "Spain's Medievalist Project in the New World," *Medievalism in Europe: Studies in Medievalism*, Vol. V, Leslie J. Workman, ed. (Cambridge: D. S. Brewer, 1994) 203.
16. Bartolomé de Las Casas, *History of the Indies*, Andrée Collard, ed. and trans. (New York: Harper Torchbooks, 1971) Book I, 48.
17. Sears 201, 206.
18. *Cross and Sword: An Eyewitness History of Christianity in Latin America*, H. McKennie Goodpasture, ed. (Maryknoll, NY: Orbis Books, 1989) 6.
19. Bernal Díaz [del Castillo], *The Conquest of New Spain*, trans. J. M. Cohen (London: The Folio Society, 1963)18.
20. Hugh Thomas, *Conquest: Montezuma, Cortés, and the Fall of Old Mexico* (New York: Simon & Schuster, 1993) 111.
21. Díaz, *Conquest* 43.
22. Hernán Cortés, *Letters from Mexico*, Anthony Pagden, ed. and trans. (New Haven: Yale University Press, 1986) 30.
23. Cortés, *Letters* 484, note 15.
24. Cortés, *Letters* 465, note 27.
25. Cortés, *Cartas de Relación de Méjico*, Tomo 1, Quinta ed. (Madrid: Espasa Calpe, 1942) 65.
26. Bartolomé de Las Casas, *A Short Account of the Destruction of the Indies*, trans. Nigel Griffin (New York: Penguin, 1992) 53.
27. Valentin Y. Mudimbe, "Romanus Pontifex (1454) and the Expansion of Europe," *Race, Discourse, and the Origins of the Americas: A New World View*, Vera Lawrence Hyatt and Rex Nettleford, eds. (Washington, D.C.: Smithsonian Institute Press, 1995) 58.
28. H. Thomas, *Rivers of Gold: The Rise of the Spanish Empire, from Columbus to Magellan* (New York: Random House, 2003) 167.
29. Qtd. in H. Thomas, *The Golden Empire: Spain, Charles V, and the Creation of America* (New York: Random House, 2010) 465.
30. Thomas, *Rivers* 341–2.
31. Cortés, *Letters* 59.
32. Las Casas, *Short Account* 33.
33. Tzvetan Todorov, *The Conquest of America: The Question of the Other*, trans. Richard Howard (New York: Harper & Row, 1984) 148.
34. Nicolás Wey Gómez, *The Tropics of Empire: Why Columbus Sailed South to the Indies* (Cambridge: MIT Press, 2008) 299.
35. Abulafia 288; Susan D. Gillespie, *The Aztec Kings: The Construction of Rulership in Mexica History* (Tucson: University of Arizona Press, 1989) 184.
36. Camilla Townsend, "Burying the White Gods: New Perspectives on the Conquest of Mexico," *The American Historical Review* 108.3 (June 2003) 669.
37. R. C. Padden, *The Hummingbird and the Hawk: Conquest and Sovereignty in the Valley of Mexico, 1503–1541* (San Francisco: Harper Torchbooks, 1967) 142.
38. Elliott, *Spain and Its World, 1500–1700* (New Haven: Yale University Press, 1989) 59–60; Cortés, *Letters* 37.
39. Cortés, *Letters* 60.
40. "Extract from Annals of Tlatelolco," *We People Here: Nahuatl Accounts of the Conquest of Mexico*, James Lockhart, ed. and trans. (Berkeley: University of California Press, 1993) 257.

41. Qtd. in H. Thomas, *Conquest* 161.
42. Don Juan de Villagutierre Soto-Mayor, *History of the Conquest of the Province of the Itza: Subjugation and Events of the Lacandon and Other Nations of Yucatan in North America*, trans. Brother Robert D. Wood (Culver City, CA: Labyrinthos, 1983) 78.
43. Padden 143.
44. Bernal Díaz del Castillo, *The History of the Conquest of New Spain*, trans. A. P. Maudslay, Davíd Carrasco, ed. (Albuquerque: University of New Mexico Press, 2008) 33.
45. Díaz, *History* 46.
46. Díaz, *History* 49.
47. Mudimbe 61.
48. Abulafia 90.
49. Andrés de Tapia, "The Chronicle of Andres de Tapia," *The Conquistadors: First-Person Accounts of the Conquest of Mexico*, Patricia de Fuentes, ed. and trans. (New York: Orion Press, 1963) 28.
50. Díaz, *History* 60.
51. Díaz, *Conquest* 125.
52. See Ross Hassig, *Mexico and the Spanish Conquest*, 2d ed. (Norman: University of Oklahoma Press, 2006) 96–97; cf. Díaz, *History* 104.
53. Díaz, *History* 114.
54. Matthew Restall, *Seven Myths of the Spanish Conquest* (New York: Oxford University Press, 2003) 46.
55. Tacitus, *The Agricola and the Germania*, trans. H. Mattingly (Baltimore: Penguin, 1970) 129.
56. Anonymous Indian observer, "The Chronicle," excerpted in *Cross and Sword* 17.
57. Díaz, *Conquest* 162–3, 178–9.
58. Andrés de Tapia, qtd. in Charles S. Braden, *Religious Aspects of the Conquest of Mexico* (Durham: Duke University Press, 1930), excerpted in *Cross and Sword* 18–19.
59. Thomas, *Conquest* 327–28.
60. Richard F. Townsend, *The Aztecs*, 3d ed. (London: Thames & Hudson, 2009) 233.
61. Cortés, *Letters* 106.
62. Thomas, *Conquest* 328.
63. O'Callaghan 204.
64. Cortés, *Letters* 106.
65. Díaz, *History* 295.
66. Padden 26; Davíd Carrasco, *Quetzalcoatl and the Irony of Empire: Myths and Prophesies in the Aztec Tradition* (Boulder: University of Colorado Press, 2000) 163–64.
67. Enrique Florescano, *The Myth of Quetzalcoatl*, trans. Lysa Hochroth (Baltimore: John Hopkins University Press, 1999) 166–67.
68. Inga Clendinnen, "The Cost of Courage in Aztec Society," *The Cost of Courage in Aztec Society: Essays on Mesoamerican Society and Culture* (New York: Cambridge University Press, 2010) 19; cf. Todorov 109–110.
69. Padden 25.
70. Anamaría Ashwell and John O'Leary, *Cholula: La Ciudad Sagrada: The Sacred City* (Puebla: Volkswagen de Mexico, 1999) 72.
71. Díaz, *Conquest* 245.
72. Gillespie xxix; C. Townsend 687.
73. Cortés, *Letters* 166, 63.
74. Cortés, *Letters* 272; cf. 485, note 27.
75. Cortés, *Letters* 351.
76. Cliff 37; Jonathan Phillips, *The Fourth Crusade and the Sack of Constantinople* (New York: Penguin, 2004) xviii–xix.
77. Geoffrey of Villhardouin, qtd. in Phillips 144.
78. "like an enchanted vision from the tale of Amadis." Díaz, *Conquest* 185.
79. Díaz, *History* 352.
80. Cortés, *Letters* 375; cf. 368.
81. Villagutierre 78, note.
82. *Cross and Sword* 21.
83. Cortés, *Letters* 333.
84. Gillespie xxxv.
85. Motolinía (Toribio de Benavente), "Christianization in Mexico," *Latin American History: Selected Problems—Identity, Integration, and Nationhood*, Frederick B. Pike, ed. (New York: Harcourt, Brace & World, 1969) excerpted in *Cross and Sword* 25.
86. Ashwell and O'Leary 47–8, 69–72.
87. Delno C. West, "Medieval Ideas of Apocalyptic Mission and the Early Franciscans in Mexico," *The Americas* 45.3 (January 1989) 293.
88. Charles C. Mann, *1493: Uncovering the New World Columbus Created* (New York: Vintage, 2011) 194–5.
89. Adorno, "Polemics" 27; Barbara Fuchs, "Religion and National Distinction in the Early Modern Atlantic," *Empires of God* 58–9, 66; Jennings 83.
90. "Pope cautions on the pitfalls of materialism" (AP), *San Francisco Chronicle* 25 July 2013: A4.
91. *New York Times* (Reuters), 28 October 2011: A11.
92. Todorov 193.

Chapter 5

1. Bartolomé de Las Casas, "Digest of Columbus's Log-Book on his First Voyage," *The Four Voyages of Christopher Columbus*, J. M. Cohen, ed. and trans. (New York: Penguin, 1969) 55.
2. Peter S. Wells, *Barbarians to Angels: The Dark Ages Reconsidered* (New York: W. W. Norton, 2008) 182–3; Riane Eisler, *The Chalice and the Blade: Our History, Our Future* (San Francisco: Harper & Row, 1987) 46–49.
3. See Figures 4.23 and 4.24 in Philip L. Kohl, *The Making of Bronze Age Eurasia* (New York: Cambridge University Press, 2007) 169, 171.

4. David W. Anthony, *The Horse, the Wheel, and Language: How Bronze-Age Riders from the Eurasian Steppes Shaped the Modern World* (Princeton: Princeton University Press, 2007) 48.

5. Jeremiah 12:12.

6. Kelly DeVries, *Medieval Military Technology* (Orchard Park, NY: Broadview Press, 1992) 7, 20.

7. Inga Clendinnen, *Aztecs: An Interpretation* (New York: Cambridge University Press, 1991) 153.

8. DeVries 21-2.

9. Wells 56; cf. 52, 57, 60.

10. Wells 63-65, 148-9, 182-83.

11. DeVries 22-24; Joseph F. O'Callaghan, *Reconquest and Crusade in Medieval Spain* (Philadelphia: University of Pennsylvania Press, 2003) 130.

12. David Nicolle, *Granada 1492: The Twilight of Moorish Spain* (Westport, CT: Praeger, 2005) 30; Pita Kelekna, *The Horse in Human History* (New York: Cambridge University Press, 2009) 320; Bernal Díaz del Castillo, *The History of the Conquest of New Spain*, Davíd Carrasco, ed., trans. A. P. Maudslay (Albuquerque: University of New Mexico Press, 2008) 40; R. C. Padden, *The Hummingbird and the Hawk: Conquest and Sovereignty in the Valley of Mexico, 1503-1541* (San Francisco: Harper Torchbooks, 1967) 136.

13. Hugh Thomas, *Conquest: Montezuma, Cortés, and the Fall of Old Mexico* (New York: Simon & Schuster, 1993) xiv.

14. See Plates 9 and 14, for example, of the *Lienzo de Tlaxcala*, reproduced in Hernán Cortés, *Letters from Mexico*, Anthony Pagden, trans. and ed. (New Haven: Yale University Press, 1986) 225-6.

15. Francisco de Aguilar, "The Chronicle of Fray Francisco de Aguilar," *The Conquistadors: First-Person Accounts of the Conquest of Mexico*, Patricia de Fuentes, trans. and ed. (New York: Orion Press, 1963) 159.

16. Jared Diamond, *Guns, Germs, and Steel: The Fates of Human Societies* (New York: W. W. Norton, 1999) 76.

17. Díaz, *History* 5, 9, 12, 41.

18. Díaz, *History* 99.

19. Informantes, *The Broken Spears: The Aztec Account of the Conquest of Mexico*, expanded and updated ed., trans. Lysander Kemp, Miguel Leon-Portilla, ed. (Boston: Beacon Press, 1992) 89.

20. Thomas, *Conquest* 168.

21. Matthew Restall, *Seven Myths of the Spanish Conquest* (New York: Oxford University Press, 2003) 143.

22. "Book Twelve of the Florentine Codex," *We People Here: Nahuatl Accounts of the Conquest of Mexico*, James Lockhart, ed. and trans. (Berkeley: University of California Press, 1993) 190.

23. Charles C. Mann, *1491: New Revelations of the Americas Before Columbus*, 2d ed. (New York: Vintage, 2011) 66.

24. Restall 142; Clendinnen, "'Fierce and Unnatural Cruelty': Cortés and the Conquest of Mexico," *Representations* 33 (Winter 1991) 77.

25. Bernal Díaz [del Castillo], *The Conquest of New Spain*, trans. J. M. Cohen (London: The Folio Society, 1963) 38-9.

26. David Abulafia, *The Discovery of Mankind: Atlantic Encounters in the Age of Columbus* (New Haven: Yale UP, 2008) 303.

27. Mann, *1493: Uncovering the New World Columbus Created* (New York: Vintage, 2011) 179, 260.

28. Thomas, *Conquest* 36, 319.

29. Thomas, *Conquest* 332.

30. Las Casas, *History of the Indies II*, Andrée Collard, trans. and ed. (New York: Harper Torchbooks, 1971) 77, 237.

31. Eisler 45-6; Mann, *1493* 94-5; Leon-Portilla, Introduction, *The Broken Spears* xxvi; Ross Hassig, *Aztec Warfare: Imperial Expansion and Political Control* (Norman: University of Oklahoma Press, 1988) 80-81, 85; Díaz *History* 169.

32. Unnamed source cited and qtd. by Gary Kamiya, "Cabrillo made his name with bold, bloody exploits," *San Francisco Chronicle* 18 October 2014: C-2.

33. Las Casas, *History* 250; Díaz, *History* 225, 255, 267, 285, 292; Cortés 156; Inga Clendinnen, "Cortés, Signs, and the Conquest of Mexico," *The Transmission of Culture in Early Modern Europe*, Anthony Grafton and Ann Blair, eds. (Philadelphia: University of Pennsylvania Press, 1990) 111.

34. Abulafia 96.

35. Hassig, *Aztec* 237-8.

36. Camilla Townsend, "Burying the White Gods: New Perspectives on the Conquest of Mexico," *The American Historical Review* 108.3 (June 2003) 678-79.

37. Padden 21.

38. Hassig, *Aztec* 101.

39. Díaz, *History* 217.

40. *The Iliad of Homer*, trans. Richmond Lattimore (Chicago: Phoenix Books, 1951) 8/ll. 268-272: 189.

41. Clendinnen, "Cortés, Signs" 108.

42. "Book Twelve" 140.

43. Clendinnen, "Cortés, Signs" 105-6, 109.

44. Clendinnen, "'Fierce'" 79-83; Clendinnen, "The Cost of Courage in Aztec Society," *The Cost of Courage in Aztec Society: Essays on Mesoamerican Society and Culture* (New York: Cambridge University Press, 2010) 21-2; Restall 144; Hassig, *Aztec* 245; Frances F. Berdan,

The Aztecs of Central Mexico: An Imperial Society, 2d ed. (Belmont, CA: Thomson Wadsworth, 2005) 114; *Broken Spears* xxvi.
45. Clendinnen, "Cortés, Signs" 112.
46. Cf. Jonathan Phillips, *The Fourth Crusade and the Sack of Constantinople* (New York: Penguin, 2004) 178; David Graeber, *Debt: The First 5,000 Years* (Brooklyn: Melville House, 2012) 240.
47. Ronald Findlay and Kevin H. O'Rourke, *Power and Plenty: Trade, War, and the World Economy in the Second Millennium* (Princeton: Princeton University Press, 2007) 144.
48. "Book Twelve" 118.
49. Clendinnen, "'Fierce'" 75, 97 note.
50. Richard F. Townsend, *The Aztecs*, 3d ed. (London: Thames & Hudson, 2009) 232.
51. C. Townsend 673.
52. Christòfol Despuig, qtd. in J. H. Elliott, *Spain and Its World, 1500–1700* (New Haven: Yale University Press, 1989) 9.
53. MacWilliam Bishop, "Medieval Weapon Finds Modern Appeal," *New York Times* 17 September 2014: B12.

Chapter 6

1. Tacitus, *The Agricola and the Germania*, trans. H. Mattingly (Baltimore: Penguin, 1970) 105.
2. Peter S. Wells, *Barbarians to Angels: The Dark Ages Reconsidered* (New York: W. W. Norton, 2008) 42, 101, 173.
3. David Graeber, *Debt: The First 5,000 Years* (Brooklyn: Melville House, 2012) 145.
4. Wells 128, 179.
5. Lotte Hedeager, "From Warrior to Trade Economy," *Vikings: The North Atlantic Saga*, William W. Fitzhugh and Elisabeth I. Ward, eds. (Washington, D.C.: Smithsonian Institute Press, 2000) 84–85.
6. James Casey, *Early Modern Spain: A Social History* (New York: Routledge, 1999) 68.
7. Bartolomé de las Casas, "Digest of Columbus's Log-Book on His First Voyage," *The Four Voyages of Christopher Columbus*, ed. and trans. J. M. Cohen (New York: Penguin, 1969) 59; cf. 56–7.
8. Las Casas, *History of the Indies I*, trans. and ed. Andrée Collard (New York: Harper Torchbooks, 1971) 48.
9. Cf. Hernando Colon, "The Life of the Admiral by his Son, Hernando Colon," *Four Voyages* 190.
10. Christopher Columbus, "Letter Written by Christopher Columbus, Viceroy and Admiral of the Indies, to the Most Christian and Mighty King and Queen of Spain, Our Sovereigns, Notifying Them of the Events of His Voyage and the Cities, Provinces, Rivers and Other Marvels, also the Many Goldfields and Other Objects of Great Riches and Value," *Four Voyages* 300.
11. John Darwin, *After Tamerlane: The Rise and Fall of Global Empires, 1400–2000* (New York: Bloomsbury Press, 2008) 58.
12. Tzvetan Todorov, *The Conquest of America: The Question of the Other*, trans. Richard Howard (New York: Harper & Row, 1984) 98.
13. Las Casas, *History of the Indies II*, trans. and ed. Andrée Collard (New York: Harper Torchbooks, 1971) 87.
14. Thomas More, *Utopia*, trans. Paul Turner (Baltimore: Penguin, 1965) 86.
15. J. M. G. LeClézio, *The Mexican Dream: Or, the Interrupted Thought of Amerindian Civilizations*, trans. Teresa Lavender Fagan (Chicago: University of Chicago Press, 1993) 14.
16. Las Casas, *A Short Account of the Destruction of the Indies*, trans. Nigel Griffin (New York: Penguin, 1992) 27–28.
17. Cf. Hugh Thomas, *Conquest: Montezuma, Cortés, and the Fall of Old Mexico* (New York: Simon & Schuster, 1993) 63.
18. Thomas, *The Golden Empire: Spain, Charles V, and the Creation of America* (New York: Random House, 2010) 137.
19. Informantes, *The Broken Spears: The Aztec Account of the Conquest of Mexico*, trans. Lysander Kemp, Miguel Leon-Portilla, ed. (Boston: Beacon Press, 1992) 51–2.
20. Todorov 111.
21. Ramón Iglesia, *Columbus, Cortés, and Other Essays*, Lesley Byrd Simpson, ed. and trans. (Berkeley: University of California Press, 1969) 195.
22. Bernal Díaz del Castillo, *The History of the Conquest of New Spain*, trans. A. P. Maudslay, Davíd Carrasco, ed. (Albuquerque: University of New Mexico Press, 2008).
23. R. C. Padden, *The Hummingbird and the Hawk: Conquest and Sovereignty in the Valley of Mexico, 1503–1541* (San Francisco: Harper Torchbooks, 1967) 139–41.
24. Díaz, *History* 54–5.
25. Qtd. in J. H. Elliott, *Imperial Spain: 1469–1716* (New York: Penguin, 2002) 65, citing Lewis Hanke, *Bartolomé de las Casas* (The Hague, 1951) 9.
26. From Erasmus, *L'Ichtyophagic* (1526), qtd. in Thomas, *Golden* 21.
27. Jonathan Phillips, *The Fourth Crusade and the Sack of Constantinople* (New York: Penguin, 2004) 260, 265.
28. Patricia Seed, *American Pentimento: The Invention of Indians and the Pursuit of Riches* (Minneapolis: University of Minnesota Press, 2001) 61.
29. Columbus, "Letter," *Four Voyages* 300.

30. Bernal Díaz, *The Conquest of New Spain*, trans. J. M. Cohen (London: The Folio Society, 1963) 209.
31. Díaz, *Conquest* 111-12.
32. Cf. Frances F. Berdan, *The Aztecs of Central Mexico: An Imperial Society*, 2d ed. (Belmont, CA: Thomson Wadsworth, 2005) 172.
33. Matthew Restall, *Seven Myths of the Spanish Conquest* (New York: Oxford University Press, 2003) 21-2.
34. Inga Clendinnen, *Aztecs: An Interpretation* (New York: Cambridge University Press, 1991) 269; cf. Claude Lévi-Strauss, *The Elementary Structures of Kinship*, rev. ed., trans. James Harle Bell, et al. (Boston: Beacon Press, 1969) 53.
35. "Book Twelve of the Florentine Codex," *We People Here: Nahuatl Accounts of the Conquest of Mexico*, James Lockhart, ed. and trans. (Berkeley: University of California Press, 1993) 122.
36. Díaz, *History* 199, 201-2.
37. Henri Pirenne, *Economic and Social History of Medieval Europe* (New York: Harcourt, Brace & World, 1937) 118-19.
38. Phillips 279.
39. *La Conquista de Tenochtitlan*, Germán Vazquez, ed. (Madrid, 1988) 105, cited in Thomas, *Conquest* 326.
40. Díaz, *History* 202.
41. Díaz, *History* 202-4; Thomas, *Conquest* 330-331.
42. Hernán Cortés, *Letters from Mexico*, Anthony Pagden, ed. and trans. (New Haven: Yale University Press, 1986) 118.
43. Cf. Díaz, *Conquest* 259; Díaz, *History* 227, 231.
44. Díaz, *History* 237-8.
45. "Book Twelve" 248.
46. "Extract from Annals of Tlatelolco," *We People Here* 271.
47. Graeber 315-17; cf. Díaz, *Conquest* 350.
48. Díaz, *Conquest* 345.
49. Díaz, *History* 305.
50. Díaz, *History* 311.
51. See, e.g., Thomas, *Conquest* 322.
52. Díaz, *Conquest* 348. My emphasis.
53. Díaz, *Conquest* 348.
54. Díaz, *History* 313.
55. Phillips 269.
56. Díaz, *Conquest* 349-50.
57. Thomas, *Golden* 5.
58. Díaz, *History* 180.
59. Graeber 113.
60. Díaz, *History* 362-71.
61. Todorov 156.
62. Cortés 94.
63. Arturo Giraldez, "Cacao Beans in Colonial Mexico: Small Change in a Global Economy," *Money in the Pre-Industrial World: Bullion, Debasements and Coin Substitutes*, John H. Munro, ed. (Brookfield, VT: Pickering & Chatto, 2012) 150-4; Deborah L. Nichols, "Artisans, Markets, and Merchants," *The Aztec World*, Elizabeth M. Brumfiel and Gary M. Feinman, eds. (New York: Abrams and the Field Museum, 2008) 113.
64. See, for example, Díaz, *History* 110, 202, 241.
65. Clendinnen, *Aztecs* 137.
66. Elliott, *Spain and Its World, 1500-1700* (New Haven: Yale University Press, 1989) 52.
67. Davíd Carrasco with Scott Sessions, *Daily Life of the Aztecs: People of the Sun and Earth* (Westport, CT: Greenwood Press, 1998) 41; cf. Richard F. Townsend, *The Aztecs*, 3d ed. (London: Thames & Hudson, 2009) 56.
68. Ronald Findlay and Kevin H. O'Rourke, *Power and Plenty: Trade, War, and the World Economy in the Second Millennium* (Princeton: Princeton University Press, 2007) 165.
69. Fernand Braudel, *The Mediterranean and the Mediterranean World in the Age of Philip II*, Vol. 1, trans. Siân Reynolds (New York: Harper & Row, 1972) 470.
70. Graeber 229-39.
71. *The Poem of the Cid: A Bilingual Edition with Parallel Text*, trans. Rita Hamilton and Janet Perry (New York: Penguin, 1975) ll. 1187-89, 84-5.
72. Casey 87.
73. Steven Gunn, "War, Religion, and the State," *Early Modern Europe: An Oxford History*, Euan Cameron, ed. (New York: Oxford University Press, 1999) 112.
74. Robert Ferguson, *The Vikings: A History* (New York: Penguin, 2009) 254.
75. Charles C. Mann, *1493: Uncovering the New World Columbus Created* (New York: Vintage, 2011) 376.
76. Abulafia 91.
77. Taylor Branch, *Parting the Waters: America in the King Years, 1954-63* (New York: Simon & Schuster, 1988) 741.
78. Braudel, *Mediterranean* 469.
79. A. J. R. Russell-Wood, "Before Columbus: Portugal's African Prelude to the Middle Passage and Contribution to Discourse on Race and Slavery," *Race, Discourse, and the Origins of the Americas: A New World View*, Vera Lawrence Hyatt and Rex Nettleford, eds. (Washington, D.C.: Smithsonian Institute Press, 1995) 137.
80. Hans Koning, *The Conquest of America: How the Indian Nations Lost Their Continent* (New York: Monthly Review, 1993) 54; Pirenne 17, 22; Eric Williams, *Capitalism & Slavery* (Chapel Hill: University of North Carolina Press, 1994) 3; Barnaby Rogerson, *The Last Crusaders: The Hundred-Year Battle for the Centre of the World* (New York: Overlook Press, 2009) 35; Robert S. Duplessis, *Transitions to*

Capitalism in Early Modern Europe (New York: Cambridge University Press, 1997) 261-2; Thomas, *Rivers of Gold: The Rise of the Spanish Empire, from Columbus to Magellan* (New York: Random House, 2003) 32-3; Nigel Cliff, *Holy War: How Vasco da Gama's Epic Voyages Turned the Tide in a Centuries-Old Clash of Civilizations* (New York: HarperCollins, 2011) 90-1.

81. Abulafia 91-95; Russell-Wood 153-54.

82. Marcus Rediker, *The Slave Ship: A Human History* (New York: Penguin, 2007) 260.

83. Rediker 98.

84. Bartolomé de Las Casas, "Digest," *Four Voyages* 58-9; "Letter of Columbus to Various Persons Describing the Results of his First Voyage and Written on the Return Journey," *Four Voyages* 118.

85. James Reston, Jr., *Dogs of God: Columbus, the Inquisition, and the Defeat of the Moors* (New York: Doubleday, 2005) 307; cf. Thomas, *Rivers* 134, 136, 155.

86. Thomas, *Rivers* 111, 184-5.

87. Anthony Pagden, "Introduction" to Las Casas, *A Short Account of the Destruction of the Indies*, trans. Nigel Griffin (New York: Penguin, 1992) xix.

88. Las Casas, *History* 79, 207; Todorov 134.

89. Las Casas, *History*, excerpted in *Cross and Sword: An Eyewitness History of Christianity in Latin America*, H. McKennie Goodpasture, ed. (Maryknoll, NY: Orbis Books, 1989) 10.

90. Graeber 315.

91. Thomas, *Golden* 113.

92. Qtd. in Todorov 161.

93. Seed 57-62; 71.

94. Lesley Byrd Simpson, *The Encomienda in New Spain: The Beginning of Spanish Mexico* (Berkeley: University of California Press, 1966) 69.

95. Fray Juan de Zumárraga, "The Bishop-elect of Mexico, Don Fray Juan de Zumárraga, to Charles V, August 27, 1529," abridged as Appendix 3 in Simpson 217-19; William Weber Johnson, *Cortés* (Boston: Little, Brown, 1975) 210-11.

96. Thomas, *Golden* 467.

97. Mann, *1493* 182.

98. Howard J. Erlichman, *Conquest, Tribute, and Trade: The Quest for Precious Metals and the Birth of Globalization* (Amherst, NY: Prometheus, 2010) 260-66; 362-65; cf. Findlay and O'Rourke 165.

99. Thomas, *Rivers* 410. Thomas repeatedly cites Las Casas as a prime example, but see Rolena Adorno, "The Polemics of Possession: Spain in America, Circa 1550," *Empires of God: Religious Encounters in the Early Modern Atlantic*, Linda Gregerson and Susan Juster, eds. (Philadelphia: University of Pennsylvania Press, 2011) 30.

100. Thomas, *Golden* 114.

101. Valentin Y. Mudimbe, "Romanus Pontifex (1454) and the Expansion of Europe," *Race, Discourse* 65.

102. Cf. Findlay and O'Rourke 155.

103. See, for example, Andre Gunder Frank, *ReOrient: Global Economy in the Asian Age* (Berkeley: University of California Press, 1998) 153-9; Elliott, *Imperial* 192-6.

104. Findlay and O'Rourke 219-20.

105. Teofilo F. Ruiz, *Spanish Society, 1400-1600* (Essex: Pearson Education, 2001) 24, 26; Restall 57; Elliott, *Imperial Spain* 193, 198, 200; Elliott, *Spain and Its* 21; Renate Pieper, "Money or Export Commodity for Asia? American Silver in the Markets of Mexico, Castile and Amsterdam From the Sixteenth to the Eighteenth Century," *Money in the Pre-Indusrial World* 137; Graeber 339.

106. Elliott, *Imperial Spain* 206-10.

107. Gunn 113.

108. Elliott, *Spain and Its* 23.

109. Pita Kelekna, *The Horse in Human History* (New York: Cambridge University Press, 2009) 365; J. M. Blaut, *The Colonizer's Model of the World: Geographic Diffusionism and Eurocentric History* (New York: The Guilford Press, 1993) 189; Mann, *1493* 33-4, 189-90.

110. Gunder Frank 143.

111. Casey 68.

112. Braudel, *Mediterranean* 480-1, 522.

113. Qtd. in Braudel, *Mediterranean* 488.

114. Giovanni Arrighi, *The Long Twentieth Century: Money, Power, and the Origins of Our Times* (New York: Verso, 1994) 126, 131.

115. Findlay and O'Rourke 185.

116. Braudel, *Mediterranean* 495-6.

117. Qtd. in Braudel, *Mediterranean* 519.

118. Elliott, *Imperial* 269.

119. Elliott, *Imperial* 285.

120. Qtd. in Elliott, *Spain and Its* 25.

121. Braudel, *The Perspective of the World*, trans. Siân Reynolds (New York: Harper & Row, 1984) 167-9, 208-9; Elliott, *Imperial* 231-3, 263; Erlichman 297-8.

122. Arrighi 152.

123. Casey 69.

124. Pieper 129.

125. Braudel, *Capitalism and Material Life: 1400-1800* (New York: Harper & Row, 1973) 345.

126. Pieper 145.

127. William Neuman, "For Miners, Increasing Risk on a Mountain at the Heart of Bolivia's Identity," *New York Times* 17 September 2014: A7.

128. Qtd. in Gunder Frank 132.

129. Elliott, *Spain and Its* 20; Findlay and O'Rourke 212, 223.

130. Findlay and O'Rourke 221.

131. Gunder Frank 141; Findlay and O'Rourke 173.

132. Braudel, *Mediterranean* 495-6.

133. Darwin 12–13, 86.
134. Ian Morris, *Why the West Rules—For Now* (New York: Picador, 2010) 275.
135. Darwin 21–2, 98.
136. Braudel, *Mediterranean* 464, 499; Gunder Frank 35, 56–7, 71, 135; Mann, *1493* 196–7; Findlay and O'Rourke 215.
137. Braudel, *Perspective* 490.
138. Qtd. in Gunder Frank 138.
139. Minqi Li, *The Rise of China and the Demise of the Capitalist World Economy* (New York: Monthly Review Press, 2008) 5.
140. Findlay and O'Rourke 220; Mann, *1493* 215 ff.
141. Herman Van der Wee, "The Amsterdam Wisselbank's Innovations in the Monetary Sphere: The Role of 'Bank Money,'" *Money in the Pre-Industrial World: Bullion, Debasements and Coin Substitutes,* John H. Munro, ed. (Brookfield, VT: Pickering & Chatto, 2012) 94–5; Pieper 140, 145; Braudel, *Capitalism* 349; Graeber 309–13.
142. Gunder Frank 138, 147, 152, 157–8, 160, 162, 164, 178; cf. Findlay and O'Rourke 213.
143. Braudel, *Perspective* 491.
144. Bruno Snell, *The Discovery of the Mind: The Greek Origins of European Thought,* trans. T. G. Rosenmeyer (New York: Harper & Row, 1960) 227–45.
145. Lewis Mumford, *Technics and Civilization* (New York: Harcourt, Brace & World, 1962) 137; Quote is from William Blake, "And did those feet in ancient time."
146. Morris 81–171.
147. Darwin 98, 104; Patrick K. O'Brien, "Metanarratives in Global Histories of Material Progress," *The International History Review* XXIII, 2 (June 2001) 354–57; William T. Rowe, rev. of Kenneth Pomeranz, *The Great Divergence: Europe, China, and the Making of the Modern World Economy* in *The International History Review* XXIII, 2 (June 2001) 409.
148. That of Angus Maddison, *The World Economy: Historical Statistics* (Paris: Organization for Economic Co-operation and Development, 2003), cited in Li 5.
149. Eric Jones, *The European Miracle: Environments, Economies and Geopolitics in the History of Europe and Asia,* 3d ed. (New York: Cambridge University Press, 2003) xiv, xx, xxix-xxx.
150. Cf. Braudel, *Capitalism* 3.
151. Jones 226–7.
152. Jones 229, 231.
153. Jones 241. But Jones also writes that when Europeans discovered the Americas, they were ready to exploit the "vast resources" of these lands "and to develop as a result." See Jones xxxiii, 228.
154. O'Brien 348, 353, 361, 366; Immanuel Wallerstein, *The Capitalist World Economy* (New York: Cambridge University Press, 1979) 26, 37, 134.
155. Darwin 50.
156. Bernard Lewis, *Cultures in Conflict: Christians, Muslims, and Jews in the Age of Discovery* (New York: Oxford University Press, 1995) 73.
157. Rediker 53.
158. Frank 354–5; Blaut 188–90.
159. Charles P. Kindleberger, *Economic Response: Comparative Studies in Trade, Finance, and Growth* (Cambridge: Harvard University Press, 1978) 142, 166.
160. Darwin 109; Werner Sombart, *Luxury and Capitalism,* trans. W. R. Dittmar (Ann Arbor University of Michigan Press, 1967).
161. In *The Great Divergence,* discussed in O'Brien 363.
162. Duplessis 47.
163. Findlay and O'Rourke 324.
164. Darwin 197.
165. Morris 515.

Chapter 7

1. Pita Kelekna, *The Horse in Human History* (New York: Cambridge University Press, 2009) 352–3; R. B. Cunninghame Graham, *The Horses of the Conquest* (Norman: University of Oklahoma Press, 1949) 20–1, 23.
2. Hugh Thomas, *Rivers of Gold: The Rise of the Spanish Empire, from Columbus to Magellan* (New York: Random House, 2003) 257.
3. Bartolomé de Las Casas, *A Short Account of the Destruction of the Indies,* trans. Nigel Griffin (New York: Penguin, 1992) 21–22.
4. Bernal Díaz del Castillo, *The History of the Conquest of New Spain,* trans. A. P. Maudslay, David Carrasco, ed. (Albuquerque: University of New Mexico Press, 2008) 42, 44–5, 73.
5. Díaz, *History* 92–4.
6. Hernán Cortés, *Letters from Mexico,* Anthony Pagden, trans. and ed. (New Haven: Yale University Press, 1986) 252.
7. Cortés 184, 242; Díaz, *History* 288; Kelekna 113.
8. Cortés 230; James Reston, Jr., *Dogs of God: Columbus, the Inquisition, and the Defeat of the Moors* (New York: Doubleday, 2005) 93.
9. Cortés 234; cf. Díaz, *History* 232, 244.
10. Summarizing these arguments is Sherpard Krech III, *The Ecological Indian: Myth and History* (New York: W. W. Norton, 1999) 29–43. Cf. *Native Americans and the Environment: Perspectives on the Ecological Indian,* Michael E. Harkin and David Rich Lewis, eds. (Lincoln University of Nebraska Press, 2007).
11. Kelekna 16–17, 42, 339–50; Krech 36.
12. David W. Anthony, *The Horse, the Wheel, and Language: How Bronze-Age Riders*

from the Eurasian Steppes Shaped the Modern World (Princeton: Princeton University Press, 2007) 197–8.

13. Kelekna 64.

14. Kelekna 40–1, 46, 65, 93, 96, 106 ff; Brian Fagan, *The Great Warming: Climate Change and the Rise and Fall of Civilizations* (New York: Bloomsbury Press, 2008) 54–6.

15. Cf. Anthony 234 ff.; Philip L. Kohl, *The Making of Bronze Age Eurasia* (New York: Cambridge University Press, 2007) 133 ff.; Cristina Biaggi, "The Roots of Patriarchy in Europe, the Middle East, and Asia (or) Why Did the Kurgans Become Warlike?" *The Rule of Mars: Readings on the Origins, History and Impact of Patriarchy,* C. Biaggi, ed. (Manchester, CT: Knowledge, Ideas & Trends, 2005) 77–93; Riane Eisler, *The Chalice and the Blade: Our History, Our Future* (San Francisco: Harper & Row, 1987).

16. Ian Morris, *Why the West Rules—For Now* (New York: Picador, 2010) 389.

17. Jared Diamond, *Guns, Germs, and Steel: The Fates of Human Societies* (New York: W. W. Norton, 1999) 164; Marcus Rediker, *The Slave Ship: A Human History* (New York: Penguin, 2007) 90; Fernand Braudel, *Capitalism and Material Life: 1400–1800* (New York: Harper & Row, 1973) 255; David Abulafia, *The Discovery of Mankind: Atlantic Encounters in the Age of Columbus* (New Haven: Yale University Press, 2008) 92.

18. Joseph F. O'Callaghan, *Request and Crusade in Medieval Spain* (Philadelphia: University of Pennsylvania Press, 2003) 146.

19. O'Callaghan 132.

20. James Casey, *Early Modern Spain: A Social History* (New York: Routledge, 1999) 12.

21. *The Poem of the Cid: A Bilingual Edition with Parallel Text,* trans. Rita Hamilton and Janet Perry (New York: Penguin, 1975) 104–7.

22. Graham 17–18; Kelekna 348; Teofilo F. Ruiz, *Spanish Society, 1400–1600* (Essex: Pearson Education, 2001) 90.

23. Kelekna 357.

24. Graham 111. The conquistadors mostly switched to cotton armor before they had gone very far.

25. Díaz, *History* 25–6.

26. Graham 56.

27. Xenophon, *The Persian Expedition,* trans. Rex Warner (New York: Penguin, 1972) 349, note.

28. Patricia Seed, *American Pentimento: The Invention of Indians and the Pursuit of Riches* (Minneapolis: University of Minnesota Press, 2001) 74; Lesley Byrd Simpson, *The Encomienda in New Spain: The Beginning of Spanish Mexico* (Berkeley: University of California Press, 1966) 75; Anamaría Ashwell and John O'Leary, *Cholula: La Cuidad Sagrada: The Sacred City* (Puebla: Volkswagen de México, 1999) 75.

29. Cortés 342–3, 346–48, 361–2, 376–7; notes 514–15; Kelekna 390–1.

30. Kelekna 363; Charles C. Mann, *1491: New Revelations of the Americas Before Columbus,* 2d ed. (New York: Vintage, 2011) 98.

31. Joseph R. Strayer and Dana C. Munro, *The Middle Ages: 395-1500* (New York: Appleton-Century-Crofts, 1959) 505.

32. Cortés 377.

33. William Weber Johnson, *Cortés* (Boston: Little, Brown, 1975) 205.

34. Juan de Villagutierre Soto-Mayor, *History of the Conquest of the Province of the Itza: Subjugation and Events of the Lacondon and Other Natives of Yucatan in North America,* trans. Brother Robert D. Wood (Culver City, CA: Labyrinthos, 1983) 72–3.

35. Villagutierre 73–77.

36. Tacitus, *The Agricola and the Germania,* trans. H. Mattingly (Baltimore: Penguin, 1970) 109–10.

37. Graham 108–9, 112; Hugh Thomas, *The Golden Empire: Spain, Charles V, and the Creation of America* (New York: Random House, 2010) 418–19.

38. Braudel, *Capitalism* 251, 255.

39. Graham 112, 114–16.

40. Diamond 164; Robert V. Hine and John Mack Faragher, *The American West: A New Interpretive History* (New Haven: Yale University Press, 2000) 137–8; Preston Holder, *The Hoe and the Horse on the Plains: A Study of Cultural Development Among North American Indians* (Lincoln: University of Nebraska Press, 1970) 140–2.

41. Holder 112–13; Hine and Faragher 139.

42. Diamond 77.

43. Strayer and Munro 472, 506; Barbara W. Tuchman, *A Distant Mirror: The Calamitous 14th Century* (New York: Ballantine, 1978) 593–4.

44. John Darwin, *After Tamerlane: The Rise and Fall of Global Empires, 1400–2000* (New York: Bloomsbury Press, 2008) 78.

45. J. H. Elliott, *Imperial Spain: 1469–1716* (New York: Penguin, 2002) 133.

46. Braudel, *Capitalism* 253–4, 274; Marcel Mazoyer and Laurence Roudart, *A History of World Agriculture: From the Neolithic Age to the Current Crisis,* trans. James H. Membrez (New York: Monthly Review Press, 2006) 268 and passim.

47. "Horses headed for slaughter" (AP), *San Francisco Chronicle* 19 April 2013: A6.

Chapter 8

1. Charles C. Mann, *1493: Uncovering the New World Columbus Created* (New York: Vintage, 2011) 100.

2. Bartolomé de Las Casas, *Historia I,* ch.

92, 376 ff., qtd. without translation in Pierre Chaunu, *European Expansion in the Later Middle Ages*, trans. Katharine Bertram (New York: North-Holland, 1979) 194 note.

3. Cf. Frances F. Berdan, *The Aztecs of Central Mexico: An Imperial Society*, 2d ed. (Belmont, CA: Thomson Wadsworth, 2005) 188.

4. Francisco de Aguilar, "The Chronicle of Fray Francisco de Aguilar," *The Conquistadors: First-Person Accounts of the Conquest of Mexico*, Patricia de Fuentes, ed. and trans. (New York: Orion Press, 1963) 149.

5. Anthony Pagden, "Introduction" to Bartolomé de Las Casas, *A Short Account of the Destruction of the Indies*, trans. Nigel Griffin (New York: Penguin, 1992) xxvi; Las Casas, *Short Account* 13.

6. Rolena Adorno, "The Polemics of Possession: Spain on America, Circa 1550," *Empires of God: Religious Encounters in the Early Modern Atlantic*, Linda Gregerson and Susan Juster, eds. (Philadelphia: University of Pennsylvania Press, 2011) 24–5.

7. Pagden, "Introduction" to Las Casas xxviii.

8. Las Casas, *History of the Indies*, Andrée Collard, ed. and trans. (New York: Harper Torchbooks, 1971) 211.

9. Las Casas, *History* 211.

10. Las Casas, *Short Account* 24.

11. David Abulafia, *The Discovery of Mankind: Atlantic Encounters in the Age of Columbus* (New Haven: Yale University Press, 2008) 293.

12. Teofilo F. Ruiz, *Spanish Society, 1400–1600* (Essex: Pearson Education, 2001) 102.

13. Qtd. in Lesley Byrd Simpson, *The Encomienda in New Spain: The Beginning of Spanish Mexico* (Berkeley: University of California Press, 1966) 13.

14. Hugh Thomas, *Rivers of Gold: The Rise of the Spanish Empire, from Columbus to Magellan* (New York: Random House, 2003) 232–4; cf. 176, 180.

15. Thomas, *Rivers* 290–1; Simpson 22–23. Simpson's numbers on labor entitlement rankings vary a little from Thomas's, used here.

16. Hernando Colon, "The Life of the Admiral by His Son, Hernando Colon," in *The Four Voyages of Christopher Columbus*, J. M. Cohen, ed. and trans. (New York: Penguin, 1969) 263; Thomas, *The Golden Empire: Spain, Charles V, and the Creation of America* (New York: Random House, 2010) 117.

17. Las Casas, *History*, excerpted in *Cross and Sword: An Eyewitness History of Christianity in Latin America*, H. McKennie Goodpasture, ed. (Maryknoll, NY: Orbis Books, 1989) 9.

18. Simpson 45–47; Thomas *Rivers* 376–8.

19. Thomas, *Rivers* 258.

20. Bernal Díaz [del Castillo], *The Conquest of New Spain*, trans. J. M. Cohen (London: The Folio Society, 1963) 26, 115.

21. Hernán Cortés, *Letters from Mexico*, Anthony Pagden, ed. and trans. (New Haven: Yale Univesity Press, 1986) 38.

22. Cortés 126.

23. Richard Lee Marks, *Cortés: The Great Adventurer and the Fate of Aztec Mexico* (New York: Alfred A. Knopf, 1993) 21.

24. Las Casas, *Short Account* 30.

25. Massimo Livi-Bacci, "Return to Hispaniola: Reassessing a Demographic Catastrophe," *The Hispanic American Historical Review* 83:1 (February 2003) 3–51.

26. Simpson 131.

27. Junot Díaz, *The Brief Wondrous Life of Oscar Wao* (New York: Riverhead Books, 2007) 1. Labor exploitation on Hispaniola (now Haiti and the Dominican Republic) has not ended. According to the Worker Rights Consortium, Haitian garment factories that make products for Gap, Target, Walmart, and other prominent retailers routinely violate labor laws by establishing hard-to-meet production quotas and failing to pay overtime, thus ensuring that the great majority of Haitian garment workers receive less than the legal minimum of 300 *gourdes* (about $6.90) that employers are obliged to offer for an eight-hour workday. See www.nytimes.com/2013/10/16.

28. Cortés, *Letters* 279–80.

29. Cortés, *Letters*, note 98, 498.

30. Cortés, *Letters* 336.

31. Ed. J. Garcia Icazbalceta, *Colección de documentos para la historia de México* I (México: El Museo, 1856–1866) 470–83, cited in Simpson 61–2.

32. Patricia Seed, *American Pentimento: The Invention of Indians and the Pursuit of Riches* (Minneapolis: University of Minnesota Press, 2001) 67; Simpson 181.

33. Thomas, *Conquest: Montezuma, Cortés, and the Fall of Old Mexico* (New York: Simon & Schuster, 1993) 576.

34. R. C. Padden, *The Hummingbird and the Hawk: Conquest and Sovereignty in the Valley of Mexico, 1503–1541* (San Francisco: Harper Torchbooks, 1967) 19–20.

35. Thomas, *Golden* 13.

36. Held by the *Museo Nacional de Antropologia* as Plate IV of *Notas* to the *residencia* of Pedro de Alvarez, according to Henry R. Wagner, *The Rise of Fernando Cortés* (Berkeley: The Cortes Society, 1944) 78.

37. Challenging the assumption that the painting depicts the killing of the Cholultecan chief over possession of gold is Lori Boornazian Diel, "*Manuscrito del aperreamiento* (Manuscript of the Dogging): A 'Dogging' and Its

Implications for Early Colonial Cholula," *Ethnohistory* 58.4 (Fall 2011) 585–611.
38. Wagner 78.
39. See Rolena Adorno, "Bernal Díaz del Castillo: Soldier, Eye-witness, Polemicist," *The History of the Conquest of New Spain by Bernal Díaz del Castillo*, Davíd Carrasco, ed. (Albuquerque: University of New Mexico Press, 2008) 389–98.
40. William Weber Johnson, *Cortés* (Boston: Little, Brown, 1975) 208, 212; Thomas, *Conquest* 577.
41. Thomas, *Golden* 13; Howard J. Erlichman, *Conquest, Tribute, and Trade: The Quest for Precious Metals and the Birth of Globalization* (Amherst, NY: Prometheus, 2010) 158; J. H. Parry, *The Age of Reconnaissaince: Discovery, Exploration and Settlement 1450 to 1650* (Berkeley: University of California Press, 1981) 169.
42. Díaz, *History* 369.
43. Cortés, *Letters* 287; cf. 284, 289, 298.
44. Díaz, *History* 324, 327.
45. Thomas, *Golden* 98; Díaz, *History* 330–31.
46. Thomas, *Golden* 78.
47. Simpson 74.
48. Wagner 436.
49. Simpson 101, 189 note.
50. "Extract from *Annals of Tlatelolco*," *We People Here: Nahuatl Accounts of the conquest of Mexico*, James Lockhart, ed. and trans. (Berkeley: University of California Press, 1993) 273.
51. Cf. Parry 169.
52. Fray Juan de Zumárraga, "The Bishop-elect of Mexico, Don Fray Juan de Zumárraga, to Charles V, August 27, 1529," abridged as Appendix 3, Simpson 226.
53. W. W. Johnson 207.
54. Cf. J. H. Elliott, *Imperial Spain: 1469–1716* (New York: Penguin, 2002) 63–4; Berdan 171–2; Richard F. Townsend, *The Aztecs*, 3d ed. (London: Thames & Hudson, 2009) 221; Las Casas, *History* 60, 78, 227; Matthew Restall, *Seven Myths of the Spanish Conquest* (New York: Oxford University Press, 2003) 35–38; Thomas, *Rivers* 440.
55. Simpson 80–1.
56. Simpson 123.
57. Simpson 129–33, 140.
58. Thomas, *Golden* 483.
59. Mann, *1493* 386, 388.
60. Thomas, *Golden* 134, 482, 484.
61. Qtd. in Simpson 138.
62. Simpson 133.
63. Thomas, *Golden* 312.
64. Díaz, *History* 371.
65. Adorno, "Bernal Díaz."
66. W. W. Johnson 219; Marks 333.
67. Thomas, *Conquest* 319–20.
68. Henry Kamen, *Empire: How Spain Became a World Power* (New York: HarperCollins, 2003) 83.
69. Chaunu 121.
70. Aristotle, *The Politics of Aristotle*, trans. Ernest Barker (New York: Oxford University Press, 1962) VII, x §13, 306.
71. Thomas, *Rivers* 281.
72. Qtd. in Robert V. Hine and John Mack Faragher, *The American West: A New Interpretative History* (New Haven: Yale University Press, 2000) 35.
73. Simpson viii; cf. 177 note.
74. Díaz, *Conquest* 232.
75. Parry 228; Philip Wayne Powell, *Soldiers, Indians & Silver: The Northward Advance of New Spain, 1550–1600* (Berkeley: University of California Press, 1952) 41.
76. Diaz, *History* 72.
77. Padden 151.
78. Díaz, *History* 291–2.
79. Alexis de Tocqueville, *Democracy in America*, Vol. 1, trans. Henry Reeve (New York: Vintage, 1945) 30.
80. Edward G. Wakefield, *England and America*, Vol. 1 (London, 1833) 17, qtd. in Karl Marx, *Capital: A Critique of Political Economy*, Vol. One, trans. Ben Fowkes (New York: Vintage, 1976) 933.
81. Jill Lepore, "The Dark Ages: Terrorism, Counterterrorism, and the Law of Torment," *The New Yorker*, March 18, 2013: 31.
82. Leonard Pitt, *The Decline of the Californios: A Social History of the Spanish-Speaking Californians, 1846–1890* (Berkeley: University of California Press, 1968) 6.
83. Qtd. in David J. Langum, "Californios and the Image of Indolence," *The Western Historical Quarterly* IX.2 (April 1978) 195.
84. Qtd. in Langum 189–90.
85. Qtd. in Langum 184.
86. Richard Henry Dana, Jr., *Two Years Before the Mast* (Hertfordshire: Wordsworth Editions, 1996) 61, 65, 66.
87. Dana 60.
88. Robert Ferguson, *The Vikings: A History* (New York: Penguin, 2009) 256.
89. Qtd. in Langum 191.
90. Pitt 12.
91. Pitt 16.
92. Pitt 23.
93. Richard Dawkins, *The Selfish Gene* (New York: Oxford University Press, 1989) 197 and passim.
94. Erlichman 449–50; Elliott, *Imperial* 292; Simpson xii; Seed 69.
95. Mann, *1493* 78.
96. Qtd. in Jill Lepore, *The Mansion of Happiness: A History of Life and Death* (New York: Vintage, 2012) 8–9.
97. Francis Jennings, *The Invasion of Amer-*

ica: Indians, Colonialism, and the Cant of Conquest (Chapel Hill: University of North Carolina Press, 1975) 15, 33, 66, 80; cf. Hine & Faragher 75–6.
98. Seed 17–18, 28.
99. Tocqueville 301–2; Hine and Faragher 110, 118. Cf. the slogan associated with the movement to establish a Jewish homeland in Palestine: "A land without people for a people without land."
100. Hugh Brogan, *The Pelican History of the United States of America* (New York: Penguin, 1985) 56.
101. Hine and Faragher 118.
102. Lepore 30.
103. Robert Hughes, *The Fatal Shore: The Epic of Australia's Founding* (New York: Vintage, 1986) 40–1.
104. Eric Williams, *Capitalism & Slavery* (Chapel Hill: University of North Carolina Press, 1994) 10.
105. Mann, *1493* 367.
106. Williams 3–29; Fernand Braudel, *The Perspective of the World*, trans. Siân Reynolds (New York: Harper & Row, 1984) 396; David Graeber, *Debt: The First 5,000 Years* (Brooklyn: Melville House, 2012) 212.

Chapter 9

1. Eric Partridge, *Origins: A Short Etymological Dictionary of Modern English* (New York: Greenwich House, 1966) 588–9.
2. J. H. Elliott, "The Discovery of America and the Discovery of Man," *Spain and Its World, 1500–1700* (New Haven: Yale University Press, 1989) 49.
3. Elliott, "Discovery" 53–56.
4. Qtd. in Jared Diamond, *Guns, Germs, and Steel: The Fates of Human Societies* (New York: W. W. Norton, 1999) 74.
5. Qtd. in Francis Jennings, *The Invasion of America: Indians, Colonialism, and the Cant of Conquest* (Chapel Hill: University of North Carolina Press, 1975) 46.
6. Qtd. in Hans Koning, *The Conquest of America: How the Indian Nations Lost Their Continent* (New York: Monthly Review Press, 1993) 85.
7. Robert Hughes, *The Fatal Shore: The Epic of Australia's Founding* (New York: Vintage, 1986) 273.
8. Marcus Rediker, *The Slave Ship: A Human History* (New York: Penguin, 2007) 266.
9. Marshall Sahlins, *The Western Illusion of Human Nature* (Chicago: Prickly Paradigm Press, 2008) 54.
10. Cf. Norbert Elias, *The History of Manners: The Civilizing Process*, Vol. 1, trans. Edmund Jephcott (New York: Pantheon, 1978)

e.g., 78, 85–6, 89; Margaret Visser, *The Rituals of Dinner: The Origins, Evolution, Eccentricities, and Meaning of Table Manners* (New York: Grove Weidenfeld, 1991) e.g., 63, 317.
11. David A. Peterson, "The Real Cholula," *Notas Mesoamericanas* 10 (1987) 71, 73.
12. Hernán Cortés, *Letters from Mexico*, Anthony Pagden, trans. and ed. (New Haven: Yale University Press, 1986) 75.
13. Peterson 96–7; Buddy Levy, *Conquistador: Hernán Cortés, King Moctezuma, and the Last Stand of the Aztecs* (New York: Bantam Dell, 2008) 87.
14. H. B. Nicholson, *Topiltzin Quetzalcoatl: The Once and Future Lord of the Toltecs* (Boulder: University Press of Colorado, 2001) 95; Peterson 75.
15. Gabriel de Rojas, "Descripción de Cholula (1581)," *Revista Mexicana de Estudios Históricos, tomo 1*, excerpted in Peterson 106.
16. Peterson 106.
17. Cortés, *Letters* 75.
18. Levy 87.
19. Geoffrey G. McCafferty, "Reinterpreting the Great Pyramid of Cholula, Puebla," *Ancient Mesoamerica* 7 (1996): 1–17; Anamaría Ashwell and John O'Leary, *Cholula: La Ciudad Sagrada: The Sacred City* (Puebla: Volkswagen de México, 1999) 22.
20. Illustration in Peterson 81. See also 73, 75, 78–9.
21. "Book Twelve of the Florentine Codex," *We People Here: Nahuatl Accounts of the Conquest of Mexico*, James Lockhart, ed. and trans. (Berkeley: University of California Press, 1993) 134.
22. Andrés de Tapia, "The Chronicle of Andrés de Tapia," *The Conquistadors: First-Person Accounts of the Conquest of Mexico*, Patricia de Fuentes, ed. and trans. (New York: Orion Press, 1963) 36; Bernal Díaz del Castillo, *The History of the Conquest of New Spain*, David Carrasco, ed. (Albuquerque: University of New Mexico Press, 2008) 141.
23. Henry R. Wagner, *The Rise of Fernando Cortés* (Berkeley: The Cortes Society, 1944) 176; Levy 92.
24. Díaz, *History* 142.
25. Cortés, *Letters* 74.
26. Cortés, *Letters* 75.
27. Rojas 107–8; Peterson 79, 84.
28. Ashwell and O'Leary 61, 63.
29. Cortés, *Letters* 70, 72.
30. Francisco López de Gómara, *Cortés: The Life of the Conqueror by His Secretary*, trans. Lesley Byrd Simpson (Berkeley: University of California Press, 1964) 123–4.
31. Tapia 33.
32. Francisco de Aguilar, "The Chronicle of Fray Francisco de Aguilar," *The Conquistadors* 144.

33. Díaz, *History* 127.
34. Cortés, *Letters* 73; Gómara 126; Aguilar 144; Díaz, *The History* 133.
35. Gómara 127.
36. Aguilar 144; Díaz, *History* 135; Gómara 126, 128.
37. Díaz, *History* 135.
38. Cortés, *Letters* 73. Malinche spoke Maya and Nahuatl, and soon learned Spanish. Gerónimo de Aguilar spoke Maya and Spanish. Malinche's importance to the expedition and to post-conquest Mexican culture far exceeds her work as an interpreter. See, for example, Frances Karttunen, "Rethinking Malinche," *Indian Women in Early Mexico*, Susan Schroeder, Stephanie Wood, and Robert Haskett, eds. (Norman: University of Oklahoma Press, 1997) 291–312; Sandra Messinger Cypress, "La Malinche as Palimpsest II," Díaz, *History* 418–438.
39. Gómara 127.
40. Díaz, *History* 136, 138–9.
41. Gómara 126.
42. Díaz, *History* 140; Gómara 128; Tapia 36.
43. Gómara 127.
44. Cortés, *Letters* 73; Aguilar 144.
45. Aguilar 144.
46. Díaz, *History* 144–5.
47. Díaz, *History* 145.
48. Levy 89, 91.
49. Peter O. Koch, *The Aztecs, the Conquistadors, and the Making of Mexican Culture* (Jefferson, NC: McFarland, 2006) 182–3, 185.
50. Richard Lee Marks, *Cortés: The Great Adventurer and the Fate of Aztec Mexico* (New York: Alfred A. Knopf, 1993) 113–14.
51. Diego Muñoz Camargo, *Historia de Tlaxcala*, Clavero, ed. (Mexico, 1892), trans. and excerpted in *The Broken Spears: The Aztec Account of the Conquest of Mexico*, expanded and updated ed., trans. Lysander Kemp, Miguel Leon-Portilla, ed. (Boston: Beacon Press, 1992) 43–47.
52. Sahagún, *General History of the Things of New Spain*, excerpt in *Broken Spears* 40.
53. William H. Prescott, *History of the Conquest of Mexico*, Vol. 1 (Philadelphia: J. B. Lippincott, 1892) 417.
54. Cortés, *Letters* 74.
55. See Ross Hassig, *Aztec Warfare: Imperial Expansion and Political Control* (Norman: University of Oklahoma Press, 1988) 254–5, 264.
56. David A. Peterson and Z. D. Green, "The Spanish Arrival and the Massacre at Cholula," *Notas Mesoamericanas* 10 (1987) 204, citing F. J. Clavijero, *Historia Antigua de México* III (1945) 78; McCafferty, "The Cholula Massacre: Factional Histories and Archaeology of the Spanish Conquest," *The Entangled Past: Integrating History and Archaeology—Proceedings of the 30th Annual Chacmool Conference* (Calgary: The Archaeological Assoc. of the University of Calgary, 2000) 349, citing Muñoz Camargo, *Historia*.
57. McCafferty, "The Cholula Massacre" 349, 352, citing Juan de Torquemada, *Monarchia Indiana*, Book 2 (Mexico DF: Instituto de Investigaciones Históricas, 1975–83) 134–141; Peterson and Green 204.
58. Díaz, *History* 141.
59. Hassig, *Mexico and the Spanish Conquest*, 2d ed. (Norman: University of Oklahoma Press, 2006) 88, 96–98.
60. Wagner 173.
61. Aguilar 144.
62. Hassig, *Mexico* 95; Hassig, *Aztec Warfare* 238.
63. Hassig, *Mexico* 95.
64. Hassig, *Aztec Warfare* 53, 243, 262; Hassig, *Mexico* 95; Inga Clendinen, *Aztecs: An Interpretation* (New York: Cambridge University Press, 1991) 91.
65. Cortés, *Letters* 72.
66. Tapia 35.
67. Cortés, *Letters* 73.
68. Bartolomé de las Casas, *The Tears of Indians: Being An Historical and True Account of the Cruel Massacres and Slaughters Committed by the Spaniards in the Islands of the West Indies, Mexico, Peru, etc.: An Eye-Witness Account*, trans. John Phillips (1656) (New York: Oriole Editions, 1972) 21–2.
69. Wagner 174; Peterson and Green 208, 210.
70. William Weber Johnson, *Cortés* (Boston: Little, Brown, 1975) 220.
71. Wagner 174–5, citing unedited documents from the Royal Archives in Madrid.
72. Muñoz Camargo 48.
73. Sahagún, *General History of the Things of New Spain, Book 12—The Conquest of Mexico*, trans. Arthur J. O. Anderson and Charles e. Dibble (Santa Fe: School of American Research and University of Utah, 1955) 30.
74. "Book Twelve of the Florentine Codex," *We People Here: Nahuatl Accounts of the Conquest of Mexico*, James Lockhart, ed. and trans. (Berkeley: University of California Press, 1993) 94.
75. Díaz, *History* 46.
76. McCafferty, "The Cholula Massacre" 348, 352, 355–7; McCafferty, "De-Colón-izing Malintzin" (Calgary, Canada: University of Calgary Chacmool Archaeological Association, 2009) 183–4.
77. Muñoz Camargo 48.
78. McCafferty, "The Cholula Massacre" 355; image from the *Lienzo de Tlaxcala* on 351.
79. Sahagún, *Historia General de las Cosas de la Nueva España* (Mexico, 1938) 4: 47, 152, cited in Wagner 177.
80. McCafferty, "The Cholula Massacre" 353. Why 671, the total number of skeletons re-

portedly found, is not used as the denominator in this fraction is unclear.

81. Peterson and Green 211, 215; McCafferty, "The Cholula Massacre" 353.
82. Prescott 418.
83. "Extract from the *Annals of Tlatelolco, We People Here* 259.
84. Bartolomé de Las Casas, *Brevissima relacion de la destrucción de las Indias* (Mexico, 1822), qtd. in Wagner 175.
85. Joseph F. O'Callaghan, *Reconquest and Crusade in Medieval Spain* (Philadelphia: University of Pennsylvania Press, 2003) 140.
86. Hugh Thomas, *Rivers of Gold: The Rise of the Spanish Empire, from Columbus to Magellan* (New York: Random House, 2003) 316.
87. Las Casas, *History of the Indies* III, 29, cited by Tzvetlan Todorov, *The Conquest of America: The Question or the Other*, trans. Richard Howard (New York: Harper & Row, 1984) 141.
88. Peter Martyr Anghiera, *De Orbe Novo*, qtd. in Todorov 141.
89. Thomas, *Rivers* 331; Todorov 141.
90. Las Casas, *A Short Account of the Destruction of the Indies*, trans. Nigel Griffin (New York: Penguin, 1992) 15, 23, and passim.
91. Pagden, "Introduction," *Short Account* xxxi.
92. Cortés, *Letters* 62.
93. Cortés, *Letters* 66.
94. "Book Twelve," *We People Here* 162.
95. Cortés, *Letters* 146.
96. Díaz, *History* 235.
97. Cortés, *Letters* 253; cf. Ramón Iglesia, *Columbus, Cortés, and Other Essays*, Lesley Byrd Simpson, ed. and trans. (Berkeley: University of California Press, 1969) 178.
98. Fernando de Alva Ixtlilxochitl, *Obras Histórica*, Book 2 (Mexico DF: Universidad Nacional Autónoma de México, 1975-1977) 215-16, cited in McCafferty 352.
99. Díaz, *History* 235.
100. Jennings 151-2.
101. http://www.nebraskastudies.org/0200/stories/0201_0211.html.
102. Mark Van de Logt, *War Party in Blue: Pawnee Scouts in the U.S. Army* (Norman: University of Oklahoma Press, 2010) 26-7, 33-35, 173.
103. Hassig, *Aztec Warfare* 114; cf. R. C. Padden, *The Hummingbird and the Hawk: Conquest and Sovereignty in the Valley of Mexico, 1503-1541* (San Francisco: Harper Torchbook, 1967) 89.
104. Cited in Hassig, *Aztec Warfare* 300.
105. Oskar Verkaaik, "Terrorism," *International Encyclopedia of the Social Sciences*, Vol. 8, 2d ed. (San Francisco: Thomson Gale, 2008) 328-330.
106. Jennings 164.
107. Jennings 153.
108. Van de Logt 35-6.
109. Caesar, *The Conquest of Gaul*, trans. S. A. Handford (Baltimore: Penguin, 1951) 128.
110. *The Poem of the Cid: A Bilingual Edition with Parallel Text*, trans. Rita Hamilton and Janet Perry (New York: Penguin, 1975) 84-5.
111. O'Callaghan 134.
112. David Nicolle, *Granada 1492: The Twilight of Moorish Spain* (Westport, CT: Praeger, 2005) 26-7.
113. Harold E. Driver, *Indians of North America* (Chicago, 1961) 384, qtd. in Jennings 150.
114. Cortés, *Letters* 37.
115. Lynn Holden, "Cannibalism," *Encyclopedia of Taboos* (Santa Barbara: ABC-CLIO, 2000) 105; Robinson Herrera, rev. of *Butterflies Will Burn: Prosecuting Sodomites in Early Modern Spain and Mexico* by Federico Garza Carvajal, *The Hispanic American Historical Review* 85: 3 (August 2005) 506; Claude Lévy-Strauss, *The Savage Mind* (Chicago: University of Chicago Press) 105.
116. Cortés, *Letters* 146.
117. Marshall Sahlins, "Culture as Protein and Profit," *New York Review of Books* 25.18 (November 23, 1978).
118. See, e. g., "Colonial cannibalism evidence discovered" (*New York Times*), *San Francisco Chronicle* 2 May 2013: A9.
119. Teofilo F. Ruiz, *Spain's Centuries of Crisis* (Malden, MA: Blackwell, 2007) 154.
120. Jennings 47.
121. Todorov 154, 149.
122. *The Iliad of Homer*, trans. Richmond Lattimore (Chicago: Phoenix Books, 1951) Book 6: 55-59, 154.
123. 1 Samuel 15: 2-3.
124. Cf. Jennings 10.
125. Ruiz, *Spanish Society, 1400-1600* (Essex: Pearson Education, 2001) 167-69, 171, 199; Ruiz, *Spain's Centuries* 38-9.
126. Ruiz, *Spanish Society* 196-7; Casey 225.
127. Tuchman 585; Nicolle 30.
128. Fernand Braudel, *Capitalism and Material Life: 1400-1800* (New York: Harper & Row, 1973) 287.
129. James Reston, Jr., *Dogs of God: Columbus, the Inquisition, and the Defeat of the Moors* (New York: Doubleday, 2005) 154, 168-9, 184-5, 190; Nicolle 24, 61, 64.
130. Díaz, *History* 102.
131. Philip Zimbardo, *The Lucifer Effect: Understanding How People Turn Evil* (New York: Random House, 2007) 307.
132. Lesley Byrd Simpson, *The Encomienda in New Spain: The Beginning of Spanish Mexico* (Berkeley: University of California Press, 1966) 91.

Chapter 10

1. Peter Martyr D'Anghera, *De Orbo Novo*, qtd. in Alfred W. Crosby, *Ecological Imperialism: The Biological Expansion of Europe, 900–1900* (New York: Cambridge University Press, 1986) 175.
2. Bernal Díaz del Castillo, *The History of the Conquest of New Spain*, David Carrasco, ed., trans. A. P. Maudslay (Albuquerque: University of New Mexico Press, 2008) 34; Rebecca Earle, *The Body of the Conquistador: Food, Race and the Colonial Experience in Spanish America* (New York: Cambridge University Press, 2012) 73.
3. Earle 73.
4. Díaz, *The History* 34; Díaz, *The Conquest of New Spain*, trans. J. M. Cohen (London: The Folio Society, 1963) 2.
5. Anthony Pagden, "Translator's Introduction," Hernán Cortés, *Letters from Mexico*, Pagden, trans. and ed. (New Haven: Yale University Press, 1986) lii.
6. Hugh Thomas, *Rivers of Gold: The Rise of the Spanish Empire, from Columbus to Magellan* (New York: Random House, 2003) 320; Díaz, *The History* 306.
7. Crosby, *Ecological* 175.
8. Earle 73.
9. In Robert V. Hine and John Mack Faragher, *The American West: A New Interpretative History* (New Haven: Yale University Press, 2000) 16; R. B. Cunninghame Graham, *The Horses of the Conquest* (Norman: University of Oklahoma Press, 1949) 27.
10. Charles C. Mann, *1493: Uncovering the New World Columbus Created* (New York: Vintage, 2011) 93–4.
11. Tacitus, *The Agricola and the Germania*, trans. H. Mattingly (Baltimore: Penguin, 1970) 139; Leo Braudy, *From Chivalry to Terrorism: War and the Changing Nature of Masculinity* (New York: Alfred A. Knopf, 2003) 39.
12. Peter Bogucki, "The Exploitation of Domestic Animals in Neolithic Central Europe," *Early Animal Domestication in its Cultural Context*, Pam J. Crabtree, Douglas Campana, and Kathleen Ryan, eds. (Philadelphia: The Museum Applied Science Center for Archaeology and Anthropology, 1989) 130; cf. Juliet Clutton-Brock, *A Natural History of Domesticated Mammals*, 2d ed. (New York: Cambridge University Press, 1999) 91–94; Annat Haber, Tamar Dayan, and Nimrod Getzo, "Pig Exploitation at Hagoshrim: A Prehistoric Site in the Southern Levant," *First Steps of Animal Domestication: New Archaeological Approaches*, J.-D. Vigne, J. Peters, and D. Helmer, eds. (Oxford: Oxbow Books, 2005) 84.
13. Robert Beverley, *The History and Present State of Virginia*, qtd. in Crosby, *Ecological* 175.
14. Clutton-Brock 94–96; Crosby 173–4.
15. Frederick E. Zeuner, *A History of Domesticated Animals* (New York: Hutchinson, 1963) 260.
16. Crosby, *Ecological* 173; cf. Clutton-Brock 95; Clive Roots, *Domestication* (Westport, CT: Greenwood Press, 2007) 182.
17. Earle 74.
18. www.nps.gov/chis/naturescience/restoring-santa-cruz-island.htm; www.sfgate.com/green/article/Pig-eradication-plan-out-of-control-2668922.php; www.articles.latimes.com/2007/ang/30/local/me-pigs30.
19. Roots 182; Crosby, *Ecological* 175.
20. Teofilo F. Ruiz, *Spanish Society, 1400–1600* (Essex: Pearson Education, 2001) 217–18.
21. William Weber Johnson, *Cortés* (Boston: Little, Brown, 1975) 6; Rebecca West, *Survivors in Mexico* (New Haven: Yale University Press, 2003) 113; Thomas, *Conquest: Montezuma, Cortés, and the Fall of Old Mexico* (New York: Simon & Schuster, 1993) 533.
22. Ruiz, *Spanish Society* 215 ff.
23. Fernand Braudel, *Capitalism and Material Life: 1400–1800* (New York: Harper & Row, 1973) 67.
24. Earle 74.
25. http://en.wikipedia.org/wiki/Jamón_ibérico.
26. http://foxnews.com/story/0,2933,575305,00.html; http://www.factory-farming.com/pig_farms.html; Henry C. Jackson, "Something Stinks in Iowa: Hog Farms" (AP) at http://washingtonpost.com/wp-dyn/content/article/2007/10/19.

Chapter 11

1. Alfred W. Crosby, "Conquistador y Pestilencia: The First New World Pandemic and the Fall of the Great Indian Empires," *Biological Consequences of the European Expansion, 1450–1800*, Kenneth F. Kiple and Stephen V. Beck, eds. (Brookfield, VT: Ashgate, 1997) 97; Noble David Cook, "Disease and the Depopulation of Hispaniola, 1492–1518," *Biological Consequences* 44–56.
2. Crosby, "Conquistador" 97; Dorothy H. Crawford, *Deadly Companions: How Microbes Shaped Our History* (New York: Oxford University Press, 2007) 109; Donald Joralemon, "New World Depopulation and the Case of Disease," *Biological Consequences* 81–87; Alan P. Zelicoff, MD, and Michael Bellomo, *Microbe: Are We Ready for the Next Plague?* (New York: AMACOM, 2005) 117.
3. Cook 41–3, 60–1; Crosby, "Conquistador" 95; J. N. Hayes, *Epidemics and Pandemics: Their Impacts on Human History* (Santa Bar-

bara: ABC-CLIO, 2005) 82, 88; Crawford 107; Joralemon 81-2.

4. "Book Twelve of the Florentine Codex," *We People Here: Nahuatl Accounts of the Conquest of Mexico,* James Lockhart, ed. and trans. (Berkeley: University of California Press, 1993) 182.

5. "Book Twelve" 180.

6. Fray Toribio Motolinía, *Motolinía's History of the Indians of New Spain,* Elizabeth Andros Foster, ed. and trans. (Berkeley: The Cortés Society, 1950) 38; Sheldon Watts, *Epidemics and History: Disease, Power and Imperialism* (New York: Yale University Press, 1997) 103.

7. See, for example, Watts 89.

8. J. M. Blaut, *The Colonizer's Model of the World: Geographic Diffusionism and Eurocentric History* (New York: The Guilford Press, 1993) 185; William H. McNeil, *Plagues and Peoples* (New York: Anchor Books, 1998) 20; William T. Sanders, "Tenochtitlan in 1519: A Pre-Industrial Megapolis," *The Aztec World,* Elizabeth M. Brumfiel and Gary M. Feinman, eds. (New York: Abrams and the Field Museum, 2008) 84.

9. Francisco de Aguilar, "The Chronicle of Fray Francisco de Aguilar," *The Conquistadors: First-Hand Accounts of the Conquest of Mexico,* Patricia de Fuentes, ed. and trans. (New York: Orion Press, 1963) 159.

10. "Book Twelve" 218.

11. Bernal Díaz del Castillo, *The History of the Conquest of New Spain,* trans. A. P. Maudslay, Davíd Carrasco, ed. (Albuquerque: University of New Mexico Press, 2008) 305-6.

12. Watts 90.

13. Qtd. in Crosby, *"Conquistador"* 93; Robert McCaa, "Revisioning Smallpox in Mexico City-Tenochtitlán, 1520-1950: What Difference did Charity, Quarantine, Inoculation and Vaccination Make?" *Proceedings of the International Conference held by [the] International Commission for Historical Demography (Ichd), Rome, September 27-29, 1999,* Eugenio Sonnino, ed. (Rome: *La Sapienza,* Università di Rome, 2004) 455.

14. Francis J. Brooks, "Revising the Conquest of Mexico: Smallpox, Sources, and Populations," *The Journal of Interdisciplinary History* XXIV.1 (Summer 1993) 29.

15. See, e.g., Jeffrey R. Parsons, "Environment and Rural Economy," *Aztec World* 23.

16. McCaa 464; James C. Riley, "Smallpox and American Indians Revisited," *Journal of the History of Medicine and Allied Sciences* 65.4 (Oct. 2010) 453, 455, 475.

17. Watts 102, 108.

18. Hernán Cortés, *Letters from Mexico,* Anthony Pagden, ed. and trans. (New Haven: Yale University Press, 1986) 472, note 69.

19. Brooks 12-13, 15; Riley 450, 469.

20. Joralemon 80-1; Crosby, *"Conquistador"* 104.

21. McCaa 457.

22. Díaz, *History* 306.

23. Sahagún, *Historia general de las cosas de Nueva España,* Angel Maria Garibay K., ed. (Mexico City, 1956), qtd. in McCaa 465.

24. Riley 453; cf. Brooks 27.

25. Suzanne Austin Alchon, "The Great Killers in Precolumbian America: A Hemispheric Perspective," *Latin American Population History Bulletin* 27, Fall 1997, www.hist.umn.edu.edu/~mccaa/laphb/27fall97/laphb 271.htm; John Noble Wilford, "Don't Blame Columbus for All the Indians' Ills," *New York Times* 29 October 2002.

26. Watts 90.

27. Hays 84; Crawford 118.

28. Hays 85.

29. Hays 84.

30. Qtd. in Watts 98.

31. Qtd. in Watts 93.

32. McNeill 217.

33. P. M. Ashburn, *The Ranks of Death: A Medical History of the Conquest of America* (New York: Coward-McCann, 1947) 98, qtd. in Joralemon 75.

34. Blaut 184.

35. Cf. Crosby, *Ecological Imperialism: The Biological Expansion of Europe, 900-1900* (New York: Cambridge University Press, 1986) 196.

36. Crawford 106-7.

37. Crawford 78-9; McNeill 130-32, 322.

38. Hays 31; McNeill 147-8, 153.

39. Crawford 19, 27; McNeill 31, 86, 132, 153, 161; Hays 87, 89; Brooks 16; Watts 91.

40. McNeill 69, 122; Crawford 106.

41. McNeill 91; Hugh Thomas, *Rivers of Gold: The Rise of the Spanish Empire, from Columbus to Magellan* (New York: Random House, 2003) 344; Howard J. Erlichman, *Conquest, Tribute, and Trade: The Quest for Precious Metals and the Birth of Globalization* (Amherst, NY: Prometheus, 2010) 179-81.

42. Nicolás Wey Gómez, *The Tropics of Empire: Why Columbus Sailed South to the Indies* (Cambridge: MIT Press, 2008) 311.

43. Wey Gómez 314.

44. Qtd. in Crawford 128.

45. Hays 69, 72; Watts 125, 128; Crosby, "The Early History of Syphilis: A Reappraisal," *American Anthropologist* 71.2 (April 1969) 124-26.

46. Watts 126.

47. Crosby, "Early History" 222-3; Watts 130; Hays 71.

48. Cf. Crosby, *The Columbian Exchange: Biological and Cultural Consequences of 1492* (Westport, CT: Praeger, 2003).

49. "Yaws," WHO Media Centre: Fact Sheet No. 316 (updated February 2014), http://www.

who.int/mediacentre/factsheets/fs316/en/; Angela Aristone, "Syphilis: Etiology, Epidemiology, and Origin Theory," *Totem: The University of Western Ontario Journal of Anthropology* 3. 1: Article 6 (June 19, 2011) 35, @ir.lib.uwo.ca/totem/vol3/iss1/6/; R. S. Morton and S. Rashid, "'The syphilis enigma': the riddle resolved?" *Sexually Transmitted Infections* 77: 322-324 (May 22, 2001) *@BMJ Open Gastroenterology*, http://sti.bmj.com/content/77/5/322.full.pdf#page=1& review=FitH.

50. Watts 126; Crawford 128.
51. Morton and Rashid; Aristone 34.
52. McNeill 187-190; Brenda J. Baker and George J. Armelagos, "The Origin and Antiquity of Syphilis: Paleopathological Diagnosis and Interpretation," *Biological Consequences of the European Expansion, 1450-1800*, Kenneth F. Kiple and Stephen V. Beck, eds. (Brookfield, VT: Ashgate, 1997) 1; Crawford 129; Crosby, "Early History" 218-19, 224-5.
53. Baker and Armelagos 1, 5; Aristone 33.
54. Charles C. Mann, *1491: New Revelations of the Americas Before Columbus*, 2d ed. (New York: Vintage, 2011) 407.
55. Baker and Armelagos 16; Mann, *1491* 407.
56. Morton and Rashid; cf. Aristone 28.
57. Baker and Armelagos 17, 30; Mary Lucas Powell, "Comments" in Baker and Armelagos 23; Watts 126-7; Margalit Fox, "George J. Armelagos, an Anthropologist Who Told Skeletons' Tales, is Dead at 77," *New York Times* 8 June 2014: 24. Cf. Richard Lee Marks, *Cortés: The Great Adventure and the Fate of Aztec Mexico* (New York: Alfred A. Knopf, 1993) 20, which states that mummies at Machu Pichu bore unmistakable signs of syphilis.
58. Hays 76; Crosby, "Early History" 225; Mann *1491* 406.
59. Aristone 34.

Chapter 12

1. R. C. Padden, *The Hummingbird and the Hawk: Conquest and Sovereignty in the Valley of Mexico, 1503-1541* (San Francisco: Harper Torchbooks, 1967) 131.
2. In Gogol's "The Inspector General."
3. "Book Twelve of the Florentine Codex," *We People Here: Nahuatl Accounts of the Conquest of Mexico*, James Lockhart, ed. and trans. (Berkeley: University of California Press, 1993) 50-56.
4. "Book Twelve" 58.
5. Susan D. Gillespie, *The Aztec Kings: The Construction of Rulership in Mexica History* (Tucson: University of Arizona Press, 1989) 198.
6. Bernal Díaz [del Castillo], *The Conquest of New Spain*, trans. J. M. Cohen (London: The Folio Society, 1963) 83.
7. Díaz del Castillo, *The History of the Conquest of New Spain* (Albuquerque: University of New Mexico Press, 2008) 187.
8. "Book Twelve" 244.
9. "Annals of Tlatelolco, Extract from," *We People Here* 265.
10. Nicolás Wey Gómez, *The Tropics of Empire: Why Columbus Sailed South to the Indies* (Cambridge: MIT Press, 2008) 316-17.
11. Gillespie 170.
12. "Book Twelve" 62-80.
13. F. Alvarado Tezozomoc, *Cronica Mexicana*, De Vigil, ed. (1944), excerpt in *The Broken Spears: The Aztec Account of the Conquest of Mexico*, expanded and updated, trans. (from Spanish) Lysander Kemp, Miguel Leon Portilla, ed. (Boston: Beacon Press, 1992) 18.
14. "Book Twelve" 82.
15. "Book Twelve" 83-4; Frances F. Berdan, *The Aztecs of Central Mexico: An Imperial Society*, 2d ed. (Belmont, CA: Thomson Wadsworth, 2005) 180.
16. "Book Twelve" 84-85.
17. "Book Twelve" 102-4.
18. "Book Twelve" 106; Inga Clendinnen, "Cortés, Signs, and the Conquest of Mexico," *The Transmission of Culture in Early Modern Europe*, Anthony Grafton and Ann Blair, eds. (Philadelphia: University of Pennsylvania Press, 1990) 98.
19. "Book Twelve" 98.
20. Hugh Thomas, *Conquest: Montesuma, Cortés, and the Fall of Old Mexico* (New York: Simon & Schuster, 1993) 285.
21. "Book Twelve" 110, 114.
22. Hernán Cortés, *Letters from Mexico*, Anthony Pagden, ed. and trans. (New Haven: Yale University Press, 1986) 85-6.
23. Glen Carman, *Rhetorical Conquests: Cortés, Gómara, and Renaissance Imperialism* (W. Lafayette: Purdue University Press, 2006) 159.
24. "Book Twelve" 116.
25. Cortés 98-99.
26. Thomas, *Conquest* 307.
27. Bernal Díaz del Castillo, *The History of the Conquest of New Spain*, Davíd Carrasco, ed. (Albuquerque: University of New Mexico Press, 2008) 204-5.
28. Cortés 106-7.
29. Díaz, *History* 205.
30. Thomas, *Conquest* 303-312, 331, 406.
31. Davíd Carrasco, *Quetzalcoatl and the Irony of Empire: Myths and Prophesies in the Aztec Tradition*, rev. ed. (Boulder: University Press of Colorado, 2000) 5, 13, 101, 158, 160; Carrasco, "When Strangers Come to Town: Millennial Discourse, Comparison, and the Return of Quetalcoatl," *Encuentros* 16 (June 1996) 13.
32. Gillespie 175.

33. Eugene R. Fingerhut, *Explorers of Pre-Columbian America? The Diffusionist-Inventionist Controversy* (Claremont, CA: Regina Books, 1994) 54.
34. Qtd. from *Anales de Tlatelolco* in Thomas, *Conquest* 185.
35. Ross Hassig, *Time, History, and Belief in Aztec and Colonial Mexico* (Austin: University of Texas Press, 2001) 58.
36. Carrasco, *Quetzalcoatl* 175, 178; Hassig, *Time, History* 58.
37. Gillespie 146-47.
38. Carrasco, *Quetzalcoatl* 150.
39. Cortés 467-69, note.
40. Enrique Florescano, *The Myth of Quetzalcoatl,* trans. Lysa Hochroth (Baltimore: John Hopkins University Press, 1999) 167-71.
41. Carrasco, *Quetzalcoatl* 11, 97.
42. Carrasco, *Quetzalcoatl* 183-85.
43. Cf. Mircea Eliade, *The Myth of the Eternal Return,* trans. Willard R. Trask (New York: Pantheon for Bollingen Foundation, 1954) 5, 34, 89.
44. Carrasco, *Quetzalcoatl* 178, 184, 204; Carrasco, "When Strangers" 13.
45. Eliade 87-88.
46. Gillespie xxiii, xxvii-xxviii.
47. Qtd. in Thomas, *Conquest* 9.
48. Clendinnen, *Aztecs: An Interpretation* (New York: Cambridge University Press, 1991) 195.
49. Carrasco, *Quetzalcoatl* 97, 102, 169, 175, 199, 204.
50. Carrasco, *Quetzalcoatl* 191-92.
51. Subchapter title in Carrasco, *Quetzalcoatl* 175.
52. Gillespie xix, xxvi-xxvii; Lockhart, "Introduction," *We People Here* 5; Camilla Townsend, "Burying the White Gods: New Perspectives on the Conquest of Mexico," *The American Historical Review* 108.3 (June 2003) 665.
53. Matthew Restall, *Seven Myths of the Spanish Conquest* (New York: Oxford University Press, 2003) 97-98.
54. Cortés 26; J. H. Elliott, "Cortés, Velázquez and Charles V," Introduction to Cortés xx-xxi.
55. Cortés 37; Elliott, "Cortés, Velázquez" xxi.
56. Cortés 118-19, 474—note.
57. Cortés 127, 139, 156-7, 479—note.
58. Cortés 52.
59. Cortés 65.
60. Díaz, *History* 102.
61. Cortés 79-81.
62. Cortés 87, 99.
63. Cortés 87-90.
64. Cortés 90-91.
65. Cortés 469—note 43.
66. See, e.g., Cortés 53; Carman 65, 70.
67. Anthony Pagden, "Translator's Introduction," Cortés liii ff.
68. "Book Twelve" 62, 64, 68; Clendinnen, "'Fierce and Unnatural Cruelty': Cortés and the Conquest of Mexico," *Representations* 33 (Winter 1991) 68.
69. E.g., at "Book Twelve" 170; cf. Lockhart, "Introduction" 27; C. Townsend 667; Gillespie xxxii-xxxiv; Tzvetan Todorov, *The Conquest of America: The Question of the Other,* trans. Richard Howard (New York: Harper & Row, 1984) 219-24.HH
70. Gillespie xxx, xxxii.
71. Lockhart, "Introduction" 19.
72. "Book Twelve" 86, 186, 216; cf. C. Townsend 668; Carrasco, *Quetzalcoatl* 180; Lockhart, "Introduction" 30.
73. "Extract from the Annals of Tlatelolco," *We People Here* 259-65.
74. "Book Twelve" 90-92.
75. C. Townsend 667.
76. Lockhart, "Introduction" 17.
77. See, e.g., Gillespie 196; Francis J. Brooks, "Motecuzoma Xocoytl, Hernán Cortés, and Bernal Díaz del Castillo: The Construction of an Arrest," *Hispanic American Historical Review* 75:2 (May 1995) 178.
78. Lockhart, "Introduction" 17.
79. Clendinnen, "Cortés, Signs" 93.
80. C. Townsend 672.
81. Díaz, *Conquest* 279, 304.
82. Lockhart, "Introduction" 14-15, 20-21.
83. "Book Twelve" 70-72.
84. Gillespie 195.
85. Hassig, *Time, History* 58.
86. Carrasco, *Quetzalcoatl* 197.
87. Lockhart, "Introduction" 17-18.
88. Hassig, *Mexico* 55.
89. Discussed in Keith Thomas, *Religion and the Decline of Magic: Studies in Popular Beliefs in Sixteenth and Seventeenth Century England* (New York: Oxford University Press, 1971) 647.
90. Elliott, "The Mental World of Hernán Cortés," *Spain and Its World, 1500-1700* (New Haven: Yale University Press, 1989) 37.
91. Díaz, *Conquest* 194.
92. Díaz, *Conquest* 91.
93. Clendinnen, "Cortés, Signs" 99, 103.
94. Díaz, *Conquest* 177.
95. C. Townsend 683; Hassig, *Mexico* 101.
96. Hassig, *Mexico* 101-02.
97. Brooks, "Motecuzoma" 162-67, 181—note.
98. "Book Twelve" 120-26.
99. See Cortés 472—n. 69; Brooks, "Motecuzoma" 166, 181.
100. Cf. Lockhart, "Introduction" 17; Clendinnen, "Cortés, Signs" 94.
101. Carman 146-47; Elliott, "Cortés, Velázquez and Charles V," Introduction to Cortés xxvii-xxviii; C. Townsend 674; Pagden, "Translator's Introduction," Cortés xlii.

102. Carman 146.
103. Cortés 468—n. 42.
104. Brooks, "Motecuzoma" 161.
105. Lockhart, "Introduction" 18; Carman 149; H. Thomas, *Conquest* 281.
106. Cortés 467-69—n. 42.
107. Joseph Campbell, *The Hero With a Thousand Faces*, 2d ed. (Princeton, NJ: Princeton UP, 1949) 246 and passim.
108. Elliott, "Cortés, Velázquez," Cortés xlviii.
109. Elliott, "The Mental World" 37.
110. H. Thomas, *Conquest* 282, 284, 324, 325.
111. Brooks, "Motecuzoma" 161, 165.
112. H. Thomas, *Conquest* 283.
113. H. Thomas, *Conquest* 322-24.
114. Gillespie 179, 182; C. Townsend 669.
115. H. Thomas, *Conquest* 183-84; Padden 77.
116. H. Thomas, *Conquest* 185.
117. Gillespie 182-190; C. Townsend 669.
118. Díaz, *Conquest* 157-58.
119. H. Thomas, *Conquest* 182.
120. Gillespie 191-92, 196-97.
121. Lockhart, "Introduction" to William H. Prescott, *History of the Conquest of Mexico* (New York: Modern Library, 2001) xxxiii.
122. Brooks, "Motecuzoma" 178, 182.
123. Clendinnen, "Cortés, Signs" 119; Brooks, "Motecuzoma" 183.
124. Gillespie 164, 172-73, 200.
125. Clendinnen, "Cortés, Signs" 124—n. 6.
126. See, e.g., Howard Zinn, *A People's History of the United States: 1492-Present* (New York: HarperCollins, 2003) 422-23; William Appleman Williams, *The Tragedy of American Diplomacy*, rev. and enlarged ed. (New York: Dell, 1962) 253 ff.

Conclusion

1. Ian Morris, *Why the West Rules—For Now* (New York: Picador, 2010) 157.
2. J. M. Blaut, "Where Was Capitalism Born?" *Antipode* 8, 2:1, qtd. in Richard Peet, with Elaine Hartwick, *Theories of Development* (New York: The Guilford Press, 1999) 89.
3. Ronald Wright, *Stolen Continents: Conquest and Resistance in the Americas* (New York: Penguin, 2003) 259-271; Ronald Takaki, *A Different Mirror: A History of Multicultural America* (Boston: Little, Brown, 1993) 334-39.
4. Inga Clendinnen, *Aztecs: An Interpretation* (New York: Cambridge University Press, 1991) 92; cf. 209.
5. Bernardino de Sahagún, *General History of the Things of New Spain, Introductory Volume*, 48-9, qtd. in Clendinnen, *Aztecs* 111.
6. See, for example, R. C. Padden, *The Hummingbird and the Hawk: Conquest and Sovereignty in the Valley of Mexico, 1503-1541* (San Francisco: Harper Torchbooks, 1967) 97.

Bibliography

Abulafia, David. *The Discovery of Mankind: Atlantic Encounters in the Age of Columbus.* New Haven: Yale University Press, 2008.

Adleman, Leonard. "Resurrecting Smallpox? Easier Than You Think." *The New York Time* 16 October 2014: A29.

Alchon, Suzanne Austin. "The Great Killers in Pre-Columbian America: A Hemispheric Perspective." *Latin American Population History Bulletin* 27: Fall 1997. www.hist.umn.edu/~mccaa/laphb/27fall97/laphb271.htm.

———. *A Pest in the Land: World Epidemics in a Global Perspective.* Albuquerque: University of New Mexico Press, 2003.

Amadis of Gaul, Books I and II. Rev. and Reworked by Garci Rodríguez de Montalvo. Edwin B. Place and Herbert C. Behm, trans. Lexington, KY: University Press of Kentucky, 1974.

Ancient American: Archaeology of the Americas Before Columbus, 16.97 (Dec. 2012).

Anthony, David W. *The Horse, the Wheel, and Language: How Bronze-Age Riders from the Eurasian Steppes Shaped the Modern World.* Princeton, NJ: Princeton University Press, 2007.

Applebaum, Herbert. *The Concept of Work: Ancient, Medieval, and Modern.* Albany, NY: State University of New York Press, 1992.

Arens, William. *TheMan-Eating Myth: Anthropology & Anthropophagy.* New York: Oxford University Press, 1979.

Aristone, Angela. "Syphilis: Etiology, Epidemiology, and Origin Theory." *Totem: The University of Western Ontario Journal of Anthropology* 3.1: Article 6 (June 19, 2011): 28–36.

Arrighi, Giovanni. *The Long Twentieth Century: Money, Power, and the Origins of Our Times.* New York: Verso, 1994.

Ashwell, Anamaría, and John O'Leary. *Cholula: La Ciudad Sagrada: The Sacred City.* Puebla, Mexico: Volkswagen de México, 1999.

Aztec World, The. Elizabeth M. Brumfiel and Gary M. Feinman, eds. New York: Abrams and the Field Museum, 2008.

Baker, Brenda J., and George J. Armelagos. "The Origin and Antiquity of Syphilis: Paleopathological Diagnosis and Interpretation." *Current Anthropology* XXIX.5 (©1988, University of Chicago Press): 703–737.

Barker, Francis, Peter Hulme, and Margaret Iversen, eds. *Cannibalism and the Colonial World.* New York: Cambridge University Press, 1998.

Baxter, Joan. "Africa's 'greatest explorer.'" BBC, December 13, 2000. News at http://news.bbc.co.uk/2/hi/Africa/1068950.st.

Bender, Thomas. "Capitalism, As Woven Through Cotton." Review of Sven Beckert, *Empire of Cotton: A Global History. New York Times* 30 December 2015: Cl, C6.

Berdan, Frances F. *The Aztecs of Central Mexico: An Imperial Society,* 2d ed. Belmont, CA: Thomson Wadsworth, 2005.

Betz, Margaret. Letter. *The New York Times Book Review* 20 March 2011: 6.

Biaggi, Cristina, ed. *The Rule of Mars: Readings on the Origins, History and*

Impact of Patriarchy. Manchester, CT: Knowledge, Ideas & Trends, 2005.

Bishop, MacWilliam. "Medieval Weapon Finds Modern Appeal." *New York Times* 17 September 2014: B12.

Blaut, J. M. *The Colonizer's Model of the World: Geographic Diffusionism and Eurocentric History*. New York: The Guilford Press, 1993.

Bogucki, Peter. "The Exploitation of Domestic Animals in Neolithic Central Europe." *Early Animal Domestication in Its Cultural Context*. Pam J. Crabtree, Douglas Campana & Kathleen Ryan, eds. Philadelphia: The Museum Applied Science Center for Archaeology and Anthropology, 1989: 118–139.

Book of John Mandeville with Related Texts, The. Iain Macleod Higgins, ed. and trans. Indianapolis: Hackett Pub., 2011.

Braudel, Fernand. *The Mediterranean and the Mediterranean World in the Age of Philip II*, Vol. 1. Siân Reynolds, trans. New York: Harper & Row, 1972.

_____. *Capitalism and Material Life: 1400–1800*. George Weidenfeld and Nicholson Ltd., trans. New York: Harper & Row, 1973.

_____. *The Perspective of the World*. Siân Reynolds, trans. New York: Harper & Row, 1984.

Braudy, Leo. *From Chivalry to Terrorism: War and the Changing Nature of Masculinity*. New York: Alfred A. Knopf, 2003.

Breitburg, Emanuel. "The Evolution of Turkey Domestication in the Greater Southwest and Mesoamerica." *Culture and Contact: Charles C. DiPeso's Gran Chichimeca*. Anne I. Woolsey and John C. Ravesloot, eds. Albuquerque: University of New Mexico Press, 1993: 153–172.

Brengle, Richard L., ed. *Arthur, King of Britain: History, Chronicle, Romance, & Criticism*. New York: Appleton-Century-Crofts, 1964.

Brooks, Francis J. "Revising the Conquest of Mexico: Smallpox, Sources, and Populations." *The Journal of Interdisciplinary History* XXIV.1 (Summer 1993): 1–29.

_____. "Motecuzoma, Xocoyotl, Hernán Cortés, and Bernal Díaz del Castillo: The Construction of an Arrest." *Hispanic American Historical Review* 75:2 (May 1995): 149–183.

Butterfield, Andrew. "They Clamor for Our Attention." *The New York Review of Books* LIX.4 (March 8, 2012): 10–12.

Caesar, Julius. *The Conquest of Gaul*. S. A. Handford, trans. Baltimore: Penguin Books, 1951.

Campbell, Joseph. *The Masks of God: Primitive Mythology*. New York: Viking Compass, 1969.

Carman, Glen. *Rhetorical Conquests: Cortés, Gómara, and Renaissance Imperialism*. W. Lafayette, IN: Purdue U. Press, 2006.

Carrasco, Davíd. "When Strangers Come to Town: Millennial Discourse, Comparison, and the Return of Quetzalcoatl." *Encuentros* 16 (June 1996).

_____. *Daily Life of the Aztecs: People of the Sun and Earth*. Westport, CT: Greenwood Press, 1998.

_____. *City of Sacrifice: The Aztec Empire and the Role of Violence in Civilization*. Boston: Beacon Press, 1999.

_____. *Quetzalcoatl and the Irony of Empire: Myths and Prophesies in the Aztec Tradition*, rev. ed. Boulder, CO: University Press of Colorado, 2000.

Casey, James. *Early Modern Spain: A Social History*. New York: Routledge, 1999.

Cervantes, Miguel de. *Don Quijote: Backgrounds and Contexts, Criticisms*. Armas Wilson, Diana de, ed., Burton Raffel, trans. New York: W. W. Norton & Co., 1999.

Chaucer, Geoffrey. *The Canterbury Tales, A Selection*. Daniel Cook, ed. Garden City, NY: Anchor Books, 1961.

_____. *The Canterbury Tales*. A. Kent Hieatt and Constance Hieatt, eds. New York: Bantam Books, 1964.

Chaunu, Pierre. *European Expansion in the Later Middle Ages*. Katharine Bertram, trans. New York: North-Holland Pub., 1979.

Christian, William A., Jr. *Apparitions in Late Medieval and Renaissance Spain*. Princeton, NJ: Princeton University Press, 1981.

Clendinnen, Inga. *Aztecs: An Interpretation*. New York: Cambridge University Press, 1991.

———. "'Fierce and Unnatural Cruelty': Cortés and the Conquest of Mexico." *Representations* 33 (Winter 1991): 65–100.

———. *The Cost of Courage in Aztec Society: Essays on Mesoamerican Society and Culture*. New York: Cambridge University Press, 2010.

Cliff, Nigel. *Holy War: How Vasco da Gama's Epic Voyage Turned the Tide in a Centuries-Old Clash of Civilizations*. New York: HarperCollins, 2011.

Clutton-Brock, Juliet. *A Natural History of Domesticated Mammals*, 2d ed. New York: Cambridge University Press, 1999.

Cohen, J. M., ed. and trans. *The Four Voyages of Christopher Columbus*. New York: Penguin Books, 1969.

Cortés, Hernan. *Cartas de Relación de la Conquista de Méjico*, Tomo 1, Quinta Ed. Madrid: Espasa Calpe, 1942.

———. *Letters from Mexico*. Anthony Pagden, ed. and trans. New Haven: Yale University Press, 1986.

Crawford, Dorothy H. *Deadly Companions: How Microbes Shaped Our History*. New York: Oxford University Press, 2007.

Crosby, Alfred W., Jr. "The Early History of Syphilis: A Reappraisal." *American Anthropologist* 71.2 (April 1969): 218–227.

———. *Ecological Imperialism: The Biological Expansion of Europe, 900–1900*. New York: Cambridge University Press, 1986.

Dana, Richard Henry, Jr. *Two Years Before the Mast*. Hertfordshire, UK: Wordsworth Editions, 1996.

Darwin, John. *After Tamerlane: The Rise and Fall of Global Empires, 1400–2000*. New York: Bloomsbury Press, 2008.

Davis, Graeme. *Vikings in America*. Edinburgh, UK: Birlinn Ltd., 2009.

Dawkins, Richard. *The Selfish Gene*. New York: Oxford University Press, 1989.

Defoe, Daniel. *Robinson Crusoe and A Journal of the Plague Year*. New York: Modern Library, 1948.

DeVries, Kelly. *Medieval Military Technology*. Orchard Park NY: Broadview Press, 1992.

Diamond, Jared. *Guns, Germs, and Steel: The Fates of Human Societies*. New York: W. W. Norton, 1999.

Díaz [del Castillo], Bernal. *The Conquest of New Spain*. J. M. Cohen, trans. London: The Folio Society, 1963.

Díaz del Castillo, Bernal. *The History of the Conquest of New Spain*. Davíd Carrasco, ed., With Additional Essays by Rolena Adorno, Carrasco, Sandra Cypress, and Karen Vieira Powers. Albuquerque, NM: University of New Mexico Press, 2008.

Diel, Lori Boornazian. "*Manuscito del aperreamiento* (Manuscript of the Dogging): A 'Dogging' and Its Implications for Early Colonial Cholula." *Ethnohistory* 58:4 (Fall 2011): 585–611.

Dumézil, Georges. *The Destiny of the Warrior*. Alf Hiltebeitel, trans. Chicago: University of Chicago Press, 1969.

Duplessis, Robert S. *Transitions to Capitalism in Early Modern Europe*. New York: Cambridge University Press, 1997.

Durán, Fray Diego. *The Aztecs: The History of the Indies of New Spain*. Doris Heyden and Fernando Horcasitas, trans. New York: Orion Press, 1964.

Earle, Rebecca. *The Body of the Conquistador: Food, Race and the Colonial Experience in Spanish America*. New York: Cambridge University Press, 2012.

Edlin, Duncan. "The Stoned Age? A Look at the Evidence for Cocaine in Mummies," undated. http://www.hallofaat.com/modules.php?name=Articles&file=article. Retrieved 4/17/2014.

Eisler, Riane. *The Chalice and the Blade: Our History, Our Future*. San Francisco: Harper & Row, 1987.

Eliade, Mircea. *The Myth of the Eternal Return*. Willard R. Trask, trans. New York: Pantheon for Bollingen Foundation, 1954.

Elliott, J. H. *Spain and Its World, 1500–1700*. New York: Yale University Press, 1989.

———. *Imperial Spain: 1469–1716*. New York: Penguin Books, 2002.

Erlichman, Howard J. *Conquest, Tribute, and Trade: The Quest for Precious Metals and the Birth of Globalization.* Amherst, NY: Prometheus Books, 2010.

Fagan, Brian. *The Great Warming: Climate Change and the Rise and Fall of Civilizations.* New York: Bloomsbury Press, 2008.

Fell, Barry. *Bronze Age America.* Boston: Little, Brown, 1982.

Ferguson, Robert. *The Vikings: A History.* New York: Penguin Books, 2009.

Findlay, Ronald, and Kevin H. O'Rourke. *Power and Plenty: Trade, War, and the World Economy in the Second Millennium.* Princeton, NJ: Princeton University Press, 2007.

Fingerhut, Eugene R. *Explorers of Pre-Columbian America? The Diffusionist-Inventionist Controversy.* Claremont, CA: Regina Books, 1994.

Fitzhugh, William W., and Elisabeth I. Ward, eds. *Vikings: The North Atlantic Saga.* Washington: Smithsonian Institute Press, 2000.

Fitzpatrick-Matthews, Keith. "Old World People in the New World Before Columbus?" 9/22/2012. http://badarchaeology.wordpress.com/tag/ogham/.

Florescano, Enrique. *The Myth of Quetzalcoatl.* Lysa Hochroth, trans. Baltimore: The John Hopkins University Press, 1999.

Fox, Margalit. "George J. Armelagos, an Anthropologist Who Told Skeletons' Tales, is Dead at 77." *New York Times* 8 June 2014: A24.

———. "Anthony Smith, Explorer with Zest for Land, Sea and Air, is Dead at 88." *New York Times* 25 July 2014: A19.

Frank, Andre Gunder. *ReOrient: Global Economy in the Asian Age.* Berkeley: University of California Press, 1998.

Frazer, James G. *The Golden Bough: A Study in Magic and Religion,* abridged ed. New York: Macmillan, 1950.

Fuentes, Patricia de, ed. and trans. *The Conquistadors: First-Person Accounts of the Conquest of Mexico.* New York: Orion Press, 1963.

Gibson, Arthur C. "Batatas, Not Potatoes," undated. http://www.botgard.ucla.edu/html/botanytextbooks/economicbotany/Ipomoea/index/html. Retrieved 4/17/2014.

Gilgamesh, The Epic of, revised ed. N. K. Sandars, trans. New York: Penguin Books, 1972.

Gillespie, Susan D. *The Aztec Kings: The Construction of Rulership in Mexica History.* Tucson: University of Arizona Press, 1989.

Goldman, Laurence R., ed. *The Anthropology of Cannibalism.* Westport, CT: Bergin & Garvey, 1999.

Gómara, Francisco López de. *Cortés: The Life of the Conqueror by His Secretary.* Lesley Byrd Simpson, trans. Berkeley: University of California Press, 1964.

Goodpasture, H. McKennie, ed. *Cross and Sword: An Eyewitness History of Christianity in Latin America.* Maryknoll, NY: Orbis Books, 1989.

Graeber, David. *Debt: The First 5,000 Years.* Brooklyn: Melville House, 2012.

Grafton, Anthony, and Ann Blair, eds. *The Transmission of Culture in Early Modern Europe.* Philadelphia: University of Pennsylvania Press, 1990.

Graham, R. B. Cunninghame. *The Horses of the Conquest.* Norman, OK: University of Oklahoma Press, 1949.

Gregerson, Linda, and Susan Juster, eds. *Empires of God: Religious Encounters in the Early Modern Atlantic.* Philadelphia: University of Pennsylvania Press, 2011.

Gunn, Steven. "War, Religion, and the State." *Early Modern Europe: An Oxford History.* Euan Cameron, ed. New York: Oxford University Press, 1999.

Haber, Annat, Tamar Dayan, and Nimrod Getzo. "Pig Exploitation at Hagoshrim: A Prehistoric Site in the Southern Levant." *First Steps of Animal Domestication: New Archaeozoological Approaches.* J.-D. Vigne, J. Peters & D. Helmer, eds. Oxford, UK: Oxbow Books, 2005: 80–85.

Halpern, Jake. "The Secret of the Temple: The Discovery of Treasure Worth Billions of Dollars Shakes Southern India." *The New Yorker,* April 30, 2012: 49–57.

Harner, Michael. "The Ecological Basis

for Aztec Sacrifice." *American Ethnologist* 4.1 (February 1977): 117–135.

Harris, Marvin. *Good to Eat: Riddles of Food and Culture.* Long Grove, IL: Waveland Press, 1985.

Hassig, Ross. *Aztec Warfare: Imperial Expansion and Political Control.* Norman, OK: University of Oklahoma Press, 1988.

_____. *Time, History, and Belief in Aztec and Colonial Mexico.* Austin, TX: University of Texas Press, 2001.

_____. *Mexico and the Spanish Conquest,* 2d ed. Norman, OK: University of Oklahoma Press, 2006.

Hays, J. N. *Epidemics and Pandemics: Their Impacts on Human History.* Santa Barbara, CA: ABC-CLIO, 2005.

Herrera, Robinson. Review of *Butterflies Will Burn: Prosecuting Sodomites in Early Modern Spain and Mexico* by Federico Garza Carvajal. *The Hispanic American Historical Review* 85:3 (August 2005): 505–507.

Hillgarth, J. N. *The Spanish Kingdoms: 1250–1516,* Vol. I. Oxford, UK: Clarendon Press, 1976.

Hine, Robert V., and John Mack Faragher. *The American West: A New Interpretive History.* New Haven: Yale University Press, 2000.

Hofmeester, Karin, and Christine Moll-Murata, eds. *The Joy and Pain of Work: Global Attitudes and Valuations, 1500–1650.* Amsterdam: International Review of Social History, Special Issue 19, 2011.

Holden, Lynn. "Cannibalism." *Encyclopedia of Taboos.* Santa Barbara, CA: ABC-CLIO, 2000: 15–20.

Holder, Preston. *The Hoe and the Horse on the Plains: A Study of Cultural Development Among North American Indians.* Lincoln, NE: University of Nebraska Press, 1970.

Hristov, Romeo H., and Santiago Genovés T. "The Roman Head from Tecaxic-Calixtlahuaca, Mexico: A Review of the Evidence." Rev. and extended version of paper presented on April 22, 2001. http://www.unm.edu/~rhistov/calixtla-huaca.html.

Hughes, Robert. *The Fatal Shore: The Epic of Australia's Founding.* New York: Vintage Books, 1986.

Huizinga, Johan. *The Waning of the Middle Ages.* Harmondsworth, UK: Penguin Books, 1955.

Hyatt, Vera Lawrence, and Rex Nettleford, eds. *Race, Discourse, and the Origins of the Americas: A New World View.* Washington: Smithsonian Institute Press, 1995.

Iglesia, Ramón. *Columbus, Cortés, and Other Essays.* Lesley Byrd Simpson, ed. & trans. Berkeley: University of California Press, 1969.

Ikegami, Eiko. *The Taming of the Samurai: Honorific Individualism and the Making of Modern Japan.* Cambridge, MA: Harvard University Press, 1995.

Iliad of Homer, The. Richmond Lattimore, trans. Chicago: Phoenix Books, 1951.

Janicot, Michael. "Rethinking History—Did the Chinese Discover America?" *Another Day in Paradise* 5.30 (January 2004). http://www.adip.info/2003_2003/jan/04-history.php.

Jennings, Francis. *The Invasion of America: Indians, Colonialism, and the Cant of Conquest.* Chapel Hill, NC: University of North Carolina Press, 1975.

Johnson, Allan G. *The Gender Knot: Unraveling Our Patriarchal Legacy.* Philadelphia: Temple University Press, 2005.

Johnson, William Weber. *Cortés.* Boston: Little, Brown, 1975.

Jones, Eric. *The European Miracle: Environments, Economies and Geopolitics in the History of Europe and Asia,* 3d ed. New York: Cambridge University Press, 2003.

Joseph, Frank. *The Lost Colonies of Ancient America: A Comprehensive Guide to the Visitors Who Really Discovered America.* Pompton Plains, NJ: New Page Books, 2014.

Jung, C. G. *Symbols of Transformation,* Vol. 5 of *The Collected Works of C. G. Jung,* 2d ed. R. F. C. Hull, trans. Princeton, NJ: Princeton University Press, 1967.

_____. *Psychology and Religion: West and East,* Vol. 11 of *Collected Works,* 2d ed. Hull, trans. Princeton, NJ: Princeton University Press, 1969.

Kamen, Henry. *Spain, 1469–1714: A Soci-*

ety of Conflict. Harlow, UK: Pearson Education Ltd., 2005.

Kamiya, Gary. "Cabrillo made his name with bold, bloody exploits." *San Francisco Chronicle* 18 October 2014: C1-2.

Karttunen, Frances. "Rethinking Malinche." *Indian Women of Early Mexico.* Susan Schroeder, Stephanie Wood, and Robert Haskett, eds. Norman, OK: University of Oklahoma Press, 1997: 291–312.

Keen, Benjamin. *The Aztec Image in Western Thought.* New Brunswick, NJ: Rutgers University Press, 1971.

Kelekna, Pita. *The Horse in Human History.* New York: Cambridge University Press, 2009.

Kilgannon, Corey. "Couple Arrives in New York from Africa, Merrily, Merrily." *New York Times* 21 June 2014: A19.

Kindleberger, Charles P. *Economic Response: Comparative Studies in Trade, Finance, and Growth.* Cambridge, MA: Harvard University Press, 1978.

Kiple, Kenneth F., and Stephen V. Beck, eds. *Biological Consequences of the European Expansion, 1450–1800.* Brookfield, VT: Ashgate Pub., 1997.

Koch, Peter O. *The Aztecs, the Conquistadors, and the Making of Mexican Culture.* Jefferson, NC: McFarland & Co., 2006.

Kohl, Philip L. *The Making of Bronze Age Eurasia.* New York: Cambridge University Press, 2007.

Kolata, Gina. "Anthropologists Suggest Cannibalism is a Myth." *Science* 232 (June 13, 1986): 1497–1500.

Koning, Hans. *The Conquest of America: How the Indian Nations Lost Their Continent.* New York: Monthly Review Press, 1993.

Krech, Shepard III. *The Ecological Indian: Myth and History.* New York: W. W. Norton, 1999.

Langum, David J. "Californios and the Image of Indolence." *The Western Historical Quarterly* IX.2 (April 1978): 181–196.

Las Casas, Bartolomé de. *History of the Indies.* Andrée Collard, ed. and trans. New York: Harper Torchbooks, 1971.

_____. *The Tears of Indians: Being An Historical and True Account of the Cruel Massacres and Slaughters Committed by the Spaniards in the Islands of the West Indies, Mexico, Peru, etc.: An Eye-Witness Account.* John Phillips, trans. (1656). _____: Oriole Editions, 1972.

_____. *The Destruction of the Indies: A Brief Account.* Herma Briffault, trans. New York: Seabury Press, 1974.

_____. *A Short Account of the Destruction of the Indies.* Nigel Griffin, trans. New York: Penguin Books, 1992.

LeClézio, J. M. G. *The Mexican Dream: Or, the Interrupted Thought of Amerindian Civilizations.* Teresa Lavender Fagan, trans. Chicago: University of Chicago Press, 1993.

Leon-Portilla, Miguel, ed. *The Broken Spears: The Aztec Account of the Conquest of Mexico,* Expanded and Updated. Lysander Kemp, trans. from Spanish. Boston: Beacon Press, 1992.

Lepore, Jill. *The Mansion of Happiness: A History of Life and Death.* New York: Vintage Books, 2012.

_____. "The Dark Ages: Terrorism, Counterterrorism, and the Law of Torment." *The New Yorker,* March 18, 2013: 28–32.

Lerner, Gerda. *The Creation of Patriarchy.* New York: Oxford University Press, 1986.

Lestringant, Frank. *Cannibals: The Discovery and Representation of the Cannibal from Columbus to Jules Verne.* Rosemary Morris, trans. Berkeley: University of California Press, 1997.

Lévy-Strauss, Claude. *The Savage Mind.* George Weidenfeld and Nicolson Ltd., trans. Chicago: University of Chicago Press, 1966.

_____. *The Elementary Structures of Kinship,* rev. ed. James Harle Bell, John Richard Sturmer, and Rodney Needham, trans. Boston: Beacon Press, 1969.

Levy, Buddy. *Conquistador: Hernán Cortés, King Montezuma, and the Last Stand of the Aztecs.* New York: Bantam Dell, 2008.

Lewis, Bernard. *Cultures in Conflict: Christians, Muslims, and Jews in the Age of Discovery.* New York: Oxford University Press, 1995.

Livi-Bacci, Massimo. "Return to Hispaniola: Reassessing a Demographic Catastrophe." *The Hispanic American Historical Review* 83:1 (February 2003): 3–51.

Lockhart, James, ed. and trans. *We People Here: Nahuatl Accounts of the Conquest of Mexico.* Berkeley: University of California Press, 1993.

Loomis, C. Grant. *White Magic: An Introduction to the Folklore of Christian Legend.* Cambridge, MA: Mediaeval Academy of America, 1948.

MacKay, Angus. *Spain in the Middle Ages: From Frontier to Empire, 1000–1500.* London: Macmillan Press, 1977.

Mallett, Michael, and Christine Shaw. *The Italian Wars: 1494–1559.* Harlow, UK: Pearson Ed. Ltd., 2012.

Mann, Charles C. *1491: New Revelations of the Americas Before Columbus,* 2d ed. New York: Vintage Books, 2011.

_____. *1493: Uncovering the New World Columbus Created.* New York: Vintage Books, 2011.

_____. "Into the Wilderness." Review of *The Barbarous Years* by Bernard Bailyn. *New York Times Book Review,* January 6, 2013: 15.

Mannheim, Karl. *Ideology and Utopia: An Introduction to the Sociology of Knowledge.* Louis Wirth and Edward Shils, trans. New York: Harcourt, Brace & World, 1964.

Mantel, Hilary. "The Magic of Keith Thomas." *New York Review of Books* LIX.10 (June 7, 2012): 38–39.

Mariscal, George. *Contradictory Subjects: Quevedo, Cervantes, and Seventeenth-Century Spanish Culture.* Ithaca, NY: Cornell University Press, 1991.

Marks, Richard Lee. *Cortés: The Great Adventurer and the Fate of Aztec Mexico.* New York: Alfred A. Knopf, 1993.

Mazoyer, Marcel, and Laurence Roudart. *A History of World Agriculture: From the Neolithic Age to the Current Crisis.* James H. Membrey, trans. New York: Monthly Review Press, 2006.

McCaa, Robert. "Revisioning Smallpox in Mexico City-Tenochtitlán, 1520–1950: What Difference Did Charity, Quarantine, Inoculation and Vaccination Make?" *Proceedings of the International Commission for Historical Demography (ICHD).* Eugenio Sonnino, ed. Rome: La Sapienza, University of Rome, 2004: 455–488.

McCafferty, Geoffrey G. "Reinterpreting the Great Pyramid of Cholula, Puebla." *Ancient Mesoamerica* 7 (1996): 1–17.

_____. "The Cholula Massacre: Factional Histories and Archaeology of the Spanish Conquest." *The Entangled Past: Integrating History and Archaeology—Proceedings of the 30th Annual Chacmool Conference.* Calgary, Canada: The Archaeological Association of the University of Calgary, 2000.

_____. "De-Colón-izing Malintzin." *Postcolonial Perspectives in Archaeology: Proceedings of the 39th (2006) Annual Chacmool Archaeological Conference.* Peter Bikoulis, Dominic Lacroix, and Meaghan Peuramaki-Brown, eds. Calgary, Canada: The Archaeological Association of the University of Calgary, 2009.

McNeill, William H. *Plagues and Peoples.* New York: Anchor Books, 1998.

Mendelsohn, Daniel. "Battle Lines: A slimmer, faster Iliad." Review of *Iliad,* Stephen Mitchell, trans. *The New Yorker,* November 7, 2011: 76–81.

Menzies, Gavin. *1421: The Year China Discovered America.* New York: Harper Perennial, 2003.

Minder, Rafael. "A Hard Sell to Tame a Name in Spain." *New York Times* 11 May 2014: 6.

Mogelson, Luke. "The River Martyrs: Day by day, a city at war with the regime collects its dead." *The New Yorker,* April 29, 2013: 40–49.

Montaigne, Michel de. "On Cannibals." *Essays.* J. M. Cohen, trans. Baltimore: Penguin Books, 1958.

Morris, Ian. *Why the West Rules—For Now.* New York: Picador, 2010.

Morton, R. S., and S. Rashid. "'The syphilis enigma': the riddle resolved?" *Sexually Transmitted Infections* 77: 322–324 (May 22, 2001). http://sti.bmj.com/content/77/5/322.full.pdf#page =1&view=FitH.

Motolinía, Fray Toribio. *Motolinía's History of the Indians of New Spain*. Elizabeth Andros Foster, ed. and trans. Berkeley: The Cortés Society, 1950.

Mumford, Lewis. *Technics and Civilization*. New York: Harcourt, Brace & World, 1963.

Munro, John H., ed. *Money in the Pre-Industrial World: Bullion, Debasements and Coin Substitutes*. Brookfield, VT: Pickering & Chatto, 2012.

Nash, June. "The Aztecs and the Ideology of Male Dominance." *SIGNS: Journal of Women in Culture and Society* 4.2 (Winter 1978) 349–362.

Neuman, William. "For Miners, Increasing Risk on a Mountain at the Heart of Bolivia's Identity." *New York Times* 17 September 2014: A7.

Nicholson, H. B. *Topiltzin Quetzalcoatl: The Once and Future Lord of the Toltecs*. Boulder, CO: University Press of Colorado, 2001.

Nicolle, David. *Granada 1492: The Twilight of Moorish Spain*. Westport, CT: Praeger, 2005.

O'Brien, Patrick K. "Metanarratives in Global Histories of Material Progress." *The International History Review* XXIII, 2 (June 2001) 345–367.

O'Callaghan, Joseph F. *Reconquest and Crusade in Medieval Spain*. Philadelphia: University of Pennsylvania Press, 2003.

Padden, R. C. *The Hummingbird and the Hawk: Conquest and Sovereignty in the Valley of Mexico, 1503–1541*. San Francisco: Harper Torchbooks, 1967.

Parry, J. H. *The Age of Reconnaissance: Discovery, Exploration and Settlement, 1450 to 1650*. Berkeley: University of California Press, 1981.

Peet, Richard, with Elaine Hartwick. *Theories of Development*. New York: The Guilford Press, 1999.

Peterson, David A. "The Real Cholula." *Notas Mesoamericanas* 10 (1987): 71–117.

_____, and Z. D. Green. "The Spanish Arrival and the Massacre at Cholula." *Notas Mesoamericanas* 10 (1987): 203–239.

Phillips, Jonathan. *The Fourth Crusade and the Sack of Constantinople*. New York: Penguin Books, 2004.

Pierson, Peter. *The History of Spain*. Westport, CT: Greenwood Press, 1999.

Pirenne, Henri. *Economic and Social History of Medieval Europe*. New York: Harcourt, Brace & World, 1937.

Pitt, Leonard. *The Decline of the Californios: A Social History of the Spanish-Speaking Californians, 1846–1890*. Berkeley: University of California Press, 1968.

Poem of the Cid, The: A Bilingual Edition with Parallel Text. Rita Hamilton and Janet Perry, trans. New York: Penguin Books, 1975.

Powell, Philip Wayne. *Soldiers, Indians & Silver: The Northward Advance of New Spain, 1550–1600*. Berkeley: University of California Press, 1952.

Powers, James F. *A Society Organized for War: The Iberian Municipal Militias in the Central Middle Ages*. Berkeley: University of California Press, 1988.

Prescott, William H. *History of the Conquest of Mexico*. New York: Modern Library, 1843.

_____. *History of the Conquest of Mexico*, Vol. 1. Philadelphia: J. B. Lippincott, 1892.

Rabasa, José. "Dialogue as Conquest: Mapping Spaces for Counter-Discourse." *Cultural Critique* 6 (Spring 1987): 137–159.

Raitt, Jill, ed. *Christian Spirituality: High Middle Ages and Reformation*. New York: Crossroad, 1987.

Rediker, Marcus. *The Slave Ship: A Human History*. New York: Penguin Books, 2007.

Reed, Clyde G. Review of Gregory Clark, *A Farewell to Alms: A Brief Economic History of the World*. *The International History Review* XXXI.1 (March 2009): 97–99.

Restall, Matthew. *Seven Myths of the Spanish Conquest*. New York: Oxford University Press, 2003.

Reston, James, Jr. *Dogs of God: Columbus, the Inquisition, and the Defeat of the Moors*. New York: Doubleday, 2005.

Riley, E. C. *Don Quixote*. Boston: Allen & Unwin, 1986.

Riley, James C. "Smallpox and American Indians Revisited." *Journal of the History of Medicine and Allied Sciences* 65.4 (October 2010): 445–477.

Riley-Smith, Jonathan. *The Crusades: A Short History.* New Haven: Yale University Press, 1987.

Roewer, Lutz, et al. "Continent-Wide Decoupling of Y-Chromosomal Genetic Variation from Language and Geography in Native South Americans," April 11, 2013. http://www. plosgenetics.org/article/info:doi/10.1371/journal.pgen.10 03460.

Rogerson, Barnaby. *The Last Crusaders: The Hundred-Year Battle for the Centre of the World.* New York: Overlook Press, 2009.

Romero, Simon. "Discoveries Challenge Beliefs on Humans' Arrival in the Americas." *New York Times International* 28 March 2014: A5.

Roots, Clive. *Domestication.* Westport, CT: Greenwood Press, 2007.

Rougemont, Denis de. *Love in the Western World.* Montgomery Belgion, trans. San Francisco: HarperColophon, 1956.

Rowe, William T. Review of Kenneth Pomeranz, *The Great Divergence: Europe, China, and the Making of the Modern World Economy. The International History Review* XXIII.2 (June 2001): 408–410.

Ruiz, Teofilo F. *Spanish Society, 1400–1600.* Essex, UK: Pearson Ed., 2001.

_____. *Spain's Centuries of Crisis.* Malden, MA: Blackwell Pub., 2007.

Sagan, Eli. *At the Dawn of Tyranny: The Origins of Individualism, Political Oppression and the State.* New York: Vintage Books, 1985.

Sahagún, Fray Bernardino de. *A History of Ancient Mexico,* Vol. 1. Fanny R. Bandelier, trans. (from Spanish). Nashville, TN: Fisk University Press, 1932.

_____. *General History of the Things of New Spain, Book 2—The Ceremonies,* 2d ed. Arthur J. O. Anderson and Charles E. Dibble, trans. Santa Fe, NM: School of American Research and University of Utah, 1981.

_____. *General History of the Things of New Spain, Book 12—The Conquest of Mexico.* Arthur J. O. Anderson and Charles E. Dibble, trans. Santa Fe: School of American Research & University of Utah, 1955.

Sahlins, Marshall. "Culture as Protein and Profit." *New York Review of Books* 25.18 (November 23, 1978).

_____. *The Western Illusion of Human Nature.* Chicago: Prickly Paradigm Press, 2008.

Sanday, Peggy Reeves. *Divine Hunger: Cannibalism as a Cultural System.* New York: Cambridge University Press, 1986.

Schmidle, Nicholas. "In the Crosshairs." *The New Yorker,* June 3, 2013: 33–45.

Schmölz-Häberlein, Michaela, and Mark H. Häberlein. "Hans Staden, Neil L. Whitehead, and the Cultural Politics of Scholarly Publishing." *Hispanic American Historical Review* 81:3-4 (August-November 2001): 745–751.

Schneider, Jane. "Of Vigilance and Virgins: Honor, Shame, and Access to Resources in Mediterranean Societies." *Ethnology* X.1 (January 1971): 1–24.

Sears, Theresa Ann. "Spain's Medievalist Project in the New World." *Medievalism in Europe: Studies in Medievalism,* Vol. V. Leslie J. Workman, ed. Cambridge, UK: D. S. Brewer, 1994: 200–208.

Seed, Patricia. Review of *Fernández de Oviedo's Chronicle of America: A New History for the New World* by Kathleen Ann Myers. *The Hispanic American Review* 89: 4 (November 2009): 678–680.

_____. *American Pentimento: The Invention of Indians and the Pursuit of Riches.* Minneapolis: University of Minnesota Press, 2001.

Simpson, Lesley Byrd. *The Encomienda in New Spain: The Beginning of Spanish Mexico.* Berkeley: University of California Press, 1966.

Singer, Peter. "Kinder and Gentler." Review of *The Better Angels of Our Nature: Why Violence Has Declined* by Steven Pinker. *The New York Times Book Review,* October 9, 2011: 1, 12–13.

Snell, Bruno. *The Discovery of the Mind: The Greek Origins of European Thought.*

T. G. Rosenmeyer, trans. New York: Harper & Row, 1960.
Song of Roland, The. Frederick Bliss Luquiens, trans. New York: Macmillan, 1952.
Strayer, Joseph R., and Dana C. Munro. *The Middle Ages: 395–1500.* New York: Appleton-Century-Crofts, 1959.
Swinton, George. *Sculpture of the Eskimo.* Toronto: McClelland & Stewart, 1972.
Tacitus. *The Agricola and the Germania.* H. Mattingly, trans. Baltimore: Penguin Books, 1970.
Takaki, Ronald. *A Different Mirror: A History of Multicultural America.* Boston: Little, Brown, 1993.
Terborgh, John. Letter. *The New York Review of Books* LIX.9 (May 24, 2012) 50.
Thomas, Hugh. *Conquest: Montezuma, Cortés, and the Fall of Old Mexico.* New York: Simon & Schuster, 1993.
_____. *Rivers of Gold: The Rise of the Spanish Empire, from Columbus to Magellan.* New York: Random House, 2003.
_____. *The Golden Empire: Spain, Charles V, and the Creation of America.* New York: Random House, 2010.
Thomas, Keith. *Religion and the Decline of Magic: Studies in Popular Beliefs in Sixteenth and Seventeenth Century England.* New York: Oxford University Press, 1971.
Thorsson, Örnólfur, ed., *The Sagas of the Icelanders: A Selection.* Keneva Kunz, trans. New York: Penguin, 1997.
Tocqueville, Alexis de. *Democracy in America,* Vol. 1. Henry Reeve, trans. New York: Vintage Books, 1945.
Todorov, Tzvetan. *The Conquest of America: The Question of the Other.* Richard Howard, trans. New York: Harper & Row, 1984.
Townsend, Camilla. "Burying the White Gods: New Perspectives on the Conquest of Mexico." *The American Historical Review* 108.3 (June 2003): 659–687.
Townsend, Richard F. *The Aztecs,* 3d ed. London: Thames & Hudson Ltd., 2009.
Tuchman, Barbara W. *A Distant Mirror: The Calamitous 14th Century.* New York: Ballantine Books, 1978.
Turner, Christy G., II, and Jacqueline A. Turner. *Man Corn: Cannibalism and Violence in the Prehistoric American Southwest.* Salt Lake City: University of Utah Press, 1999.
Tyerman, Christopher. *Fighting for Christendom: Holy War and the Crusades.* New York: Oxford University Press, 2004.
Ullmann, Walter. *A History of Political Thought: the Middle Ages.* Baltimore: Penguin Books, 1965.
Van de Logt, Mark. *War Party in Blue: Pawnee Scouts in the U.S. Army.* Norman, OK: University of Oklahoma Press, 2010.
Verhaaik, Oskar. "Terrorism." *International Encyclopedia of the Social Sciences,* 2d ed., Vol. 8. San Francisco: Thomson Gale, 2008: 328–330.
Vilar, Pierre. *Spain: A Brief History,* 2d ed. Brian Tate, trans. New York: Pergamon Press, 1977.
Villagutierre Soto-Mayor, Don Juan de. *History of the Conquest of the Province of the Itza: Subjugation and Events of the Lacandon and Other Nations of Yucatan in North America.* Brother Robert D. Wood, trans. Culver City, CA: Labyrinthos, 1983.
Viviano, Frank. "The Eunuch Admiral." *California* 122.3 (Fall 2011): 40–45.
Vree, Wilbert Van. *Meetings, Manners and Civilization: The Development of Modern Meeting Behaviour.* Kathleen Bell, trans. New York: Leicester University Press, 1999.
Wagner, Henry R. *The Rise of Fernando Cortés.* Berkeley: The Cortés Society, 1944.
Wallerstein, Immanuel. *The Capitalist World Economy.* New York: Cambridge University Press, 1979.
Walton, Priscilla L. *Our Cannibals, Ourselves.* Chicago: University of Illinois Press, 2004.
Watts, Sheldon. *Epidemics and History: Disease, Power and Imperialism.* New Haven: Yale University Press, 1997.
Weber, Max. *The Protestant Ethic and the Spirit of Capitalism.* Talcott Parsons, trans. New York: Chas. Scribner's Sons, 1958.

Wells, Peter S. *Barbarians to Angels: The Dark Ages Reconsidered.* New York: W. W. Norton, 2008.

West, Delno C. "Medieval Ideas of Apocalyptic Mission and the Early Franciscans in Mexico." *The Americas* 45.3 (January 1989): 293–313.

West, Rebecca. *Survivors in Mexico.* New Haven: Yale University Press, 2003.

Wey Gómez, Nicolás. *The Tropics of Empire: Why Columbus Sailed South to the Indies.* Cambridge, MA: MIT Press, 2008.

White, Luise. *Speaking With Vampires: Rumor and History in Colonial Africa.* Berkeley: University of California Press, 2000.

Whitehead, Neil L. "Hans Staden and the Cultural Politics of Cannibalism." *Hispanic American Historical Review* 80:4 (November 2000): 721–751.

Wilford, John Noble. "Don't Blame Columbus for All the Indians' Ills." *New York Times* 29 October 2002.

Williams, Eric. *Capitalism & Slavery.* Chapel Hill, NC: University of North Carolina Press, 1994.

Wright, Ronald. *Stolen Continents: Conquest and Resistance in the Americas.* New York: Penguin Books, 2003.

"Yaws." WHO Media Centre: Fact Sheet No. 316 (Updated February 2014). http://www.who.int/mediacentre/factsheets/fs316/en/.

Zelicoff, Alan P., MD, and Michael Bellomo. *Microbe: Are We Ready for the Next Plague?* New York: AMACOM, 2005.

Zeuner, Frederick E. *A History of Domesticated Animals.* New York: Hutchinson & Co., 1963.

Zinn, Howard. *A People's History of the United States: 1492-Present.* New York: HarperCollins, 2003.

Index

Numbers in **_bold italics_** indicate pages with photographs.

Abulafia, David 37
Acapulco 71, 91
Achaians 47, 69
Achilles 47
Africa 6, 13, 18, 26, 30, 83, 92; East Africa 3, 91; Northwest Africa 32; South Africa 15; sub-Saharan 30, 82, 38; tropical 161; West Africa 26, 31, 38, 52, 57, 81, 91, 101, 161, 190; *see also* Cape Bojador; Cape Branco; Cape Hope; Cape Verde; the Gold Coast; the Grain Coast; the Ivory Coast; North Africa; the Slave Coast; slavery
Africans 13, 26, 27, 86, 125, 161; in Mesoamerica 26, 80; *see also* slavery
Agamemnon 145
Age of Discovery 41, 49, 52, 64, 86, 101
Agobard of Lyon 51
"agricultural revolution" 107
agriculturalists 101, 150; *see also* peasants
agriculture, plantation 87, 94, 95, 124; and slavery 96–97, 118; techniques 123; *see also* cotton; sugar; tobacco
Aguilar, Francisco de 113, 128, 130, 131, 132, 136; *see also* Cholula massacre
Aguilar, Gérónimo 175, 185, 211n38
AIDs 160
Alaska 22
Alexander VI, Pope 33, 55
Alfonso VIII, King of Castile 44
Algiers 91
Almería *see* Nautla
Almíndez Chirino, Pedro 114
alphabet 125
The Alphabet: A Key to the History of Mankind 11; *see also* Diringer, David
altepetl (community) 115, 170, 180; *see also* Aztecs, enemies
Alva Ixtlixochitl, Fernando de 142
Alvarado, Jorge de 114
Alvarado, Pedro de 9, 19, 41, 46–47, 58, 66, 74, 76, 114, 141, 152, 176; *see also* Tonatiuh
Alvarez Osorio, Pedro 43

Amadis of Gaul 41, 43, 184; *see also* chivalric novels; Montalvo, Garci Rodríguez de
Amalek 145
ambush 69, 134; *see also* tactics, comparative military
America 32, 38, 53, 54, 62, 153; American South 96, 124; British America 95, 122, 124; tropical 95, 161; *see also* Americas; Western Hemisphere
the American dream 120
Americas 7, 13, 15, 16, 17, 18, 27, 33, 34, 51, 92, 94, 95, 96, 141, 189; and European divergence 92–97, 191; and horses 100; and pigs 150–*151*; and syphilis 164; *see also* New World
Amsterdam 95; account entries 89
Amur River 101
Anacaona, Queen 98; *see also* massacres, gratutious
"anachronistic feudalism" 116
Anales de Cuauhtitlan 186; *see also* Quetzalcoatl
Ancient American 13, 15
Andean civilization 16
the Andes 34, 82, 103, 160; expedition 43; *see also* Pizarro, Francisco
angels 45; *see also* victories, miraculous
Anglo Saxons 120–122
Annals of Tlatelolco 56, 115, 141, 179, 186
L'Anse aux Meadows 19, 20, 23
Antequera, Bishop of *see* Zárate, Don Juan de
anthropologists 156, 164
antibodies *see* immunity
Antilles 53, 72, 82, 85, 112, 113, 154, 155; Greater Antilles 73; *see also* Caribbean
Antioch 45; *see also* victories, miraculous
anti-Semitism 35; *Castrillo Matajudos* 35
Antwerp 88, 89
Apahida 65
Arabian Peninsula 163
Arabic commentators 159; *see also* Ibn Fadlan
Aragon 33, 34, 72

229

archaeologists 128, 140–141, 143, 164
Arctic 16, 22, 26
Argentina 24, 105
Arica 90
aristocracy 42; military 42, 193; patrons 146; and privilege 79; work ethic 5, 108–124
Aristotle 46, 108, 118
Arizona 105
armor 6, 43, 70, 107, 150, 170, 190; cotton 66, 70; metal 65–66, 168
Army of Flanders 88
arrows 55, 64, 66, 67, 77, 99, 102, 147
Arthur, King 13, 44, 64
artillery 47, 70, 146–147
Arubakari II 17, 18
Ashburn, P.M. 159
Asia 92; Asians 159; goods 191; markets 92, 95; outlets 97; ports 91; producers 96
Asia, East 6, 16, 30, 60, 88, 91, 159; *see also* China; Japan
Asia, South 3, 6, 60; *see also* India
Asia, Southeast 3, 91
asientos 88; *see also* bankruptcies
Atlantic trade winds 26, *28*, 31, 96; 190; currents 26, 27
atlatl see spear-thrower
Augustinian doctrine 56; friary 164; "political Augustinism" 125
Augustinians 116, 185
Australia 13, 92, 124, 125, 150, 151
Austria 87
autos-de-fe 145
Ávila, Alonso de 79, 114
Azcapotzalco 34, 114
Azores 31, 32, 37, 42, 80
Aztec Empire 3, 8, 9, 10, 18, 45, 48, 57, 58, 143, 156, 159, 172, 178, 182, 184, 185; capital 4, 40, 182; nation 46, 171, 191–192; world 183, 192; *see also* Tenochtitlán; Triple Alliance
Aztec military tactics 68–69
Aztec Studies 75
Aztec theology 144, 192; *see also* Aztecs, cosmology; Aztecs, pantheon
Aztecs 4, 7, 18, 32, 34, 40, 58, 99, 188, 189; affluent 78; calendar 192; communities (*altepetl*) 115, 170, 180; corn grinders 141; cosmology 173–175; cruelty 143; "cultural illegitimacy" 172; culture 192; and development 191; drawings (pictographs) 150, 175; elders 168; enemies 180; festivals 192; forced labor 113, 116; gods 67, 174, 192; history 187; icons 59; ingenuity 66, 137; land 184; merchants 81, 143, 192; and Moctezuma 70; nobles 135, 141, 169, 175, 177, 185; pantheon 59, 171–174, 186; pre–Hispanic history 143; priests 32, 58, 59, 61, 169, 192; and Quetzalcoatl 172–175; records 35; rulers 172; rules of warfare 68–69; and smallpox 155–159; survivors 73, 75, 77, 114, 156, 174, 183; sweepers 141; and Tlaxcala 128, 135, 136; treasure 41, 75–80; tribute,

collection of 81, 143, 170, 177, 180; warriors 46,119, 130, 131, 132, 134, 138, 142, 143, 168, 171, 178, 192; water carriers 141; weapons 64, 67; witches 168; wizards 168–169, 181; *see also* Coyohuehuetzin; Huitzilopochtli; Tezcatlipoca; Tiplacazin; Tlappanecatl Ecatzin; Toxcatl massacre

Baffin Island **20**
baggage slaves *see tamemes*
Bahamas 36, 64
Balabanova, Svetlana 15
Balboa, Vasco Nuñez de 118, 141, 152
Balkans 52
Baltic 94
Bangladesh 165
bankers 87–89; European financiers 92; Genoese 87
bankruptcies and royal revenue deficits 87–89; *see also* Charles V; Philip II
Baptism 58, 62
Barbados 27
Barcelona 88, 116
barley 153
Barrientos, Hernán de 118
Barros, João de 30
bathing 109, 144, 155; *see also* Europe, taboos; smallpox
beans 118
bearers *see tamemes*
bejel 162; *see also* treponema spirochetes
Benavente, Fray Toribio de *see* Motolinía
Benedict XVI, Pope 62
Benedictines 61
Bengal 96; *see also* India
Ben Laden, Osama 50
Beothuks 22
Beowulf 65
Berbers 36, 38, 82; *see also* slavery
Berdan, Frances 10
Beringia 5, 100, 189
the berserker 46
Béthencourt, Jean de 37, 52
the Bible 72, 82
bills of exchange 88
bison 106
the Black Death 83, 94, 163
Blaut, J. M. 95, 159
Blučina 65
boars *see* pigs
boats, Spanish *see* brigantines
Bobtail (*La Rabona*) 102; *see also* horses, of the conquistadors
Bolivia 85
Bombard, Alain 27
bombards *see* artillery
Book Twelve 48, 166–170; 175, 178–183, 185; *see also Florentine Codex*; Greek and Latin texts; Sahagún, Bernardino de
Boone, Daniel 123

Bosnians 82; *see also* slavery
Bosporus 29
bowmen 99
bows 47, 64, 67; crossbows 45, 47, 66, 68, 72, 106, 168; Cupid's bow 47; long bow 47, 106; "recurved" bow 47
Braudel, Fernand 88, 91, 146, 153
Brazil 6, 11, 14, 17, 18, 26, 54, 86, 91, 116
bridges 103; *see also* Honduran expedition
brigantines 6, 43, 68, 78, 113, 137, 179; *see also* launches
Britain 13, 59, 61; British government 123; manufacturers 96; *see also* England
British East India Company 96
Britons 27
bronze 67, 71; *see also* precious metals
Bronze Age 14, 64, 67
Brooks, Francis J. 156-159, 182-183, 185
bubonic plague 18, 37; *see also* epidemics
Buddhist missionaries 159
Buenos Aires 105
bullfighting 102
Bush, George W. 63
Byzantine Empire 52; *see also* Constantinople
Byzantine mapmakers 29
caballero (gentleman) 101, 109; *see also* horses, and hierarchy

Cabot, John 26
Cabral, Pedro Álvares 11, 54
cacao beans 80, 89, 118, 128
caciques 135; *see also* indigenous leaders
Caesar, Gaius Julius 15; and economic warfare 144
Cairo 29
Cajamarca 98, 151; *see also* Pizarro, Francisco
Calacoyan 142; *see also* massacres, gratuitous
California 16; Alta California 120; pre-Gold Rush 120-122; southern 152
Californios 120-122; culture 121-122; women 121-122
Callao 90
Calvinists 120
camelpox 160; *see also* smallpox
camels 18, 100, 145; caravans 30
Canada 119
Canary Islanders 68; *see also* Guanches
Canary Islands 15, 27, 30, 36-38, 42, 52, 55, 98, 149, 190; "Fortunate Isles" 36; Gomera 37; Grand Canary 37; Lanzarote 37; Tenerife 37
Canek 105; *see also* Honduran expedition
cannibalism 39, 43, 56, 84, 86, 144, 192; "famine cannibalism" 144; and the Irish 145; and Muslims 145; and slavery 144
cannon 5, 6, 47, 66, 68, 147, 168; balls 146, 147
Cano, Juan 185
The Canterbury Tales 72
Canton 91
Canton, the ulcer of *see* syphilis
Caonao 141; *see also* massacres, gratuitous

Cape Bojador 30
Cape Branco 30
Cape Hope 31, 91
Cape Horn 120
Cape Verde 30; Cape Verde Islands 38
capitalism 87, 95; and "proto-capitalists" 94, 95
Carbajal, Antonio de 113
carbon dating 164
Caribbean 5, 6, 15, 18, 26, 27, 32, 33, 36, 54, 57, 91, 98, 182; Caribbean Islands 36, 86, 111, 149, 161; natives 72, 112, 126, 154; plantations 124; *see also* Antilles; Bahamas; Cuba; Greater Antilles; Hispaniola; slave markets, Caribbean
Carman, Glen 170
Carmelites 37
Carolinas 95
Carrasco, Davíd 59, 171-174, 181
Cartas de Relación de la Conquista de Méjico (Letters to the Crown) 7; *see also* Cortés, writings
Caspian Sea 90
cassava 83
Castile 3, 6, 7, 10, 29, 30, 31, 33, 34, 35, 37, 48, 52, 62, 63, 72, 83, 86, 87, 166, 191; army 115; and Charles V 87-88; court and academy 147; cultural productions 145; discoveries 108, 190; empire 113, 116, 149, 154, 184; exports to colonies 115; Greater Castile 110; legal charter 184; merchants 153; monks 153; nobles 102, 118, 146, 152, 190; peasants 152-153, 193; and Philip II 88-89; and reform 111-113; slavery 82; and syphilis 162; *see also* Reconquest; *Siete Partidas*; Spain
Castrillo Matajudíos 35; *see also* anti-Semitism
catapults, Ferdinand's 146; French 106
the "Catholic army" *see* Army of Flanders
"the Catholic Monarchs" 53; *see also* Ferdinand; Isabel
Catholicism 5, 55, 62; missionaries 62; monarchs 33; *see also* the Church; the Faith
cattle, cows 24, 36, 38, 101, 119, 149, 150, 152
Ceiba tree 57, 65
Celtics 13, 17
Cempoala 8, 43, 131
Central Park 107
ceramics 30, 90
Cerezo, Gonzalo de 113
El Cerrito de la Virgin de los Remedios see the Little Hill
Cervantes Saavedra, Miguel de 49; *see also* Don Quixote; Sancho Panza
Ceuta 30, 52; *see also* North Africa
Chac Mool 173
Chagas' disease 161
Chalco 114
Chaldean doctrine 174; the "Great Year" 174; *see also* Aztecs, cosmology
chansons de geste 39, 43
chariot 101, 105

Index

Charles I of Spain 87; *see also* Charles V
Charles V, Holy Roman Emperor 8, 40, 43, 44, 59, 61, 65, 75, 76, 80, 81, 86, 87, 103, 114, 128, 131, 142, 149, 162; as deficit spender 87–88; and Quetzalcoatl story 170, 175–177, 184, 185; reformer 84, 112, 115–116; *see also* Charles I of Spain; Cortés, H., writings; the "sword of Christianity"
Charles VIII, King of France 161, 162
the Chatti 47; *see also* German tribes
Chavero, Alfedo 3; *see also* Historia Antigua y de la conquista
Cheyenne 143–144
Chiapas 61, 63; Bishop of; *see also* de Las Casas, Bartolomé
chichimecas 119, 171
chicken pox 160
chickens 18
Childeric 65
childhood, diseases of *see* immunity
China 3, 16–18, 30, 32, 41, 56, 94, 190; epidemics 159–160; and forced labor 124; industrialization 95; influence 16, 191; Han majority 160; mariners 18; markets 96; and Mongols 102; sailing vessels 13; as silver terminus 90–92; silks 17, 29; *see also* Ming Dynasty; Qing Dynasty; Shang Dynasty
chivalry 39, 42, 43; the Age of Chivalry 47; chivalric code 42, 43; novels 5, 43, 184
chocolate 95
cholera 18, 154
Cholollan 173
Cholula 8, 46, 54, 59, 60, 61, 62, 103, 126–142, 177; barrios 135; cult of Quetzalcoatl 172, 186; as *encomienda* 113; leaders 132, 135, 138; as "litmus test" 135; merchants 130; Office of Culture 148; pilgrims 126–127; pre–Hispanic 126–127, 139–140; priests 127, 132, 135; pyramids 126; slaves 127; temples 126–127; today 147–148; Toltec-Chichimeca rulers 127; *see also* Cholula massacre; Quetzalcoatl
Cholula massacre 66, 113, 114, 127–148, 169; archeological evidence 127; conspiracy 128–129, 132, 138, 147; food supply 130–131, 136, 138; nobles 138; skeletons 140; today 147–148; warning 130, 134–136; women and children 128, 131, 132, 134, 140–141, 146; *see also* Aztecs, warriors; Malintzin; noncombatants
Cholultecas 62, 127
Christ 32, 42, 45, 56; image of 52; Jesus 181, 186; Son of God 51
Christianity 5, 22, 29, 32, 33, 34, 37, 40, 51, 53, 55, 58, 60, 73, 74, 110, 126; armies 62, 144, 146 (*see also* crusaders); "Christians" 44; converts 35, 37, 158, 178, 185; *Conversos* 35; doctrine 56, 57, 105, 171; icons 57, 58, 74, 171 (*see also* cross; Virgin Mary); merchants 30; *Moriscos* 35; Nestorian Christians 31; rulers 33, 51; Spaniards 35, 52, 103, 109; warriors 81;

see also Catholicism; the Church; the Faith; Protestantism
Chumash Indians 152
the Church 5, 21, 22, 32, 34, 37, 51–52, 55; as lender 76; as repository of wealth 76; and slavery 82; *see also* Catholicism; Christianity; the Faith
Church doctrine 33; *see also* Hostiensis doctrine; *terra nullis*
Churchmen 51
Cibao 73
the Cid (Ruy Días de Vivar) 81, 102, 144
Cihuacoatl (Snake Woman) 174
Cintla 57; *see also* the Gulf Coast
Circassions 82; *see also* slavery
civilization 86, 145; agrarian 160; civilizations 96, 102; *see also* "diseases of civilization"
Clark, George Rogers 16
the classical world 102, 174, 191; *see also* Greece; Romans
Clement, Pope 32, 37
Clendinnen, Inga 180, 187
cloth 90; as booty 128
clubs, wooden *see macama*
coal, English 93, 96
Coateocalli temple 59; *see also* Aztecs, pantheon
cocaine 12, 15
cocoa 95, 119
Codex Ríos 186; *see also* Quetzalcoatl; "Red Sea"
Cologne 71
Colombia 161
Colón, Cristóbal *see* Columbus, Christopher
Colón, Ferdinand 161
colonialism 95
colonies, American 94
colonists *see* settlers
the Columbian Exchange 12, 93, 162
"Columbian" position 164; *see also* syphilis
Columbus, Bartolomeo 83
Columbus, Christopher 3, 6, 18, 19, 26, 31, 36, 42, 71, 86, 159, 167; before 163, 164; and China 41; as Christian 53–54, 57; as colonizer 82; as discoverer 11, 12, 13, 14, 15, 17, 27, 91, 109, 154, 155, 160, 189, 190; as disease bearer 161–162; and expulsion of Jews 35; first voyage 53, 55, 64, 159, 161; fourth voyage 45, 73; as gold seeker 72, 73, 74; Indian captives 161; logbook 33, 37, 54, 72; as military commander 44, 108; plan 32; second voyage 43, 88, 98, 149, 150, 154; ships 13, 29, 52; as slave hunter 83; *see also* Santa Maria
Comanche 106
commercial revolution 95–97
The Communist Manifesto 92; *see also* Engels; Marx
A Complete Collection of Voyages and Travels see Harris, John
Concentrated Animal Feeding Operation (CAFO) 153; *see also* pigs

Conquest: Montezuma, Cortés, and the Fall of Old Mexico 4; *see also* Thomas, Hugh
"The Conquest of Jerusalem" 62
La Conquesta (Dance of the Conquest) 61
Conquista de México 3; *see also* Gómera, Francisco López de
conquistadors *see* Cortés expedition
Constantine, Emperor 51
Constantinople 35, 52, 53, 61, 76, 79, 145
copper 14, 24, 71, 86; axes 67, 80; coins 89; *see also* money
Córdoba, Francisco Hernandez de 10, 54, 62, 66, 149
Córdoba, Gonzalo de 47, 106; *see also* the *Gran Capitan*
Cortes (Castile's parliament) 89
Cortés, Hernán 9, 18, 19, 34, 54, 155; arrival 167–168; captured 66; defiant 56, 176; as dispenser of booty 76–80; and *encomiendas* 112–117; as evangelist 58, 60; as Grand Master of Rhodes 80; and gold lust 74; as hero 43, 48, **49**, 185; historical portrayals 3, 4,10, **49**; in Honduras 85, **104**, 149, 151; and horses 99, 102–105; leadership 3, 8, 40–41, 44, 46, 47, 48, 50, 69, 75, 108, 128, 132–138, 166; as Malinche 139; as Marques del Valle 80, 118; and Moctezuma 168–171, 175–178; origins 35–36, 39–40, 152; and Quetzalcoatl 166–187; *recidencia* 41, 55, 113, 138, 185; ships 176; and smallpox 156, 157–158; as "true knight" 39; and Velázquez 111; veracity 175–178; virility 45; as witness 175–178; writings 7, 8, 40, 44, 45, 56, 59, 61, 76, 103, 126, 130, 135, 137, 175–178, 182; *see also* Honduran expedition
Cortés, Martín 36, 68, 117
Cortés expedition 5, 6, 8, 22, 34, 44, 45, 47, 49, 54, 62, 66, 87, 98, 119, 149, 156, 157–158, 166, 170, 189, 192; accounts 125–138, 175, 182; arrival and predicted arrival 167, 174; arrogance and audacity 70, 182; banner 179; in Cholula 125–142; Christians 181; fear of cannibalism 86; gold seeking 73, 75, 76, 80; in Honduras 103; and horses 106; indebtedness 77; and knights 43; nobles and captains 136; notaries 77, 170, 185; and Quetzalcoatl story 185
Cortés the Conqueror: The Exploits of the Earliest and Greatest of the Gentleman Adventurers see Sedgwick, Henry D.
cotton 6, 26, 86, 90, 95–97; plantations 114, 124; textiles 94
Council of the Indies 84, 105, 117
Cow Creek 143
cowpox 160
Coyahuehuetzin 48
Coyoacán 114
Cozumel 57, 59, 149
criminals 69, 123
Crónica Mexicana 143
Crosby, Alfred 151–152

cross 5, 8, 52–62, 105, 128, 171; the "Cross Patee" 52; *see also* Christian icons
the Crown 8, 39, 41, 53, 55, 75, 76, 83, 84, 111, 116, 118, 146, 178; *see also* Charles V; Philip II
crucifixion 51, 128; *see also* the Crucifixion
the Crucifixion 55
the Crusade, Commissioner of 60
crusaders 51, 52–61, 74, 76
crusades 23, 30, 45, 48, 52, 98; Fourth Crusade 61
Crusading Order of Christ 52
"Crusading Tithe" 23; crusade tax 26
the *cruzado* 52; *see also* money
Cuauhpopoca 177–178; *see also* Cortés, H., veracity
Cuauhtémoc *see* Guatemoc
Cuautitlan 114
Cuba 8, 10, 39, 48, 49, 54, 56, 67, 73, 84, 102, 111, 112, 114, 141, 149, 155, 175; Cuban settlers 111
cuddling 163; and yaws 163
Cuetlachtlán 143
Culua 8, 9, 74, 186; *see also* Mexico
Czech Republic 65

da Gama, Vasco 31, 52
Dakota Indians 106
Dalmatian coast 82
Dana, Richard Henry 121
Danube Basin 53
Darien 118
darts 68
Darwin, John 94
Davis, Graeme 20, 22, 24
Dawkins, Richard 122
debt peonage 122
Defoe, Daniel 119
de Gaulle, Charles 50
demographic collapse 111; *see also* labor, forced
de Soto, Hernando 152
Diamond, Jared 66, 106
Dias, Bartolomeu 31
Díaz, Bernal del Castillo 7; author 7, 39, 40, 43, 45, 48, 50, 57, 61, 66, 69, 74, 79, 80, 86, 99, 111, 119, 128, 131, 132, 133, 134, 135, 139, 140, 149, 157, 167, 171, 175, 177, 181, 182, 186; as conquistador 62, 102; as *encomendero* 114, 115, 117; and Quetzalcoatl 186; "teules" 167, 180; *see also True History of the Conquest of Mexico*
Díaz, Fr. Juan 54
Diffusionists 14, 16
Diringer, David 11; *see also The Alphabet*
disease *see* microbes
"diseases of civilization" 160; *see also* cowpox; smallpox
diseases, tropical *see* Chagas' disease; sleeping fever; yellow fever
"Divine Favor" 105; *see also* victories, miraculous

DNA testing 162; *see also* trepenoma spirochetes
dogs, attack 44, 45, 66, 106, 113, 141, 168; mastiffs 72; other 150
Dominicans 114, 116, 130
dominium jurisdictionis 184
Don Quixote 43, 45, 49, 75, 184; *Don Quixote* (the book) 72; *see also* de Cervantes
doomsday machines *see* artillery
Dorset people 16, 22, 24, 25
Driver, Harold 144
drugs 90, 96
Duarte, King of Portugal 37
Duhaut-Cilly, Auguste 120
Durán, Fr. Diego 56, 175, 183, 185
Durán, Rodrigo 84
the Dutch Revolt 89
Dutch ships 89; traders 96; *see also* the VOC
dysentery 158

eagles, golden 152
Early Modern period 92, 141
the East Indies 30, 91, 190
Easter mass 57
Eastern Hemisphere 64, 189
Ebola 160
Ecatepec 114
Ecatl *see* Quetzalcoatl, Mesoamerican god, wind god
Ecuador 16
Eguia, Francisco 155; *see also* smallpox
Egypt 12, 15, 29, 35, 52, 163; boat 27; harems 82; language 16
Egyptians 13, 16, 30
Eiricksson, Leif 15; Leif the Lucky 23
Eiricksson, Thorvald 21, 25
Eirik the Red 23
"Eirik the Red's Saga" 24
Elizabeth I 62
Elliott, J. H. 181, 185
encomendero (labor lord) 59, 84, 109, 111, 114, 117; *see also* encomiendas
encomiendas 80, 83, 109–117, 150; *see also* labor, forced
Engels, Frederick 92
England 62, 88, 89, 90, 119; colonists 122, 143, 150, 158; the English 106; English gentlemen 123
English Channel 15
English ideology 125
English ships 89
epidemics 7, 9, 18; European diseases 37, 154–160; *see also* bubonic plague; cholera; measles; meningitis; mumps; plague; smallpox; typhus; whooping cough
"epidemiological adjustment" *see* immunity
equestrian tactics 70; *see also* horses
Erasmus 74
"eruptive fevers" 154
Erythroxylum species 15; *see also* cocaine

Escalante, Juan de 111
escudos, gold 91; *see also* money
Ethiopia 31
Eugenius IV, Pope 37, 82
Eurasia 92, 160, 190; cemeteries of 163; Eurasians 11, 14, 16, 17, 18
Eurasian steppes 6, 47, 64, 94, 99, 100, 101
Europe 3–7, 10, 17, 19, 21, 26, 28, 29, 31, 32, 34, 37, 51, 56, 59, 60, 62, 64, 65, 69, 71–73, 86, 120, 127, 160, 192, 193; cities 182; and crusaders 163; domestic animals 150–152; Eastern Europe 94; economic divergence 92–97; endemic violence 145; and epidemics 158–159, 161–162; history 34, 48, 51, 191; and horses 100, 103; in Ice Age 100; immigrants 124; languages 101; luxuries 21; manufacturers 92; mariners 27; medieval Europe 42; merchants 94; military advances 70; perception of others 125; propaganda 144; "proto-capitalists 94; rivers 94; and St. Thomas cult 186; silver imports 87–90, 96; southeastern Europe 35, 101; and syphilis 161–164; taboos 144; terror tactics 143; trade in bulk goods 94; wars 85–89, 107; and world economy 92; *see also* Cortés expedition; northwestern Europe; violence; Western Europe
The European Miracle see Jones, Eric
the Evangelist 61
Excalibur 44, 64; *see also* Arthur, King
explorers 152
Extremadura 35, 111, 152–153

the Faith 7, 33, 39, 42, 48, 51, 55, 56, 60, 62, 74; *see also* Catholicism; Christianity; the Church
Far East *see* Asia, East
farming 113, 115, 118
Faulkner, William 173
the feathered serpent *see* Quetzalcoatl
Fell, Barry 11, 13
Ferdinand II, King of Aragon 33, 41, 53, 146, 161
Ferdinand III, King of Castile 65 *see* St. Ferdinand
Fernandez, Joao 26; *see also* pirates
the Fertile Crescent 35
feudalism 93
Fez 30
"fifth sun" 173–174; *see also* Aztecs, cosmology
financiers *see* bankers
the Fire Drill 167; *see also* omens; Quetzalcoatl
First *Audiencia* 85
Flanders 28
Florentine Codex 8, 150, 166; *see also* Book Twelve; Sahagún, Bernardino de
Florentines 88; *see also* bankers
Florescano, Enrique 59, 173
Florin, Jean 80; *see also* pirates
Flower Wars 135

1421: The Year China Discovered America see Menzies, Gavin
fox species, dwarf 152
France 87, 88, 90, 100, 114, 146; the French 106, 124
Francis I, King of France 43, 80
Franciscans 7, 31, 37, 60, 61, 62, 84, 116, 120, 133, 140, 155 158, 178, 180; see also "metaphysical terror"
Frank, Andre Gunder 92
Fraser, George 11
Free Trade 97
the French disease *see* syphilis
Fuensalida, Fr. 105
Fuggers of Augsburg 88; *see also* bankers
furs 90

Ganges River 186
the Gap *see* Haitian garment factories
Garay, Francisco de 178
Garibay Kintana, Fr. Ángel María 4
garnets 65, 71
General History of the Things of New Spain see the *Florentine Codex*
Genesis 55, 174
Genghis Khan 94, 101
Genoa 28, 30, 87–88, 91; *see also* bankers
genocide 159
Geoffrey of Monmouth 49
gerbilpox 160; *see also* smallpox
germ theory 158; germs 25, 94, 159; *see also* epidemics; microbes; microorganisms
the German disease *see* syphilis
German financiers 162; *see also* bankers
German tribes 47, 105, 150; *see also* the Chatti; the Suiones
German troops 88; *see also* mercenaries
Germany 87, 146; a G. missionary 156; Rhineland nobles 103
Ghana 31
Gibralfaro fortress 146
Gibraltar, Strait of 30, 52
gift-women 130, 139; *see also* Malintzin
Gilgamesh 44
Gillespie, Susan 178, 185, 187
glory 44, 48, 50, 69
goats 24, 150, 152
God 45, 51, 53, 54, 56, 57, 58, 60, 64, 65, 74, 82, 115, 125; and natural law 86; and Quetzalcoatl 187; and smallpox 156, 158; *see also* holy war; slavery; victories, miraculous
gold 5, 6, 7, 8, 9, 23, 29, 53, 54, 55, 56, 60, 61, 87, 91, 113; African gold 30, 52; Aztec sacred objects 73, 75, 77; as booty 79, 128, 176, 178, 191; Castilian export 89; exported from Spanish America 81, 88; and forced labor 109; forced labor *as* gold 109; as ingots 75, 76; as offering 127; Old World usages 71–72; ornamental use 65, 67, 71, 75; quest for 71–81, 108; and royal favor 75; as tribute 76, 177; and "worthless islands" 85; *see also* precious metals
"gold famine" 29, 73, 190
the Gold Rush 122; *see also* California
Gómera, Francisco López de 3, 39, 74, 128, 130, 131, 132, 137, 175; *see also* Cholula massacre; *Conquista de México*
Gonsalves Zarco, João 57
the Gospel 63
Goths 12
Graeber, David 77, 80, 81
graffiti war 79; *see also* gold, as booty
grain 94, 115; grain yields 107
the Grain Coast 31
the *Gran Capitan* 47; *see also* Córdoba, Gonzalo de
Granada 34, 35, 43, 53; *see also* Moors
Gratian's *Decretum* 51
Great Basin 106
"Great Cairo" 54
the great pox *see* syphilis
the Great Pyramid 127, 128, 148; and the Cheops pyramid 127
the Great Temple 59, 80, 173
Greece 82; ancient Greek language 93; *see also* the classical world
Greek and Latin texts 180; *see also* Book Twelve
Green, Z.D. 140
Greenland 15, 19, **20**, 21, 22, 24–26
Greider, Terence 16
Grijalva, Juan de 10, 46, 48, 54, 66, 73, 74, 80, 111, 149, 167, 180, 181
Grijalva expedition *see* Grijalva, Juan de
guaic wood 162
Guanajuato 85
Guanches 36–38, 82, 83; *see also* Canary Islands; slavery
Guatemala 47, 103, 126
Guatemoc **78**, 79, 167
Guinea 32
"Guinea hogs" 18
the Gulf Coast 8, 46, 47, 54, 57, 74, 75, 98, 119, 131, 172, 177, 183; *see also* Vera Cruz
Gunder Frank, Andre 95
gunpowder 146, 147
guns 7, 66, 68, 96, 106, 158; *see also* cannon; harquebuses; pistol
Gutenberg, Johannes 43; *see also* printing press
Guzman, Nuño de 85

the Hague Tribunal 147
Haitian garment factories 208*n*27
Hakluyt, Richard 3
ham 153; *jamon iberica* 153; *see also* pork
Ham 82; *see also* slavery
Hamburg 95
hammocks 133, 137; *see also tamemes*
Hansen's disease *see* leprosy

Hapsburgs 84, 103; *see also* Charles V; Philip II
harquebuses 8, 45, 66, 72, 104, 132, 158, 169; harquebusiers 99, 107
Harris, J. Rendel 16
Harris, John 3; *see also A Complete Collection of Voyages and Travels*
harvest 136, 137; *see also* warfare, seasonal
Hasan, Aziza 90
hashish 12, 15
Hassig, Ross 58, 68, 135, 136-137, 143, 172, 181, 182
Havana 90
hay 101
Hector 44, 47; *see also* the *Iliad*
Helluland **20**
Henry III, King of Castile 37
Henry IV, King of Castile and Leon 53
Henry the Navigator of Portugal 52, 82
Hera, a bronze 76
hermandades 35
Hernan Cortés: Conqueror of Mexico see Madariaga, Salvador de
the hero 41-42, 45, 46; heroic warrior 5, 41, 44-50, 65, 69; return of 184; romantic heroes 45
Herodotus 13
Heyerdahl, Thor 27
hidalgos 34, 36, 115, 118
Hindu deities 59
Hiroshima 187
Hispaniola 44, 54, 67, 73, 82, 83, 85, 86, 98, 108, 109, 112, 122, 141, 149, 154, 155, 161, 162; *see also* Caribbean; Tainos
Historia Antigua y de la conquista see Chavero, Alfredo
Historia de los Mexicanos por sus Pinturas see Olmos, Fr. A. de
"historiographical ventriloquism" 184; *see also* Moctezuma, his "donation"; Quetzalcoatl
History of the Conquest of Mexico see Prescott, William H.
Hittite language 13
hogs *see* pigs
Holland *see* the Netherlands
holocaust 164
the Holy Land 53
Holy Roman Empire 63
the Holy Sepulcher 54
holy war 34, 51; holy warriors 60
"Holy Wood" *see* guaic wood
Homer 44
homosexuality 144; *see also* Europe, taboos
Honduran expedition 61, 103-105, 114; *see also* Cortés, Hernán, in Honduras; horses
Honduras 14
Hong Kong 126
Honshu 159; *see also* epidemics
Hop 21
"horse latitudes" 98
horses 5, 6, 8, 18, 24, 36, 37, 44, 45, 48, 58, 64, 66, 115, 146, 149, 150, 168; ancestral 100, 189; and Californios 120-121; in Castile 101-102; of conquistadors 102, 178, 191; deified 104-105; equestrian warriors 101; in European warfare 106-107; expense of 77; and hierarchy 101, 103; in Honduras 103-105; horse sausages 107; mounted police 98; in New World conquest 98-99; plow horse 107; in prehistory 100-101; proliferation 105-106, 152; shoulder harness 107; and silver 88; as targets of attack 67, 68; traps 130, 131, 136; as treasure bearers 77; *see also* chariot; equestrian tactics; Huns; Mongols; Parrthians; Persians; saddle; Sarmatians; Scythians
Hostiensis doctrine 32
Hudson Bay 22
Huitzilopochtli 59, 74, 132, 171, 174, 187; temple of 167; *see also* Aztecs, gods
Huizinga, Johan 42
Hull, England 164
human rights 145
Humbaba 44; *see also* Gilgamesh
the Hundred Years War 47, 106
Huns 101
Hygelac 65

Iberia 19, **28**, 31, 32, 36, 47, 52, 53, 65, 80, 189; and slave labor 82, 118; voyagers 26, 29, 33, 52, 91, 189; and yaws 163
Ibn Fadlan 121
Ice Age 189
Iceland 19, 22 26
Icelandic Sagas 19, 22, 23; *see also* "Eirik the Red's Saga"; "The Saga of the Greenlanders"
idols 8, 39, 56, 58, 61, 104, 133, 171
Iglesia, Ramón 40
"*ignorantes*" 56; *see also* pagans
the *Iliad* 44, 48, 64, 69, 72
immunity 160, 190; *see also* epidemics
Inca 67, 99, 184; empire 149; "roads" 103
India 30, 31, 59, 64, 72, 91, 95, 96, 160, 191; Mughal India 90, 93, 94; northern India 101; and silver; *see also* Bengal
Indian Ocean 29, 31, 32, 88, 91, 96, 190
Indians 6, 8, 16, 41, 43, 45, 46, 55, 56, 59, 63, 73, 83, 89, 98, 176; American Indians 143; Amerindians 14, 18; assessed tribute 85, 117; burial practices 140; of central Mexico 157; and disease 154-161; in European perceptions 125, 144, 180; food sources 150; and forced labor 108-124; Gulf Coast 167; and hierarchy 145; indigenous Americans 6, 7, 18, 19, 21, 34, 189, 191; Mesoamerican 145, 150, 189; as mine workers 84-90; and Muslims 144; Native Americans 12, 17, 106, 193; of New Spain 103; Paleoindians 100; in Panama 141; Plains Indians 106; warriors 99, 106; women 106, 110, 111; Yucatan 175
the Indies 7, 33, 36, 73, 74, 85, 106, 108, 110, 154, 162, 167; as slave importer 85, 86; West

Index 237

Indies 94, 96; *see also* Caribbean, East Indies; labor, forced
indigenous leaders *see* caciques
indigo 30
indulgences 60, 73
Indus River 101
industrialization 93, 94; the industrial revolution 95
infanticide 35
Innocent IV, Pope 32
the Inquisition 5, 35, 60
"intelligent animals" 125
Inter Caetera bull 55
Inuits 16, 22, 24
inventionists 14, 18
inventions, European 93
the Invincible Armada 89
Iraq 133
the Irish 125, 145
iron 6, 22, 23, 24, 67, 94
Iroquois 143
Isabel, daughter of Moctezuma 114
Isabel, Queen 33, 35, 53, 83, 109, 144, 145, 161
Isla, Ruy Diaz de 161
Islam 6, 23, 31, 51, 81; empires 51–52; and horses 101; Islamic Iberia 52; I. territory 30; Muslim world 31; *see also* Muslims
Israelites 13, 17
Italy 53, 87, 88, 89, 106, 146, 160; merchants 96; *see also* Florentines; Genoa; Venetians
Itzas 104–105
ivory 22, 30
Ivory Coast 31
Ixlilxochitl, Alva 58, 185, 187

Jackson, Andrew 50
Jamaica *see* Garay, Francisco de
Jamestown 122–123
Japan 16, 91, 159, 160, 161, 187
Jason *see* the hero, return of
javelin *see* spears
Jennings, Francis 143
Jérez, Francisco de 43
Jerusalem 34, 52, 53, 54, 60, 61, 126, 145; *see also* the Holy Land
Jesuits 56
Jett, Stephen G. 11, 14
Jews 35, 54; *Conversos* 35; *see also* Christian converts
João, King of Portugal 52
João II, King of Portugal 161
Joint Special Operations Command 50; *see also* Ben Laden, O.
Jones, Eric 94; *see also The European Miracle*
Joseph, Frank 15, 16, 17, 18
juros 87; *see also* Charles V, as deficit spender

Karlsefni, Thorfinn 23
the Katvan Steppe, Battle of 31
Kelley, David 17

Kensington Stone 12, 13, 15, 22
Kindleberger, Charles 95
knights 5, 42, 43, 44, 61, 65, 80, 81, 106, 118; knight-errant 40, 45; the "true knight" 42, 47, 48
Knights Templar 15, 52
Koch, Peter O. 133
Kyle, Chris 50

labor demand 123; and indentured servitude 123–124; "transportation" 124
labor, forced 82–87, 108–124; and hierarchy 109–110, 119; no-cost workers 158; and production costs 94; as tribute 109; *see also encomiendas*; mines; *mita* system; slavery
labor lord *see encomendero*
labor shortages 94
labor, unpaid *see* labor, forced
Labrador *20*, 22
Lake Petén *104*
Lake Superior 14
Lake Texcoco 77, 102, 113, 137, 182
lance *see* spear
land acquisition, North America 123
land owning 119–120, 123–124; *see also* North America
Landa, Diego de 81
Las Casas, Bartolomé de 33, 54, 55, 63, 67, 73, 84, 98, 108, 109, 111, 117, 123, 137–138, 141, 145, 149, 154, 161, 162; and Quetzalcoatl 186; *see also* Chiapas, Bishop of; *A Short Account of the Destruction of the Indies*; Valladolid
latifundios *see* agriculture, plantation
launches 9; *see also* brigantines
Lazarote Island 15
lead coins 89; *see also* money
"learned helplessness" *see* Stockholm syndrome
"legend formation" 175, 181; *see also* Quetzalcoatl
leprosy 163; cemeteries 163–164; leprosaria 163; *see also* syphilis
Letters to the Crown 7, 8; *see also* H. Cortés, writings
the Levant 90
Levy, Buddy 133
El Lienzo de Tlaxcala 139; *see also* Malinche
Lipsius, Justus 89
Lisbon 36
the Little Hill of the Virgin of Remedies 148; *see also* the Great Pyramid
the Little Ice Age 26
Liverpool 95
llamas 90, 160, 189
Lockhart, James 178–180
London 95
Long Island 21
Lothar I, King of France 65
Louis IX, King of France 52

Low Countries *see* the Netherlands
Luther, Martin 62

macama 67, 99
MacArthur, Douglas 50
Macchiavelli 41
Madagascar 15
Madariaga, Salvador de 4; *see also Hernan Cortés: Conqueror of Mexico*
Madeira 31, 32, 37, 38, 52, 57
Madrid 153
maize 92, 93, 118, 150, 153, 158; corn fields 144
Majorca 37
Málaga 146
malaria 108
Mali 30
malinalli see Malintzin, "Lady Grass"
Malinowski, Bronislaw 181
Malintzin 77, 113, 131–132, 133, 138, 139–140, 175, 211n38; Doña Marina 131, 139; "Lady Grass" 139; Malinche 131; *see also* gift women; H. Cortés, as Malinche; *tecpillahtolli* 175; twisted-grass motif
Malocello, Lancellotto 36
mammoths 100, 189
Mandeville, John 31; *see also* Prester John
Manila 62, 71, 91
manufacturers 92, 95, 113; British 96; European 92; goods 96; North American 121, 123; of shoes 121; *see also* Europe
Marco Polo 6, 53
Marin, Luis 61
Maritime Provinces 16, 25
Markland **20**, 21
Marks, Richard Lee 134
Marrakesh 30
Martin, Paul S. 100
Martyr, Peter 149
Marx, Karl 92, 119
Marx, Robert F. 11
masks, mosaic 180
Massachusetts colony 158; *see also* Winthrop, John
Massacre Canyon 143
massacres, gratuitous 98, 141–142; *see also* Calacoyan; Caonao; Toxcatl
mastodons 100, 189
Matamoros 35
Matienzo, Juan de 25
Maudslay, A.P. 102
Mauretania Tingitana 30
Mauritius 15
Maya Indians 61, 103, 169; Chontal Maya 175
Maya language 211n38
Mayan sites 173; traditions 186
McCafferty, Geoffrey 139
measles 18, 158, 159, 160; German measles 158; *see also* epidemics
Medellín 36, 115
Medina Sidonia, Duke of 104

Mediterranean 30, 35, 88, 90; crossings 98; merchants 28; sailors 28; shipbuilding 189
"megafauna" 5, 100; *see also* mammoths; mastodons
Meggers, Betty 14
Meknes 30
memes 120, 122; meme complex 122; *see also* Dawkins, Richard
Mendez, Diego 45
Mendieta, Fr. Gerónimo de 158
Mendoza, Diego Hurtado de 74
Mendoza, Don Antonio de 80, 116; *see also* New Spain, Viceroy of
Mendoza, Pedro de 105
Menelaus 145
meningitis 158
Menzies, Gavin 15, 18, 29, 30; *see also 1421: The Year China Discovered America*
mercenaries 87, 89, 162
merchants, European 85, 87, 90; North American 123
mercury 85, 163; poisoning 122
mermaids 41
Mesoamerica 14, 18, 27, 33, 34, 36, 39, 52, 61, 67, 69, 74, 80, 82, 94, 143, 146, 154, 155, 191; cities 182; man-gods 174
Mesopotamia 159, 163
metal weapons 66–68, 190; *see also* armor, metal; steel
metallurgy, Indian 67
"metaphysical terror" 62
Mexica 8, 67, 69, 174, 179; *see also* Aztecs; Tenocha; Tlatelolca
Mexican War 128
Mexico 3, 4, 6, 8, 10 13, 16, 18, 19, 26, 32, 35, 37, 39, 41, 44, 45, 49, 66, 67, 91, 98, 106, 111, 118, 119, 155, 166, 178, 191; as booty source 74, 76, 191; central 157, 172; and Cortés, H., writings 176; mines 82–89; National Palace 192; natives 112, 120, 122, 154; Quetzalcoatl 168, 187–188; today 115; *see also* Culua; New Spain
Mexico City 80, 114, 116, 126; site of French Embassy 121; and smallpox 156; *see also* Tenochtitlan; Valley of Mexico
Michoacan 67
Micmac Indians 16
microbes 5, 6, 45, 48, 86, 106, 111; disease 122, 189, 190, 193; microorganisms 25; Old World microbes 86; viruses 178; *see also* epidemics; germs; smallpox
Middle Ages 41, 64, 76, 144, 146, 163
Middle East 64, 82, 94, 150
Middle Swedish 12
Midwest 15
Milan 89
militarism 81, 85; and slavery 81
mine operators 84, 86
mines: Central European 30; of New Spain 85, 88, 90, 110, 113, 114; silver 85–90, 95, 122; in

Spain 115; Spanish American 84–90; and work regime 84–87
Ming Dynasty 3, 18, 29, 91, 93, 94; *see also* Zhu Di
Minnesota 12, 22
Minoans 13
Minorca 82
Mississippi 106
mita system, Inca 86; *see also* labor, forced; mines, silver
Mixtecs 67
moa 100
Moclin 146
Moctezuma 3, 4, 8, 9, 10, 29, 40, 44, 56, 57, 59, 130, 134, 179; "angry lord" 168, 171; and Aztec gods 132; as captive 75, 170–171,177, 182–183; and Cholula 142; conquistador disrespect 70; deference to 70; diplomatic language 175; "donation" and speech 108, 169–170, 175, 181, 183–187; his emissaries 73, 74, 99, 142, 167, 168, 180; as host 75, 76; as Patty Hearst 171; post-conquest portrayal 166–181; priests 171; and Quetzalcoatl 166–187; as Spaniards' puppet 183; as *tlatoani* 174, 182; treasure 75–79, 81
Moctezuma, First Emperor 174
Moctezuma III 187
Mofras, Duflot de 121
Moll Flanders 119, 124
money 72, 87, 90–92, 117; bronze coins 91; in China 92; Indian use of 80–81; paper currency 91; playing cards 89; and royal indebtedness 87–88; *see also* Amsterdam account entries; bronze; cacao beans; copper axes; *escudos*; gold; lead coins; precious metals; *reales*; silver
Mongols 101, 102
Montalvo, Garci Rodríguez de 43; *see also Amadis of Gaul*
Montejo, Francisco de 114
Moors 34, 36, 54, 55, 184, 190; Moorish Spain 34, 35; *see also* Granada
More, Thomas 73; *see also* Utopians
Morelos, José María 192
Morini 144; *see also* Caesar
Morocco 27, 35
Morris, Ian 18, 93; *see also Why the West Rules—For Now*
Morte D'Arthur 72; *see also* Arthur, King
mosques 54, 59, 147
Motolinía 61, 84, 133, 155, 156, 157, 158, 175, 186; *see also* Benavente, Toribio de; Quetzalcoatl, Mesoamerican god of air; smallpox
Mount Badon 44; *see also* Arthur, King
Mughals *see* India
Muhammed 59
mules 101
mummies 15; Egyptian mummies 159
mumps 158, 160
Muñoz Camargo, Diego 134, 138

Muslims 23, 34, 35, 38, 39, 62, 63, 190; districts in Valencia 146; enslavement of 82; Iberia 109; infidels 33; and Mecca 126; merchants 94, 96; middlemen 30; military tactic 99; Moriscos 35, 146; trade routes 42; *see also* Christian converts; Reconquest
mutinies, troop 88–89; *see also* mercenaries
Mycenae 64

Nagasaki 187
Nahuatl 6, 133, 171, 175; sources 157; speakers 186, 211*n*38; traditions 4, 186; world 180
nakedness 36,144; *see also* Europe, taboos
Naples 89
Naples, the disease of *see* syphilis
Napoleon Bonaparte 50
Narragansett Bay 12
Narragansett people 12, 15
Narváez, Panfilo de 9, 41, 44, 46, 60, 76, 102, 176, 183; and Indian labor 111; and smallpox 155
Narváez expedition *see* Narváez, Panfilo de
the National Park Service 152
natural law 33, 86
Nautla 177–178; *see also* Cortés, H., veracity
Navajo Mountain 11, 14
Navarre 72
Las Navas de Tolosa, battle of 44, 82; *see also* victories, miraculous
Nebraska 143
necromancy 35
Neolithic people 100
the Netherlands 87, 88, 89, 90; Spanish Netherlands 88
New Brunswick 21
New England 15, 66, 120, 121
New Guinea 13
the New Laws of 1542 84, 112, 116, 117
New Mexico 105
New Spain 3, 6, 60, 61, 65, 67, 119, 130, 133; and *encomenderos* 111–120; farming 118; its mines 85–87; money shortage 89; police 115; Puebla 148; and slave trading 85; Viceroy of 80
New Testament 32
New World 4, 5, 6, 14, 15, 25, 36, 38, 49, 56, 61, 62, 72, 73, 74, 81, 83, 84, 87, 125; and disease 154–165; as destination 115, 141, 191; food crops 92; horses 99–100, 105; "lords and masters" 153; natives 145; paradise 172; precious metals 85–97; and pre–Hispanic massacres 142–143; products 93; and syphilis 164; *see also* St. Brendan; Western Hemisphere
New Zealand 100
Newberry Tablet 13
Newfoundland 19, *20*, 22, 24, 26
Newport tower 13
Nice, Treaty of 80
Nicholas V, Pope 33

240 INDEX

nicotine 12, 15
the Nile 31
Noah 152
Noche Triste 9, 40, 41, 46, 66, 77, 102, 136, 142, 156, 157, 176, 184
nomadism 101
Nombre de Dios 90
non-combatants, killing of 143–147; *see also* massacres, gratuitous; women and children
Norse people 15, 22, 24; *see also* Vikings
North Africa 37, 53, 82, 150; *see also* Ceuta; Egypt; Oran; Tlemcen; Tripoli
North America 12, 19, 21, 91, 100, 106; land ownership in 119–120, 123–124
Northwest Passage 91
northwestern Europe 92, 107
Norway 21; Norwegians 12
nuclear option 147
Nuestra Señora de los Remedios 128; *see also* the Great Pyramid; the Little Hill
Nuñez Vela, Blasco 117

oats 101
Oaxaca 114
obsidian 67
"Oedipus Rex" 185
Ohio Valley 16
Olaf, King of Norway 22
Olbes, Fr. Ramón 120
Old Testament 32, 64
Old World 4, 5, 7, 10, 12, 14, 17, 18, 24, 48, 65, 70, 71, 87, 88, 106, 189, 191; armies 146–147; diseases 154–160, 178; warfare 144; *see also* Eastern Hemisphere, "eruptive fevers"
olive oil 153
Olmec civilization 14, 26
Olmeca-Xicallnca people 139–140; *see also* Cholula, pre-Hispanic
Olmos, Fr. Andrés de 186
Omaha 106
omens 167, 180; *see also* Quetzalcoatl
1-Reed, year of 167, 174; Ce Catl 186
1-Wind, year of 169
opium 96
Oran 53; *see also* North Africa
Orbita, Fr. Juan de 105
orchil 37
Ordaz, Diego de 118
the Orient *see* Asia, East
Otomis 77, 179, 180
Ottomans 29, 35, 87, 94, 106; "gunpowder army" 106; Ottoman Empire 31, 93; and slave labor 82; *see also* Turks
Otumba 114
Ovando, Nicholás de 109, 111
Oviedo y Valdes, G. Fernández de 56, 162
oxen 18, 76, 100, 105, 145; in land allotments 81

Padden, R.C. 59, 74
pagans 32, 35, 44, 48, 60, 73; infidels 33, 57;
non-believers 33; non-Christians 32, 33, 82, 190; and slavery 82–86
Pagden, Anthony 176
Palm Sunday 57
the Pampas 105, 152; *see also* Argentina
Panama 17, 45, 85, 90, 118, 141, 150, 161, 182
Pánuco 85
paper, invention of 83
Parthians 101
Pascal's wager 181
Patlahuatzin 134
Patroklos 47; *see also* the *Iliad*
Paul I, Pope 65
Paul III, Pope 85
Pawnees 143–144; buffalo hunters 144
Pearl Coast 85
pearls 72, 74, 75
peasants 42, 87, 103, 115, 118, 137, 145, 192, 193; *see also* Castile, peasants; pork
peccary 149
Pedro, son of Moctezuma 114
penicillin 162
Pennsylvania 13
Pentecostal church 62
Persia 90, 91, 93; and Persians 101; *see also* Safavids
the Persian Gulf 35, 91
Peru 18, 87, 91, 103, 122, 150, 191; and encomenderos 111, 117
the Petén 103; *see also* Honduran expedition
Peterson, David A. 140
petroglyphs 11
Philadelphia 124
Philip II 84, 85, 88–89; Prince Philip 117
Phoenicians 13, 17
pigs 5, 6, 18, 24, 38, 73, 100, 149–153, 154; environmental damage 151–152; a "harvestable meat source" 150; Old World pigs 149, 150; "razorbacks" 152; *Sus scofa* 149; wild pigs 149
pikemen, Swiss 106; pikes 107
Pillars of Hercules 13
pinta 162; *see also* treponema spirochetes
the *Pinta* 161
Pinzón, Martín Alonso 161, 162
Pippin, King of the Franks 65
pirates 26, 37, 80, 94, 152
Pirsig, Wolfgang 15
pistol 102
Pizarro, Francisco 118, 125, 149, 151, 152
Pizarro, Gonzalo 103, 152
Pizarro, young 119
plague 154; Antonine 159; of Athens 159; pneumonic plague 158
the Plains 106; Central Plains people 143
playing cards *see* money
Pleistocene animals *see* megafauna
the "plunder frontier" 87
Poles 82; *see also* slavery
Polynesians 14, 18
Pomeranz, Kenneth 95

porcelain 91, 191
pork 152; in New World 153; and peasant diets 152–153
porters *see* tamemes
Portugal 28, 29, 32, 33, 36–38, 42, 52, 55, 161; and African slave trade 82, 86, 101; fishermen 26; and gunboat diplomacy 88; mariners 26–31, 57, 90, 190 (*see also* da Gama, Vasco; Dias, Batholomeu; Iberian voyagers); monarchs 52 (*see also* João; Henry the Navigator)
post-traumatic stress 147
potatoes 93
potlatch, Europeanized *see* "Roman Circus"
Potonchan 139
Potosí 85, 86, 87, 88, 89; *Cerro Rico* 90
precious metals 49, 60; in the Antilles 72–74, 82; as booty and its division 76–80, 81; as burial goods 71–72, 74–75; as currency 71–72, 76; and European divergence 93, 95; hoarding 72, 75; inflation 87; Moctezuma's missing treasure 78–79; ornamental usage 71, 73; as plunder 72–80; prestige of 72; and slave labor 84–90, 108; *see also* gold; money; silver
preemptive strike 147
Prescott, William H. 3, 40, 133, 135, 140; *see also History of the Conquest of Mexico*
Prester, John 31; Mandeville, John 31
printing press 6, 43
prisons 124, 133
Proaño, A. 113
the proletariat 93
property, private 125; peasant property 145; *see also* land
Protestant army 88
Protestantism 81; "international Protestantism" 89
Ptolemy 29
public executions 145
Puebla 126, 148
"Pueblo Morisco" 54
Puerto Rico 112
the Puritans 62

Qing dynasty 94; *see also* China
Queen of Cities *see* Constantinople
"queen of weapons" 70; *see also* sword
Quetzalcoatl 56, 126, 127, 166–187; cult of 172; feathered serpent 166, 174; Lord Quetzalcoatl 172; return as "emollient myth" 187; Topiltzin Quetzalcoatl 167, 168, 172, 178, 186; vestments 180; *see also* Tollan, the man-god of
Quetzalcoatl, Mesoamerican god 172; of air 186; Ecatl 173; of merchants 172; of twins 172; Venus 172; wind god 172; *see also* St. Thomas; "white god"
Quetzalcoatl Pyramid 126, 127, 128, 140; *see also* San Gabriel convent

Quetzalcoatl Temple 127
quicksand 103
quicksilver 91
quinto real see the royal fifth

racism 17, 124, 166, 172, 187; *see also* St. Thomas; white supremacy
Raleigh, Walter 62
ranchers 152
Rangel, Rodrigo 113
reales, silver 91; *see also* money
Recidencia see H. Cortés, *recidencia*
Reconquest 30, 34, 35, 53, 54, 59, 60, 65, 81, 101, 146; and economic warfare 144; Muslim lands as plunder 81; *see also* Castile; Spain
Red Sea 29, 90, 91; "Red Sea" 186; *see also Codex Ríos*; Quetzalcoatl
reform, forced labor 111–120
the Reformation 62
Relación de la Genealogía 186; *see also* Quetzalcoatl, Topiltzin
"religious synchretism" 59
the Renaissance 35, 145, 184
repartimentos 109; *see also encomiendas*
requirimiento 55, 56
Restall, Matthew 66, 75
Revelation 31
the Revolt of the *Germanías* 146; *see also* Valencia
the Revolutionary War 123
Rhineland *see* Germany
Rhode Island 12, 13, 18
Richard III, King of England 150
Rig Veda 44, 45
Riley, James C. 158
Rio de Janeiro 11
Rio Grande 62, 106
Rip van Winkle *see* the hero, return of
River of Gold 36, 42
Rivera, Diego 192
Robinson Crusoe 55, 86
Roman amphorae 11
Roman coins 15, 71–72
"Roman Circus" 80; *see also* potlatch, Europeanized
Roman Empire 51, 91, 159; republic 159; *see also* epidemics
Roman head 13
Roman legal doctrine 34
Roman soldiers 64, 144; the testudo 47
romance 43, 44
Romania 65
Romans 13, 15, 16, 17, 29, 40, 44, 47, 71, 150, 191
Romanus Pontifex 32, 55
Rome 29, 60, 65, 82; *see also* the classical world
Ronda 144, 146; and siege warfare 144
Roosevelt, Teddy 50
the royal fifth 75, 77, 86, 87, 176; *see also quinto real*

the Royal Treasury, officials of 79
the Rus *see* Vikings
Russia 82, 90; *see also* silver; slavery

sacrifice, human 39, 56, 57, 59, 61, 113, 130, 131, 132, 133, 135, 143, 145, 171, 174, 192; and cannibalism 144, 192; military tactics 68–69; Quetzalcoatl Topiltzin 172, 186, 187; *see also* Aztecs, cosmology
saddle 101, 102; Moorish saddle 102
Safavids 93; *see also* Persia
"The Saga of the Greenlanders" 19, 20, 24
Sahagún, Bernardino de 8, 46, 77, 133, 134, 138, 140, 155, 166–170, 178–179, 185, 192; academy 179; Aztec informants 178–180; *see also* Book Twelve; *Florentine Codex*; Quetzalcoatl
Sahara Desert 30; trade route 31
sahasramuska 45
St. Brendan 172; *see also* New World, paradise; Quetzalcoatl, the Mesoamerican god
St. Ferdinand *see* Ferdinand III
St. James 45; Santiago 45
St. Lawrence River Valley 20; *see also* Vinland
St. Thomas 56, 172, 186; *see also* racism; "white god"
saints 45, 76; *see also* victories, miraculous
Salle, de la 52
salt 128
Samuel 145
samurai 42, 46
San Gabriel convent 128, 148; Cathedral 140; *see also* Quetzalcoatl Pyramid
San Jorge da Mina 31
San Juan de Ulúa 57, 74, 76, 167; *see also* the Gulf Coast; Yucatan
San Salvador Island *see* Watling Island
Sancho Panza 49, 75, 83; *see also* Cervantes Saavedra, M. de
Sandoval, Francisco Tello de 116, 117
Santa Barbara 120
Santa Cruz Island 152
Santa Maria 29
Santistevan 114
São Tomé 38
Saramago, José 28; *see also The Stone Raft*
Sarmatians 101
Satan 3, 56
savagery 5, 25; *see also* savages, violence
savages 5, 86, 125, 145, 192
Saxons 44; *see also* Arthur, King
scalp taking 143
Scandinavia 90
scarlet fever 159
scientific method 93
Scythians 101
sea power 95
sealskins 37
Sears, Theresa Ann 54
the Second Coming 61

Sedgwick, Henry Dwight 4; *see also Cortés the Conqueror*
Seed, Patricia 84
Sepúlveda, Juan Ginés de 62, 80, 109, 123, 145
serfdom *see* labor, forced
servants 145; indentured 123; *see also* labor demand
settlers 83–88, 109–112, 149–150, 176; and forced labor 108–124, 150
Seville 71, 81, 87, 88, 90, 154
Seville Cathedral 65
sexual promiscuity 144; *see also* Europe, taboos
Shakespeare, William 41
Shang Dynasty 14
Shao, Paul 14, 16
sheep 24, 81, 101, 145, 149, 150, 152, 153
shellac 30
Shia 90
ships 28–29, 96, 190; barque 28; caravel 28–29, 52; cogs 28; lateen sails 28; shipbuilding 95, 189; slave ships 95; square-riggers 28; *see also Pinta*; *Santa Maria*
A Short Account of the Destruction of the Indies 141; *see also* Las Casas, B. de
Shoshone 106
Siberia 5, 120, 189
Sicily 89
siege 5, 6, 9, 69, 99, 113, 119, 141, 144, 146–147, 156, 179, 191; *see also* tactics, military; Tenochtitlán; warfare
Sierra Leone 30
Siete Partidas 184; *see also* Moctezuma, "donation"
"signature strikes" 147
silk 29, 30, 88, 90, 91, 94, 97, 191; *see also* China
Silk Road 29
silver 5, 6, 7, 23, 60, 71–72, 79, 80; and Aztecs 81; and China 90–91; commercial expansion 92–97; family silver 92; global distribution 90–92; as New World's prime export 85–97; smelting 67; *see also* precious metals
Sioux 143
skeletons 158, 163–164
skraelings 21, 22, 23, 24; *see also* Vikings
the Slave Coast 31
slave hunters 37, 82–83, 85, 110, 142; *see also* Columbus, C.; Tepeaca
slave markets, Caribbean 38
slave trading 52, 82–85, 91, 124, 125, 163; *see also* agriculture, plantation; Portugal
slaves 10, 25, 30, 31, 32, 37–39, 52, 56, 77, 80–87, 96, 109, 112, 118, 123, 145, 155; African 82, 86, 95, 96, 116, 124; and agriculture, plantation 96; in Argentina 105; as booty 128, 191; in classical world 82; in Middle Ages 82; militarism 81; and Moctezuma's "donation" 185; in Peru 117; racialization 82–83; self-financing 95; as wages 85; and yaws 163; *see*

also Indians, and forced labor; labor, forced; pagans
sleeping sickness 161
smallpox 7, 9, 18, 154–160, 164–165; communication and progression 154–155; and dehydration 157–158; epidemic 155–158; *Variola major* 160, 164; *see also* epidemics; microbes
Smith, Adam 93
Smith, John 123
Snake Woman *see* Cihuacoatl
soap 163; *see also* syphilis; yaws
Soconusco 114
sodomy 35, 39, 56, 61, 134, 144; *see also* Europe, taboos
Solís, Antonio de 3
The Song of Roland 39, 72; *see also* chansons de geste
South America 11, 12, 14, 18, 26, 27, 152
South Dakota 143
the Southwest 11, 14, 106
sows *see* pigs
Spain 5, 7, 10, 23, 34, 36–38, 42–43, 45–46, 48, 52–55, 58–59, 62, 71, 72, 76, 101, 112, 115, 116, 117; armies 141, 161; *autos-de-fe* 145; and Charles V 87; Christian Spain 144; cities 126; and colonies 92, 123; colonists 63, 83 (*see also* settlers); conquest 96; in decline 87–89; domestic animals 152; galleons 91; as gold importer 81; infantry 106; and land 120; language 55, 175, 211*n*38; as measure of human status 125; missionaries 104–105; monarchs 56 (*see also* Alfonso VIII; Ferdinand; Henry III; Henry IV; Isabel); Moorish Spain 103; silver for gold 91; as slave importer 83; *see also* Castile; horses, in Castile
the Spaniards *see* Cortés expedition
Spanish America 5, 34, 63, 65, 81, 84, 88, 116, 118
Spanish Christians 53
the Spanish disease *see* syphilis
Sparta 46
spear-thrower (*atlatl*) 67
spears 64, 67, 99, 102, 138, 168
Spice Islands 30, 41; *see also* Indies, East
spices 29, 30, 31, 54, 88, 90, 91, 94, 190, 191
spirochete *see* treponema
Spoehr, Alexander 164
"The Star Spangled Banner" 128
steam engine 93; steam power 96
steel 66–67, 159; helmets 66; *see also* sword; armor
Stewart, T. D. 164
Stockholm syndrome 171
Stone Age 36
The Stone Raft see Saramago, José
stones 67; rocks 77; as tributes 67; as weapons 67, 131, 137
Strabo 36
strategic bombing 147
sugar 31–32, 37, 38, 86, 95; plantations 114, 124

Suiones 150; *see also* Germanic tribes
Sumerians 13, 17
Sunni 90
Sutherland, Patricia 24
Swedes 82; *see also* slave hunters
sweet potatoes 14, 92
swine *see* pigs
swine flu 154
Swiss cantons 103
sword 5, 6, 7, 8, 10, 23, 44, 46, 48, 51, 56, 59, 102, 107; at Caonao 141; captured by Indians 65, 68; Childeric's 65; and the cross 51, 65; European obsolescence 70, 146; of iron 65; manufacture 65; provenance and prestige 64–65, 70; steel 65, 70; symbolic importance 65; use against Indians 66–69, 72, 99, 138, 158, 178; *see also* Excalibur; "queen of weapons"
the "sword of Christianity" *see* Charles V
syphilis 161–164; endemic 162, 163; the "enigma of syphilis" 162, 164, "error of reclassification" 163; *Treponema pallidum* 162, 164; venereal 162, 164; *see also* bejel; "Columbian" position; Hull; leprosy; pinta; treponema spirochetes; unitarian theory; yaws
Syria 12, 82, 90, 163

Tabasco coast 65, 114, 139
Tacitus 47, 58, 150
tactics, military 68–69, 191, 193; *see also* sacrifice, human
Tacuba 114
Tacuba, the Lord of 79
Tainos 38, 83, 86, 98, 108, 112, 154, 155, 162
tamemes 133, 137, 138; *see also* hammocks
Tampico 114
Tangier 52
Tapia, Andrés de 58, 59, 76, 113, 128, 130, 131, 132, 133, 137, 138, 183, 186; *see also* Cholula massacre; Quetzalcoatl; St. Thomas
Tapia, Bernardino Vásquez de 54, 138; *see also* Cortés, *recidencia*
Tapia, Cristóbal de 111
tapirs 100
Target *see* Haitian garment factories
Tarrascans 67
Tasmania 124
tax assessments 87, 88; collection 118; and European development 94; exemptions 118; *see also* bankruptcies
tea 91, 97
technology, military 67–68, 81, 159, 181; Europeans' edge 67–68, 191; modern 152
tecpllahtolli 175; *see also* Moctezuma, diplomatic language
Templo Mayor see the Great Temple
Tennessee 16
Tenocha 10, 179; lords 183; women 179; *see also* Mexica

Tenochtitlán 6, 9, 18, 40, 41, 45, 46, 48, 57, 58, 59, 60, 61, 69, 76, 102, 127, 132, 134, 137, 145, 168, 177, 182, 191; assault on 66, 68, 99, 113, 119, 136, 142, 144, 147, 156; canals 66, 77, 179; and Cholula 138; destined fall 171–174, 187; lost with 192–193; "Mexico" 136; Narváez's arrival 176; as political entity 179; post-conquest 74, 87, 114, 149, 167; priesthood schools 173; and Quetzalcoatl 172–173; reborn as Mexico City 80; smallpox 155–159; and starvation 158; trap for conquistadors 77, 182; as vision 169; see also Toxcatl; women and children
Teotihuacán 173
Tepeaca 142, 144; "slave town" 142; as Villa Segura de la Frontera 142; see also cannibals
the *tercio* 107; see also Córdoba, Gonzalo de
terra nullis 33
terror 134, 138, 193; terrorism 36, 39, 142, 143
"teules" 167, 181; *"teotl"* 180
Texas 105
Texcoco 58, 99; see also Lake Texcoco
Tezcatlipoca 132, 169, 171, 172, 174; see also Aztecs, gods
Thames 65
"thistle people" 167; see also omens
Thomas, Hugh 4, 36, 80, 86, 113, 118, 185, 186; see also *Conquest: Montezuma, Cortés, and the Fall of Old Mexico*
Tigris River 101
timber 21, 90, 94, 95
time, cyclical view of 174, 187; see also Aztecs, cosmology; "fifth sun"
Tiplacatzin 48
Tirant lo Blanc 43; see also chivalric novels
Tlappanecatl Ecatzin 48; see also Aztecs, warriors
Tlatelolca 10, 59, 179; see also Mexica
Tlatelolco 179
tlatoani 174; the Great Speaker 174, 182; see also Moctezuma
Tlaxcala 8, 9, 45, 57, 58, 61, 62, 66, 99, 113, 128, 134, 135, 136, 142, 147, 169, 176–177, 179, 180; campaign 44; as conquistador allies 77, 79, 115, 128, 130, 131, 142, 180; epidemics 158; nobles 134, 186; and Quetzalcoatl 186; revanchism 140; in Sahagún's account 179; salt blockade 128; Tlaxcalan warriors 47, 66, 67, 136, 137, 139
Tlemcen 53; see also North Africa
Tlolac 173
tobacco 86, 95, 124
Tocqueville, Alexsis de 119, 123
Todorov, Tvestan 4
Toledo y Rojas, Maria 86; see also slave trading
Tollan 172, 173, 186, 187; the "man-god of Tollan" 172, 185; see also Quetzalcoatl, Topitzin
Toltec-Chichimeca people 139; see also Cholula, pre-Hispanic

Toltecs 172, 191; Toltec sites 173
tomatoes 93
Tonatiuh (the Sun) 46; see also Alvarado, Pedro de
Torquemada 135
torture 7, 39, 56, 79, 133, 141, 143
Totonac Indians 54
Townsend, Camilla 29, 68
Toxcatl festival 46, 127; and massacre 69, 141, 142, 176, 181
trade, globalized 91; in luxuries 91, 95, 96; world economy 92; world market 93; see also commercial revolution; Europe, economic divergence
transvestites, Indian 141; see also dogs, attack; Europe, taboos
treasure fleets 88, 90, 92; see also silver
treponema spirochetes 162; treponemal diseases 163; treponematosis 164; see also bejel; DNA testing; syphilis; pinta; yaws
Triple Alliance 9, 10, 57, 182; see also Aztec Empire
Tripoli 53; see also North Africa
Trojans 145
True History of the Conquest of New Spain 7, 40, 43, 80, 114, 117, 128, 130, 167; see also Díaz, Bernal, author
Trujillo 117
Tuckahoe 150
Tula see Toltecs
Turkey 91
turkeys 131
Turks 29, 52, 69, 80, 88, 146; see also Ottomans
Twelve Peers of France 43
twisted-grass motif 139; see also Malintzin
Two Years Before the Mast see Dana, Richard Henry
typhus 154, 158, 159
Tziminchac 104–105; see also horses, deified

"ungulate eruption" 152
unitarian theory 162; see also syphilis
the United States 12, 96, 119, 122, 133, 153, 187, 192; Army 128; Congress 123; western 124
United States Exploring Expedition 121
University of London 11
Urganda the Unknown 43
Utopians 73; see also More, Thomas

Valdivian civilization 16
Valencia 81, 144, 145–146; see also Revolt of the Germanías
Valladolid 123, 126, 145
Valley of Mexico 34, 156, 157, 158, 171, 173
Van Sertima, Ivan 26; see also Africans, in Mesoamerica
Variola major see smallpox
Velázquez, Diego 8, 9, 39, 48, 56, 111, 114, 176; see also Cuba
Velez-Málaga 146

Index

Venetians 19, 30, 36, 82, 88, 91; *see also* bankers; slave traders
Venezuela 17, 85, 161
Vera Cruz 8, 54, 76, 119, 176, 177
Veragua 74
La verdadera historia de la conquista de la Nueva España see *True History of the Conquest of New Spain*
Verranzzano, Giovanni de 12, 15
Vespucci, Amerigo 72
victories, miraculous 44–45, 62
Vikings 13, 14, 17, 19–25, 72, 82, 189, 191; reports 32; the Rus 82, 121; *see also* Norse people, slave hunters
Villa Rica de la Vera Cruz *see* Vera Cruz
Villagutierre Soto-Mayor, Juan de 104–105
Vinland 12, 19, **20**, 22, 23; *see also* St. Lawrence River Valley; Vikings
violence 6, 7, 42, 51, 145, 190; Europeans' comparative advantage 70; micro-violence 145
the Virgin Mary 12, 31, 44, 57, 59, 61, 62, 171
Virginia 95, 122, 143, 150
"virus factories" 155; *see also* smallpox
Visigoths 30
Vitoria, Francisco de 108, 145
Vivaldi brothers 30
Vivar, Ruy Días de *see* the Cid
the VOC 96
Volga River 90, 101
Volkswagen plant 147; *see also* Cholula, today

Wallace, Birgitta 21
Walmart *see* Haitian garment factories
walruses 22, 26
War on Terror 63
warfare, asymmetrical 44; economic 143–144; seasonal 69, 137; *see also* siege; tactics
warrior mystique 119
warrior society 193
Washington, George 50, 125
"water folk" 167; *see also* omens
Watling Island 64; *see also* San Salvador Island
the West 107
West, Rebecca 40
Western Europe 51, 61, 90, 91, 93, 94

Western Hemisphere 6, 13, 14, 16, 26, 71, 94, 149; *see also* Americas; New World; syphilis
Westerners 178, 187
whalers 152
wheat 37
wheel of fortune 41
White, John Manchip 4
"white god" *see* St. Thomas
white supremacy 16; *see also* racism
whooping cough 158, 160
Why the West Rules—For Now see Morris, Ian
Wilkes, Charles, U.S. Navy lieutenant 121–122
wine 90, 115, 121, 149
Winthrop, John 158
Wolof kingdom 101
wolves 125
women and children 142, 143, 144, 146; and hierarchy 145; *see also* Cholula massacre; massacre, gratuitous; non-combatants, killing of
woolens 163; and yaws 163
Worker Rights Consortium 208*n*27
World War I 106

Xaltocan 114
Xicotencatl **129**
Xochimilco 114

Yancuitlán 143
"Yankee Doodle Dandy" 128
Yankees *see* Anglo Saxons
yaws 162–164; *see also* treponema spirochetes
yellow fever 160–161
Yucatan 6, 8, 29, 54, 57, 62, 68, 81, 103, 111, 114, 149, 151, 155, 157, 168; *see also* the Gulf Coast

Zacatecas 85, 88
Zapata, Emiliano 192
Zapoteca territory 118
Zárate, Don Juan de 117; *see also* Antequera
Zheng He 3, 18
Zhu Di 18; *see also* Ming Dynasty
Zhukov, Georgy 50
the Zócolo 80
Zumárraga, Fray Juan de 85, 115
Zumpango 114

www.ingramcontent.com/pod-product-compliance
Ingram Content Group UK Ltd.
Pitfield, Milton Keynes, MK11 3LW, UK
UKHW041938140426
5217IPUK00014B/548